Philosophers Speak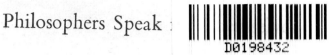

From Descartes to Locke

Edited by

T. V. SMITH

AND

MARJORIE GRENE

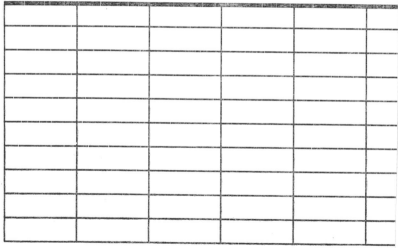

DATE DUE					

DEMCO, I

CHICAGO AND LONDON

International Standard Book Number: 0–226–76481–8

Library of Congress Catalog Card Number: 57–7904

THE UNIVERSITY OF CHICAGO PRESS, CHICAGO 60637
The University of Chicago Press, Ltd., London

PREFACE

THIS book—together with its companion volume, *Berkeley, Hume, and Kant*—is intended to furnish guides and readings in the philosophy of the seventeenth and eighteenth centuries. Wherever possible, whole works have been chosen; but where, as in the case of Locke's *Essay* or Hume's *Treatise*, that plan was obviously not feasible, fairly substantial selections have been substituted. The limited scope of the volumes unfortunately does not permit the inclusion of readings bearing on all aspects of the philosophy of each major author. Fundamental problems of method and of metaphysics have been treated in each case; ethical problems appear in the selections from Hobbes, Hume, and Kant, and the philosophy of civil society in the parallel passages from Hobbes and Locke. In the case of the remaining authors, the introductions attempt to suggest briefly how these gaps are filled, although their chief aim is to elucidate for the student the selections actually included.

The lists of suggested readings make no claim to completeness but enumerate, for students interested in reading further, some of the books that are easily available in English. Since the first appearance of the materials in this book, a number of useful and important works have come to our attention that ought to be added to these lists. Chief among these are the following: Bayle's *Dictionary*, ed. Beller and Lee (Princeton, 1952); A. Vartanian, *Diderot and Descartes* (Princeton, 1953); Elizabeth Haldane, *Descartes, His Life and Times* (London, 1903); Leo Strauss, *Natural Right and History* (Chicago, 1953), chap. v; Stuart Hampshire, *Spinoza* (Penguin ed. [London, 1951]); Leibniz' *Philosophical Papers and Letters*, ed. L. E. Loemker (2 vols.; Chicago, 1956); *Leibniz-Clarke Correspondence*, ed. Alexander (Manchester, England, 1956); H. W. B. Joseph, *Lectures on the Philosophy of*

Leibniz (Oxford, 1949); R. Saw, *Leibniz* (Penguin ed. [London, 1954]); Locke's *Essays on the Law of Nature* (Oxford, 1954); J. W. Gough, *John Locke's Political Philosophy: Eight Studies* (Oxford, 1950); and D. J. O'Connor, *John Locke* (Penguin ed. [London, 1952]).

Acknowledgment is made in the appropriate places for the following permissions: to the Open Court Publishing Company for the translation of Descartes's *Meditations;* to the Dial Press for permission to reprint selections from Wolf's translation of Spinoza's letters; and to Félix Alcan for permission to translate two selections from Couturat's *Fragments inédits de Leibniz.*

T. V. SMITH
MARJORIE GRENE

TABLE OF CONTENTS

INTRODUCTION

THE development of physics in the seventeenth century, culminating in the work of "the incomparable Mr. Newton" (1642–1727), suggested to scientists a number of cognate philosophic problems. The method of physics effectively united contributions from reason and observation. To account theoretically for this practically successful union was the more difficult task left to philosophers. As to its content, physics gave a diagrammatic picture of a world-machine running smoothly according to mathematical formulas; philosophers were concerned to relate that mechanical world to the mind knowing it and, in general, to phenomena usually called mental or spiritual. Or to put the problem again in terms of method: the procedure of physical science reduced certain phenomena of the natural world to expressions of a few simple mathematical laws; philosophers were interested in discovering how far and on what basis human reason could be applied with similar success in other fields. The statement of such problems varied widely, of course, with the men propounding them. Some emphasized the role of "reason" in knowledge, some that of "experience," with both terms interpreted in a variety of ways. Some thought the world ultimately more akin to matter, some to mind; many divided it radically into two disunited parts. A few despaired of extending scientific method beyond mathematical physics; but many attempted such extensions—some to a universal science, some to various particular fields like politics or morality or religion. The situation was complicated, further, by the survival of traditional terms and principles. Physics made, in a sense, a fresh start with the adoption of its new method. Philosophy, using language as its only tool, was slower in effecting anything like so radical a transformation. In a new age old terms do indeed acquire new meanings. But the process is very gradual; and the strong line of continuity sometimes almost overshadows the novelty of emphasis. Thus Spinoza, to take one example, may equally well be interpreted as "the last of the medievals" or as one of Descartes's successors in dealing with the problem of method in its seventeenth-century guise. Still, out of the wide diversities of emphasis and out of the varying entanglements of old and new, one may draw without too much unfairness the conclusion that the dominant theme of philosophy in the seventeenth and eighteenth centuries centers in the problem of understanding and generalizing the method and doctrines of physical science. Before we look separately at some of the major representatives of the period, we may illustrate more specifically the three aspects of the central problem stated above: (1) the problem of analyzing the method of scientific knowledge; (2) the problem of stating the relation of the physical world, as Galilean-Newtonian mechanics depicts it, to the realm of mind or spirit; and (3) the problem of generalizing the method of physics or a method similarly rational to apply to other fields.

The method of the new physics involved, as we have seen, the joint use of deductive and observational procedures. Hence every philosophical interpretation of scientific knowledge took some account of both these factors. Each term was subject, however, to a variety of interpretations. For Hobbes, for example, reasoning is just as important a factor in scientific method as for Descartes; but the power and function and significance of reason are very differently conceived in the two.

Moreover, the degree to which the importance of one or other of the two sides is emphasized forms one of the major lines of variation among philosophic interpreters of science. We shall notice some such variants in our account of particular philosophers. For the moment we may take as illustrative the disagreement between the Dutch philosopher

Spinoza and the English chemist Robert Boyle (1627–91) as to the significance of Boyle's experiments on niter. In October, 1661, Henry Oldenburg, soon to be first secretary of the Royal Society, sent to Spinoza a copy of Boyle's *Physiological Essays*, including reports of experiments on the composition of niter.[1] By showing, through carefully planned experiments, the difference in physical and chemical properties between spirit of niter and niter, Boyle asserted that he had proved the heterogeneity of these two compounds. Spinoza, replying to Oldenburg on the subject of "the book of the very talented Boyle," offered a simpler hypothesis: to wit, that niter and spirit of niter are homogeneous, but that in spirit of niter the particles are in motion, whereas in niter (or, as he would say, the dregs of niter) they are at rest. The difference in properties, Spinoza declared, could just as well be accounted for on this simpler theory. For instance, niter is inflammable; since, its particles being at rest, it at first resists fire, until at last, when the flame has surrounded all the particles on every side, the whole thing catches fire at once. Spirit of niter, on the other hand, is noninflammable; since, its particles being in motion, they are quickly driven in all directions by a little heat, dissipate themselves before the fire can thoroughly surround them, and thus help to extinguish rather than to feed the flame. In experimental illustration of this principle Spinoza allowed some spirit of niter to be absorbed (and hence rendered motionless in the solid medium) by some ordinary sand—and showed that in this condition the substance became inflammable. (He also executed two other experiments in illustration of his general thesis.) Boyle replied, through Oldenburg, (1) that his intention had not been to give a philosophic account of the very nature of niter but to show that it was not necessary to assume "occult qualities" or "substantial forms" to explain the phenomena and (2) that Spinoza's experiments were not

[1] See Spinoza's correspondence, ed. Wolf (New York: Dial Press, 1928), Letters III, IV, V, VI, VII, XI, XIII, XIV, XVI.

cogent because, unlike his own, they were not made under artificial conditions in which extraneous factors are eliminated. Spinoza replied to the first objection that he had no idea Boyle was merely trying to refute a puerile doctrine already amply refuted, but thought he was rather showing something about the nature of niter. To the second he replied, that if one already knew the principles of mechanical philosophy, then Boyle's experiments might be excellent to illustrate the nature of niter, though still no better than certain common experiments, which, however, did not prove Boyle's thesis. Now the significance of this controversy lies not in the question of the composition of niter—which has been settled to the satisfaction of experimental scientists in Boyle's favor—but in the question it raises concerning the place of experiment and observation as such in science. Boyle and his friends of the Royal Society (at the opening of the Oldenburg correspondence still the "Invisible College") were especially interested, Oldenburg tells Spinoza, in the new techniques of advancing natural knowledge by careful experiment. Boyle does, indeed, recognize the co-operation of reasoning and experiment in scientific procedure, even calling observation the handmaid of reason.[2] But it appears that his chief attention is to the handmaid rather than to the mistress, for, as Oldenburg says of him, "our Boyle" is one of those who are modest enough to hope the phenomena will agree with their reason. For Spinoza, on the other hand, science is essentially rational explanation, of which mathematics is the type; that is, it is knowledge obtained deductively from premises self-evidently true. But for science in this sense nothing is ever *proved* by observation. Experiment may indeed suggest premises for scientific reasoning or confirm deductions from general theories. For that minor purpose, however, many common experiments will do as well as more elaborate ones; since the end of scientific procedure is the construction of a true system of knowledge, not, as it

[2] *Works*, V, 539.

seems to be for Boyle-Oldenburg, the obtaining of experimental results.

But the development of physical science raised other questions as well as those directly concerned in the analysis of scientific method. Galileo declared, and succeeding scientists like Boyle and Newton agreed with him, that nature was written in mathematical letters. They agreed, that is, that mathematics is not only to be used as an instrument in physics but that the physical world really *is* the mechanical-mathematical system physics describes. Galileo's distinction, moreover, between the qualities of shape, size, etc., present in bodies and the qualities of color, sound, etc., produced in our experience by unknown operations of those "primary" characters of shape, size, and the like was generally accepted by his successors. In other words, the picture of the world as a great system of extended matter moving according to mechanical laws soon became, among scientists and philosophers, the standard view of the physical universe. But what is the place of mind in such a universe? What is the relation to such a radically non-mental world of the very mind that knows it? More generally, how do human values as well as human thought, or how does the God of traditional religion fit into such a bare mechanized scheme? So the old problem of the place of mind or soul in the cosmos gets a new twist by virtue of the widespread acceptance of "the new mechanical philosophy." But, again, the statements of the problem run the gamut of philosophic temperaments and traditions. Some, like Gassendi (1592–1655), resorted to an Epicurean atomism which legislated non-material "mind" out of existence. At another extreme, in contrast, is a man like the Cambridge Platonist Henry More (1614–87; *Encheiridon metaphysicum*, 1671). More, although accepting the mechanical world-view, conceived of the vehicle of extended matter, empty space, as a spiritual entity constituting a sort of vague, confused representation of the divine essence. Empty space has, he pointed out, many of the attributes of the Deity. It is eternal, perfect, immense, existing by itself, incorporeal, omnipresent, etc. So, he concluded, space expresses, though not the life or activity of God, at least his bare essence and existence. A common view, expounded as we shall see by Descartes and accepted by such men as Boyle and Newton, was one which divided the world into two parts: extended matter and cogitating mind. The variants on this separation were legion. For the narrower problem of the relation of human mind and body Pierre Crousaz's *Traité du beau* (1712) may serve as example of one solution. Crousaz (1663–1748) distinguishes between feelings, which are of the body, and ideas, which are of the mind. These two, body and mind, and their corresponding affections, ideas and feelings, are, Crousaz holds, so basically different as to have no causal influence on one another. Each works independently of the other according to its own laws. The apparent relation we sometimes observe between them is actually the result of a harmony established by the fiat of a benevolent creator.

Put in terms of method, thirdly, the problem of the relation between the world of physics and the world of mind or spirit becomes the problem of extending procedures like those of physical science to disciplines such as metaphysics, ethics, politics, criticism, or religion. If physical "nature" can be accounted for so successfully by a few simple laws, why not try a similar reduction for "first philosophy" or for the science of human nature or of God? As we shall see, Descartes intended, by generalizing the demonstrative method of mathematics, to construct a universal mathematics which should include the whole of human knowledge. And Descartes's aim typifies the fundamental belief of his contemporaries—a belief which motivated many of them to attempt the construction of particular sciences comparable in simplicity and certainty to mathematical physics. Locke, for example, began philosophizing in the endeavor to discover whether it was possible to formulate a moral science possessing the same certainty as mathematics. There were, of course, men like Pascal (1623–62) for whom the pattern of mathematics appeared impossible of application in matters human or divine. Yet it is optimism like Descartes's that is dominant. For in men of the most varying opinions in ethics, criticism, politics, or religion, one finds not only faith in the power of human reason but a kindred faith in the ultimate simplicity of the subject matters to be analyzed. One finds, that is, a faith that the phenomena in question exhibit basic uniformity sufficient to allow reduction by reason to a few simple principles as their source. To take one example, Francis Hutcheson (1694–1747), in his *Inquiry into the Original of Our Ideas of Beauty and Virtue*, defines "taste" as an "internal sense"; that is, as a simple and immediate feeling of pleasure arising from the perception of certain sights and sounds. Now one might think that such an equation makes taste a matter of purely private experience, with no sufficient communion between the experience of various individuals to allow any generalizing of treatment. When tastes disagree, they simply disagree, and there is an end of the matter. In fact, however, Hutcheson declares that, where there is disagreement between two people in the simple perceptions of taste, there must be some corresponding difference in what they actually perceive. For one cannot but assume that the senses operate uniformly for all mankind. Where the object is the same, therefore, the resulting act of sensing will be similar, and where the acts of sensing are dissimilar, the objects perceived must differ. The degree to which taste is developed may vary enormously between individuals, but its basic principles must be the same for all. Such faith in the simplicity and uniformity of the phenomena is the correlate of the belief that reason can successfully reduce any subject matter to a system. Keeping both correlatives in mind, we may mention briefly a few of the many attempts to reduce to disciplines analogous to "natural philosophy" the studies of man, of the state, and of God.

We shall discover in Hobbes, Descartes, and Spinoza instances of the reduction of the human passions to a basic few from which others are derived by combination and variation. (Spinoza makes most explicit his use of scientific demonstration in this field when he declares that he is dealing with human emotions as if he were treating of lines, planes, and angles.) Building on such analyses of the passions, and later on the "associational psychology" expounded by David Hartley (1704–57), philosophers gave varying pictures of the springs and standards of human action. For Hobbes (as for Spinoza) the standards of moral conduct follow solely from the endeavor of the individual being to preserve itself. In order to combat this "selfish system," moralists like Shaftesbury (1671–1713) insisted that men possess by nature a feeling for or with their fellow-men (sometimes called a "moral sense") which makes them act with a view to the benefit of others as well as themselves. For Shaftesbury this moral sense is identical with the sense of beauty: virtue is the perception of beauty or order in society. Joseph Butler (1692–1752) added to the passions and benevolence two further principles: rational self-love and conscience; and, by distinguishing sharply between power and authority, demonstrated the natural authority of conscience over all other principles. Of the innumerable formulations of standards in the sphere of taste, Hutcheson's statement may be supplemented by one of a different type. In Crousaz's *Traité du beau*, also mentioned above, taste is accounted for by the co-operation of the rational idea of beauty with certain bodily feelings of pleasure. The phenomenon of poor taste (discord between idea and feeling) is due to the Fall of Man. God had decreed that mind and body, idea and feeling, should work harmoniously in their parallel spheres; that concord was disjointed at the Fall. Good taste, consequently, is but the restoration of man's original harmony.

In dependence on their varying interpretations of the individual man, secondly, philosophers endeavored to enunciate fundamental principles for politics. Again, their formulations were based on the assertion of basic principles common to all men at all times; i.e., on the assertion of a fundamental Law of Nature, from which all the subordinate principles of politics could be obtained by rational deduction. Grotius (1583–1645), in his treatise *On the Law of War and Peace* (1645), made the basic principle of politics the statement of man's needs relative to his existence in society. Whatever reason deduces from the social nature of man constitutes natural right (*jus naturale*)—a right superior to and serving as the basis for all positive law. Puffendorf (1632–94), by his use of a rigidly geometrical method, stresses even more strikingly the deductive character of political theory. (At the same time Puffendorf combines the doctrines of Grotius and Hobbes in his insistence that the endeavor for self-preservation can be rationally expressed only in the satisfaction of social needs.) This line of development as well as the allied concepts of sovereignty and of a social contract as the basis for political association will recur in our study of Hobbes and Locke. It must suffice here to point out the importance for the period of the doctrine that political theory can be stated in the form of a demonstrative science whose principles are laws of human nature valid for all men in all conditions in all ages. The writings of such Americans as John Adams, Hamilton, and their contemporaries offer fruitful indications, at the close of the period, of the various strands of this development.

In the theories of "natural religion," thirdly, the theological field was invaded by the attempt to discover uniform principles natural to all humanity. Of the long and bitter controversy in this field, we may take the views of Lord Herbert of Cherbury (1581–1648) as an example. Lord Herbert is considered in Leland's *View of the Deistical Writers in England* (1754), for example, as the first of the line of "Deistical" authors whose doctrines, in more or less extreme forms, obtained wide notoriety in France and England. The essence of religion, Lord Herbert declared, consists not in the special revelation of a given religion but in five general beliefs natural to all men: (1) that there is one supreme God; (2) that he is chiefly to be worshiped; (3) that piety and virtue constitute the principal part of his worship; (4) that we must repent of our sins and that, if we do so, God will pardon them; and (5) that there are rewards for good men and punishments for bad in a future state, "both here and hereafter." This insistence on a natural rather than a revealed basis for religion formed one of the main tenets of Deism. As a matter of fact, the earlier Deists did not, in their formulations of such uniform rational principles, stress the analogy with the demonstrative method of mathematics or physics; it was rather the more orthodox divines who emphasized this relation. Especially in the later Deists, however, the statement of the principle of natural religion was modified in the direction of greater emphasis on the importance of the world-machine of physics. In the more extreme of such later statements the function of God sometimes became that of the original mechanic who has, indeed, invented the cosmic machine and so is worthy of worship, but who is less concerned with directing its operation.[3]

We have remarked as typical three aspects of seventeenth- and eighteenth-century thought: the interest in analyzing scientific method and knowledge in general, the problem of relating mechanical to mental phenomena in the world and in man, and the attempt to deduce phenomena other than those of physics from simple and universal laws. All these factors will recur in more detailed contexts in our examination of the major philosophers of these two centuries with their divergent statements of its major problems.

[3] Among the most famous of the English Deistic writers were John Toland (1670–1722; *Christianity Not Mysterious*, 1696); Anthony Collins (1676–1729); Matthew Tindal (1656–1733; *Christianity as Old as Creation*, 1730); and Thomas Chubb (1679–1747).

SUGGESTED READINGS

BUTLER, *The Analogy of Religion* (various eds.); HOLBACH, *System of Nature*, trans. ROBINSON (Boston, 1889); LA METTRIE, *Man a Machine*, trans. BUSSEY (Chicago, 1912); LELAND, *A View of the Deistical Writers in England* (London, 1754); PASCAL, *Thoughts* (various eds.); SHAFTESBURY, *Characteristics* (various eds.); ADAM SMITH, *The Theory of Moral Sentiments* (various eds.); VOLTAIRE, *Candide* (various eds.); *Philosophical Dictionary* (various eds.).

MORRIS BISHOP, *Pascal: The Life of Genius* (New York, 1936); G. S. BRETT, *Philosophy of Gassendi* (London, 1908); C. D. BROAD, *Five Types of Ethical Theory* (New York, 1930); E. A. BURTT, *see* readings for chap. ii; J. G. HIBBEN, *The Philosophy of the Enlightenment* (New York, 1910); KINGSLEY MARTIN, *French Liberal Thought in the Eighteenth Century* (1929); J. M. MORLEY, *Diderot and the Encyclopedists* (London, 1923); *Voltaire* (London, 1903, 1923); DANIEL MORNET, *French Thought in the Eighteenth Century* (New York, 1929); F. J. POWICKE, *The Cambridge Platonists* (Cambridge, Mass., 1927); LESLIE STEPHEN, *English Thought in the Eighteenth Century* (New York and London, 1902).

CHAPTER I

RENE DESCARTES

René Descartes was born in Touraine in 1596 and educated at the Jesuit school at La Flèche. From 1618 to 1621 he served in various military campaigns abroad. On one of these occasions he was returning from the coronation of the emperor to the army, when the beginning of the winter overtook him, as he says, in a place where "finding no conversation which diverted him and happily having, besides, no cares or passions which troubled him," he spent the whole day shut up by himself with his thoughts for entertainment; and it was here that he conceived the idea of a philosophic method to which he was to devote the rest of his life. After 1621 he spent some time in Paris, then withdrew in 1628 to a life of scholarly retirement in the Netherlands. In 1649 he accepted an invitation of Queen Christina to come to her court in Sweden. He died there in 1650. Chief works: *The World or a Treatise on Light* (first published 1654); *Rules for the Direction of the Understanding* (first published 1701, probably written between 1619 and 1628); *Discourse on Method* (1637); *Meditations on First Philosophy* (1641); *Principles of Philosophy* (1644); *The Passions of the Soul* (1650). Suggested readings: *Philosophical Works*, trans. Haldane and Ross (Cambridge, 1912, 1931); *Correspondence of Descartes and Constantyn Huygens*, ed., Roth (Oxford, 1926); *Geometry of René Descartes*, trans. Smith and Latham (Chicago, 1925). Kuno Fischer, *Descartes and His School* (New York, 1887); A. B. Gibson, *The Philosophy of Descartes* (London, 1932); E. S. Haldane, *Descartes: His Life and Times* (New York, 1905); Jacques Maritain, *Three Reformers: Luther—Descartes—Rousseau* (London, 1928); Leon Roth, *Spinoza, Descartes, and Maimonides* (Oxford, 1924); Norman Kemp Smith, *Studies in the Cartesian Philosophy* (London and New York, 1902).

Like Bacon's projected *Instauration*, Descartes's philosophy proclaimed itself as something completely different from the mistaken Aristotelianism of the schools. Its aim was, reasoning from a few premises clearly and distinctly apprehended, to construct a universal science possessing the certainty of mathematics; and this aim, Descartes believed, could be supported only by the wholesale rejection of traditional views. But accustomed doctrines are not so easily sloughed off; and to us Descartes's philosophy appears as a combination of certain new principles with other presuppositions characteristic of the very tradition he thought himself rejecting. True, as a mathematician and physicist, Descartes was entirely convinced of the correctness of the new worldviews, and he found the reasonings of his teachers on these subjects woefully inadequate. Yet he had grown up in the old ways of thinking, and his natural piety made him sympathetic, in spite of himself, to many of the beliefs fundamental to inherited philosophies.

The direction of Descartes's philosophizing is determined by his faith in the possibility of a rational science. It was his conviction that, if only he could arrive at some very clear and distinct premises from which other propositions could be just as clearly deduced, he would be able to construct a system of universal knowledge valid for all men at all times. Abandoning the subtle reasonings of the schools, he therefore determined to doubt everything that could possibly be doubted until he got to some absolutely clear and simple principle that no man in or even out of his senses possibly could doubt. From that first most certain premise he would then proceed with deductions of a straightforward and simple nature, making sure that at each step his understanding of the inference and conclusion was just as clear as his apprehension of the first proposition had been. The model for this procedure, of course, was mathematics. His purpose, in fact, was to construct a "universal mathematics," that is, a science of wider scope possessing the same absolute validity which mathematics attains in the limited field of numbers and figures. The form of exposition, however, according to Descartes, should not always be that of a finished mathematical theory. The ancient geometers have published their discoveries in a form which Descartes called *synthetic;* that is, they start with axioms which are logically prior and from them construct the succeeding theorems. But for the actual procedure of learning and discovering (as against the finished exposition) Descartes prefers the method of *analysis;* that is, the method whereby one starts with a simple, self-evident truth near at hand (which may not turn out to be logically first in the completed system) and from it works in simple steps to more difficult and remote principles. Both methods, however, Descartes holds, give absolutely certain knowledge if only they are correctly applied; and they can be used in such a way as to embrace within one system the whole compass of human knowledge. Descartes set down the rules for constructing such a system in the *Discourse* and the *Rules;* he proceeded to carry out the construction in the *Meditations;* and summarized the resulting universal knowledge in the *Principles*.

Now in the ideal of a rational science possessing absolute and universal validity Descartes was expressing a principle characteristic both of his philosophic predecessors and of his scientific contemporaries. That knowledge, to be knowledge, must be certain has been the belief of most philosophers almost up to the present century. Even Hume's "scepticism," as we shall see, is motivated by that conviction. And that knowledge can be certain only if it is attained by rigorous deduction from clearly intuited premises has been the belief of a long line of philosophers whose faith in the power of human reason has encouraged them to seek such knowledge. With that principle common to past and present, however, Descartes combined divergent beliefs drawn separately from the two sources. He accepted—again, in agreement with most philosophers, and notably with all those who descend from Aristotle—the idea of *substance* as the basic concept in philosophy. Descartes accepted, that is, the axiom explicitly formulated by Spinoza: everything that is, is either in itself or in another. Everything is either a substance, the supporting basis for passing qualities, itself existing independently; or it is an accident, that is a quality of a substance, which can exist only in a substance, not in itself. But substance, being independent, is more ultimate than accident; and when we ask, in philosophy, what the world is really like, we are asking what kinds of substances there are, how many, how they react on one another, etc. Besides the Aristotelian notion of substance, in the second place, Descartes inherited the Platonistic notion of the world as hierarchically constructed. Accident, being dependent on substance, seems somehow less real than substance. And, even among substances, some are more real than others in proportion as they are more "perfect." Man has greater reality than the lower animals, angels more than man, and God is most real of all—or most perfect: the meaning is the same. Descartes's anomalous position is evident, moreover, from the fact that he retains the principle of degrees of reality side by side with its opposite: the belief in a uniform, mechanized, physical world, where bodies are or are not, move or are at rest. He retains, in the third place, the view that God has done all with a benevolent purpose, a belief in what Aristotle called final causes. But again the new scientist's emphasis on mechanical cause makes itself felt: for Descartes insists that, while final causes exist, there is no good in our asking for them. We had better concentrate on the measurements of force and velocity with which the physicist can deal and leave God's inscrutable purposes alone.

He retains, fourthly, the belief in a non-corporeal, immortal human mind. And yet, again, the new mechanism leads him to regard the body, and even the "lower" functions of mind, the senses and imagination, as purely mechanical. Man has a mind mysteriously injected somewhere into his body; but except for that one spark he is as much machine as any instrument he himself contrives. Influences of mind on body and body on mind occur, according to Descartes, through "a little gland at the base of the brain" (the pineal body) which stands in especially intimate relation to the mind. The "passions of the soul" (of which the basic ones are admiration, love, hate, desire, joy, and sorrow) are said to be "perceptions or sentiments or emotions of the soul, which we refer particularly to the soul itself," but which have as their proximate cause the movements set up by "animal spirits" in the little gland. Again, although Descartes begins his treatise on the passions by announcing his disregard of all previous analyses, this picture of man does not differ essentially from earlier views. The distinction between the animal spirits whose movements account for the highest corporeal functions and a wholly incorporeal mind (*animus*) was a familiar and important one to medieval writers. Still Descartes's insistence that the new mechanical principles can exhaustively explain all the functions of the lower animals and all the lower functions of man puts a somewhat different light on the old picture.

We may conclude, then, that, although Descartes considered himself an innovator in his construction of a universal mathematics, he was, like most philosophic innovators, combining in many ways the terminology and principles of his predecessors in philosophic speculation with the views of his contemporaries in mathematics and physical science.

SELECTIONS FROM *RULES FOR THE DIRECTION OF THE UNDERSTANDING*[1]

RULE I.—*The end of all studies should be to direct the mind toward the enunciation of solid and true judgments on all things which are presented to it.*

Men are accustomed, whenever they observe any similarity between two things, to attribute to both of them, even in those respects in which they differ, whatever they have found to be true of either one. So they have made a false comparison between the sciences, which consist entirely in the cognition of the mind, and the arts, which demand some practice and a certain disposition of the body. For they have seen that one man cannot learn all the arts at the same time, but that a man who practises only one art more easily emerges an excellent artist (since the same hands cannot so conveniently be applied both to the cultivation of the fields and to the strumming of the lyre, or to several different employments of this kind, as to a single one of them). Hence they have held the same opinion of the sciences, and distinguishing them from one another by the diversity of their objects they have thought it proper to pursue each one of them singly to the neglect of all the others.

[1] Translated from *Regulae ad directionem ingenii*. For the standard text see the Adam and Tannery edition (Paris, 1908), X, 359 ff.

But in this they are certainly mistaken. For all the sciences are nothing else but human wisdom, which always remains one and the same, however different the subjects to which it is applied, and which receives no more alteration from those subjects than does the light of the sun from the variety of things it illumines. Hence there is no need to impose any boundaries upon the mind: the knowledge of one truth does not, like the practise of one art, keep us from the discovery of another, but rather helps us. Indeed it amazes me, how most people study with the greatest diligence the customs of men, the properties of plants, the motions of the stars, the transformations of metals, and the objects of other such disciplines, while at the same time almost no one gives thought to good sense, or to that universal knowledge, although as a matter of fact all other things ought to be valued not for themselves but because they contribute something to it. Thus it is not without reason that we set down this first of all our rules, since nothing takes us farther afield from the right road for seeking truth, than the direction of our studies to particular ends rather than to one general one. I do not speak of perverted and reprehensible ends, like vain glory or the base desire for gain; it is obvious that pretended reasonings and sophistries suited to vulgar minds open a much shorter road to them than the solid knowledge of truth could do. But I am thinking even of honest and laudable ends, since we are often more subtly deceived by these: as, for example, if we pursue sciences useful either for the comforts of life, or for that pleasure which is found in the contemplation of truth, and which is almost the only happiness in this life that is pure and untroubled by pain. For these legitimate fruits of the sciences we can certainly expect to attain; but, if we think about these things in the midst of our studies, they often make us omit much that is necessary to the knowledge of other things,—whether because such material appears at first sight of little use, or of little interest. It must be recognized, however, that all the sciences are so related to one another, that it is much easier to learn them all at one time than to separate one from the others. If therefore any one wishes seriously to investigate the truth of things, he ought not to choose any single science; for they are all interconnected and reciprocally dependent. He should rather think only of increasing the natural light of reason, not in order to resolve this or that scholastic problem, but in order that in every particular situation of his life his intellect may show his will what choice to make. Soon he will be amazed to find that he has made much greater progress than those who study particular things, and that he has attained not only what others desire, but also higher things which they could not expect to reach.

RULE II.—*We should concern ourselves only with those objects, for the certain and indubitable knowledge of which our minds appear to be adequate.*

All science is certain and evident knowledge. He who doubts of many things is not more learned than he who has never thought about them. Indeed the former seems even more ignorant than the latter, if he has conceived a false opinion of any of them. So it is better not to study at all, than to occupy oneself with objects so difficult that, in our inability to distinguish true from false, we are forced to admit doubtful things for certain; for in these matters there is not so much hope of increasing our learning as there is danger of diminishing it. And so through this proposition we reject all knowledge that is only probable, and we declare that only those things ought to be believed which are perfectly known and which cannot be doubted. Learned men may perhaps have convinced themselves that such knowledge is very rare, because, according to a vice common to mankind, they have neglected to reflect on it as being too easy and open to any one at all. But I warn them that it is much more plentiful than they think, and sufficient to demonstrate with certainty innumerable propositions on which they have been able until now to argue only with probability. And because they have thought it unworthy of a learned man to admit ignorance of anything, they have been accustomed to adorn their false reasons so well that they have finished by persuading themselves, and so they have given them out as true.

Indeed if we observe this rule well there will be very few things which we may undertake to learn. For there is scarcely one question in the sciences on which clever men have not often disagreed. But each time the judgments of two men on a single point diverge, it is certain that at least one of them is wrong; and not even one of them, it seems, has scientific knowledge: for if the reasons of the one were certain and evident, he would be able to expound them to the other in such a way as finally to convince his intellect also.

Therefore we see that in all such probable opinions we cannot acquire perfect science, for we may not without rashness hope for more than others have achieved. Consequently, if our reckoning is correct, there remain of all the sciences already discovered only arithmetic and geometry to which the observation of this rule reduces us.

Nevertheless we do not therefore condemn that method of philosophizing which others have already invented, the scholastics' military machines of probable syllogisms. They do indeed train young minds and stimulate them by a certain emulation. It is much better to mould them with opinions of this kind, uncertain though they seem when argued among scholars, than to leave them free to themselves. For perhaps without a guide they might cast themselves into some abyss; but while they follow in their masters' footsteps, they may indeed deviate somewhat from the truth, yet they will certainly take a road that is at least in this sense more secure, that it has already been tried by more prudent people. We ourselves rejoice, that we have formerly been thus trained in the schools. But since we are now freed of that obligation which bound us to our master's words, and since we have reached a sufficient age to withdraw our hand from the ferule, if we wish seriously to set ourselves rules whereby we may ascend to the height of human knowledge, we must surely admit among the first the one that warns us not to abuse our leisure, as many do, who neglect everything simple and are occupied only with arduous matters. They certainly make the subtlest conjectures on such subjects, and devise very probable arguments; but after many labors they finally find too late that they have only increased the number of their doubts, without learning any science.

But now, since we said just previously that of all the disciplines known by others, only arithmetic and geometry are pure from every taint of falsity and incertitude: we should examine more carefully the reason why this is so. And for this purpose we must observe that we can arrive at a knowledge of things by a double path, namely by experience, or by deduction. We must observe, further, that experiences of things are often deceptive; that deduction, however, or a pure inference of one thing from another, can indeed be passed over if it is not noticed, but can never be erroneously executed by an intellect even minimally rational. But I find of little use for this purpose those bonds by which the dialecticians seek to rule human reason, although I do not deny that they are most suitable for other uses. For all the error to which men are subject (men, I say, not beasts), results, never from faulty inference, but only from the fact that experiments insufficiently understood are admitted, or that judgments are asserted rashly and without basis.

From this the explanation is evident, why arithmetic and geometry are much more certain than other disciplines. The reason is, that they alone are concerned with an object so pure and simple that they suppose absolutely nothing which experience has rendered uncertain, but consist entirely in consequences rationally deduced. They are therefore the easiest and clearest of all the sciences, and have an object such as we require, since in them it is almost impossible for men to err except by inattention. Nevertheless we ought not to wonder if the minds of many apply themselves more spontaneously to other arts or to philosophy. For this happens, because every one gives himself the liberty of guessing with greater confidence in an obscure than in an evident subject matter, and because it is much easier to make conjectures on any random question than to arrive at truth itself in a single one, however simple.

From all this one must conclude, not, indeed, that one must learn nothing but arithmetic and geometry, but only that those who seek the right road of truth ought not to occupy themselves with any object, concerning which they cannot possess a certainty equal to that of the demonstrations of arithmetic and geometry.

RULE III.—*Concerning the objects presented to us we should investigate not what others have thought nor what we ourselves conjecture, but what we can intuit clearly and evidently or deduce with certainty, since by no other means is knowledge acquired.*

The books of the ancients should be read, since it is a tremendous advantage to us to be able to use the labors of so many men: as much to learn what has been correctly discovered in the past, as to be counselled what more remains to be thought out in all the disciplines. On the other hand there is great danger that perhaps some blemishes in the shape of errors acquired by too attentive a reading of those authors may remain with us however unwilling we may be and however much we guard against them. For writers are in fact so minded that whenever, through thoughtless credulity, they have slipped into a judgment on some controversial subject, they always try by the subtlest arguments to draw us along in the same direction. Whenever, on the contrary, they have happily discovered something certain and evident, they never display it except in a wrapping of various detours, fearing no doubt lest the dignity of their discovery be diminished by the simplicity of the explanation, or else because they grudge us the open truth.

Yet even if they were all guileless and open, and never imposed upon us any doubtful opinions as true, but expounded every subject in good faith, we should still be perpetually uncertain which of them to believe,—since scarcely anything has been pronounced by one, the contrary of which has not been asserted by another. And it would avail nothing to count votes, that we might follow the opinion held by the greater number of authorities; for in the matter of a difficult question it is more likely that the truth should have been discovered by few than by many. But even if all of them should agree, their doctrine would still be inadequate. For we shall not, for example, turn out to be mathematicians, even though we keep in mind all the demonstrations of others, unless we are equipped intellectually for the solution of any kind of problem. Nor shall we turn out to be philosophers if we have read all the arguments of Plato and Aristotle but are unable to form a solid judgment on a given question. In fact we seem in this fashion to have learned not sciences but histories.

We are warned, further, never at any time to admit any conjectures whatsoever as an admixture to our judgments on the truth of things. This counsel is of no small importance. For the chief reason why nothing is found in the vulgar philosophy so evident and certain as to be incapable of controversial treatment, is this: scholars, not content with knowing what is clear and certain, have first hazarded further affirmations about obscure and unknown matters, at which they have arrived only by probable conjectures; and then gradually attaching to such matters a complete faith, and mixing them indiscriminately with what is true and evident, they have finally grown unable to draw any conclusion which does not appear to depend on some such proposition, and so is not uncertain.

But in order that we may not fall into the same error, let us here enumerate all the acts of our intellect through which we can arrive at the cognition of things without any fear of error. There are only two: namely intuition and induction.

By *intuition* I understand, not the fleeting testimony of the senses, nor the deceptive judgment of the imagination with its false constructions; but a conception of a pure and attentive mind so easy and so distinct, that no doubt at all remains about that which we are understanding. Or, what comes to the same thing, intuition is the undoubting conception of a pure and attentive mind, which arises from the light of reason alone, and is more certain even than deduction, because simpler,—although, as we noted above, men cannot err in deduction either. Thus every one can see by mental intuition that he exists, that he thinks, that a triangle is bounded by only three lines, the globe by a single surface, and the like. Such facts are much more numerous than most people think, because they scorn to turn their minds toward matters so easy.

But that others may not be disturbed by the term intuition in this new sense, or still others by my being forced to depart in the same way from common meanings in the following pages, I add here the general warning: that I pay no heed to the way in which particular terms have recently been employed in the schools, since it would have been very difficult to use the same words for ideas so entirely different. I consider only what each word means in Latin, so that when proper words are lacking I may transform to suit my meaning whatever terms appear to me most suitable.

This evidence and certitude of intuition is required, however, not only for single statements, but also for discursive reasoning of every kind. Thus, for example, given this conclusion: 2 and 2 amount to the same as 3 and 1; one must see by intuition not only that 2 and 2 make 4, and that 3 and 1 also make 4, but also that from these two propositions the third is a necessary conclusion.

Thus there may now be some doubt as to why we should here have added another mode of knowledge besides intuition, i.e. one proceeding by *deduction*, by which we understand all that is necessarily concluded from other facts certainly known. But this procedure was necessary since many things are known with certainty, which nevertheless are not themselves evident, simply because they are deduced from true and known principles by the continuous and uninterrupted movement of a mind which clearly intuits each step.

Thus we know that the last link of a long chain is connected with the first, even though we do not take in all the intermediate links, on which the connection depends, with a single glance (*intuitu*) of the eyes,—provided only that we run through them successively, and remember that from first to last each one was attached to the one next it. Therefore we here distinguish intuition from certain deduction by the fact that some movement or succession is conceived in the latter but not in the former. Moreover, evidence is not necessarily present for deduction, as it is for intuition, but deduction rather acquires its certitude, in a sense, from memory. From all this we may conclude that those propositions which follow immediately from first principles are known, according to the way we look at it, now by intuition, now by deduction; but that the first principles themselves are known only by intuition; and the remote conclusions, in contrast, only by deduction.

These then are the two most certain paths to scientific knowledge. No others should be admitted by the mind, but all the rest rejected as suspect and liable to error. This does not, however, prevent our believing those matters which are divinely revealed to be more certain than all knowledge. For faith in these, although it concerns obscure matters, is not an act of intellect but of will, and if they have a basis in the intellect, they can and ought to be, more than all other things, discovered by one or other of the two ways already mentioned, as we shall perhaps indicate some time at greater length.

RULE IV.—*Method is necessary for the investigation of truth.*

Mortals are possessed by such blind curiosity, that they often lead their minds through unknown paths, without any ground for hope, but simply venturing on the chance that what they seek might lie that way: as if a man were burning with so stupid a desire to find a treasure, that he constantly roamed about the roads to see if by chance he might find some article lost by a traveller. It is in this manner that almost all the chemists, most geometers, and not a few philosophers work. To be sure, I do not deny that they sometimes stray so fortunately as to find something true; still I do not therefore hold them more efficient, but only more fortunate. And it is much better never to think of investigating the truth of anything at all, than to do it without method. For it is very certain, that through such disorderly studies and obscure meditations the natural light is troubled and our minds blinded. Thus all those who get used to walking in the dark weaken the acuteness of their eyes so much that afterward they cannot bear the open light. This is also confirmed by experience; for how often do we not see those who have never devoted themselves to letters judging much more solidly and clearly of the things that come their way than do those who have spent all their time in the schools. By method, then, I understand certain and simple rules, such that if a man follows them exactly, he will never suppose anything false to be true, and, spending no useless mental effort, but gradually and steadily increasing his knowledge, will arrive at the true knowledge of all those things to which his powers are adequate.

Two things should be noted here: never to suppose true what is false, and to arrive at the knowledge of all things. For if we are ignorant of some one of all the things which we can know, that happens only because we have never discovered any way which would lead us to such knowledge, or because we have slipped into the contrary error. But if the method explains correctly how the intuition of the mind is to be used, and how deductions are to be made, that we may arrive at the knowledge of all things, nothing more seems to me to be required to make it complete, since we have already said that there can be no scientific knowledge except through mental intuition or deduction. Nor indeed must it extend to showing how these operations themselves are to be conducted, since they are the first and simplest of all,—so much so that, unless our intellect already knew how to use them, it could understand none of the precepts of the method itself, however simple. As to the other operations of the mind, moreover, which dialectic struggles to direct with the aid of these prior ones, they are useless here,—or rather they may be counted as obstructions, since nothing can be added to the pure light of reason without in some way obscuring it.

Since therefore the usefulness of this method is so great, that without it it seems more harmful than useful to devote oneself to the study of the sciences, I am readily convinced that, doubtless with the sole guide of nature, the greatest minds have formerly perceived it in some fashion. For the human mind possesses an I-know-not-what that is divine, in which the first seeds of useful thoughts are scattered, so that often, although neglected and suffocated by perverse studies, they bear spontaneous fruit. Of this we have experience in the simplest of the sciences, arithmetic and geometry; for we have sufficient evidence that the ancient geometers used a certain analysis, which they extended to the resolution of all problems, even though they begrudged it to posterity. And now there also exists a kind of arithmetic, called algebra, made to do with numbers what the ancients did with figures. And these two are nothing but spontaneous fruits, born of the innate principles of this method. Nor do I wonder that, with regard to the extremely simple objects of these arts, these fruits have developed more happily than in others, where greater obstacles usually stifle them. Even there, however, if only they are cultivated with the greatest care, they can without doubt arrive at full maturity.

This, then, is what I have principally undertaken to do in this treatise. Indeed, I should not make much of these rules, if they were adapted only to the solution of the vain problems with which logicians and geometers are wont to play when at leisure; for in that case I should think I had succeeded only in playing with trifles perhaps more subtly than others had done. True, I shall often speak here of figures and of numbers (since one cannot expect from any disciplines examples so evident or so certain), yet whoever considers my meaning attentively will easily perceive, that there is nothing of which I am here thinking less than of vulgar mathematics; but that I am expounding another discipline, of which these are the integument rather than the parts. This science should in fact contain the first rudiments of human reason, and should need only to extend itself in order to elicit truths on any subject whatsoever; and to speak freely, I am convinced that it is more powerful than all the other knowledge that mankind has taught us, because it is its source. But I said integument, not because I want to wrap up this doctrine and hide it to keep off the crowd, but rather in order to clothe and ornament it, that it may be more suitable for the human mind.

When I first applied my mind to the mathematical disciplines I first read most of those things, which the mathematical authors usually teach, and I paid most attention to arithmetic and geometry, since they were said to be simplest and at the same time roads to the others. But in neither case did I at that time lay my hand on authors who fully satisfied me. I did indeed read in their works several statements about numbers which after making calculations I found to be true; and even with regard to figures, they set, so to speak, many things before my eyes, and inferred them from certain consequences. But why these matters stood thus, and how they had been discovered, they did not seem to my mind to exhibit satisfactorily. So it did not surprise me that after tasting these arts, most men of talent and knowledge at once put them aside as puerile and vain, or on the contrary are deterred at the very beginning from learning them as being very difficult and intricate. For indeed nothing is more futile than to occupy oneself with bare numbers and imaginary figures, in such a way as to appear willing to rest content with the knowledge of such trifles; nor is anything more futile than so to attach oneself to those superficial demonstrations, which are more frequently discovered by chance than by art, and which have more to do with the eyes and imagination than with the intellect, that one becomes in a sense unaccustomed to the use of reason. At the same time nothing is more complicated than to dispose with this method of new difficulties hidden by the confusion of numbers. But then when I went on to think that the first discoverers of philosophy were long ago unwilling to admit to the study of wisdom any one untrained in mathematics, as if this discipline seemed to them the easiest and most necessary of all in training minds and preparing them to understand other and higher sciences, I strongly suspected that they knew some mathematics very different from the vulgar mathematics of our age. Not that I think they knew it very perfectly, for their mad rejoicings and thanksgivings for trifling discoveries indicate clearly how little advanced they were. Nor do certain machines of theirs which are celebrated by historians move me from my opinion; for although they were doubtless very simple, they could be praised to a degree of fame befitting miracles by the ignorant and astonished crowd. But I am convinced that the first seeds of truth, sown by nature in the human mind, but which we stifle in ourselves by reading and hearing every day so many errors of every kind, had such force in that rude and simple antiquity that, by the same light of the mind which made them see that they ought to prefer virtue to pleasure and the honest to the useful, although they were ignorant why it should be so, men had true ideas of philosophy and mathematics, although they had not yet been able to acquire perfectly these sciences themselves. In fact it seems to me that traces of that true mathematics are still visible in Pappus and Diophantus, who, though not of the first age, still lived many centuries before our time. But this I believe was later suppressed, with a sort of evil cunning, by these authors themselves. For, as many artisans have certainly done for their inventions, they feared perhaps that being very easy and simple their method might lose its price if given to the crowd. In order that we should wonder at them they preferred to give us instead of their discoveries a few sterile verities, subtly deduced, as the fruits of their art, rather than to teach the art itself, which would clearly dispel the wonder. Finally there were some very ingenious men who tried in this century to revive this art. For that art which is called by the barbarous name of algebra seems to be nothing else, provided only one could disentangle it from the multitudinous numerals and inexplicable figures with which it is encumbered, so that it might no longer lack that clarity and that supreme facility which ought, as we have said, to be present in true mathematics. When these thoughts had led me from the particular study of arithmetic and geometry to a general study of mathematics, I inquired first of all precisely what every one means by this word, and why not only those two sciences of which we have already spoken, but also music, optics, mechanics and several others are called parts of mathematics. For it is not enough in this case to consider the etymology of the word; since, as the term *mathesis* signifies simply science, the other sciences would have no less right than geometry itself to be called mathematics. Moreover we see no one who, if he has so much as touched the threshold of the schools, fails to distinguish easily among those subject matters which are presented to him what belongs to mathematics and what belongs to the other disciplines. And if one reflects on this matter more attentively, one finally observes that all those and only those subjects in which order and measurement are investigated are referred to mathematics, no matter whether such measure is sought in numbers, in figures, in stars, in sounds, or in what object so-ever. One concludes, therefore, that there must be some general science explaining all that can be investigated concerning order and measure, without application to a particular material; and that this science is called, not by a strange name, but by a name already ancient and received by usage, universal mathematics, because it includes all that material by virtue of which other sciences are called parts of mathematics. How much it excels in usefulness and facility the sciences which depend on it is clear from the fact that it extends to all the objects which they treat and to many others; and that all the difficulties which it involves are found also in the other sciences, accompanied in addition by many other difficulties, which arise from their particular objects, and which it for its part does not possess. But now, since every one knows its name and knows, even without applying it, of what it treats, how does it happen that most men try to learn the other sciences which depend on it, while no one takes the trouble to study it in itself? I should certainly be amazed at this, if I did not know that it is considered by every one to be very simple, and if I had not long since observed that the human mind, leaving aside what it thinks easy of attainment, hurries straight on to new and loftier things.

But I, conscious of my weakness, have decided constantly to observe in the investigation of truth an order such that, always beginning with the simplest and easiest matters, I never pass to others, before it seems to me that nothing remains to be desired in the first. That is why I have up to now cultivated, as much as in me lay, this universal mathematics; hence I believe that when I go on, as I hope to do soon, to deal in turn with more profound sciences, my efforts will not be premature. But before I take this step I shall try to unite and to set in order all that I have found worthy of notice in my earlier studies: both in order to find them without trouble in this book, if need be, at the time when with increasing age my memory shall fail, and in order by discharging my memory of them now to be able to carry a freer mind to other things.

RULE V.—*All method consists in the order and disposition of those things toward which our mental vision must be directed if we are to discover any truth. And we follow this method exactly if we reduce involved and obscure propositions step by step to simpler ones, and then attempt to ascend by the same steps from the intuition of all those that are entirely simple to the cognition of all the others.*

In this alone lies the sum total of human endeavor, and this rule must be followed no less carefully by one who would enter into a knowledge of things, than the thread of Theseus by him who would penetrate the labyrinth. But many people either do not reflect on what this precept teaches, or are completely ignorant of it, or suppose they do not need it. Hence they often examine the most difficult questions with so little order, that they seem to me to behave as if they were trying to get from the bottom to the top of a building with one jump, either taking no account of the stairs intended for this use, or failing to notice them. That is what all the astrologers do, who, without knowing the nature of the heaven and without even having observed its motions adequately, hope to be able to indicate its effects. That is what many do, who study mechanics apart from physics, and rashly manufacture new instruments for the production of motions. That is also what those philosophers do, who make no tests but think that truth will spring from their own brains, like Minerva from the head of Jupiter.

Indeed it is evident that all these err with respect to the present rule. But since the order here required is so obscure and intricate that not every one can make out what it is, they can scarcely take care enough to avoid error, unless they observe diligently what is expounded in the following proposition.

RULE VI.—*To distinguish the simplest things from those which are complex, and to follow them out in order, it is necessary, in every sequence of things in which we have directly deduced certain truths from others, to observe what constituent has the greatest simplicity, and in what way all the others are more or less or equally removed from it.*

Although this proposition appears to teach nothing now, it contains nevertheless the chief secret of this art, nor is there any more useful proposition in all this treatise; for it counsels that all things can be arranged in certain sequences. Not indeed, that they can be so arranged in so far as they are referred to some genus of being, as the philosophers have divided them into their categories, but in so far as certain ones can be known through others. Thus, each time any difficulty occurs, we can see immediately whether it will be of profit to run through certain other matters first, and which, and in what order.

In order that this may be correctly done, however, it must first be noted that all things, in the degree to which they can be useful to our project (when we do not consider their natures in isolation but compare them with one another, in order that certain ones may be known through others) may be said to be either absolute or relative.

I call absolute everything which contains within itself the pure and simple nature that is in question: as all that is considered independent, cause, simple, universal, equal, similar, straight or the like; and I call this the simplest and easiest of all, so that we may use it for resolving questions.

The relative, on the other hand, is that which participates in the same nature, or at least in something of it, in accordance with which it can be referred to the absolute, and deduced from it through some sequence; but which, in addition, involves in its conception other things, which I call relations. Such is all that is called dependent, effect, compounded, particular, many, unequal, dissimilar, oblique, etc. These relatives are removed from absolutes in proportion to the number of mutually subordinate relations they contain. And it is the necessity of distinguishing such relations that the present rule teaches. It also teaches the need of observing the pattern of interconnections between them and their natural order in such fashion that we can proceed from the last of them to the most absolute, passing through all the rest.

The secret of all our art consists in noticing carefully in all things what is most absolute in them. For some things are more absolute than others from one point of view, but more relative from another. Thus the universal is indeed more absolute than the particular, since it has a simpler nature, but at the same time one can say it is more relative since it depends on individuals for its existence. Again, there are sometimes things that are really more absolute than others, even though they are never the most absolute of all. Thus, if we consider individuals, the species is an absolute, and if we consider the genus, it is a relative; among measurable things, extension is an absolute, but among extensions length, etc. In the same way, finally, in order to make it clearer that we are here considering the sequences of things as objects of knowledge and not the nature of each one of them, we have purposely counted cause and equal among the absolutes, although their nature is really relative,—for among the philosophers cause and effect are in fact correlatives. But here, if we are in fact inquiring into the nature of the effect, we must first know the cause, and not the reverse. Equals likewise correspond with one another; but we know unequals only by comparison with equals, and not the reverse, etc.

It should be noted, secondly, that there are only a few pure and simple natures, which we may intuit in themselves, independently of all others, whether in trials by experience, or by the light that is implanted in us. Moreover we declare that these must be painstakingly observed; for it is these which we call the simplest in every sequence. All others, in contrast, can be perceived only in so far as they are deduced from these, either immediately or proximately, or through the mediation of two or three or more different conclusions. And the number of these conclusions must also be noted, that we may know if they are removed from the first and simplest propositions by a smaller or greater number of steps. And such is everywhere the nexus of consequences, from which arise those sequences of objects of investigation, to which every question is to be reduced in order that it may be examined by a sure method. But because it is not easy to review them all, and since, besides, they need not be so much retained by the memory as distinguished by some insight of the mind, we must seek for something which will so form the mind as to let it perceive these sequences whenever it needs to do so. For this purpose, I can say from experience, nothing is more effective than to reflect with some sagacity on the very smallest of the facts one has already perceived.

Finally, it should be noted in the third place, that we ought not to begin an inquiry with the investigation of difficult matters. Rather, before we set out to attack any definite questions, we must first collect indiscriminately all the truths which spontaneously present themselves, then gradually see if others can be deduced from them, and from these last others, and so on. That done, we must reflect attentively on the truths we have discovered, and consider carefully why we have been able to find some sooner and more easily than others, and which they are. This we do that we may also be able to judge, when we begin some definite question, to what other inquiries we could profitably apply ourselves first. For example, if it occurred to me that 6 is the double of 3, I should look further for the double of 6, that is to say, 12; then I should look, if I liked, for the double of that, that is to say 24, and the double of that, that is 48, etc. . . . . ; and thence I should conclude, as it is easy to do, that there is the same proportion between 3 and 6 as between 6 and 12, and the same between 12 and 24 etc. . . . . and that consequently the numbers 3, 6, 12, 24, 48 etc. are in a continuous proportion. Thence, although all these things are so clear as to appear almost childish, I understand, on attentive reflection, in what way all questions are involved which can be posed about proportions or the relations of things, and in what order they should be investigated: and this alone embraces the whole of the science of pure mathematics. . . . .

Rule VII.—*In order to attain complete scientific knowledge, it is necessary to run through, one by one, in a movement of thought which is continuous and nowhere interrupted, all those matters which bear upon our end; they must also be included in an enumeration at once sufficient and ordered.*

The observation of what is here propounded is necessary for the admission among certain truths of those which, as we have said above, are not immediately deduced from first principles known through themselves. Sometimes, in fact, this deduction is made by a chain of consequences so long that, when we get to the end, we do not easily remember the whole road which has conducted us to this point; and that is why we said that it is necessary to aid the weakness of the memory by a continuous movement of thought. Thus if I have found out by separate operations, for example, what relation there is between the magnitudes A and B, next between B and C, and then between C and D, and finally between D and E, I do not therefore see what relation there is between A and E, nor can I understand it with accuracy from the facts I have already learned, unless I remember them all. To remedy this, I should run over them several times with a continuous movement of the imagination which gives an intuition of every single one and at the same time passes to others, until I had learned to pass from the first to the last so rapidly that next to no part was left to memory, but I seemed to intuit the whole thing at once. For by this means, while it helps the memory, the sluggishness of the mind is corrected, and its capacity in a certain sense extended.

We add, moreover, that the movement must be nowhere interrupted. For often those who wish to deduce something too quickly and from distant principles do not run through the whole chain of intermediate propositions with sufficient care to prevent their rashly overlooking many points. But surely, wherever even the smallest point is omitted, the chain is immediately broken, and the whole certainty of the conclusion falls.

We may say here, further, that enumeration is required for the complete attainment of science. To be sure, other precepts are of assistance in the solution of many questions; but only the aid of enumeration can bring it about that, to whatever question we may apply our minds, we should always make a true and certain judgment, and that therefore nothing at all should escape us, but we should appear to know something about everything.

This enumeration, then, or induction, is an inventory of everything that bears on any given question—an inventory so painstaking and accurate that from it we conclude with certainty and evidence that nothing has mistakenly been omitted by us. Thus every time we have used it, if the thing we are looking for escapes us, we are at least wiser in this respect: that we perceive with certainty that it can be found by no way known to us; and if perchance, as often happens, we have succeeded in reviewing all the ways to it that are open to men, we may boldly affirm that knowledge of it lies entirely beyond the reach of human intelligence.

It should be noted, further, that by sufficient enumeration or induction, we understand only the means by which truth is more certainly inferred than by any other kind of proof except simple intuition. As often as a cognition cannot be reduced to intuition, since we have thrown off all the syllogistic bonds, there remains to us only this one way to which we should fasten all our faith. For whatever single propositions we have deduced immediately from others, are already reduced to a true intuition, if the inference was evident. If, however, we infer some one thing from many and disconnected facts, the capacity of our intellect is often insufficient to embrace them all in a single intuition; in which case the certitude of the present operation should suffice. In the same way we are unable to distinguish with a single glance of the eyes all the links of a very long chain; yet if we see the connection of each one to the next, that is enough to let us say we have seen how the last is connected with the first.

I have said that this operation ought to be sufficient, because it can often be defective and in consequence liable to error. For sometimes, even though we review by enumeration a great number of things which are really evident, if nevertheless we omit even the smallest point, the chain is broken, and the whole certainty of the conclusion falls. Sometimes, moreover, we embrace the whole with certainty in an enumeration, but we do not distinguish the single points from one another; and so know the whole only confusedly.

Besides, this enumeration should sometimes be complete, sometimes distinct, but sometimes neither is necessary; and that is why it has only been stated that it ought to be sufficient. For if I want to prove by enumeration, how many genera of things are corporeal, or fall in some way under sense, I shall not declare that there are so many and no more, until I know for certain that I have included them all in my enumeration, and have distinguished each from the others. But if I wish to show by the same means that the rational soul is not corporeal, it will not be necessary that the enumeration be complete, but it will be sufficient if I include all bodies at once in certain classes, in such a way as to demonstrate that the rational soul can be referred to none of them. And finally if I wish to show by enumeration that the area of the circle is greater than the area of other figures whose perimeter is equal, it is not necessary to review all the figures, but it is sufficient to demonstrate this of some particular figures, in order by induction to reach this same conclusion concerning all the others.

I have also added that enumeration should be ordered, not only because there is no better remedy for the defects already enumerated than to examine everything with order, but also because it often happens that, if it were necessary to examine separately every one of the things which bear on a given question, no human life would suffice for it, either because these things are too numerous, or because the same things would too often meet us for renewed consideration. But if we dispose of all things in the best order, they will (for the most part) be (as far as possible) reduced to definite classes. It will then be enough to examine carefully either a single one of them, or something from each, or some rather than others; or at least we shall not review the same thing twice to no purpose. This procedure is so helpful, that often because of a well-established order one traverses in a short time and with little effort a great many things which at first sight look immense.

This order of things to be enumerated, however, can often vary, and it depends on the choice of each person. So, to grasp it more accurately, one must recall what was said in the fifth proposition. There are also many of the more trivial inventions of men, for the discovery of which the whole method consists in this disposing of order. Thus if you wish to construct a perfect anagram by transposing the letters of a name, there is no need to pass from the easy to the difficult, nor to distinguish absolute from relative. Here there is no place for these things; but it will be sufficient to adopt an order for transposing the letters under examination, such that one never comes twice to the same one, and that their number, for instance, is distributed in fixed classes, so that it may immediately appear in which there is the best hope of finding what is sought. In this fashion the work will often not be too long, but only child's play.

On the other hand, these three last propositions are not to be separated, because for the most part we must think of them at the same time, and because all concur equally in the perfection of our method. It made no great difference, which was given first; and we explain them here in few words, because we have practically nothing left to do in the rest of the treatise, except to show in particular what we have here considered in general.

RULE VIII.—*If in the series of things to be examined something presents itself which our intellect is unable sufficiently well to perceive by intuition, we must stop there; nor ought we to examine what follows, but to abstain from superfluous labor.*

The three preceding rules prescribe order and explain it; this one shows when it is absolutely necessary, when only useful. Thus whatever constitutes a complete step in that series by which we must pass from relatives to some absolute or the reverse, must necessarily be examined before anything which follows it. If however, as often happens, many things belong to the same step, it is indeed always useful to run through them all in order, but in this case we are not forced to observe order so strictly nor so rigidly. Often, although we do not know clearly all these things, but only a small number of them or just one, it is still possible to pass beyond them.

This rule follows necessarily from the reasons given for the second. However it must not be supposed that it contains nothing new for the advancement of science, even though it appears only to keep us from the discussion of certain things and to propound no truth. As for beginners, indeed, it teaches them only not to waste their time, in almost the same way as the second rule. But to those who have perfectly learned the seven preceding rules, it shows how in any science whatsoever they can so satisfy themselves as to desire nothing further. For whoever shall have observed the preceding rules exactly in the solution of any difficulty and shall nevertheless have received from this rule the order to halt, will then know with certainty that he cannot by any device discover the knowledge he is seeking,—and that not by the fault of his mind, but because the nature of the difficulty itself or the condition of humanity prevents. This knowledge is no less a science than is that which exhibits the nature of the thing itself; and he would not appear of sound mind, who should extend his curiosity further.

All this should be illustrated by one or two examples. If some one who studies only mathematics looks for that line which in dioptrics is called anaclastic, and in which parallel lines are refracted in such fashion that all of them, after the refraction, meet in a single point, he will easily observe, according to rules five and six, that the determination of this line depends on the proportion of the angles of refraction to the angles of incidence. But as he will not be capable of investigating this matter, since it belongs not to mathematics but to physics, he will have to stop immediately. And it would avail him nothing if he wished to hear from the philosophers or draw from experience the knowledge of this truth; for he would be sinning against the third rule. Besides, this proposition is still compounded and relative; but it is only in things that are perfectly simple and absolute that experience can be considered certain, as we shall show in the proper place. Moreover, it would be useless for him to postulate, between angles of this kind, some proportion which he suspected to be truest of all; for then he would no longer be looking for the anaclastic line, but only for the line which should follow out the ground of his supposition.

On the other hand, if some one who does not study mathematics alone, but who tries, according to the first rule, to look for truth on all subjects which present themselves, should fall into the same difficulty, he will go farther and discover that this proportion between the angles of incidence and the angles of refraction depends on the variation of these same angles in virtue of the difference of the media; that this variation in its turn depends on the manner in which the ray penetrates into the transparent body; that the knowledge of the property of penetrating into a body supposes equally that the nature of illumination is known; and that finally to understand illumination one must know what a natural power is in general,—and this is the last and most absolute term in this whole sequence. Then when he has perceived this clearly by intuition, he will repeat the same steps, according to the fifth rule; and if in the second step he cannot at once recognize the nature of illumination, he will enumerate all the other natural powers, in accordance with the seventh rule, in order that, thanks to the knowledge of some one of them, he will understand it also, at least by analogy (of which I shall speak later). This done, he will investigate the manner in which the ray penetrates through the whole transparent body; and in this way he will run through the rest in order, until he has arrived at the anaclastic itself. Although up to now this has been vainly attempted by many people, I see nothing to keep some one who makes perfect use of our method from the evident knowledge of this line.

But let us give the most noble example of all. If a man proposes to himself the problem of examining all the truths for the knowledge of which human reason suffices—a task which should be undertaken at least once in his life, it seems to me, by any one who is in all seriousness eager to attain to excellence of mind—he will certainly discover by the rules given above that nothing can be known before the understanding, since the knowledge of all other things depends on this, and not the reverse. Then, when he has examined everything that follows immediately after the knowledge of the pure understanding, he will enumerate, among other things, all the other instruments of knowledge we possess besides the understanding; and these are only two: namely, imagination and the senses. He will then devote all his care to distinguishing and examining these three modes of knowledge; and seeing that strictly speaking truth or falsity can exist only in the understanding, but that they often take their source also from the other two, he will attend carefully to everything by which he can be deceived, that he may be on guard against it. And he will enumerate exactly all the paths to truth which are open to men, that he may follow the sure one,—for they are not so many that he cannot discover them all easily through a sufficient enumeration. And, what will seem marvellous and incredible to the inexpert, as soon as he has distinguished, for each object, those cognitions which only fill and embellish the memory, from those in virtue of which one may truly be said to be more learned, a distinction which it is also easy to make, ...[2] he will feel that there is absolutely nothing of which he is ignorant through a defect of mind or art, and that nothing further can be known by any man, which he is not also capable of knowing, provided only that he applies his mind to it as he ought. And although many things can often be proposed to him the investigation of which will be forbidden by this rule, he will nevertheless not think himself more ignorant for having clearly understood that they exceed the bounds of the human mind; but this knowledge itself, that no one can know the thing in question, will amply satisfy his curiosity if he is reasonable.

But that we may not always be uncertain of what our mind is capable, and that we may not labor wrongly and rashly, before we set ourselves to learn things in detail; we ought to inquire carefully, once in our lives, of what knowledge human reason is capable. In order better to accomplish this task, we ought among things that are equally simple to investigate those which are more useful.

Indeed, this method resembles those of the mechanical arts which need no outside help, and which themselves teach how to construct their instruments. Thus if one wished to practice one of them, the art of the smith, for example, one would be forced at first to use as an anvil a hard stone or a rough lump of iron, to take a piece of rock in place of a hammer, to shape pieces of wood into tongs, and to collect other materials of this sort according to need. Thus equipped, one would not then at once try to forge swords or helmets or any object of iron for the use of others; but one would first of all manufacture hammers, an anvil, tongs, and the other things useful to oneself. This example teaches us that, if we have at the outset been able to find only some confused principles, which

[2] There seems to be a lacuna here in the original text.

seem to be innate in our minds rather than prepared by art, we must not use them to try to settle immediately the controversies of the philosophers or to solve the puzzles of the mathematicians. We must rather use them first for seeking with the greatest care all that is more necessary for the examination of truth; since there is surely no reason why this should seem more difficult to discover than any of the questions usually propounded in geometry or physics or the other disciplines.

Now nothing is more useful here than to inquire what human knowledge is and how far it extends. That is why we now embrace these problems in a single question, which we hold should be examined first of all questions in accordance with the rules previously stated. This must be done once in his life by every one of those who have even the faintest love for truth, since in this inquiry the true instruments of knowledge and the whole of method are contained. Nothing seems to me more absurd, on the other hand, than to dispute boldly on the mysteries of nature, on the influence of the heavens on our earth, on the prediction of the future, and the like, as many do, and yet never to have inquired whether human reason is adequate for the discovery of these things. Nor ought it to seem arduous or difficult to determine the limits of the mind, which we perceive within ourselves, since often we do not hesitate to make judgments on things which are outside us and quite foreign to us. Nor is it an immense task to attempt to embrace in thought all the things contained in this universe, in order that we may recognize how each one is subjected to the examination of our minds; for nothing can be so multiple or so scattered that it cannot, by means of the enumeration with which we have been dealing, be circumscribed in definite limits and disposed under a certain number of heads. In order to have experience of this in the question at hand, we first divide everything that pertains to it into two parts; for it ought either to be referred to us who are capable of knowledge, or to those things which can be known; and we discuss these two parts separately.

Now in ourselves we notice that the understanding alone is capable of scientific knowledge; but that it can be helped or hindered by three other faculties, namely by imagination, sense and memory. We must therefore see, in order, what hindrance each of these faculties can be, that we may be on our guard; or of what use each can be, that we may use all its resources. Thus this part will be treated by a sufficient enumeration, as we shall show in the following rule.

We must then proceed to the things themselves, which are to be examined only in so far as they are touched by the understanding. In this connection we divide them into maximally simple natures and natures that are complex or composite. Simple natures must be either spiritual or corporeal, or related to both. Then among the composites the understanding realizes some to be complex before it judges that it can determine anything about them; but others it compounds itself. All this will be expounded at greater length in the twelfth rule, where it will be proved that there can be no falsity except in these last natures which are compounded by the intellect. That is why we distinguish them again into two kinds: those which are deduced from natures that are of the greatest simplicity and known through themselves, of which we shall treat in the following book; and those which likewise presuppose others which the facts themselves show us to be composite, for the exposition of which we destine the whole of the third book.

And indeed in all this treatise we shall try to follow through with so much care and to make so easy all the paths which are open to men for the knowledge of truth, that any one who has perfectly learned the whole of this method, however mediocre his mind, may yet see that none of these paths is more closed to him than to others, and that he is no longer ignorant of anything through a defect of mind or art. But as often as he applies his mind to the knowledge of anything, he will either reach it entirely; or he will clearly understand that it depends on some experience which is not in his power, and then he will not make his mind responsible, although he be forced to stop at that place; or finally he will demonstrate that what he is seeking exceeds the bounds of the human mind, and consequently he will not think therefore himself more ignorant, because this result is no less scientific knowledge than the knowledge of anything else.

RULE IX.—*We ought to turn the whole force of our minds to the smallest and simplest things, and to stop there for a long time, until we become accustomed clearly and distinctly to intuit the truth.*

We have now expounded the two operations of our intellect, intuition and deduction, which alone we have said we must employ in learning the sciences. We continue in this and the following rule to explain by what procedure we can become more skilled in using them and at the same time in developing the two principal faculties of our mind, perspicacity, in having a distinct intuition of each thing, and sagacity, in deducing easily certain facts from others.

Indeed, we learn the manner in which mental intuition should be used, by comparing it with vision. For he who wishes to look at many objects at a time with one and the same glance, sees none of them distinctly; and similarly he who is used to attending to many objects at the same time in a single act of thought, is confused in mind. But those artisans who practise delicate operations, and are accustomed to direct the force of their eyes attentively to single points, acquire by use the ability to distinguish perfectly things as tiny and subtle as may be. In the same way, likewise, those who never disperse their thought among different objects at one time, but always occupy all its attention in considering the simplest and easiest matters, become perspicacious.

But it is a failing common to mortals to consider difficult things lovelier. And most men think they know nothing when they find a cause for something that is really clear and simple; while they admire certain sublime and profound theories of the philosophers, although these rest for the most part on foundations never adequately examined by any one. Fools, indeed, who prefer darkness to light! It should be noted, however, that those who really know, discern the truth with equal facility whether they have drawn it from a simple or an obscure subject. For they comprehend each truth by an act that is similar, single, and distinct, once they have arrived at it, but the whole difference is in the road, which should certainly be longer if it leads to a truth remote from the first and most absolute principles.

RULE X.—*In order that the mind may acquire sagacity, it is necessary to give it practice in investigating what others have already discovered; and it ought to traverse methodically even the most trifling inventions of men, but especially those which best explain or suppose order.*

I confess that I was born with a mind such that I have always found the greatest pleasure of study not in hearing the explanations of others, but in finding them by my own devices. This alone attracted me, while I was still young, to the study of the sciences. So whenever a book promised by its title a new discovery, before going farther I tried if by chance I should not succeed in finding something analagous by natural sagacity; and I took good care not to deprive myself of this innocent pleasure by a precipitous reading. I succeeded in this so often that I finally noticed that I was no longer arriving at the truth of things, as others usually do, by vague and blind disquisitions, by the help of fortune rather than art; but that by long experience I had perceived certain rules, which are of no little help in this study and which I afterward used to think out many others. And so I have diligently elaborated this whole method, and have become convinced that I had followed from the beginning the most useful mode of studying.

But since not all minds are equally inclined by their nature to discover things of their own power, this proposition teaches, that we ought not to occupy ourselves at once with the more difficult and arduous matters, but should first discuss those disciplines which are easiest and simplest, and those above all in which order most prevails. Such are the arts of the craftsmen who make cloth and tapestries, those of women who embroider or make lace, as well as all the games with numbers, and all that relates to arithmetic, and the like. All these arts give the mind excellent practice, provided we do not learn them from others, but discover them ourselves. For, since nothing in them remains hidden, and they are entirely adjusted to the capacity of human knowledge, they show us very distinctly innumerable arrangements, all different from one another and yet regular, in the scrupulous observation of which the whole of human sagacity consists. . . . .

Perhaps, however, some may wonder that in this place, where we are looking for the means to make us more skilful in deducing truths one from another, we should omit all the precepts by which the dialecticians think to govern human reason. They prescribe to it certain forms of argument which conclude with such necessity that reason, if confined to them, although it does not take the trouble to consider the inference itself in an attentive and evident manner, can nevertheless sometimes arrive, by virtue of the form, at a sure conclusion. The thing is that, as a matter of fact, we are aware that truth often escapes these bonds, while those, meanwhile, who have used them remain entangled. That does not happen so frequently to other men; and experience shows that ordinarily the subtlest sophisms refute, not ever those who use only pure reason, but the sophists themselves.

That is why here, fearing above all things that our reason should go on holiday while we are examining the truth of some matter, we reject these forms of reasoning as contrary to our end, and we search rather for all the aids by which our thought may be kept attentive, as we shall show in what follows. But that it may appear with even greater evidence that this method of argument is of no use for the knowledge of truth, it must be noted that the dialecticians can find by their art no syllogism which yields a true conclusion unless they first have the material for it, i.e. unless they have already learned the truth itself which they are deducing in their syllogism. Hence it is clear that they themselves learn nothing new from such a form; and that vulgar dialectic is therefore entirely useless for those who wish to seek for truth. On the contrary, its only use is that now and then it can expound more easily to others explanations already known; hence it should be transferred from philosophy to rhetoric.

RULE XI.—*If, after we have grasped by intuition a certain number of simple propositions, we wish to infer some other proposition from them, it is useful to run over them in a continuous and uninterrupted movement of thought, to reflect on their relations to one another, and as far as possible to conceive distinctly several at a time. For it is in this way that our knowledge becomes much more certain and the power of our mind is greatly increased.*

This is the occasion to expound more clearly what has already been said of intuition in rules three and seven. For in one place we have opposed it to deduction, and in another to enumeration only, which we have defined as an inference drawn from many and diverse things. But we said in the same place that the simple deduction of one thing from another is executed by intuition.

It was necessary to proceed in this way, because we demand two conditions of intuition, to wit: that the proposition be clearly and distinctly understood, and, further, that it be understood in its entirety at one time and not successively. Deduction, on the other hand, if we are thinking of its execution, as in rule three, does not seem to occur all at one time, but it involves a certain movement of our mind, which infers one thing from another. So we were right in distinguishing it from intuition. But if we consider deduction as already accomplished, as in what we said in rule seven, then it no longer designates any movement, but rather the end of a motion. Therefore we suppose that it is perceived by intuition when it is simple and clear, but not when it is complex and obscured. To the latter situation we give the name of enumeration, or induction, because it cannot then be comprehended by the intellect all at one time, but its certainty depends to some extent on memory, in which our judgments about the individual points enumerated must be retained if some one single judgment is to be drawn from all of them.

All these distinctions were necessary for the interpretation of this rule. For after the ninth rule had treated only of intuition, and the tenth only of enumeration, this one explains how these two operations mutually assist and complete one another, to the point of seeming to merge into one by a certain movement of thought which perceives each fact attentively by intuition and at the same time passes to others.

To this we designate a double use: namely for the more certain knowledge of the conclusion with which we are concerned; and for rendering the mind more skilful in other discoveries. The fact is that memory (on which, we have said, depends the certainty of conclusions that embrace more than we can grasp in one intuition) though unstable and infirm, can be renewed and strengthened by this continuous and repeated movement of thought. Thus if by several operations I have first discovered the relation which exists between a first and a second magnitude, then between the second and a third, then between the third and a fourth, and finally between the fourth and a fifth, I do not therefore see what relation exists between the first and fifth, and I cannot deduce it from the relations already known if I do not remember them all. That is why it is necessary for me to run through them repeatedly in thought, until I have passed so rapidly from the first to the last that practically no parts of the process are left to memory, and I seem to grasp the whole thing at once by intuition.

Every one must see that by this scheme the sluggishness of the mind is corrected and its comprehension likewise enlarged. But it must be noted, further, that the greatest utility of this rule consists in the fact that, in reflecting on the mutual dependence of simple propositions, we get the habit of distinguishing immediately what is more or less relative and by what degrees it is reduced to the absolute. For example, if I run through several magnitudes that are in continuous proportion, I shall reflect on all the following facts: to wit, that it is by a similar mental act—neither more nor less easy—that I recognize the relation which exists between the first magnitude and the second, the second and the third, the third and the fourth, and so on; but that I cannot grasp so easily what is the dependence of the second on the first and third at the same time; and that it is still more difficult to grasp the dependence of the same second on the first and fourth, and so on. Hence I see for what reason I can easily find the third and fourth if only the first and second are given, and so on: it is because that is accomplished by particular and distinct conceptions. But if only the first and third are given, I do not so easily learn the intermediate magnitude, because that can be done only by an effort of thought which embraces at once the two given magnitudes. If only the first and the fourth are given, I shall have still more trouble in getting an intuitive grasp of the two intermediates, because here three concepts at once are involved. Thus it would seem, in consequence, more difficult still to find the three intermediates between the first and fifth. But there is another scheme by which this can be achieved in another way. Although four concepts are here conjoined, they can nevertheless be separated, since four can be divided by another number. Thus, I can look for the third by itself from the first and fifth, then the second from the first and third, and so on. Whoever accustoms himself to reflect on these and similar matters, every time he examines a new question, immediately discovers what produces a difficulty in it, and what of all ways is the very simplest one for solving it, and this is a very great aid to the knowledge of truth.

RULE XII.—*Finally we ought to use all the aids of intellect, imagination, sense, and memory, partly in order to have a distinct intuition of simple propositions; partly to compare correctly what we seek with what we know, that we may recognize it; partly in order to discover those things which should be so compared with one another that none of the devices in the power of men may be omitted.*

This rule gives the conclusion of all that has been said above, and teaches in general the points that were there explained in particular, in this wise.

In what concerns the knowledge of things, only two matters

have to be considered: namely, ourselves who know and the objects themselves which are to be known. In us there are only four faculties which we can use for this purpose, namely, understanding, imagination, sense, and memory. To be sure, the understanding alone is capable of perceiving truth; but it must nevertheless be assisted by imagination, sense, and memory, lest perchance we should omit anything that lies in our power. On the side of the objects it is enough to examine three things: first, what presents itself spontaneously; secondly, how we learn one fact from another; and thirdly, what deductions one can make from each. This enumeration seems to me to be complete, and to omit nothing to which human powers can extend. . . . .

RULE XIII.—*If we understand a question perfectly, we must abstract it from every superfluous concept, simplify it as much as possible, and divide it by enumeration into as small parts as possible.* . . . .

RULE XIV.—*The same question must be transferred to the real extension of bodies, and represented in its entirety to the imagination through bare figures; for in this way it will be much more distinctly perceived by the understanding.*

If we wish also to use the aid of the imagination, we must notice that whenever we deduce something unknown from something else already known, we do not for all that discover a new genus of being; but it only happens that the knowledge we have is extended to the point of making us see that the thing sought participates in one way or another in the nature of those things which are given in the question. For example, if some one is blind from birth, he need not hope that we can ever by any argument bring it about that he should perceive true ideas of colors such as we have received from the senses. On the other hand, if some one has already seen the fundamental colors, but does not know the intermediate and mixed colors, it is possible for him by a sort of deduction to invent for himself the images even of those he has not seen, according to their similarity with the others. In the same way, if there exists in the magnet some genus of being, to which our understanding has so far seen nothing similar, we need not hope ever to know it by reasoning. For that we should need either some new sense or a divine mind. All that the human mind can do in this matter, we shall think we have done if we see very distinctly the mixture of beings or of natures already known which produces the same effects which appear in the magnet.

In fact, whatever be the difference of subjects, it is by the same idea that we know all those beings already known, such as extension, figure, motion, and the like, which it is not the place to list here; and we do not imagine differently the figure of a crown, whether it be of silver or of gold. This common idea passes from one subject to another only by means of a simple comparison, through which we affirm that the thing sought is, in one respect or another, similar, identical, or equal to the thing given, in such a way that in all ratiocination it is only by comparison that we know the truth with precision. For example in this: all A is B, all B is C, therefore all A is C: we compare with one another the thing sought and the thing given, that is to say, A and C, with respect to the question whether either one is B, etc. But since, as we have often warned, the forms of the syllogisms are of no help in perceiving the truth of things, it will be of advantage to the reader, if, after he has completely rejected them, he grasps the fact that every cognition whatsoever which is not got by a simple and pure intuition of one isolated object, is got by the comparison of two or more objects with one another. Indeed almost all the labor of human reason consists in preparing this operation; for, when it is open and simple, there is no need for any aid of art, but only of the light of nature alone, for the intuition of the truth which is got through it.

It must be noted, that comparisons are not called simple and open except whenever the thing sought and the thing given participate equally in a certain nature; that all other comparisons, on the other hand, need preparation only because this common nature is not equally present in the one and the other, but with respect to other relations or proportions in which it is involved; and that the principal part of human contriving consists only in reducing these proportions in such a way as to see clearly an equality between what is sought and something known.

It must be noted, further, that nothing can be reduced to this equality except what admits of more and less, and that all this is comprised under the name of magnitude. Thus when the terms of the difficulty have been abstracted from every subject, according to the preceding rule, we understand that we have nothing further to occupy us except magnitudes in general.

But if we wish to imagine something more here, and to make use, not of the pure understanding, but of the understanding aided by images painted on the imagination, we must note, finally, that nothing is said about magnitudes in general which cannot also be referred to some one in particular.

Hence it is easy to conclude that there will be great advantage in transferring what we understand to be said about magnitudes in general to that species of magnitude which among all will be painted most easily and most distinctly in our imagination. But, that this magnitude is the real extension of a body, abstracted from everything else but its figure, results from what has been said in rule 12, where we have seen that imagination itself, with the ideas which exist in it, is only a true, real, extended, and figured body. This is also evident in itself, because all the differences in proportion are in no other subject exhibited more distinctly. For although one thing can be called more or less white than another, or again one sound more or less acute, and so of other things, still we cannot define exactly whether this more or less is in double or triple proportion, except by a certain analogy with the extension of a figured body. It remains sure and certain, therefore, that perfectly determined questions contain scarcely any difficulty beyond that which consists in resolving proportions into equalities; and that everything in which just this difficulty is discovered can and should be easily separated from every other subject, and then transferred to extension and figures, of which, for this reason, we shall later treat exclusively up to the twenty-fifth rule. . . . .

RULE XV.—*It is also useful in many cases to describe these figures and to exhibit them to the external senses, in order that by this device our thought should more easily be kept attentive.* . . . .

RULE XVI.—*As for the things which do not demand the immediate attention of the mind, although they are necessary for the conclusion, it is better to designate them by very brief signs rather than by complete figures; for thus the memory can not err, and meanwhile the thought will not be distracted for the purpose of retaining them, while it is applying itself to deducing other things.* . . . .

RULE XVII.—*A given difficulty should be run through directly, in abstraction from the fact that some of its terms are known and others unknown, and with the intuition, obtained by taking the right road, of the mutual dependence of each term on the others.* . . . .

RULE XVIII.—*For this only four operations are required, addition, subtraction, multiplication and division, among which the last two often do not need to be carried out here, as much to keep from complicating things rashly as because they can be executed more easily later.* . . . .

RULE XIX.—*By this method of ratiocination we should seek out as many magnitudes expressed in two different modes, as we suppose unknown terms directly bearing on the difficulty in place of known ones: for thus we shall have so many comparisons between two equals.*

RULE XX.—*When the equations have been found, we must finish the operations which we have left aside, never making use of multiplication whenever there is room for division.*

RULE XXI.—*If there are several equations of this sort, we should reduce them all to one single one, that is to say, to the one whose terms will occupy the least number of degrees in the sequence of magnitudes in continuous proportion, according to which they are to be ordered.*

MEDITATIONS ON FIRST PHILOSOPHY[3]

PREFACE TO THE READER

I have already slightly touched upon the questions respecting the existence of God and the nature of the human soul, in the "Discourse on the Method of rightly conducting the Reason, and seeking truth in the Sciences," published in French in the year 1637; not, however, with the design of there treating of them fully, but only, as it were, in passing, that I might learn from the judgments of my readers in what way I should afterwards handle them: for these questions appeared to me to be of such moment as to be worthy of being considered more than once, and the path which I follow in discussing them is so little trodden, and so remote from

[3] From *The Meditations and Selections from the Principles of René Descartes*, trans. John Veitch (La Salle, Ill.: Open Court Publishing Co., 1937). By permission of the publishers.

the ordinary route, that I thought it would not be expedient to illustrate it at greater length in French, and in a discourse that might be read by all, lest even the more feeble minds should believe that this path might be entered upon by them.

But, as in the Discourse on Method, I had requested all who might find aught meriting censure in my writings, to do me the favour of pointing it out to me, I may state that no objections worthy of remark have been alleged against what I then said on these questions, except two, to which I will here briefly reply, before undertaking their more detailed discussion.

The first objection is that though, while the human mind reflects on itself, it does not perceive that it is any other than a thinking thing, it does not follow that its nature or essence consists only in its being a thing which thinks; so that the word *only* shall exclude all other things which might also perhaps be said to pertain to the nature of the mind.

To this objection I reply, that it was not my intention in that place to exclude these according to the order of truth in the matter (of which I did not then treat), but only according to the order of thought (perception); so that my meaning was, that I clearly apprehended nothing, so far as I was conscious, as belonging to my essence, except that I was a thinking thing, or a thing possessing in itself the faculty of thinking. But I will show hereafter how, from the consciousness that nothing besides thinking belongs to the essence of the mind, it follows that nothing else does in truth belong to it.

The second objection is that it does not follow, from my possessing the idea of a thing more perfect than I am, that the idea itself is more perfect than myself, and much less that what is represented by the idea exists.

But I reply that in the term *idea* there is here something equivocal; for it may be taken either materially for an act of the understanding, and in this sense it cannot be said to be more perfect than I, or objectively, for the thing represented by that act, which, although it be not supposed to exist out of my understanding, may, nevertheless, be more perfect than myself, by reason of its essence. But, in the sequel of this treatise I will show more amply how, from my possessing the idea of a thing more perfect than myself, it follows that this thing really exists.

Besides these two objections, I have seen, indeed, two treatises of sufficient length relating to the present matter. In these, however, my conclusions, much more than my premises, were impugned, and that by arguments borrowed from the commonplaces of the atheists. But, as arguments of this sort can make no impression on the minds of those who shall rightly understand my reasonings, and as the judgments of many are so irrational and weak that they are persuaded rather by the opinions on a subject that are first presented to them, however false and opposed to reason they may be, than by a true and solid, but subsequently received, refutation of them, I am unwilling here to reply to these strictures from a dread of being, in the first instance, obliged to state them.

I will only say, in general, that all which the atheists commonly allege in favour of the non-existence of God, arises continually from one or other of these two things, namely, either the ascription of human affections to Deity, or the undue attribution to our minds of so much vigour and wisdom that we may essay to determine and comprehend both what God can and ought to do; hence all that is alleged by them will occasion us no difficulty, provided only we keep in remembrance that our minds must be considered finite, while Deity is incomprehensible and infinite.

Now that I have once, in some measure, made proof of the opinions of men regarding my work, I again undertake to treat of God and the human soul, and at the same time to discuss the principles of the entire First Philosophy, without, however, expecting any commendation from the crowd for my endeavours, or a wide circle of readers. On the contrary, I would advise none to read this work, unless such as are able and willing to meditate with me in earnest, to detach their minds from commerce with the senses, and likewise to deliver themselves from all prejudice; and individuals of this character are, I well know, remarkably rare. But with regard to those who, without caring to comprehend the order and connection of the reasonings, shall study only detached clauses for the purpose of small but noisy criticism, as is the custom with many, I may say that such persons will not profit greatly by the reading of this treatise; and although perhaps they may find opportunity for cavilling in several places, they will yet hardly start any pressing objections, or such as shall be deserving of reply.

But since, indeed, I do not promise to satisfy others on all these subjects at first sight, nor arrogate so much to myself as to believe that I have been able to foresee all that may be the source of difficulty to each one, I shall expound, first of all, in the *Meditations*, those considerations by which I feel persuaded that I have arrived at a certain and evident knowledge of truth, in order that I may ascertain whether the reasonings which have prevailed with myself will also be effectual in convincing others. I will then reply to the objections of some men, illustrious for their genius and learning, to whom these Meditations were sent for criticism before they were committed to the press; for these objections are so numerous and varied that I venture to anticipate that nothing, at least nothing of any moment, will readily occur to any mind which has not been touched upon in them.

Hence it is that I earnestly entreat my readers not to come to any judgment on the questions raised in the Meditations until they have taken care to read the whole of the Objections, with the relative Replies.

Synopsis of the Six Following Meditations

In the First Meditation I expound the grounds on which we may doubt in general of all things, and especially of material objects, so long, at least, as we have no other foundations for the sciences than those we have hitherto possessed. Now, although the utility of a doubt so general may not be manifest at first sight, it is nevertheless of the greatest, since it delivers us from all prejudice, and affords the easiest pathway by which the mind may withdraw itself from the senses; and, finally, makes it impossible for us to doubt wherever we afterwards discover truth.

In the Second, the mind which, in the exercise of the freedom peculiar to itself, supposes that no object is, of the existence of which it has even the slightest doubt, finds that, meanwhile, it must itself exist. And this point is likewise of the highest moment, for the mind is thus enabled easily to distinguish what pertains to itself, that is, to the intellectual nature, from what is to be referred to the body. But since some, perhaps, will expect, at this stage of our progress, a statement of the reasons which establish the doctrine of the immortality of the soul, I think it proper here to make such aware, that it was my aim to write nothing of which I could not give exact demonstration, and that I therefore felt myself

obliged to adopt an order similar to that in use among the geometers, viz., to premise all upon which the proposition in question
depends, before coming to any conclusion respecting it. Now, the
first and chief pre-requisite for the knowledge of the immortality
of the soul is our being able to form the clearest possible conception
(*conceptus*—concept) of the soul itself, and such as shall be absolutely distinct from all our notions of body; and how this is to be
accomplished is there shown. There is required, besides this, the
assurance that all objects which we clearly and distinctly think are
true (really exist) in that very mode in which we think them; and
this could not be established previously to the Fourth Meditation.
Farther, it is necessary, for the same purpose, that we possess a
distinct conception of corporeal nature, which is given partly in the
Second and partly in the Fifth and Sixth Meditations. And, finally,
on these grounds, we are necessitated to conclude, that all those
objects which are clearly and distinctly conceived to be diverse
substances, as mind and body, are substances really reciprocally
distinct; and this inference is made in the Sixth Meditation. The
absolute distinction of mind and body is, besides, confirmed in
this Second Meditation, by showing that we cannot conceive body
unless as divisible; while, on the other hand, mind cannot be conceived unless as indivisible. For we are not able to conceive the
half of a mind, as we can of any body, however small, so that the
natures of these two substances are to be held, not only as diverse,
but even in some measure as contraries. I have not, however, pursued this discussion further in the present treatise, as well for the
reason that these considerations are sufficient to show that the
destruction of the mind does not follow from the corruption of the
body, and thus to afford to men the hope of a future life, as also
because the premises from which it is competent for us to infer the
immortality of the soul, involve an explication of the whole principles of Physics: in order to establish, in the first place, that generally all substances, that is, all things which can exist only in
consequence of having been created by God, are in their own nature incorruptible, and can never cease to be, unless God himself,
by refusing his concurrence to them, reduce them to nothing; and,
in the second place, that body, taken generally, is a substance, and
therefore can never perish, but that the human body, in as far as
it differs from other bodies, is constituted only by a certain con-

figuration of members, and by other accidents of this sort, while the human mind is not made up of accidents, but is a pure substance. For although all the accidents of the mind be changed— although, for example, it think certain things, will others, and perceive others, the mind itself does not vary with these changes; while, on the contrary, the human body is no longer the same if a change take place in the form of any of its parts: from which it follows that the body may, indeed, without difficulty perish, but that the mind is in its own nature immortal.

In the Third Meditation, I have unfolded at sufficient length, as appears to me, my chief argument for the existence of God. But yet, since I was there desirous to avoid the use of comparisons taken from material objects, that I might withdraw, as far as possible, the minds of my readers from the senses, numerous obscurities perhaps remain, which, however, will, I trust, be afterwards entirely removed in the Replies to the Objections: thus, among other things, it may be difficult to understand how the idea of a being absolutely perfect, which is found in our minds, possesses so much objective reality [*i.e.*, participates by representation in so many degrees of being and perfection] that it must be held to arise from a cause absolutely perfect. This is illustrated in the Replies by the comparison of a highly perfect machine, the idea of which exists in the mind of some workman; for as the objective (*i.e.*, representative) perfection of this idea must have some cause, viz., either the science of the workman, or of some other person from whom he has received the idea, in the same way the idea of God, which is found in us, demands God himself for its cause.

In the Fourth, it is shown that all which we clearly and distinctly perceive (apprehend) is true; and, at the same time, is explained wherein consists the nature of error; points that require to be known as well for confirming the preceding truths, as for the better understanding of those that are to follow. But, meanwhile, it must be observed, that I do not at all there treat of Sin, that is, of error committed in the pursuit of good and evil, but of that sort alone which arises in the determination of the true and the false. Nor do I refer to matters of faith, or to the conduct of life, but only to what regards speculative truths, and such as are known by means of the natural light alone.

In the Fifth, besides the illustration of corporeal nature, taken generically, a new demonstration is given of the existence of God, not free, perhaps, any more than the former, from certain difficulties, but of these the solution will be found in the Replies to the Objections. I further show, in what sense it is true that the certitude of geometrical demonstrations themselves is dependent on the knowledge of God.

Finally, in the Sixth, the act of the understanding (*intellectio*) is distinguished from that of the imagination (*imaginatio*); the marks of this distinction are described; the human mind is shown to be really distinct from the body, and, nevertheless, to be so closely conjoined therewith, as together to form, as it were, a unity. The whole of the errors which arise from the senses are brought under review, while the means of avoiding them are pointed out; and, finally, all the grounds are adduced from which the existence of material objects may be inferred; not, however, because I deemed them of great utility in establishing what they prove, viz., that there is in reality a world, that men are possessed of bodies, and the like, the truth of which no one of sound mind ever seriously doubted: but because, from a close consideration of them, it is perceived that they are neither so strong nor clear as the reasonings which conduct us to the knowledge of our mind and of God; so that the latter are, of all which come under human knowledge, the most certain and manifest—a conclusion which it was my single aim in these Meditations to establish; on which account I here omit mention of the various other questions which, in the course of the discussion, I had occasion likewise to consider.

MEDITATIONS ON THE FIRST PHILOSOPHY, IN WHICH THE EXISTENCE OF GOD, AND THE REAL DISTINCTION OF MIND AND BODY, ARE DEMONSTRATED

MEDITATION I. OF THE THINGS OF WHICH WE MAY DOUBT

Several years have now elapsed since I first became aware that I had accepted, even from my youth, many false opinions for true, and that consequently what I afterwards based on such principles was highly doubtful; and from that time I was convinced of the necessity of undertaking once in my life to rid myself of all the opinions I had adopted, and of commencing anew the work of building from the foundation, if I desired to establish a firm and abiding superstructure in the sciences. But as this enterprise appeared to me to be one of great magnitude, I waited until I had attained an age so mature as to leave me no hope that at any stage of life more advanced I should be better able to execute my design. On this account, I have delayed so long that I should henceforth consider I was doing wrong were I still to consume in deliberation any of the time that now remains for action. To-day, then, since I have opportunely freed my mind from all cares, [and am happily disturbed by no passions]4 and since I am in the secure possession of leisure in a peaceable retirement, I will at length apply myself earnestly and freely to the general overthrow of all my former opinions. But, to this end, it will not be necessary for me to show that the whole of these are false—a point, perhaps, which I shall never reach; but as even now my reason convinces me that I ought not the less carefully to withhold belief from what is not entirely certain and indubitable, than from what is manifestly false, it will be sufficient to justify the rejection of the whole if I shall find in each some ground for doubt. Nor for this purpose will it be necessary even to deal with each belief individually, which would be truly an endless labour; but, as the removal from below of the foundation necessarily involves the downfall of the whole edifice, I will at once approach the criticism of the principles on which all my former beliefs rested.

All that I have, up to this moment, accepted as possessed of the highest truth and certainty, I received either from or through the senses. I observed, however, that these sometimes misled us; and it is the part of prudence not to place absolute confidence in that by which we have even once been deceived.

But it may be said, perhaps, that, although the senses occasionally mislead us respecting minute objects, and such as are so far removed from us as to be beyond the reach of close observation, there are yet many other of their informations (presentations), of the truth of which it is manifestly impossible to doubt; as for example, that I am in this place, seated by the fire, clothed in a winter dressing-gown, that I hold in my hands this piece of paper, with other intimations of the same nature. But how could I deny that I possess these hands and this body, and withal escape being

4 Square brackets [. . . .] indicate additions in the French edition.

classed with persons in a state of insanity, whose brains are so disordered and clouded by dark bilious vapours as to cause them
pertinaciously to assert that they are monarchs when they are in
the greatest poverty; or clothed [in gold] and purple when destitute
of any covering; or that their head is made of clay, their body of
glass, or that they are gourds? I should certainly be not less insane
than they, were I to regulate my procedure according to examples
so extravagant.

Though this be true, I must nevertheless here consider that I
am a man, and that, consequently, I am in the habit of sleeping,
and representing to myself in dreams those same things, or even
sometimes others less probable, which the insane think are presented to them in their waking moments. How often have I dreamt
that I was in these familiar circumstances,—that I was dressed, and
occupied this place by the fire, when I was lying undressed in bed?
At the present moment, however, I certainly look upon this paper
with eyes wide awake; the head which I now move is not asleep;
I extend this hand consciously and with express purpose, and I
perceive it; the occurrences in sleep are not so distinct as all this.
But I cannot forget that, at other times, I have been deceived in
sleep by similar illusions; and, attentively considering those cases,
I perceive so clearly that there exist no certain marks by which the
state of waking can ever be distinguished from sleep, that I feel
greatly astonished; and in amazement I almost persuade myself
that I am now dreaming.

Let us suppose, then, that we are dreaming, and that all these
particulars—namely, the opening of the eyes, the motion of the
head, the forth-putting of the hands—are merely illusions; and
even that we really possess neither an entire body nor hands such
as we see. Nevertheless, it must be admitted at least that the objects which appear to us in sleep are, as it were, painted representations which could not have been formed unless in the likeness of
realities; and, therefore, that those general objects, at all events,—
namely, eyes, a head, hands, and an entire body—are not simply
imaginary, but really existent. For, in truth, painters themselves,
even when they study to represent sirens and satyrs by forms the
most fantastic and extraordinary, cannot bestow upon them natures absolutely new, but can only make a certain medley of the
members of different animals; or if they chance to imagine some-

thing so novel that nothing at all similar has ever been seen before, and such as is, therefore, purely fictitious and absolutely false, it is at least certain that the colours of which this is composed are real.

And on the same principle, although these general objects, viz. [a body], eyes, a head, hands, and the like, be imaginary, we are nevertheless absolutely necessitated to admit the reality at least of some other objects still more simple and universal than these, of which, just as of certain real colours, all those images of things, whether true and real, or false and fantastic, that are found in our consciousness (*cogitatio*), are formed.

To this class of objects seem to belong corporeal nature in general and its extension; the figure of extended things, their quantity or magnitude, and their number, as also the place in and the time during which they exist, and other things of the same sort. We will not, therefore, perhaps reason illegitimately if we conclude from this that Physics, Astronomy, Medicine, and all the other sciences that have for their end the consideration of composite objects, are indeed of a doubtful character; but that Arithmetic, Geometry, and the other sciences of the same class, which regard merely the simplest and most general objects, and scarcely inquire whether or not these are really existent, contain somewhat that is certain and indubitable: for whether I am awake or dreaming, it remains true that two and three make five, and that a square has but four sides; nor does it seem possible that truths so apparent can ever fall under a suspicion of falsity [or incertitude].

Nevertheless, the belief that there is a God who is all-powerful, and who created me, such as I am, has, for a long time, obtained steady possession of my mind. How, then, do I know that he has not arranged that there should be neither earth, nor sky, nor any extended thing, nor figure, nor magnitude, nor place, providing at the same time, however, for [the rise in me of the perceptions of all these objects, and] the persuasion that these do not exist otherwise than as I perceive them? And further, as I sometimes think that others are in error respecting matters of which they believe themselves to possess a perfect knowledge, how do I know that I am not also deceived each time I add together two and three, or number the sides of a square, or form some judgment still more simple, if more simple indeed can be imagined? But perhaps Deity has not been willing that I should be thus deceived, for He is said to be supremely good. If, however, it were repugnant to the goodness of Deity to have created me subject to constant deception, it would seem likewise to be contrary to his goodness to allow me to be occasionally deceived; and yet it is clear that this is permitted. Some, indeed, might perhaps be found who would be disposed rather to deny the existence of a Being so powerful than to believe that there is nothing certain. But let us for the present refrain from opposing this opinion, and grant that all which is here said of a Deity is fabulous: nevertheless in whatever way it be supposed that I reached the state in which I exist, whether by fate, or chance, or by an endless series of antecedents and consequents, or by any other means, it is clear (since to be deceived and to err is a certain defect) that the probability of my being so imperfect as to be the constant victim of deception, will be increased exactly in proportion as the power possessed by the cause, to which they assign my origin, is lessened. To these reasonings I have assuredly nothing to reply, but am constrained at last to avow that there is nothing of all that I formerly believed to be true of which it is impossible to doubt, and that not through thoughtlessness or levity, but from cogent and maturely considered reasons; so that henceforward, if I desire to discover anything certain, I ought not the less carefully to refrain from assenting to those same opinions than to what might be shown to be manifestly false.

But it is not sufficient to have made these observations; care must be taken likewise to keep them in remembrance. For those old and customary opinions perpetually recur—long and familiar usage giving them the right of occupying my mind, even almost against my will, and subduing my belief; nor will I lose the habit of deferring to them and confiding in them so long as I shall consider them to be what in truth they are, viz., opinions to some extent doubtful, as I have already shown, but still highly probable, and such as it is much more reasonable to believe than deny. It is for this reason I am persuaded that I shall not be doing wrong, if, taking an opposite judgment of deliberate design, I become my own deceiver, by supposing, for a time, that all those opinions are entirely false and imaginary, until at length, having thus balanced my old by my new prejudices, my judgment shall no longer be turned aside by perverted usage from the path that may conduct to the perception of truth. For I am assured that, meanwhile, there will arise neither peril nor error from this course, and that I cannot for the present yield too much to distrust, since the end I now seek is not action but knowledge.

I will suppose, then, not that Deity, who is sovereignly good and the fountain of truth, but that some malignant demon, who is at once exceedingly potent and deceitful, has employed all his artifice to deceive me; I will suppose that the sky, the air, the earth, colours, figures, sounds, and all external things, are nothing better than the illusions of dreams, by means of which this being has laid snares for my credulity; I will consider myself as without hands, eyes, flesh, blood, or any of the senses, and as falsely believing that I am possessed of these; I will continue resolutely fixed in this belief, and if indeed by this means it be not in my power to arrive at the knowledge of truth, I shall at least do what is in my power, viz., [suspend my judgment], and guard with settled purpose against giving my assent to what is false, and being imposed upon by this deceiver, whatever be his power and artifice.

But this undertaking is arduous, and a certain indolence insensibly leads me back to my ordinary course of life; and just as the captive, who, perchance, was enjoying in his dreams an imaginary liberty, when he begins to suspect that it is but a vision, dreads awakening, and conspires with the agreeable illusions that the deception may be prolonged; so I, of my own accord, fall back into the train of my former beliefs, and fear to arouse myself from my slumber, lest the time of laborious wakefulness that would succeed this quiet rest, in place of bringing any light of day, should prove inadequate to dispel the darkness that will arise from the difficulties that have now been raised.

MEDITATION II. OF THE NATURE OF THE HUMAN MIND; AND THAT IT IS MORE EASILY KNOWN THAN THE BODY

The Meditation of yesterday has filled my mind with so many doubts, that it is no longer in my power to forget them. Nor do I see, meanwhile, any principle on which they can be resolved; and, just as if I had fallen all of a sudden into very deep water, I am so greatly disconcerted as to be unable either to plant my feet firmly on the bottom or sustain myself by swimming on the surface. I will, nevertheless, make an effort, and try anew the same path on which I had entered yesterday, that is, proceed by casting aside all that admits of the slightest doubt, not less than if I had discovered it to be absolutely false; and I will continue always in this track until I shall find something that is certain, or at least, if I can do nothing more, until I shall know with certainty that there is nothing certain. Archimedes, that he might transport the entire globe from the place it occupied to another, demanded only a point that was firm and immoveable; so also, I shall be entitled to entertain the highest expectations, if I am fortunate enough to discover only one thing that is certain and indubitable.

I suppose, accordingly, that all the things which I see are false (fictitious); I believe that none of those objects which my fallacious memory represents ever existed; I suppose that I possess no senses; I believe that body, figure, extension, motion, and place are merely fictions of my mind. What is there, then, that can be esteemed true? Perhaps this only, that there is absolutely nothing certain.

But how do I know that there is not something different altogether from the objects I have now enumerated, of which it is impossible to entertain the slightest doubt? Is there not a God, or some being, by whatever name I may designate him, who causes these thoughts to arise in my mind? But why suppose such a being, for it may be I myself am capable of producing them? Am I, then, at least not something? But I before denied that I possessed senses or a body; I hesitate, however, for what follows from that? Am I so dependent on the body and the senses that without these I cannot exist? But I had the persuasion that there was absolutely nothing in the world, that there was no sky and no earth, neither minds nor bodies; was I not, therefore, at the same time, persuaded that I did not exist? Far from it; I assuredly existed, since I was persuaded. But there is I know not what being, who is possessed at once of the highest power and the deepest cunning, who is constantly employing all his ingenuity in deceiving me. Doubtless, then, I exist, since I am deceived; and, let him deceive me as he may, he can never bring it about that I am nothing, so long as I shall be conscious that I am something. So that it must, in fine, be maintained, all things being maturely and carefully considered, that this proposition (*pronunciatum*) I am, I exist, is necessarily true each time it is expressed by me, or conceived in my mind.

But I do not yet know with sufficient clearness what I am, though assured that I am; and hence, in the next place, I must take care, lest perchance I inconsiderately substitute some other object in room of what is properly myself, and thus wander from truth, even in that knowledge (cognition) which I hold to be of all others the most certain and evident. For this reason, I will now consider anew what I formerly believed myself to be, before I entered on the present train of thought; and of my previous opinion I will retrench all that can in the least be invalidated by the grounds of doubt I have adduced, in order that there may at length remain nothing but what is certain and indubitable. What then did I formerly think I was? Undoubtedly I judged that I was a man. But what is a man? Shall I say a rational animal? Assuredly not; for it would be necessary forthwith to inquire into what is meant by animal, and what by rational, and thus, from a single question, I should insensibly glide into others, and these more difficult than the first; nor do I now possess enough of leisure to warrant me in wasting my time amid subtleties of this sort. I prefer here to attend to the thoughts that sprung up of themselves in my mind, and were inspired by my own nature alone, when I applied myself to the consideration of what I was. In the first place, then, I thought that I possessed a countenance, hands, arms, and all the fabric of members that appears in a corpse, and which I called by the name of body. It further occurred to me that I was nourished, that I walked, perceived, and thought, and all those actions I referred to the soul; but what the soul itself was I either did not stay to consider, or, if I did, I imagined that it was something extremely rare and subtile, like wind, or flame, or ether, spread through my grosser parts. As regarded the body, I did not even doubt of its nature, but thought I distinctly knew it, and if I had wished to describe it according to the notions I then entertained, I should have explained myself in this manner: By body I understand all that can be terminated by a certain figure; that can be comprised in a certain place, and so fill a certain space as therefrom to exclude every other body; that can be perceived either by touch, sight, hearing, taste, or smell; that can be moved in different ways, not indeed of itself, but by something foreign to it by which it is touched [and from which it receives the impression]; for the power of self-motion, as likewise that of perceiving and thinking, I held as by no means pertaining to the nature of body; on the contrary,

I was somewhat astonished to find such faculties existing in some bodies.

But [as to myself, what can I now say that I am], since I suppose there exists an extremely powerful, and, if I may so speak, malignant being, whose whole endeavours are directed towards deceiving me? Can I affirm that I possess any one of all those attributes of which I have lately spoken as belonging to the nature of body? After attentively considering them in my own mind, I find none of them that can properly be said to belong to myself. To recount them were idle and tedious. Let us pass, then, to the attributes of the soul. The first mentioned were the powers of nutrition and walking; but, if it be true that I have no body, it is true likewise that I am capable neither of walking nor of being nourished. Perception (*sentire*) is another attribute of the soul; but perception too is impossible without the body: besides, I have frequently, during sleep, believed that I perceived objects which I afterwards observed I did not in reality perceive. Thinking is another attribute of the soul; and here I discover what properly belongs to myself. This alone is inseparable from me. I am—I exist: this is certain; but how often? As often as I think; for perhaps it would even happen, if I should wholly cease to think, that I should at the same time altogether cease to be. I now admit nothing that is not necessarily true: I am therefore, precisely speaking, only a thinking thing, that is, a mind (*mens sive animus*), understanding, or reason, —terms whose signification was before unknown to me. I am, however, a real thing, and really existent; but what thing? The answer was, a thinking thing. The question now arises, am I aught besides? I will stimulate my imagination with a view to discover whether I am not still something more than a thinking being. Now it is plain I am not the assemblage of members called the human body; I am not a thin and penetrating air diffused through all these members, or wind, or flame, or vapour, or breath, or any of all the things I can imagine; for I supposed that all these were not, and, without changing the supposition, I find that I still feel assured of my existence.

But it is true, perhaps, that those very things which I suppose to be non-existent, because they are unknown to me, are not in truth different from myself whom I know. This is a point I cannot determine, and do not now enter into any dispute regarding it. I can only judge of things that are known to me: I am conscious that I exist, and I who know that I exist inquire into what I am. It is, however, perfectly certain that the knowledge of my existence, thus precisely taken, is not dependent on things, the existence of which is as yet unknown to me: and consequently it is not dependent on any of the things I can feign in imagination. Moreover, the phrase itself, I frame an image (*effingo*), reminds me of my error; for I should in truth frame one if I were to imagine myself to be anything, since to imagine is nothing more than to contemplate the figure or image of a corporeal thing; but I already know that I exist, and that it is possible at the same time that all those images, and in general all that relates to the nature of body, are merely dreams [or chimeras]. From this I discover that it is not more reasonable to say, I will excite my imagination that I may know more distinctly what I am, than to express myself as follows: I am now awake, and perceive something real; but because my perception is not sufficiently clear, I will of express purpose go to sleep that my dreams may represent to me the object of my perception with more truth and clearness. And, therefore, I know that nothing of all that I can embrace in imagination belongs to the knowledge which I have of myself, and that there is need to recall with the utmost care the mind from this mode of thinking, that it may be able to know its own nature with perfect distinctness.

But what, then, am I? A thinking thing, it has been said. But what is a thinking thing? It is a thing that doubts, understands, [conceives], affirms, denies, wills, refuses, that imagines, also, and perceives (*res . . . . sentiens*). Assuredly it is not little, if all these properties belong to my nature. But why should they not belong to it? Am I not that very being who now doubts of almost everything; who, for all that, understands and conceives certain things; who affirms one alone as true, and denies the others; who desires to know more of them, and does not wish to be deceived; who imagines many things, sometimes even despite his will; and is likewise percipient of many, as if through the medium of the senses. Is there nothing of all this as true as that I am, even although I should be always dreaming, and although he who gave me being employed all his ingenuity to deceive me? Is there also any one of these attributes that can be properly distinguished from my thought, or that can be said to be separate from myself? For it is of itself so evident that it is I who doubt, I who understand, and I who desire, that it is here unnecessary to add anything by way of rendering it more clear. And I am as certainly the same being who imagines; for, although it may be (as I before supposed) that nothing I imagine is true, still the power of imagination does not cease really to exist in me and to form part of my thought. In fine, I am the same being who perceives, that is, who apprehends certain objects as by the organs of sense, since, in truth, I see light, hear a noise, and feel heat. But it will be said that these presentations are false, and that I am dreaming. Let it be so. At all events it is certain that I seem to see light, hear a noise, and feel heat; this cannot be false, and this is what in me is properly called perceiving (*sentire*), which is nothing else than thinking. From this I begin to know what I am with somewhat greater clearness and distinctness than heretofore.

But, nevertheless, it still seems to me, and I cannot help believing, that corporeal things, whose images are formed by thought, [which fall under the senses], and are examined by the same, are known with much greater distinctness than that I know not what part of myself which is not imaginable; although, in truth, it may seem strange to say that I know and comprehend with greater distinctness things whose existence appears to me doubtful, that are unknown, and do not belong to me, than others of whose reality I am persuaded, that are known to me, and appertain to my proper nature; in a word, than myself. But I see clearly what is the state of the case. My mind is apt to wander, and will not yet submit to be restrained within the limits of truth. Let us therefore leave the mind to itself once more, and, according to it every kind of liberty, [permit it to consider the objects that appear to it from without], in order that, having afterwards withdrawn it from these gently and opportunely, [and fixed it on the consideration of its being and the properties it finds in itself], it may then be the more easily controlled.

Let us now accordingly consider the objects that are commonly thought to be [the most easily, and likewise] the most distinctly known, viz., the bodies we touch and see; not, indeed, bodies in general, for these general notions are usually somewhat more confused, but one body in particular. Take, for example, this piece of wax; it is quite fresh, having been but recently taken from the bee-hive; it has not yet lost the sweetness of the honey it contained; it still retains somewhat of the odour of the flowers from which it was gathered; its colour, figure, size, are apparent (to the sight); it is hard, cold, easily handled; and sounds when struck upon with the finger. In fine, all that contributes to make a body as distinctly known as possible, is found in the one before us. But, while I am speaking, let it be placed near the fire—what remained of the taste exhales, the smell evaporates, the colour changes, its figure is destroyed, its size increases, it becomes liquid, it grows hot, it can hardly be handled, and, although struck upon, it emits no sound. Does the same wax still remain after this change? It must be admitted that it does remain; no one doubts it, or judges otherwise. What, then, was it I knew with so much distinctness in the piece of wax? Assuredly, it could be nothing of all that I observed by means of the senses, since all the things that fell under taste, smell, sight, touch, and hearing are changed, and yet the same wax remains. It was perhaps what I now think, viz., that this wax was neither the sweetness of honey, the pleasant odour of flowers, the whiteness, the figure, nor the sound, but only a body that a little before appeared to me conspicuous under these forms, and which is now perceived under others. But, to speak precisely, what is it that I imagine when I think of it in this way? Let it be attentively considered, and, retrenching all that does not belong to the wax, let us see what remains. There certainly remains nothing, except something extended, flexible, and movable. But what is meant by flexible and movable? Is it not that I imagine that the piece of wax, being round, is capable of becoming square, or of passing from a square into a triangular figure? Assuredly such is not the case, because I conceive that it admits of an infinity of similar changes; and I am, moreover, unable to compass this infinity by imagination, and consequently this conception which I have of the wax is not the product of the faculty of imagination. But what now is this extension? Is it not also unknown? for it becomes greater when the wax is melted, greater when it is boiled, and greater still when the heat increases; and I should not conceive [clearly and] according to truth, the wax as it is, if I did not suppose that the piece we are considering admitted even of a wider variety of extension than I ever imagined. I must, therefore, admit that I cannot even comprehend by imagination what the piece of wax is, and that it is the mind alone (*mens*, Lat., *entendement*, F.) which perceives it. I speak of one piece in particular; for, as to wax in general, this is still more evident. But what is the piece of wax that can be perceived only by the [understanding or] mind? It is certainly the same which I see, touch, imagine; and, in fine, it is the same which, from the beginning, I believed it to be. But (and this it is of moment to observe) the perception of it is neither an act of sight, of touch, nor of imagination, and never was either of these, though it might formerly seem so, but is simply an intuition (*inspectio*) of the mind, which may be imperfect and confused, as it formerly was, or very clear and distinct, as it is at present, according as the attention is more or less directed to the elements which it contains, and of which it is composed.

But, meanwhile, I feel greatly astonished when I observe [the weakness of my mind, and] its proneness to error. For although, without at all giving expression to what I think, I consider all this in my own mind, words yet occasionally impede my progress, and I am almost led into error by the terms of ordinary language. We say, for example, that we see the same wax when it is before us, and not that we judge it to be the same from its retaining the same colour and figure: whence I should forthwith be disposed to conclude that the wax is known by the act of sight, and not by the intuition of the mind alone, were it not for the analogous instance of human beings passing on in the street below, as observed from a window. In this case I do not fail to say that I see the men themselves, just as I say that I see the wax; and yet what do I see from the window beyond hats and cloaks that might cover artificial machines, whose motions might be determined by springs? But I judge that there are human beings from these appearances, and thus I comprehend, by the faculty of judgment alone which is in the mind, what I believed I saw with my eyes.

The man who makes it his aim to rise to knowledge superior to the common, ought to be ashamed to seek occasions of doubting from the vulgar forms of speech: instead, therefore, of doing this, I shall proceed with the matter in hand, and inquire whether I had a clearer and more perfect perception of the piece of wax when I first saw it, and when I thought I knew it by means of the external sense itself, or, at all events, by the common sense (*sensus communis*), as it is called, that is, by the imaginative faculty; or whether I rather apprehend it more clearly at present, after having examined with greater care, both what it is, and in what way it can be known. It would certainly be ridiculous to entertain any doubt on this point. For what, in that first perception, was there distinct? What did I perceive which any animal might not have perceived? But when I distinguish the wax from its exterior forms, and when, as if I had stripped it of its vestments, I consider it quite naked, it is certain, although some error may still be found in my judgment, that I cannot, nevertheless, thus apprehend it without possessing a human mind.

But, finally, what shall I say of the mind itself, that is, of myself? for as yet I do not admit that I am anything but mind. What, then! I who seem to possess so distinct an apprehension of the piece of wax,—do I not know myself, both with greater truth and certitude, and also much more distinctly and clearly? For if I judge that the wax exists because I see it, it assuredly follows, much more evidently, that I myself am or exist, for the same reason: for it is possible that what I see may not in truth be wax, and that I do not even possess eyes with which to see anything; but it cannot be that when I see, or, which comes to the same thing, when I think I see, I myself who think am nothing. So likewise, if I judge that the wax exists because I touch it, it will still also follow that I am; and if I determine that my imagination, or any other cause, whatever it be, persuades me of the existence of the wax, I will still draw the same conclusion. And what is here remarked of the piece of wax, is applicable to all the other things that are external to me. And further, if the [notion or] perception of wax appeared to me more precise and distinct, after not only sight and touch, but many other causes besides, rendered it manifest to my apprehension, with how much greater distinctness must I now know myself, since all the reasons that contribute to the knowledge of the nature of wax, or of any body whatever, manifest still better the nature of my mind? And there are besides so many other things in the mind itself that contribute to the illustration of its nature, that those dependent on the body, to which I have here referred, scarcely merit to be taken into account.

But, in conclusion, I find I have insensibly reverted to the point I desired; for, since it is now manifest to me that bodies themselves are not properly perceived by the senses nor by the faculty of imagination, but by the intellect alone; and since they are not perceived because they are seen and touched, but only because they are understood [or rightly comprehended by thought], I readily discover that there is nothing more easily or clearly apprehended than my own mind. But because it is difficult to rid one's self so promptly of an opinion to which one has been long accustomed, it will be desirable to tarry for some time at this stage, that, by long continued meditation, I may more deeply impress upon my memory this new knowledge.

MEDITATION III. OF GOD: THAT HE EXISTS

I will now close my eyes, I will stop my ears, I will turn away my senses from their objects, I will even efface from my consciousness all the images of corporeal things; or at least, because this can hardly be accomplished, I will consider them as empty and false; and thus, holding converse only with myself, and closely examining my nature, I will endeavour to obtain by degrees a more intimate and familiar knowledge of myself. I am a thinking (conscious) thing, that is, a being who doubts, affirms, denies, knows a few objects, and is ignorant of many,—[who loves, hates], wills, refuses,—who imagines likewise, and perceives; for, as I before remarked, although the things which I perceive or imagine are perhaps nothing at all apart from me [and in themselves], I am nevertheless assured that those modes of consciousness which I call perceptions and imaginations, in as far only as they are modes of consciousness, exist in me. And in the little I have said I think I have summed up all that I really know, or at least all that up to this time I was aware I knew. Now, as I am endeavouring to extend my knowledge more widely, I will use circumspection, and consider with care whether I can still discover in myself anything further which I have not yet hitherto observed. I am certain that I am a thinking thing; but do I not therefore likewise know what is required to render me certain of a truth? In this first knowledge, doubtless, there is nothing that gives me assurance of its truth except the clear and distinct perception of what I affirm, which would not indeed be sufficient to give me the assurance that what I say is true, if it could ever happen that anything I thus clearly and distinctly perceived should prove false; and accordingly it seems to me that I may now take as a general rule, that all that is very clearly and distinctly apprehended (conceived) is true.[5]

Nevertheless I before received and admitted many things as wholly certain and manifest, which yet I afterwards found to be doubtful. What, then, were those? They were the earth, the sky, the stars, and all the other objects which I was in the habit of perceiving by the senses. But what was it that I clearly [and distinctly] perceived in them? Nothing more than that the ideas and the thoughts of those objects were presented to my mind. And even now I do not deny that these ideas are found in my mind. But there was yet another thing which I affirmed, and which, from having been accustomed to believe it, I thought I clearly perceived, although, in truth, I did not perceive it at all; I mean the existence of objects external to me, from which those ideas proceeded, and to which they had a perfect resemblance; and it was here I was mistaken, or if I judged correctly, this assuredly was not to be traced to any knowledge I possessed (the force of my perception, Lat.).

But when I considered any matter in arithmetic and geometry, that was very simple and easy, as, for example, that two and three added together make five, and things of this sort, did I not view them with at least sufficient clearness to warrant me in affirming their truth? Indeed, if I afterwards judged that we ought to doubt of these things, it was for no other reason than because it occurred to me that a God might perhaps have given me such a nature as that I should be deceived, even respecting the matters that appeared to me the most evidently true. But as often as this pre-

---

[5] "Illud omne esse verum quod valde clare et distincte percipio." *Percipio* is in the present text sometimes rendered "conceive," and *perceptio*, "conception." Since Descartes makes no sharp distinction between the two (where "perception" is taken in its broadest sense), this translation has been retained. Cf. *Principles*, I, 45:

"*What constitutes clear and distinct perception.*

"There are indeed a great many persons who, through their whole lifetime, never perceive anything in a way necessary for judging of it properly; for the knowledge upon which we can establish a certain and indubitable judgment must be not only clear, but also distinct I call that clear which is present and manifest to the mind giving attention to it, just as we are said clearly to see objects when, being present to the eye looking on, they stimulate it with sufficient force, and it is disposed to regard them; but the distinct is that which is so precise and different from all other objects as to comprehend in itself only what is clear."

conceived opinion of the sovereign power of a God presents itself to my mind, I am constrained to admit that it is easy for him, if he wishes it, to cause me to err, even in matters where I think I possess the highest evidence; and, on the other hand, as often as I direct my attention to things which I think I apprehend with great clearness, I am so persuaded of their truth that I naturally break out into expressions such as these: Deceive me who may, no one will yet ever be able to bring it about that I am not, so long as I shall be conscious that I am, or at any future time cause it to be true that I have never been, it being now true that I am, or make two and three more or less than five, in supposing which,. and other like absurdities, I discover a manifest contradiction.

And in truth, as I have no ground for believing that Deity is deceitful, and as, indeed, I have not even considered the reasons by which the existence of a Deity of any kind is established, the ground of doubt that rests only on this supposition is very slight, and, so to speak, metaphysical. But, that I may be able wholly to remove it, I must inquire whether there is a God, as soon as an opportunity of doing so shall present itself; and if I find that there is a God, I must examine likewise whether he can be a deceiver; for, without the knowledge of these two truths, I do not see that I can ever be certain of anything. And that I may be enabled to examine this without interrupting the order of meditation I have proposed to myself [which is, to pass by degrees from the notions that I shall find first in my mind to those I shall afterwards discover in it], it is necessary at this stage to divide all my thoughts into certain classes, and to consider in which of these classes truth and error are, strictly speaking, to be found.

Of my thoughts some are, as it were, images of things, and to these alone properly belongs the name *idea;* as when I think [represent to my mind] a man, a chimera, the sky, an angel, or God. Others, again, have certain other forms; as when I will, fear, affirm, or deny, I always, indeed, apprehend something as the object of my thought, but I also embrace in thought something more than the representation of the object; and of this class of thoughts some are called volitions or affections, and others judgments.

Now, with respect to ideas, if these are considered only in themselves, and are not referred to any object beyond them, they cannot, properly speaking, be false; for, whether I imagine a goat or a chimera, it is not less true that I imagine the one than the other. Nor need we fear that falsity may exist in the will or affections; for, although I may desire objects that are wrong, and even that never existed, it is still true that I desire them. There thus remain only our judgments, in which we must take diligent heed that we be not deceived. But the chief and most ordinary error that arises in them consists in judging that the ideas which are in us are like or conformed to the things that are external to us; for assuredly, if we but considered the ideas themselves as certain modes of our thought (consciousness), without referring them to anything beyond, they would hardly afford any occasion of error.

But, among these ideas, some appear to me to be innate, others adventitious, and others to be made by myself (factitious); for, as I have the power of conceiving what is called a thing, or a truth, or a thought, it seems to me that I hold this power from no other source than my own nature; but if I now hear a noise, if I see the sun, or if I feel heat, I have all along judged that these sensations proceeded from certain objects existing out of myself; and, in fine, it appears to me that sirens, hippogryphs, and the like, are inventions of my own mind. But I may even perhaps come to be of opinion that all my ideas are of the class which I call adventitious, or that they are all innate, or that they are all factitious, for I have not yet clearly discovered their true origin; and what I have here principally to do is to consider, with reference to those that appear to come from certain objects without me, what grounds there are for thinking them like these objects.

The first of these grounds is that it seems to me I am so taught by nature: and the second that I am conscious that those ideas are not dependent on my will, and therefore not on myself, for they are frequently presented to me against my will,—as at present, whether I will or not, I feel heat; and I am thus persuaded that this sensation or idea (*sensum vel ideam*) of heat is produced in me by something different from myself, viz., by the heat of the fire by which I sit. And it is very reasonable to suppose that this object impresses me with its own likeness rather than any other thing.

But I must consider whether these reasons are sufficiently strong and convincing. When I speak of being taught by nature in this matter, I understand by the word nature only a certain spontaneous impetus that impels me to believe in a resemblance between ideas and their objects, and not a natural light that affords a knowledge of its truth. But these two things are widely different; for what the natural light shows to be true can be in no degree doubtful, as, for example, that I am because I doubt, and other truths of the like kind: inasmuch as I possess no other faculty whereby to distinguish truth from error, which can teach me the falsity of what the natural light declares to be true, and which is equally trustworthy; but with respect to [seemingly] natural impulses, I have observed, when the question related to the choice of right or wrong in action, that they frequently led me to take the worse part; nor do I see that I have any better ground for following them in what relates to truth and error. Then, with respect to the other reason, which is that because these ideas do not depend on my will, they must arise from objects existing without me, I do not find it more convincing than the former; for, just as those natural impulses, of which I have lately spoken, are found in me, not withstanding that they are not always in harmony with my will, so likewise it may be that I possess some power not sufficiently known to myself capable of producing ideas without the aid of external objects, and, indeed, it has always hitherto appeared to me that they are formed during sleep, by some power of this nature, without the aid of aught external. And, in fine, although I should grant that they proceeded from those objects, it is not a necessary consequence that they must be like them. On the contrary, I have observed, in a number of instances, that there was a great difference between the object and its idea. Thus, for example, I find in my mind two wholly diverse ideas of the sun; the one, by which it appears to me extremely small, draws its origin from the senses, and should be placed in the class of adventitious ideas; the other, by which it seems to be many times larger than the whole earth, is taken up on astronomical grounds, that is, elicited from certain notions born with me, or is framed by myself in some other manner. These two ideas cannot certainly both resemble the same sun; and reason teaches me that the one which seems to have immediately emanated from it is the most unlike. And these things sufficiently prove that hitherto it has not been from a certain and deliberate judgment, but only from a sort of blind impulse, that I believed in the existence of certain things different from myself, which, by the organs of sense, or by whatever other means it might be, conveyed their ideas or images into my mind [and impressed it with their like-nesses].

But there is still another way of inquiring whether, of the objects whose ideas are in my mind, there are any that exist out of me. If ideas are taken in so far only as they are certain modes of consciousness, I do not remark any difference or inequality among them, and all seem, in the same manner, to proceed from myself; but, considering them as images, of which one represents one thing and another a different, it is evident that a great diversity obtains among them. For, without doubt, those that represent substances are something more, and contain in themselves, so to speak, more objective reality [that is, participate by representation in higher degrees of being or perfection], than those that represent only modes or accidents; and again, the idea by which I conceive a God [sovereign], eternal, infinite, [immutable], all-knowing, all-powerful, and the creator of all things that are out of himself,—this, I say, has certainly in it more objective reality than those ideas by which finite substances are represented.

Now, it is manifest by the natural light that there must be at least as much reality in the efficient and total cause as in its effect; for whence can the effect draw its reality if not from its cause? and how could the cause communicate to it this reality unless it possessed it in itself? And hence it follows, not only that what is cannot be produced by what is not, but likewise that the more perfect,—in other words, that which contains in itself more reality, —cannot be the effect of the less perfect: and this is not only evidently true of those effects, whose reality is actual or formal, but likewise of ideas, whose reality is only considered as objective. Thus, for example, the stone that is not yet in existence, not only cannot now commence to be, unless it be produced by that which possesses in itself, formally or eminently, all that enters into its composition, [in other words, by that which contains in itself the same properties that are in the stone, or others superior to them]; and heat can only be produced in a subject that was before devoid of it, by a cause that is of an order [degree or kind], at least as perfect as heat; and so of the others. But further, even the idea of the heat, or of the stone, cannot exist in me unless it be put there by a cause that contains at least as much reality as I conceive existent in the heat or in the stone: for, although that cause may not transmit into my idea anything of its actual or formal reality, we ought not on this account to imagine that it is less real; but we ought to consider that, [as every idea is a work of the mind], its nature is such as of itself to demand no other formal reality than that which it borrows from our consciousness, of which it is but a mode, [that is, a manner or way of thinking]. But in order that an idea may contain this objective reality rather than that, it must doubtless derive it from some cause in which is found at least as much formal reality as the idea contains of objective; for, if we suppose that there is found in an idea anything which was not in its cause, it must of course derive this from nothing. But, however imperfect may be the mode of existence by which a thing is objectively [or by representation] in the understanding by its idea, we certainly cannot, for all that, allege that this mode of existence is nothing, nor, consequently, that the idea owes its origin to nothing. Nor must it be imagined that, since the reality which is considered in these ideas is only objective, the same reality need not be formally (actually) in the causes of these ideas, but only objectively: for, just as the mode of existing objectively belongs to ideas by their peculiar nature, so likewise the mode of existing formally appertains to the causes of these ideas (at least to the first and principal), by their peculiar nature. And although an idea may give rise to another idea, this regress cannot, nevertheless, be infinite; we must in the end reach a first idea, the cause of which is, as it were, the archetype in which all the reality [or perfection] that is found objectively [or by representation] in these ideas is contained formally [and in act]. I am thus clearly taught by the natural light that ideas exist in me as pictures or images, which may in truth readily fall short of the perfection of the objects from which they are taken, but can never contain anything greater or more perfect.

And in proportion to the time and care with which I examine all those matters, the conviction of their truth brightens and becomes distinct. But, to sum up, what conclusion shall I draw from it all? It is this;—if the objective reality [or perfection] of any one of my ideas be such as clearly to convince me, that this same reality exists in me neither formally nor eminently, and if, as follows from this, I myself cannot be the cause of it, it is a necessary consequence that I am not alone in the world, but that there is besides myself some other being who exists as the cause of that idea; while, on the contrary, if no such idea be found in my mind, I shall have no sufficient ground of assurance of the existence of any other being besides myself; for, after a most careful search, I have, up to this moment, been unable to discover any other ground.

But, among these my ideas, besides that which represents myself, respecting which there can be here no difficulty, there is one that represents a God; others that represent corporeal and inanimate things; others angels; others animals; and, finally, there are some that represent men like myself. But with respect to the ideas that represent other men, or animals, or angels, I can easily suppose that they were formed by the mingling and composition of the other ideas which I have of myself, of corporeal things, and of God, although there were, apart from myself, neither men, animals, nor angels. And with regard to the ideas of corporeal objects, I never discovered in them anything so great or excellent which I myself did not appear capable of originating; for, by considering these ideas closely and scrutinising them individually, in the same way that I yesterday examined the idea of wax, I find that there is but little in them that is clearly and distinctly perceived. As belonging to the class of things that are clearly apprehended, I recognise the following, viz., magnitude or extension in length, breadth, and depth; figure, which results from the termination of extension; situation, which bodies of diverse figures preserve with reference to each other; and motion or the change of situation; to which may be added substance, duration, and number. But with regard to light, colours, sounds, odours, tastes, heat, cold, and the other tactile qualities, they are thought with so much obscurity and confusion, that I cannot determine even whether they are true or false; in other words, whether or not the ideas I have of these qualities are in truth the ideas of real objects. For although I before remarked that it is only in judgments that formal falsity, or falsity properly so called, can be met with, there may nevertheless be found in ideas a certain material falsity, which arises when they represent what is nothing as if it were something. Thus, for example, the ideas I have of cold and heat are so far from being clear and distinct, that I am unable from them to discover whether cold is only the privation of heat, or heat the privation of cold; or whether they are not real qualities: and since, ideas being as it were images, there can be none that does not seem to us to represent some object, the idea which represents cold as something real and positive will not improperly be called false, if it be correct to say that cold is nothing but a privation of heat; and so in other cases. To ideas of this kind, indeed, it is not necessary that I should assign any author besides myself: for if they are false, that is, represent objects that are unreal, the natural light teaches me that they proceed from nothing; in other words, that they are in me only because something is wanting to the perfection of my nature; but if these ideas are true, yet because they exhibit to me so little reality that I cannot even distinguish the object represented from non-being, I do not see why I should not be the author of them.

With reference to those ideas of corporeal things that are clear and distinct, there are some which, as appears to me, might have been taken from the idea I have of myself, as those of substance, duration, number, and the like. For when I think that a stone is a substance, or a thing capable of existing of itself, and that I am likewise a substance, although I conceive that I am a thinking and non-extended thing, and that the stone, on the contrary, is extended and unconscious, there being thus the greatest diversity between the two concepts,—yet these two ideas seem to have this in common that they both represent substances. In the same way, when I think of myself as now existing, and recollect besides that I existed some time ago, and when I am conscious of various thoughts whose number I know, I then acquire the ideas of duration and number, which I can afterwards transfer to as many objects as I please. With respect to the other qualities that go to make up the ideas of corporeal objects, viz., extension, figure, situation, and motion, it is true that they are not formally in me, since I am merely a thinking being; but because they are only certain modes of substance, and because I myself am a substance, it seems possible that they may be contained in me eminently.

There only remains, therefore, the idea of God, in which I must consider whether there is anything that cannot be supposed to originate with myself. By the name God, I understand a substance infinite, [eternal, immutable], independent, all-knowing, all-powerful, and by which I myself, and every other thing that exists, if any such there be, were created. But these properties are so great and excellent, that the more attentively I consider them the less I feel persuaded that the idea I have of them owes its origin to myself alone. And thus it is absolutely necessary to conclude, from all that I have before said, that God exists: for though the idea of substance be in my mind owing to this, that I myself am a substance, I should not, however, have the idea of an infinite substance, seeing I am a finite being, unless it were given me by some substance in reality infinite.

And I must not imagine that I do not apprehend the infinite by a true idea, but only by the negation of the finite, in the same way that I comprehend repose and darkness by the negation of motion and light: since, on the contrary, I clearly perceive that there is more reality in the infinite substance than in the finite, and therefore that in some way I possess the perception (notion) of the infinite before that of the finite, that is, the perception of God before that of myself, for how could I know that I doubt, desire, or that something is wanting to me, and that I am not wholly perfect, if I possessed no idea of a being more perfect than myself, by comparison of which I knew the deficiencies of my nature?

And it cannot be said that this idea of God is perhaps materially false, and consequently that it may have arisen from nothing, [in other words, that it may exist in me from my imperfection], as I before said of the ideas of heat and cold, and the like: for, on the contrary, as this idea is very clear and distinct, and contains in itself more objective reality than any other, there can be no one of itself more true, or less open to the suspicion of falsity.

The idea, I say, of a being supremely perfect, and infinite, is in the highest degree true; for although, perhaps, we may imagine that such a being does not exist, we cannot, nevertheless, suppose that his idea represents nothing real, as I have already said of the idea of cold. It is likewise clear and distinct in the highest degree, since whatever the mind clearly and distinctly conceives as real or true, and as implying any perfection, is contained entire in this idea. And this is true, nevertheless, although I do not comprehend the infinite, and although there may be in God an infinity of things that I cannot comprehend, nor perhaps even compass by thought in any way; for it is of the nature of the infinite that it should not be comprehended by the finite; and it is enough that I rightly understand this, and judge that all which I clearly perceive, and in which I know there is some perfection, and perhaps also an infinity of properties of which I am ignorant, are formally or eminently in God, in order that the idea I have of him may become the most true, clear, and distinct of all the ideas in my mind.

But perhaps I am something more than I suppose myself to be, and it may be that all those perfections which I attribute to God, in some way exist potentially in me, although they do not yet show themselves, and are not reduced to act. Indeed, I am already conscious that my knowledge is being increased [and perfected] by degrees; and I see nothing to prevent it from thus gradually increasing to infinity, nor any reason why, after such increase and perfection, I should not be able thereby to acquire all the other perfections of the Divine nature; nor, in fine, why the power I possess of acquiring those perfections, if it really now exist in me, should not be sufficient to produce the ideas of them. Yet, on looking more closely into the matter, I discover that this cannot be; for, in the first place, although it were true that my knowledge daily acquired new degrees of perfection, and although there were potentially in my nature much that was not as yet actually in it, still all these excellences make not the slightest approach to the idea I have of the Deity, in whom there is no perfection merely potentially [but all actually] existent; for it is even an unmistakeable token of imperfection in my knowledge, that it is augmented by degrees. Further, although my knowledge increase more and more, nevertheless I am not, therefore, induced to think that it will ever be actually infinite, since it can never reach that point beyond which it shall be incapable of further increase. But I conceive God as actually infinite, so that nothing can be added to his perfection. And, in fine, I readily perceive that the objective being of an idea cannot be produced by a being that is merely potentially existent, which, properly speaking, is nothing, but only by a being existing formally or actually.

And, truly, I see nothing in all that I have now said which it is not easy for any one, who shall carefully consider it, to discern by the natural light; but when I allow my attention in some degree to relax, the vision of my mind being obscured, and, as it were, blinded by the images of sensible objects, I do not readily remember the reason why the idea of a being more perfect than myself, must of necessity have proceeded from a being in reality more perfect. On this account I am here desirous to inquire further, whether I, who possess this idea of God, could exist supposing there were no God. And I ask, from whom could I, in that case, derive my existence? Perhaps from myself, or from my parents, or from some other causes less perfect than God; for anything more perfect, or even equal to God, cannot be thought or imagined. But if I [were independent of every other existence, and] were myself the author of my being, I should doubt of nothing, I should desire nothing, and, in fine, no perfection would be wanting to me; for I should have bestowed upon myself every perfection of which I possess the idea, and I should thus be God. And it must not be imagined that what is now wanting to me is perhaps of more difficult acquisition than that of which I am already possessed; for on the contrary, it is quite manifest that it was a matter of much higher difficulty that I, a thinking being, should arise from nothing, than it would be for me to acquire the knowledge of many things of which I am ignorant, and which are merely the accidents of a thinking substance; and certainly, if I possessed of myself the greater perfection of which I have now spoken, [in other words, if I were the author of my own existence], I would not at least have denied to myself things that may be more easily obtained, [as that infinite variety of knowledge of which I am at present destitute]. I could not, indeed, have denied to myself any property which I perceive is contained in the idea of God, because there is none of these that seems to me to be more difficult to make or acquire; and if there were any that should happen to be more difficult to acquire, they would certainly appear so to me (supposing that I myself were the source of the other things I possess), because I should discover in them a limit to my power. And though I were to suppose that I always was as I now am, I should not, on this ground, escape the force of these reasonings, since it would not follow, even on this supposition, that no author of my existence needed to be sought after. For the whole time of my life may be divided into an infinity of parts, each of which is in no way dependent on any other; and, accordingly, because I was in existence a short time ago, it does not follow that I must now exist, unless in this moment some cause create me anew as it were,—that is, conserve me. In truth, it is perfectly clear and evident to all who will attentively consider the nature of duration, that the conservation of a substance, in each moment of its duration, requires the same power and act that would be necessary to create it, supposing it were not yet in existence; so that it is manifestly a dictate of the natural light that conservation and creation differ merely in respect of our mode of thinking [and not in reality]. All that is here required, therefore, is that I interrogate myself to discover whether I possess any power by means of which I can bring it about that I, who now am, shall exist a moment afterwards; for, since I am merely a thinking thing (or since, at least, the precise question, in the meantime, is only of that part of myself), if such a power resided in me, I should, without doubt, be conscious of it; but I am conscious of no such power, and thereby I manifestly know that I am dependent upon some being different from myself.

But perhaps the being upon whom I am dependent, is not God, and I have been produced either by my parents, or by some causes less perfect than Deity. This cannot be: for, as I said before, it is perfectly evident that there must at least be as much reality in the cause as in its effect; and accordingly, since I am a thinking thing, and possess in myself an idea of God, whatever in the end be the cause of my existence, it must of necessity be admitted that it is likewise a thinking being, and that it possesses in itself the idea and all the perfections I attribute to Deity. Then it may again be inquired whether this cause owes its origin and existence to itself, or to some other cause. For if it be self-existent, it follows, from what I have before laid down, that this cause is God; for, since it possesses the perfection of self-existence, it must likewise, without doubt, have the power of actually possessing every perfection of which it has the idea,—in other words, all the perfections I conceive to belong to God. But if it owe its existence to another cause than itself, we demand again, for a similar reason, whether this second cause exists of itself or through some other, until, from stage to stage, we at length arrive at an ultimate cause, which will be God. And it is quite manifest that in this matter there can be no infinite regress of causes, seeing that the question raised respects not so much the cause which once produced me, as that by which I am at this present moment conserved.

Nor can it be supposed that several causes concurred in my production, and that from one I received the idea of one of the perfections I attribute to Deity, and from another the idea of some other, and thus that all those perfections are indeed found somewhere in the universe, but do not all exist together in a single being who is God; for, on the contrary, the unity, the simplicity or inseparability of all the properties of Deity, is one of the chief perfections I conceive him to possess; and the idea of this unity of all the perfections of Deity could certainly not be put into my mind by any cause from which I did not likewise receive the ideas of all the other perfections; for no power could enable me to embrace them in an inseparable unity, without at the same time giving me the knowledge of what they were [and of their existence in a particular mode].

Finally, with regard to my parents [from whom it appears I sprung], although all that I believed respecting them be true, it does not, nevertheless, follow that I am conserved by them, or even that I was produced by them, in so far as I am a thinking being. All that, at the most, they contributed to my origin was the giving of certain dispositions (modifications) to the matter in which I have hitherto judged that I or my mind, which is what alone I now consider to be myself, is enclosed; and thus there can here be no difficulty with respect to them, and it is absolutely necessary to conclude from this alone, that I am and possess the idea of a being absolutely perfect, that is, of God, that his existence is most clearly demonstrated.

There remains only the inquiry as to the way in which I received this idea from God; for I have not drawn it from the senses, nor is it even presented to me unexpectedly, as is usual with the ideas of sensible objects, when these are presented or appear to be presented to the external organs of the senses; it is not even a pure production or fiction of my mind, for it is not in my power to take from or add to it; and consequently there remains but the alternative that it is innate, in the same way as is the idea of myself. And, in truth, it is not to be wondered at that God, at my creation, implanted this idea in me, that it might serve, as it were, for the mark of the workman impressed on his work; and it is not also necessary that the mark should be something different from the work itself; but considering only that God is my creator, it is highly probable that he in some way fashioned me after his own image and likeness, and that I perceive this likeness, in which is contained the idea of God, by the same faculty by which I apprehend myself,—in other words, when I make myself the object of reflection, I not only find that I am an incomplete, [imperfect] and dependent being, and one who unceasingly aspires after something better and greater than he is; but, at the same time, I am assured likewise that he upon whom I am dependent possesses in himself all the goods after which I aspire, [and the ideas of which I find in my mind], and that not merely indefinitely and potentially, but infinitely and actually, and that he is thus God. And the whole force of the argument of which I have here availed myself to establish the existence of God, consists in this, that I perceive I could not possibly be of such a nature as I am, and yet have in my mind the idea of a God, if God did not in reality exist,—this same God, I say, whose idea is in my mind—that is, a being who possesses all those lofty perfections, of which the mind may have some slight conception, without, however, being able fully to comprehend them —and who is wholly superior to all defect, [and has nothing that marks imperfection]: whence it is sufficiently manifest that he cannot be a deceiver, since it is a dictate of the natural light that all fraud and deception spring from some defect.

But before I examine this with more attention, and pass on to the consideration of other truths that may be evolved out of it, I think it proper to remain here for some time in the contemplation of God himself—that I may ponder at leisure his marvellous attributes—and behold, admire, and adore the beauty of this light so unspeakably great, as far, at least, as the strength of my mind, which is to some degree dazzled by the sight, will permit. For just as we learn by faith that the supreme felicity of another life consists in the contemplation of the Divine majesty alone, so even now we learn from experience that a like meditation, though incomparably less perfect, is the source of the highest satisfaction of which we are susceptible in this life.

MEDITATION IV. OF TRUTH AND ERROR

I have been habituated these past days to detach my mind from the senses, and I have accurately observed that there is exceedingly little which is known with certainty respecting corporeal objects,—that we know much more of the human mind, and still more of God himself. I am thus able now without difficulty to abstract my mind from the contemplation of [sensible or] imaginable objects, and apply it to those which, as disengaged from all matter, are purely intelligible. And certainly the idea I have of the human mind in so far as it is a thinking thing, and not extended in length, breadth, and depth, and participating in none of the properties of body, is incomparably more distinct than the idea of any corporeal object; and when I consider that I doubt, in other words, that I am an incomplete and dependent being, the idea of a complete and independent being, that is to say of God, occurs to my mind with so much clearness and distinctness,—and from the fact alone that this idea is found in me, or that I who possess it exist, the conclusions that God exists, and that my own existence, each moment of its continuance, is absolutely dependent upon him, are so manifest,—as to lead me to believe it impossible that the human mind can know anything with more clearness and certitude. And now I seem to discover a path that will conduct us from the contemplation of the true God, in whom are contained all the treasures of science and wisdom, to the knowledge of the other things in the universe.

For, in the first place, I discover that it is impossible for him ever to deceive me, for in all fraud and deceit there is a certain imperfection: and although it may seem that the ability to deceive is a mark of subtlety or power, yet the will testifies without doubt of malice or weakness; and such, accordingly, cannot be found in God. In the next place, I am conscious that I possess a certain faculty of judging [or discerning truth from error], which I doubtless received from God, along with whatever else is mine; and since it is impossible that he should will to deceive me, it is likewise certain that he has not given me a faculty that will ever lead me into error, provided I use it aright.

And there would remain no doubt on this head, did it not seem to follow from this, that I can never therefore be deceived; for if all I possess be from God, and if he planted in me no faculty that is deceitful, it seems to follow that I can never fall into error. Accordingly, it is true that when I think only of God (when I look upon myself as coming from God, Fr.), and turn wholly to him, I discover [in myself] no cause of error or falsity: but immediately thereafter, recurring to myself, experience assures me that I am nevertheless subject to innumerable errors. When I come to inquire into the cause of these, I observe that there is not only present to my consciousness a real and positive idea of God, or of a being supremely perfect, but also, so to speak, a certain negative idea of nothing,—in other words, of that which is at an infinite distance from every sort of perfection, and that I am, as it were, a mean between God and nothing, or placed in such a way between absolute existence and non-existence, that there is in truth nothing in me to lead me into error, in so far as an absolute being is my creator; but that, on the other hand, as I thus likewise participate in some degree of nothing or of non-being, in other words, as I am not myself the supreme Being, and as I am wanting in many perfections, it is not surprising I should fall into error. And hence I discern that error, in so far as it is error, is not something real, which depends for its existence on God, but is simply defect; and therefore that, in order to fall into it, it is not necessary God should have given me a faculty expressly for this end, but that my being deceived arises from the circumstance that the power which God has given me of discerning truth from error is not infinite.

Nevertheless this is not yet quite satisfactory; for error is not a pure negation, [in other words, it is not the simple deficiency or want of some knowledge which is not due], but the privation or want of some knowledge which it would seem I ought to possess. But, on considering the nature of God, it seems impossible that he should have planted in his creature any faculty not perfect in its kind, that is, wanting in some perfection due to it: for if it be true, that in proportion to the skill of the maker the perfection of his work is greater, what thing can have been produced by the supreme Creator of the universe that is not absolutely perfect in all its parts? And assuredly there is no doubt that God could have created me such that I should never be deceived; it is certain, likewise, that he always wills what is best; is it better, then, that I should be capable of being deceived than that I should not?

Considering this more attentively, the first thing that occurs to me is the reflection that I must not be surprised if I am not always capable of comprehending the reasons why God acts as he does; nor must I doubt of his existence because I find, perhaps, that there are several other things besides the present respecting which I understand neither why nor how they were created by him; for, knowing already that my nature is extremely weak and limited, and that the nature of God, on the other hand, is immense, incomprehensible, and infinite, I have no longer any difficulty in discerning that there is an infinity of things in his power whose causes transcend the grasp of my mind: and this consideration alone is sufficient to convince me, that the whole class of final causes is of no avail in physical [or natural] things; for it appears to me that I cannot, without exposing myself to the charge of temerity, seek to discover the [impenetrable] ends of Deity.

It further occurs to me that we must not consider only one creature apart from the others, if we wish to determine the perfection of the works of Deity, but generally all his creatures together; for the same object that might perhaps, with some show of reason, be deemed highly imperfect if it were alone in the world, may for all that be the most perfect possible, considered as forming part of the whole universe: and although, as it was my purpose to doubt of everything, I only as yet know with certainty my own existence and that of God, nevertheless, after having remarked the infinite power of Deity, I cannot deny that he may have produced many other objects, or at least that he is able to produce them, so that I may occupy a place in the relation of a part to the great whole of his creatures.

Whereupon, regarding myself more closely, and considering what my errors are (which alone testify to the existence of imperfection in me), I observe that these depend on the concurrence of two causes, viz., the faculty of cognition which I possess, and that of election or the power of free choice,—in other words, the understanding and the will. For by the understanding alone, I [neither affirm nor deny anything, but] merely apprehend (*percipio*) the ideas regarding which I may form a judgment; nor is any error, properly so called, found in it thus accurately taken. And although there are perhaps innumerable objects in the world of which I have no idea in my understanding, it cannot, on that account, be said that I am deprived of those ideas [as of something that is due to my nature], but simply that I do not possess them, because, in truth, there is no ground to prove that Deity ought to have endowed me with a larger faculty of cognition than he has actually bestowed upon me; and however skilful a workman I suppose him to be, I have no reason, on that account, to think that it was obligatory on him to give to each of his works all the perfections he is able to bestow upon some. Nor, moreover, can I complain that God has not given me freedom of choice, or a will sufficiently ample and perfect, since, in truth, I am conscious of a will so ample and extended as to be superior to all limits. And what appears to me here to be highly remarkable is that, of all the other properties I possess, there is none so great and perfect that I do not clearly discern it could be still greater and more perfect. For, to take an example, if I consider the faculty of understanding which I possess, I find that it is of very small extent, and greatly limited, and at the same time I form the idea of another faculty of the same nature, much more ample and even infinite; and seeing that I can frame the idea of it, I discover, from this circumstance alone, that it pertains to the nature of God. In the same way, if I examine the faculty of memory or imagination, or any other faculty I possess, I find none that is not small and circumscribed, and in God immense [and infinite]. It is the faculty of will only, or freedom of choice, which I experience to be so great that I am unable to conceive the idea of another that shall be more ample and extended; so that it is chiefly my will which leads me to discern that I bear a certain image and similitude of Deity. For although the faculty of will is incomparably greater in God than in myself, as well in respect of the knowledge and power that are conjoined with it, and that render it stronger and more efficacious, as in respect of the object, since in him it extends to a greater number of things, it does not, nevertheless, appear to me greater, considered in itself formally and precisely: for the power of will consists only in this, that we are able to do or not to do the same thing (that is, to affirm or deny, to pursue or shun it), or rather in this alone, that in affirming or denying, pursuing or shunning, what is proposed to us by the understanding, we so act that we are not conscious of being determined to a particular action by any external force. For, to the possession of freedom, it is not necessary that I be alike indifferent towards each of two contraries; but, on the contrary, the more I am inclined towards the one, whether because I clearly know that in it there is the reason of truth and goodness, or because God thus internally disposes my thought, the more freely do I choose and embrace it; and assuredly divine grace and natural knowledge, very far from diminishing liberty, rather augment and fortify it. But the indifference of which I am conscious when I am not impelled to one side rather than to another for want of a reason, is the lowest grade of liberty, and manifests defect or negation of knowledge rather than perfection of will; for if I always clearly knew what was true and good, I should never have any difficulty in determining what judgment I ought to come to, and what choice I ought to make, and I should thus be entirely free without ever being indifferent.

From all this I discover, however, that neither the power of willing, which I have received from God, is of itself the source of my errors, for it is exceedingly ample and perfect in its kind; nor even the power of understanding, for as I conceive no object unless by means of the faculty that God bestowed upon me, all that I conceive is doubtless rightly conceived by me, and it is impossible for me to be deceived in it.

Whence, then, spring my errors? They arise from this cause alone, that I do not restrain the will, which is of much wider range than the understanding, within the same limits, but extend it even to things I do not understand, and as the will is of itself indifferent to such, it readily falls into error and sin by choosing the false in room of the true, and evil instead of good.

For example, when I lately considered whether aught really existed in the world, and found that because I considered this question, it very manifestly followed that I myself existed, I could not but judge that what I so clearly conceived was true, not that I was forced to this judgment by any external cause, but simply because great clearness of the understanding was succeeded by strong inclination in the will; and I believed this the more freely and spontaneously in proportion as I was less indifferent with respect to it. But now I not only know that I exist, in so far as I am a thinking being, but there is likewise presented to my mind a certain idea of corporeal nature; hence I am in doubt as to whether the thinking nature which is in me, or rather which I myself am, is different from that corporeal nature, or whether both are merely one and the same thing, and I here suppose that I am as yet ignorant of any reason that would determine me to adopt the one belief in preference to the other: whence it happens that it is a matter of perfect indifference to me which of the two suppositions I affirm or deny, or whether I form any judgment at all in the matter.

This indifference, moreover, extends not only to things of which the understanding has no knowledge at all, but in general also to all those which it does not discover with perfect clearness at the moment the will is deliberating upon them; for, however probable the conjectures may be that dispose me to form a judgment in a particular matter, the simple knowledge that these are merely conjectures, and not certain and indubitable reasons, is sufficient to lead me to form one that is directly the opposite. Of this I lately had abundant experience, when I laid aside as false all that I had before held for true, on the single ground that I could in some degree doubt of it. But if I abstain from judging of a thing when I do not conceive it with sufficient clearness and distinctness, it is plain that I act rightly, and am not deceived; but if I resolve to deny or affirm, I then do not make a right use of my free will; and if I affirm what is false, it is evident that I am deceived: moreover, even although I judge according to truth, I stumble upon it by chance, and do not therefore escape the imputation of a wrong use of my freedom; for it is a dictate of the natural light, that the knowledge of the understanding ought always to precede the determination of the will.

And it is this wrong use of the freedom of the will in which is found the privation that constitutes the form of error. Privation, I say, is found in the act, in so far as it proceeds from myself, but it does not exist in the faculty which I received from God, nor even in the act, in so far as it depends on him; for I have assuredly no reason to complain that God has not given me a greater power of intelligence or more perfect natural light than he has actually bestowed, since it is of the nature of a finite understanding not to comprehend many things, and of the nature of a created understanding to be finite; on the contrary, I have every reason to render thanks to God, who owed me nothing, for having given me all the perfections I possess, and I should be far from thinking that he has unjustly deprived me of, or kept back, the other perfections which he has not bestowed upon me.

I have no reason, moreover, to complain because he has given me a will more ample than my understanding, since, as the will consists only of a single element, and that indivisible, it would appear that this faculty is of such a nature that nothing could be taken from it [without destroying it]; and certainly, the more extensive it is, the more cause I have to thank the goodness of him who bestowed it upon me.

And, finally, neither ought I to complain that God concurs with me in forming the acts of this will, or the judgments in which I am deceived, because those acts are wholly true and good, in so far as they depend on God; and the ability to form them is a higher degree of perfection in my nature than the want of it would be. With regard to privation, in which alone consists the formal reason of error and sin, this does not require the concurrence of Deity, because it is not a thing [or existence], and if it be referred to God as to its cause, it ought not to be called privation, but negation, [according to the signification of these words in the schools]. For in truth it is no imperfection in Deity that he has accorded to me the power of giving or withholding my assent from certain things of which he has not put a clear and distinct knowledge in my understanding; but it is doubtless an imperfection in me that I do not use my freedom aright, and readily give my judgment on matters which I only obscurely and confusedly conceive.

I perceive, nevertheless, that it was easy for Deity so to have constituted me that I should never be deceived, although I still remained free and possessed of a limited knowledge, viz., by implanting in my understanding a clear and distinct knowledge of all the objects respecting which I should ever have to deliberate; or simply by so deeply engraving on my memory the resolution to judge of nothing without previously possessing a clear and distinct conception of it, that I should never forget it. And I easily understand that, in so far as I consider myself as a single whole, without reference to any other being in the universe, I should have been much more perfect than I now am, had Deity created me superior to error; but I cannot therefore deny that it is not somehow a greater perfection in the universe, that certain of its parts are not exempt from defect, as others are, than if they were all perfectly alike.

And I have no right to complain because God, who placed me in the world, was not willing that I should sustain that character which of all others is the chief and most perfect; I have even good reason to remain satisfied on the ground that, if he has not given me the perfection of being superior to error by the first means I have pointed out above, which depends on a clear and evident knowledge of all the matters regarding which I can deliberate, he has at least left in my power the other means, which is, firmly to retain the resolution never to judge where the truth is not clearly known to me: for, although I am conscious of the weakness of not being able to keep my mind continually fixed on the same thought, I can nevertheless, by attentive and oft-repeated meditation, impress it so strongly on my memory that I shall never fail to recollect it as often as I require it, and I can acquire in this way the habitude of not erring; and since it is in being superior to error that the highest and chief perfection of man consists, I deem that I have gained not a little by this day's meditation, in having discovered the source of error and falsity.

And certainly this can be no other than what I have now explained: for as often as I so restrain my will within the limits of my knowledge, that it forms no judgment except regarding objects which are clearly and distinctly represented to it by the understanding, I can never be deceived; because every clear and distinct conception is doubtless something, and as such cannot owe its origin to nothing, but must of necessity have God for its author—God, I say, who, as supremely perfect, cannot, without a contradiction, be the cause of any error; and consequently it is necessary to conclude that every such conception [or judgment] is true. Nor have I merely learned to-day what I must avoid to escape error, but also what I must do to arrive at the knowledge of truth; for I will assuredly reach truth if I only fix my attention sufficiently on all the things I conceive perfectly, and separate these from others which I conceive more confusedly and obscurely: to which for the future I shall give diligent heed.

MEDITATION V. OF THE ESSENCE OF MATERIAL THINGS AND, AGAIN, OF GOD; THAT HE EXISTS

Several other questions remain for consideration respecting the attributes of God and my own nature or mind. I will, however, on some other occasion perhaps resume the investigation of these. Meanwhile, as I have discovered what must be done and what avoided to arrive at the knowledge of truth, what I have chiefly to do is to essay to emerge from the state of doubt in which I have for some time been, and to discover whether anything can be known with certainty regarding material objects. But before considering whether such objects as I conceive exist without me, I must examine their ideas in so far as these are to be found in my consciousness, and discover which of them are distinct and which confused.

In the first place, I distinctly imagine that quantity which the philosophers commonly call continuous, or the extension in length, breadth, and depth that is in this quantity, or rather in the object to which it is attributed. Further, I can enumerate in it many diverse parts, and attribute to each of these all sorts of sizes, figures, situations, and local motions; and, in fine, I can assign to each of these motions all degrees of duration. And I not only distinctly know these things when I thus consider them in general; but besides, by a little attention, I discover innumerable particulars respecting figures, numbers, motion, and the like, which are so evidently true, and so accordant with my nature, that when I now discover them I do not so much appear to learn anything new, as to call to remembrance what I before knew, or for the first time to remark what was before in my mind, but to which I had not hitherto directed my attention. And what I here find of most importance is, that I discover in my mind innumerable ideas of certain objects, which cannot be esteemed pure negations, although perhaps they possess no reality beyond my thought, and which are not framed by me though it may be in my power to think, or not to think them, but possess true and immutable natures of their own. As, for example, when I imagine a triangle, although there is not perhaps and never was in any place in the universe apart from my thought one such figure, it remains true nevertheless that this figure possesses a certain determinate nature, form, or essence, which is immutable and eternal, and not framed by me, nor in any degree dependent on my thought; as appears from the circumstance, that diverse properties of the triangle may be demonstrated, viz., that its three angles are equal to two right, that its greatest side is subtended by its greatest angle, and the like, which, whether I will or not, I now clearly discern to belong to it, although before I did not at all think of them, when, for the first time, I imagined a triangle, and which accordingly cannot be said to have been invented by me. Nor is it a valid objection to allege, that perhaps this idea of a triangle came into my mind by the medium of the senses, through my having seen bodies of a triangular figure; for I am able to form in thought an innumerable variety of figures with regard to which it cannot be supposed that they were ever objects of sense, and I can nevertheless demonstrate diverse properties of their nature no less than of the triangle, all of which are assuredly true since I clearly conceive them: and they are therefore something, and not mere negations; for it is highly evident that all that is true is something, [truth being identical with existence]; and I have already fully shown the truth of the principle, that whatever is clearly and distinctly known is true. And although this had not been demonstrated, yet the nature of my mind is such as to compel me to assent to what I clearly conceive while I so conceive it; and I recollect that even when I still strongly adhered to the objects of sense, I reckoned among the number of the most certain truths those I clearly conceived relating to figures, numbers, and other matters that pertain to arithmetic and geometry, and in general to the pure mathematics.

But now if because I can draw from my thought the idea of an object, it follows that all I clearly and distinctly apprehend to pertain to this object, does in truth belong to it, may I not from this derive an argument for the existence of God? It is certain that I no less find the idea of a God in my consciousness, that is, the idea of a being supremely perfect, than that of any figure or number whatever: and I know with not less clearness and distinctness that an [actual and] eternal existence pertains to his nature than that all which is demonstrable of any figure or number really belongs to the nature of that figure or number; and, therefore, although all the conclusions of the preceding Meditations were false, the existence of God would pass with me for a truth at least as certain as I ever judged any truth of mathematics to be—although indeed such a doctrine may at first sight appear to contain more sophistry than truth. For, as I have been accustomed in every other matter to distinguish between existence and essence, I easily believe that the existence can be separated from the essence of God, and that thus God may be conceived as not actually existing. But, nevertheless, when I think of it more attentively, it appears that the existence can no more be separated from the essence of God, than the idea of a mountain from that of a valley, or the equality of its three angles to two right angles, from the essence of a [rectilineal] triangle; so that it is not less impossible to conceive a God, that is, a being supremely perfect, to whom existence is wanting, or who is devoid of a certain perfection, than to conceive a mountain without a valley.

But though, in truth, I cannot conceive a God unless as existing, any more than I can a mountain without a valley, yet, just as it does not follow that there is any mountain in the world merely because I conceive a mountain with a valley, so likewise, though I conceive God as existing, it does not seem to follow on that account, that God exists; for my thought imposes no necessity on things; and as I may imagine a winged horse, though there be none such, so I could perhaps attribute existence to God, though no God existed. But the cases are not analogous, and a fallacy lurks under the semblance of this objection: for because I cannot conceive a mountain without a valley, it does not follow that there is any mountain or valley in existence, but simply that the mountain or valley, whether they do or do not exist, are inseparable from each other; whereas, on the other hand, because I cannot conceive God unless as existing, it follows that existence is inseparable from him, and therefore that he really exists: not that this is brought about by my thought, or that it imposes any necessity on things, but, on the contrary, the necessity which lies in the thing itself, that is, the necessity of the existence of God, determines me to think in this way: for it is not in my power to conceive a God without existence, that is, a being supremely perfect, and yet devoid of an absolute perfection, as I am free to imagine a horse with or without wings.

Nor must it be alleged here as an objection, that it is in truth necessary to admit that God exists, after having supposed him to possess all perfections, since existence is one of them, but that my original supposition was not necessary; just as it is not necessary to think that all quadrilateral figures can be inscribed in the circle, since, if I supposed this, I should be constrained to admit that the rhombus, being a figure of four sides, can be therein inscribed, which, however, is manifestly false. This objection is, I say, incompetent; for although it may not be necessary that I shall at any time entertain the notion of Deity, yet each time I happen to think of a first and sovereign being, and to draw, so to speak, the idea of him from the storehouse of the mind, I am necessitated to attribute to him all kinds of perfections, though I may not then enumerate them all, nor think of each of them in particular. And this necessity is sufficient, as soon as I discover that existence is a perfection, to cause me to infer the existence of this first and sovereign being: just as it is not necessary that I should ever imagine any triangle, but whenever I am desirous of considering a rectilineal figure composed of only three angles, it is absolutely necessary to attribute those properties to it from which it is correctly inferred that its three angles are not greater than two right angles, although perhaps I may not then advert to this relation in particular. But when I consider what figures are capable of being inscribed in the circle, it is by no means necessary to hold that all quadrilateral figures are of this number; on the contrary, I cannot even imagine such to be the case, so long as I shall be unwilling to accept in thought aught that I do not clearly and distinctly conceive: and consequently there is a vast difference between false suppositions, as is the one in question, and the true ideas that were born with me, the first and chief of which is the idea of God. For indeed I discern on many grounds that this idea is not factitious, depending simply on my thought, but that it is the representation of a true and immutable nature: in the first place, because I can conceive no other being, except God, to whose essence existence [necessarily] pertains; in the second, because it is impossible to conceive two or more gods of this kind; and it being supposed that one such God exists, I clearly see that he must have existed from all eternity, and will exist to all eternity; and finally, because I apprehend many other properties in God, none of which I can either diminish or change.

But, indeed, whatever mode of probation I in the end adopt, it always returns to this, that it is only the things I clearly and distinctly conceive which have the power of completely persuading me. And although, of the objects I conceive in this manner, some, indeed, are obvious to every one, while others are only discovered after close and careful investigation; nevertheless, after they are once discovered, the latter are not esteemed less certain than the former. Thus, for example, to take the case of a right-angled triangle, although it is not so manifest at first that the square of the base is equal to the squares of the other two sides, as that the base is opposite to the greatest angle; nevertheless, after it is once apprehended, we are as firmly persuaded of the truth of the former as of the latter. And, with respect to God, if I were not preoccupied by prejudices, and my thought beset on all sides by the continual presence of the images of sensible objects, I should know nothing sooner or more easily than the fact of his being. For is there any truth more clear than the existence of a Supreme Being, or of God, seeing it is to his essence alone that [necessary and eternal] existence pertains? And although the right conception of this truth has cost me much close thinking, nevertheless at present I feel not only as assured of it as of what I deem most certain, but I remark further that the certitude of all other truths is so absolutely dependent on it, that without this knowledge it is impossible ever to know anything perfectly.

For although I am of such a nature as to be unable, while I possess a very clear and distinct apprehension of a matter, to resist the conviction of its truth, yet because my constitution is also such as to incapacitate me from keeping my mind continually fixed on the same object, and as I frequently recollect a past judgment without at the same time being able to recall the grounds of it, it may happen meanwhile that other reasons are presented to me which would readily cause me to change my opinion, if I did not know that God existed; and thus I should possess no true and certain knowledge, but merely vague and vacillating opinions. Thus, for example, when I consider the nature of the [rectilineal] triangle, it most clearly appears to me, who have been instructed in the principles of geometry, that its three angles are equal to two right angles, and I find it impossible to believe otherwise, while I apply my mind to the demonstration; but as soon as I cease from attending to the process of proof, although I still remember that I had a clear comprehension of it, yet I may readily come to doubt of the truth demonstrated, if I do not know that there is a God: for I may persuade myself that I have been so constituted by nature as to be sometimes deceived, even in matters which I think I apprehend with the greatest evidence and certitude, especially when I recollect that I frequently considered many things to be true and certain which other reasons afterwards constrained me to reckon as wholly false.

But after I have discovered that God exists, seeing I also at the same time observed that all things depend on him, and that he is no deceiver, and thence inferred that all which I clearly and distinctly perceive is of necessity true: although I no longer attend to the grounds of a judgment, no opposite reason can be alleged sufficient to lead me to doubt of its truth, provided only I remember that I once possessed a clear and distinct comprehension of it. My knowledge of it thus becomes true and certain. And this same knowledge extends likewise to whatever I remember to have formerly demonstrated, as the truths of geometry and the like: for what can be alleged against them to lead me to doubt of them? Will it be that my nature is such that I may be frequently deceived? But I already know that I cannot be deceived in judgments of the grounds of which I possess a clear knowledge. Will it be that I formerly deemed things to be true and certain which I afterwards discovered to be false? But I had no clear and distinct knowledge of any of those things, and, being as yet ignorant of the rule by which I am assured of the truth of a judgment, I was led to give my assent to them on grounds which I afterwards discovered were less strong than at the time I imagined them to be. What further objection, then, is there? Will it be said that perhaps I am dreaming (an objection I lately myself raised), or that all the thoughts of which I am now conscious have no more truth than the reveries of my dreams? But although, in truth, I should be dreaming, the rule still holds that all which is clearly presented to my intellect is indisputably true.

And thus I very clearly see that the certitude and truth of all science depends on the knowledge alone of the true God, insomuch that, before I knew him, I could have no perfect knowledge of any other thing. And now that I know him, I possess the means of acquiring a perfect knowledge respecting innumerable matters, as well relative to God himself and other intellectual objects as to corporeal nature, in so far as it is the object of pure mathematics [which do not consider whether it exists or not].

MEDITATION VI. OF THE EXISTENCE OF MATERIAL THINGS
AND OF THE REAL DISTINCTION BETWEEN THE
MIND AND BODY OF MAN

There now only remains the inquiry as to whether material things exist. With regard to this question, I at least know with certainty that such things may exist, in as far as they constitute the object of pure mathematics, since, regarding them in this aspect, I can conceive them clearly and distinctly. For there can be no doubt that God possesses the power of producing all the objects I am able distinctly to conceive, and I never considered anything impossible to him, unless when I experience a contradiction in the attempt to conceive it aright. Further, the faculty of imagination which I possess, and of which I am conscious that I make use when I apply myself to the consideration of material things, is sufficient to persuade me of their existence: for, when I attentively consider what imagination is, I find that it is simply a certain application of the cognitive faculty (*facultas cognoscitiva*) to a body which is immediately present to it, and which therefore exists.

And to render this quite clear, I remark, in the first place, the difference that subsists between imagination and pure intellection [or conception]. For example, when I imagine a triangle I not only conceive (*intelligo*) that it is a figure comprehended by three lines, but at the same time also I look upon (*intueor*) these three lines as present by the power and internal application of my mind (*acie mentis*), and this is what I call imagining. But if I desire to think of a chiliogon, I indeed rightly conceive that it is a figure composed of a thousand sides, as easily as I conceive that a triangle is a figure composed of only three sides; but I cannot imagine the thousand sides of a chiliogon as I do the three sides of a triangle, nor, so to speak, view them as present [with the eyes of my mind]. And although, in accordance with the habit I have of always imagining something when I think of corporeal things, it may happen that, in conceiving a chiliogon, I confusedly represent some figure to myself, yet it is quite evident that this is not a chiliogon, since it in no wise differs from that which I would represent to myself, if I were to think of a myriogon, or any other figure of many sides; nor would this representation be of any use in discovering and unfolding the properties that constitute the difference between a chiliogon and other polygons. But if the question turns on a pentagon, it is quite true that I can conceive its figure, as well as that of a chiliogon, without the aid of imagination; but I can likewise imagine it by applying the attention of my mind to its five sides, and at the same time to the area which they contain. Thus I observe that a special effort of mind is necessary to the act of imagination, which is not required to conceiving or understanding (*ad intelligendum*); and this special exertion of mind clearly shows the difference between imagination and pure intellection (*imaginatio et intellectio pura*). I remark, besides, that this power of imagination which I possess, in as far as it differs from the power of conceiving, is in no way necessary to my [nature or] essence, that is, to the essence of my mind; for although I did not possess it, I should still remain the same that I now am, from which it seems we may conclude that it depends on something different from the mind. And I easily understand that, if some body exists, with which my mind is so conjoined and united as to be able, as it were, to consider it when it chooses, it may thus imagine corporeal objects; so that this mode of thinking differs from pure intellection only in this respect, that the mind in conceiving turns in some way upon itself, and considers some one of the ideas it possesses within itself; but in imagining it turns towards the body, and contemplates in it some object conformed to the idea which it either of itself conceived or apprehended by sense. I easily understand, I say, that imagination may be thus formed, if it is true that there are bodies; and because I find no other obvious mode of explaining it, I thence, with probability, conjecture that they exist, but only with probability; and although I carefully examine all things, nevertheless I do not find that, from the distinct idea of corporeal nature I have in my imagination, I can necessarily infer the existence of any body.

But I am accustomed to imagine many other objects besides that corporeal nature which is the object of pure mathematics, as, for example, colours, sounds, tastes, pain, and the like, although with less distinctness; and, inasmuch as I perceive these objects much better by the senses, through the medium of which and of memory, they seem to have reached the imagination, I believe that, in order the more advantageously to examine them, it is proper I should at the same time examine what sense-perception is, and inquire whether from those ideas that are apprehended by this mode of thinking (consciousness), I cannot obtain a certain proof of the existence of corporeal objects.

And, in the first place, I will recall to my mind the things I have hitherto held as true, because perceived by the senses, and the foundations upon which my belief in their truth rested; I will, in the second place, examine the reasons that afterwards constrained me to doubt of them; and, finally, I will consider what there is in them that I ought now to believe.

First, then, I perceived that I had a head, hands, feet, and other members composing that body which I considered as part, or perhaps even as a whole, of myself. I perceived further, that that body was placed among many others, by which it was capable of being affected in diverse ways, both beneficial and hurtful; and what was beneficial I remarked by a certain sensation of pleasure and what was hurtful by a sensation of pain. And, besides this pleasure and pain, I likewise felt within me hunger, thirst, and other appetites, as well as certain corporeal inclinations towards joy, sadness, anger, and similar passions. And, outside, besides the extension, figure, and motions of bodies, I likewise perceived in them hardness, heat, and the other tactile qualities, and, in addition, light, colours, odours, tastes, and sounds, the variety of which gave me the means of distinguishing the sky, the earth, the sea, and generally all the other bodies, from one another. And certainly, considering the ideas of all these qualities, which were presented to my mind, and which alone I properly and immediately perceived, it was not without reason that I thought I perceived certain objects wholly different from my thought, namely, bodies from which those ideas proceeded; for I was conscious that the ideas were presented to me without my consent being required, so that I could not perceive any object, however desirous I might be, unless it were present to the organ of sense; and it was wholly out of my power not to perceive it when it was thus present. And because the ideas I perceived by the senses were much more lively and clear, and even, in their own way, more distinct than any of those I could of myself frame by meditation, or which I found impressed on my memory, it seemed that they could not have proceeded from myself, and must therefore have been caused in me by some other objects; and as of those objects I had no knowledge beyond what the ideas themselves gave me, nothing was so likely to occur to my mind as the supposition that the objects were similar to the ideas which they caused. And because I recollected also that I had formerly trusted to the senses, rather than to reason, and that the ideas which I myself formed were not so clear as those I perceived by sense, and that they were even for the most part composed of parts of the latter, I was readily persuaded that I had no idea in my intellect which had not formerly passed through the senses. Nor was I altogether wrong in likewise believing that that body which, by a special right, I called my own, pertained to me more properly and strictly than any of the others; for in truth, I could never be separated from it as from other bodies: I felt in it and on account of it all my appetites and affections, and in fine I was affected in its parts by pain and the titillation of pleasure, and not in the parts of the other bodies that were separated from it. But when I inquired into the reason why, from this I know not what sensation of pain, sadness of mind should follow, and why from the sensation of pleasure joy should arise, or why this indescribable twitching of the stomach, which I call hunger, should put me in mind of taking food, and the parchedness of the throat of drink, and so in other cases, I was unable to give any explanation, unless that I was so taught by nature; for there is assuredly no affinity, at least none that I am able to comprehend, between this irritation of the stomach and the desire of food, any more than between the perception of an object that causes pain and the consciousness of sadness which springs from the perception. And in the same way it seemed to me that all the other judgments I had formed regarding the objects of sense, were dictates of nature; because I remarked that those judgments were formed in me, before I had leisure to weigh and consider the reasons that might constrain me to form them.

But, afterwards, a wide experience by degrees sapped the faith I had reposed in my senses; for I frequently observed that towers, which at a distance seemed round, appeared square when more closely viewed, and that colossal figures, raised on the summits of these towers, looked like small statues, when viewed from the bottom of them; and, in other instances without number, I also discovered error in judgments founded on the external senses; and not only in those founded on the external, but even in those that rested on the internal senses; for is there aught more internal than pain? and yet I have sometimes been informed by parties whose arm or leg had been amputated, that they still occasionally seemed to feel pain in that part of the body which they had lost,—a circumstance that led me to think that I could not be quite certain even that any one of my members was affected when I felt pain in it. And to these grounds of doubt I shortly afterwards also added two others of very wide generality: the first of them was that I believed I never perceived anything when awake which I could not occasionally think I also perceived when asleep, and as I do not believe that the ideas I seem to perceive in my sleep proceed from objects external to me, I did not any more observe any ground for believing this of such as I seem to perceive when awake; the second was that since I was as yet ignorant of the author of my being, or at least supposed myself to be so, I saw nothing to prevent my having been so constituted by nature as that I should be deceived even in matters that appeared to me to possess the greatest truth. And, with respect to the grounds on which I had before been persuaded of the existence of sensible objects, I had no great difficulty in finding suitable answers to them; for as nature seemed to incline me to many things from which reason made me averse, I thought that I ought not to confide much in its teachings. And although the perceptions of the senses were not dependent on my will, I did not think that I ought on that ground to conclude that they proceeded from things different from myself, since perhaps there might be found in me some faculty, though hitherto unknown to me, which produced them.

But now that I begin to know myself better, and to discover more clearly the author of my being, I do not, indeed, think that I ought rashly to admit all which the senses seem to teach, nor, on the other hand, is it my conviction that I ought to doubt in general of their teachings.

And, first, because I know that all which I clearly and distinctly conceive can be produced by God exactly as I conceive it, it is sufficient that I am able clearly and distinctly to conceive one thing apart from another, in order to be certain that the one is different from the other, seeing they may at least be made to exist separately, by the omnipotence of God; and it matters not by what power this separation is made, in order to be compelled to judge them different; and, therefore, merely because I know with certitude that I exist, and because, in the meantime, I do not observe that aught necessarily belongs to my nature or essence beyond my being a thinking thing, I rightly conclude that my essence consists only in my being a thinking thing, [or a substance whose whole essence or nature is merely thinking]. And although I may, or rather, as I will shortly say, although I certainly do possess a body with which I am very closely conjoined; nevertheless, because, on the one hand, I have a clear and distinct idea of myself, in as far as I am only a thinking and unextended thing, and as, on the other hand, I possess a distinct idea of body, in as far as it is only an extended and unthinking thing, it is certain that I, [that is, my mind, by which I am what I am], is entirely and truly distinct from my body, and may exist without it.

Moreover, I find in myself diverse faculties of thinking that have each their special mode: for example, I find I possess the faculties of imagining and perceiving, without which I can indeed clearly and distinctly conceive myself as entire, but I cannot reciprocally conceive them without conceiving myself, that is to say, without an intelligent substance in which they reside, for [in the notion we have of them, or to use the terms of the schools] in their formal concept, they comprise some sort of intellection; whence I perceive that they are distinct from myself as modes are from things. I remark likewise certain other faculties, as the power of changing place, of assuming diverse figures, and the like, that cannot be conceived and cannot therefore exist, any more than the preceding, apart from a substance in which they inhere. It is very evident, however, that these faculties, if they really exist, must belong to some corporeal or extended substance, since in their clear and distinct concept there is contained some sort of extension, but no intellection at all. Farther, I cannot doubt but that there is in me a certain passive faculty of perception, that is, of receiving and taking knowledge of the ideas of sensible things; but this would be useless to me, if there did not also exist in me, or in some other thing, another active faculty capable of forming and producing those ideas. But this active faculty cannot be in me [in as far as I am but a thinking thing], seeing that it does not presuppose thought, and also that those ideas are frequently produced in my mind without my contributing to it in any way, and even frequently contrary to my will. This faculty must therefore exist in some substance different from me, in which all the objective reality of the ideas that are produced by this faculty, is contained formally or eminently, as I before remarked; and this substance is either a body, that is to say, a corporeal nature in which is contained formally [and in effect] all that is objectively [and by representation] in those ideas; or it is God himself, or some other creature,

of a rank superior to body, in which the same is contained eminently. But as God is no deceiver, it is manifest that he does not
of himself and immediately communicate those ideas to me, nor
even by the intervention of any creature in which their objective
reality is not formally, but only eminently, contained. For as he
has given me no faculty whereby I can discover this to be the
case, but, on the contrary, a very strong inclination to believe that
those ideas arise from corporeal objects, I do not see how he could
be vindicated from the charge of deceit, if in truth they proceeded
from any other source, or were produced by other causes than
corporeal things: and accordingly it must be concluded, that corporeal objects exist. Nevertheless they are not perhaps exactly
such as we perceive by the senses, for their comprehension by the
senses is, in many instances, very obscure and confused; but it is
at least necessary to admit that all which I clearly and distinctly
conceive as in them, that is, generally speaking, all that is comprehended in the object of speculative geometry, really exists external
to me.[6]

[6] On corporeal objects as substances, cf. the *Principles*, Part I, pars. li to liv:

"LI. *What substance is, and that the term is not applicable to God and the creatures
in the same sense.*

"But with regard to what we consider as things or the modes of things, it is worth
while to examine each of them by itself. By substance we can conceive nothing else
than a thing which exists in such a way as to stand in need of nothing beyond itself
in order to its existence. And, in truth, there can be conceived but one substance
which is absolutely independent, and that is God. We perceive that all other things
can exist only by help of the concourse of God. And, accordingly, the term substance
does not apply to God and the creatures *univocally*, to adopt a term familiar in the
schools; that is, no signification of this word can be distinctly understood which is
common to God and them.

"LII. *That the term is applicable univocally to the mind and the body, and how
substance itself is known.*

"Created substances, however, whether corporeal or thinking, may be conceived
under this common concept; for these are things which, in order to their existence,
stand in need of nothing but the concourse of God. But yet substance cannot be
first discovered merely from its being a thing which exists independently, for existence by itself is not observed by us. We easily, however, discover substance itself
from any attribute of it, by this common notion, that of nothing there are no attributes, properties, or qualities: for, from perceiving that some attribute is present,
we infer that there exists some existing thing or substance to which it may be attributed is also
of necessity present.

"LIII. *That of every substance there is one principal attribute, as thinking of the
mind, extension of the body.*

"But, although any attribute is sufficient to lead us to the knowledge of substance,
there is, however, one principal property of every substance, which constitutes its

But with respect to other things which are either only particular, as, for example, that the sun is of such a size and figure, etc., or are conceived with less clearness and distinctness, as light, sound, pain, and the like, although they are highly dubious and uncertain, nevertheless on the ground alone that God is no deceiver, and that consequently he has permitted no falsity in my opinions which he has not likewise given me a faculty of correcting, I think I may with safety conclude that I possess in myself the means of arriving at the truth. And, in the first place, it cannot be doubted that in each of the dictates of nature there is some truth: for by nature, considered in general, I now understand nothing more than God himself, or the order and disposition established by God in created things; and by my nature in particular I understand the assemblage of all that God has given me.

But there is nothing which that nature teaches me more expressly [or more sensibly] than that I have a body which is ill affected when I feel pain, and stands in need of food and drink when I experience the sensations of hunger and thirst, etc. And therefore I ought not to doubt but that there is some truth in these informations.

Nature likewise teaches me by these sensations of pain, hunger,

---

nature or essence, and upon which all the others depend. Thus, extension in length, breadth, and depth, constitutes the nature of corporeal substance; and thought the nature of thinking substance. For every other thing that can be attributed to body, presupposes extension, and is only some mode of an extended thing; as all the properties we discover in the mind are only diverse modes of thinking. Thus, for example, we cannot conceive figure unless in something extended, nor motion unless in extended space, nor imagination, sensation, or will, unless in a thinking thing. But, on the other hand, we can conceive extension without figure or motion, and thought without imagination or sensation, and so of the others; as is clear to any one who attends to these matters.

"LIV. *How we may have clear and distinct notions of the substance which thinks, of that which is corporeal, and of God.*

"And thus we may easily have two clear and distinct notions or ideas, the one of created substance, which thinks, the other of corporeal substance, provided we carefully distinguish all the attributes of thought from those of extension. We may also have a clear and distinct idea of an uncreated and independent thinking substance, that is, of God, provided we do not suppose that this idea adequately represents to us all that is in God, and do not mix up with it anything fictitious, but attend simply to the characters that are comprised in the notion we have of him, and which we clearly know to belong to the nature of an absolutely perfect Being. For no one can deny that there is in us such an idea of God, without groundlessly supposing that there is no knowledge of God at all in the human mind."

thirst, etc., that I am not only lodged in my body as a pilot in a vessel, but that I am besides so intimately conjoined, and as it were intermixed with it, that my mind and body compose a certain unity. For if this were not the case, I should not feel pain when my body is hurt, seeing I am merely a thinking thing, but should perceive the wound by the understanding alone, just as a pilot perceives by sight when any part of his vessel is damaged; and when my body has need of food or drink, I should have a clear knowledge of this, and not be made aware of it by the confused sensations of hunger and thirst: for, in truth, all these sensations of hunger, thirst, pain, etc., are nothing more than certain confused modes of thinking, arising from the union and apparent fusion of mind and body.

Besides this, nature teaches me that my own body is surrounded by many other bodies, some of which I have to seek after, and others to shun. And indeed, as I perceive different sorts of colours, sounds, odours, tastes, heat, hardness, etc., I safely conclude that there are in the bodies from which the diverse perceptions of the senses proceed, certain varieties corresponding to them, although, perhaps, not in reality like them; and since, among these diverse perceptions of the senses, some are agreeable, and others disagreeable, there can be no doubt that my body, or rather my entire self, in as far as I am composed of body and mind, may be variously affected, both beneficially and hurtfully, by surrounding bodies.

But there are many other beliefs which, though seemingly the teaching of nature, are not in reality so, but which obtained a place in my mind through a habit of judging inconsiderately of things. It may thus easily happen that such judgments shall contain error: thus, for example, the opinion I have that all space in which there is nothing to affect [or make an impression on] my senses is void; that in a hot body there is something in every respect similar to the idea of heat in my mind; that in a white or green body there is the same whiteness or greenness which I perceive; that in a bitter or sweet body there is the same taste, and so in other instances; that the stars, towers, and all distant bodies, are of the same size and figure as they appear to our eyes, etc. But that I may avoid everything like indistinctness of conception, I must accurately define what I properly understand by being taught by nature. For nature is here taken in a narrower sense than when it signifies the sum of all the things which God has given me; seeing that in that meaning the notion comprehends much that belongs only to the mind [to which I am not here to be understood as referring when I use the term nature]; as, for example, the notion I have of the truth, that what is done cannot be undone, and all the other truths I discern by the natural light [without the aid of the body]; and seeing that it comprehends likewise much besides that belongs only to body, and is not here any more contained under the name nature, as the quality of heaviness, and the like, of which I do not speak,—the term being reserved exclusively to designate the things which God has given to me as a being composed of mind and body. But nature, taking the term in the sense explained, teaches me to shun what causes in me the sensation of pain, and to pursue what affords me the sensation of pleasure, and other things of this sort; but I do not discover that it teaches me, in addition to this, from these diverse perceptions of the senses, to draw any conclusions respecting external objects without a previous [careful and mature] consideration of them by the mind; for it is, as appears to me, the office of the mind alone, and not of the composite whole of mind and body, to discern the truth in those matters. Thus, although the impression a star makes on my eye is not larger than that from the flame of a candle, I do not, nevertheless, experience any real or positive impulse determining me to believe that the star is not greater than the flame; the true account of the matter being merely that I have so judged from my youth without any rational ground. And, though on approaching the fire I feel heat, and even pain on approaching it too closely, I have, however, from this no ground for holding that something resembling the heat I feel is in the fire, any more than that there is something similar to the pain; all that I have ground for believing is, that there is something in it, whatever it may be, which excites in me those sensations of heat or pain. So also, although there are spaces in which I find nothing to excite and affect my senses, I must not therefore conclude that those spaces contain in them no body; for I see that in this, as in many other similar matters, I have been accustomed to pervert the order of nature, because these perceptions of the senses, although given me by nature merely to signify to my mind what things are beneficial and hurtful to the composite whole of which it is a part, and being sufficiently clear and distinct for that purpose, are nevertheless used by me as infallible rules by which to determine immediately the essence of the bodies that exist outside me, of which they can of course afford me only the most obscure and confused knowledge.

But I have already sufficiently considered how it happens that, not withstanding the supreme goodness of God, there is falsity in my judgments. A difficulty, however, here presents itself, respecting the things which I am taught by nature must be pursued or avoided, and also respecting the internal sensations in which I seem to have occasionally detected error, [and thus to be directly deceived by nature]: thus, for example, I may be so deceived by the agreeable taste of some viand with which poison has been mixed, as to be induced to take the poison. In this case, however, nature may be excused, for it simply leads me to desire the viand for its agreeable taste, and not the poison, which is unknown to it; and thus we can infer nothing from this circumstance beyond that our nature is not omniscient; at which there is assuredly no ground for surprise, since, man being of a finite nature, his knowledge must likewise be of limited perfection. But we also not infrequently err in that to which we are directly impelled by nature, as is the case with invalids who desire drink or food that would be hurtful to them. It will here, perhaps, be alleged that the reason why such persons are deceived is that their nature is corrupted; but this leaves the difficulty untouched, for a sick man is not less really the creature of God than a man who is in full health; and therefore it is as repugnant to the goodness of God that the nature of the former should be deceitful as it is for that of the latter to be so. And, as a clock, composed of wheels and counter weights, observes not the less accurately all the laws of nature when it is ill made, and points out the hours incorrectly, than when it satisfies the desire of the maker in every respect; so likewise if the body of man be considered as a kind of machine, so made up and composed of bones, nerves, muscles, veins, blood, and skin, that although there were in it no mind, it would still exhibit the same motions which it at present manifests involuntarily, and therefore without the aid of the mind, [and simply by the dispositions of its organs], I easily discern that it would also be as natural for such a body, supposing it dropsical, for example, to experience the parchedness of the throat that is usually accompanied in the mind by the sensation of thirst, and to be disposed by this parchedness to move its nerves and its other parts in the way required for drinking, and thus increase its malady and do itself harm, as it is natural for it, when it is not indisposed, to be stimulated to drink for its good by a similar cause; and although looking to the use for which a clock was destined by its maker, I may say that it is deflected from its proper nature when it incorrectly indicates the hours, and on the same principle, considering the machine of the human body as having been formed by God for the sake of the motions which it usually manifests, although I may likewise have ground for thinking that it does not follow the order of its nature when the throat is parched and drink does not tend to its preservation, nevertheless I yet plainly discern that this latter acceptation of the term nature is very different from the other; for this is nothing more than a certain denomination, depending entirely on my thought, and hence called extrinsic, by which I compare a sick man and an imperfectly constructed clock with the idea I have of a man in good health and a well made clock; while by the other acceptation of nature is understood something which is truly found in things, and therefore possessed of some truth.

But certainly, although in respect of a dropsical body, it is only by way of exterior denomination that we say its nature is corrupted, when, without requiring drink, the throat is parched; yet, in respect of the composite whole, that is, of the mind in its union with the body, it is not a pure denomination, but really an error of nature, for it to feel thirst when drink would be hurtful to it: and, accordingly, it still remains to be considered why it is that the goodness of God does not prevent the nature of man thus taken from being fallacious.

To commence this examination accordingly, I here remark, in the first place, that there is a vast difference between mind and body, in respect that body, from its nature, is always divisible, and that mind is entirely indivisible. For in truth, when I consider the mind, that is, when I consider myself in so far only as I am a thinking thing, I can distinguish in myself no parts, but I very clearly discern that I am somewhat absolutely one and entire; and although the whole mind seems to be united to the whole body, yet, when a foot, an arm, or any other part is cut off, I am conscious that nothing has been taken from my mind; nor can the faculties of willing, perceiving, conceiving, etc., properly be called its parts, for it is the same mind that is exercised [all entire] in willing, in perceiving, and in conceiving, etc. But quite the opposite holds in corporeal or extended things; for I cannot imagine any one of them [how small soever it may be], which I cannot easily sunder in thought, and which, therefore, I do not know to be divisible. This would be sufficient to teach me that the mind or soul of man is entirely different from the body, if I had not already been apprised of it on other grounds.

I remark, in the next place, that the mind does not immediately receive the impression from all the parts of the body, but only from the brain, or perhaps even from one small part of it, viz., that in which the common sense (*sensus communis*) is said to be, which as often as it is affected in the same way, gives rise to the same perception in the mind, although meanwhile the other parts of the body may be diversely disposed, as is proved by innumerable experiments, which it is unnecessary here to enumerate.

I remark, besides, that the nature of body is such that none of its parts can be moved by another part a little removed from the other, which cannot likewise be moved in the same way by any one of the parts that lie between those two, although the most remote part does not act at all. As, for example, in the cord A, B, C, D, [which is in tension], if its last part D, be pulled, the first part A, will not be moved in a different way than it would be were one of the intermediate parts B or C to be pulled, and the last part D meanwhile to remain fixed. And in the same way, when I feel pain in the foot, the science of physics teaches me that this sensation is experienced by means of the nerves dispersed over the foot, which, extending like cords from it to the brain, when they are contracted in the foot, contract at the same time the inmost parts of the brain in which they have their origin, and excite in these parts a certain motion appointed by nature to cause in the mind a sensation of pain, as if existing in the foot: but as these nerves must pass through the tibia, the leg, the loins, the back, and neck, in order to reach the brain, it may happen that although their extremities in the foot are not affected, but only certain of their parts that pass through the loins or neck, the same movements, nevertheless, are excited in the brain by this motion as would have been caused there by a hurt received in the foot, and hence the mind will necessarily feel pain in the foot, just as if it had been hurt; and the same is true of all the other perceptions of our senses.

I remark, finally, that as each of the movements that are made in the part of the brain by which the mind is immediately affected, impresses it with but a single sensation, the most likely supposition in the circumstances is, that this movement causes the mind to experience, among all the sensations which it is capable of impressing upon it, that one which is the best fitted, and generally the most useful for the preservation of the human body when it is in full health. But experience shows us that all the perceptions which nature has given us are of such a kind as I have mentioned; and accordingly, there is nothing found in them that does not manifest the power and goodness of God. Thus, for example, when the nerves of the foot are violently or more than usually shaken, the motion passing through the medulla of the spine to the innermost parts of the brain affords a sign to the mind on which it experiences a sensation, viz., of pain, as if it were in the foot, by which the mind is admonished and excited to do its utmost to remove the cause of it as dangerous and hurtful to the foot. It is true that God could have so constituted the nature of man that the same motion in the brain would have informed the mind of something altogether different: the motion might, for example, have been the occasion on which the mind became conscious of itself, in so far as it is in the brain, or in so far as it is in some place intermediate between the foot and the brain, or, finally, the occasion on which it perceived some other object quite different, whatever that might be; but nothing of all this would have so well contributed to the preservation of the body as that which the mind actually feels. In the same way, when we stand in need of drink, there arises from this want a certain parchedness in the throat that moves its nerves, and by means of them the internal parts of the brain; and this movement affects the mind with the sensation of thirst, because there is nothing on that occasion which is more useful for us than to be made aware that we have need of drink for the preservation of our health; and so in other instances.

Whence it is quite manifest that, notwithstanding the sovereign goodness of God, the nature of man, in so far as it is composed of mind and body, cannot but be sometimes fallacious. For, if there is any cause which excites, not in the foot, but in some one of the parts of the nerves that stretch from the foot to the brain, or even in the brain itself, the same movement that is ordinarily created when the foot is ill affected, pain will be felt, as it were, in the foot, and the sense will thus be naturally deceived; for as the same movement in the brain can but impress the mind with the same sensation, and as this sensation is much more frequently excited by a cause which hurts the foot than by one acting in a different quarter, it is reasonable that it should lead the mind to feel pain in the foot rather than in any other part of the body. And if it sometimes happens that the parchedness of the throat does not arise, as is usual, from drink being necessary for the health of the body, but from quite the opposite cause, as is the case with the dropsical, yet it is much better that it should be deceitful in that instance, than if, on the contrary, it were continually fallacious when the body is well-disposed; and the same holds true in other cases.

And certainly this consideration is of great service, not only in enabling me to recognize the errors to which my nature is liable, but likewise in rendering it more easy to avoid or correct them: for, knowing that all my senses more usually indicate to me what is true than what is false, in matters relating to the advantage of the body, and being able almost always to make use of more than a single sense in examining the same object, and besides this, being able to use my memory in connecting present with past knowledge, and my understanding which has already discovered all the causes of my errors, I ought no longer to fear that falsity may be met with in what is daily presented to me by the senses. And I ought to reject all the doubts of those past days, as hyperbolical and ridiculous, especially the general uncertainty respecting sleep, which I could not distinguish from the waking state: for I now find a very marked difference between the two states, in that our memory can never connect our dreams with each other and with the course of life, as it is in the habit of doing with events that occur when we are awake. And, in truth, if some one, when I am awake, appeared to me all of a sudden and as suddenly disappeared, as do the images I see in sleep, so that I could not observe either whence he came or whither he went, I should not without reason esteem it either a spectre or phantom formed in my brain, rather than a real man. But when I perceive objects with regard to which I can distinctly determine both the place whence they come, and that in which they are, and the time at which they appear to me, and when, without interruption, I can connect the perception I have of them with the whole of the other parts of my life, I am perfectly sure that what I thus perceive occurs while I am awake and not during sleep. And I ought not in the least degree to doubt of the truth of those presentations, if, after having called together all my senses, my memory, and my understanding for the purpose of examining them, no deliverance is given by any one of these faculties which is repugnant to that of any other: for since God is no deceiver, it necessarily follows that I am not herein deceived. But because the necessities of action frequently oblige us to come to a determination before we have had leisure for so careful an examination, it must be confessed that the life of man is frequently obnoxious to error with respect to individual objects; and we must, in conclusion, acknowledge the weakness of our nature.[7]

---

[7] Cf. *Principles*, Part IV:

"CXCVIII: *That by our senses we know nothing of external objects beyond their figure [or situation], magnitude, and motion.*

"Besides, we observe no such difference between the nerves as to lead us to judge that one set of them convey to the brain from the organs of the external senses anything different from another, or that anything at all reaches the brain besides the local motion of the nerves themselves. And we see that local motion alone causes in us not only the sensation of titillation and of pain, but also of light and sounds. For if we receive a blow on the eye of sufficient force to cause the vibration of the stroke to reach the retina, we see numerous sparks of fire, which, nevertheless, are not out of our eye; and when we stop our ear with our finger, we hear a humming sound, the cause of which can only proceed from the agitation of the air that is shut up within it. Finally, we frequently observe that heat [hardness, weight], and the other sensible qualities, as far as they are in objects, and also the forms of those bodies that are purely material, as, for example, the forms of fire, are produced in them by the motion of certain other bodies, and that these in their turn likewise produce other motions in other bodies. And we can easily conceive how the motion of one body may be caused by that of another, and diversified by the size, figure, and situation of its parts, but we are wholly unable to conceive how these same things (viz., size, figure, and motion), can produce something else of a nature entirely different from themselves, as, for example, those substantial forms and real qualities which many philosophers suppose to be in bodies; nor likewise can we conceive how these qualities or forms possess force to cause motions in other bodies. But since we know, from the nature of our soul, that the diverse motions of body are sufficient to produce in it all the sensations which it has, and since we learn from experience that several of its sensations are in reality caused by such motions, while we do not discover that anything besides these motions ever passes from the organs of the external senses to the brain, we have reason to conclude that we in no way

SELECTIONS FROM THE *SECOND REPLIES TO OBJECTIONS*[8]

. . . . Finally as to your counsel about *propounding my arguments in geometrical fashion, so that they could be perceived by the reader as it were in a single intuition*, it is worth my trouble to explain here how far I have already followed it, and how far I shall seek to follow it henceforth. I distinguish two things in the geometric method of writing, to wit, the order and the method of proof (*ratio demonstrandi*).

The order consists solely in this: that those things which are first propounded, should be known without any aid from the things that follow; and that all the rest should then be so arranged that they are demonstrated from the preceding material alone. And I have certainly tried, in my *Meditations*, to follow this order as accurately as possible. The observation of it was responsible for my treating of the distinction of mind from body, not in the second, but finally in the sixth Meditation; and for my voluntary and conscious omission of many other things, because they required the explanation of a number of other matters.

The method of demonstration, moreover, is twofold, to wit, one through analysis, another through synthesis.

Analysis shows the true way by which a thing has been methodically, and as it were a priori, discovered, so that, if the reader wishes to follow it and to attend sufficiently to all the points, he will understand the material and make it his no less perfectly than if he himself had discovered it. However, it has nothing by which to urge into belief a less attentive or a hostile reader. For if even the slightest point among the matters it propounds be unnoticed, the necessity of its conclusion fails to be visible. And often there are many things it scarcely touches on, because they are clear to a sufficiently attentive reader,—things which should nevertheless be specially noticed.

---

likewise apprehend that in external objects, which we call light, colour, smell, taste, sound, heat or cold, and the other tactile qualities, or that which we call their substantial forms, unless as the various dispositions of these objects which have the power of moving our nerves in various ways."

[8] Translated from the *Secundae responsiones*. For the standard text see the Adam and Tannery edition (Paris, 1904), VII, 155 ff.

DESCARTES   115

Synthesis, on the contrary, by the opposite road and inquiring as it were a posteriori (although the proof itself is in this method often more a priori than in the former), does indeed demonstrate clearly what has been concluded. And it uses a long sequence of definitions, postulates, axioms, theorems, and problems, so that if one of its own consequences be denied, it may point out immediately that it is contained in the antecedents, and thus extort assent from the reader however hostile and stubborn. But it is not so satisfactory as the other method, nor does it fill the minds of eager learners, since it does not teach the fashion in which the matter in question was discovered.

The ancient geometers were accustomed in their works to use this method alone, not because they were wholly ignorant of the other, but, in my opinion, because they thought so highly of it, that they wished to reserve it as something secret for themselves alone.

But for my part, I have followed in my *Meditations* analysis alone, which is the true and best way for teaching. But as for synthesis, which is doubtless what you require of me here, although it is indeed, in geometrical matters, very appropriately placed after analysis, yet it cannot in these metaphysical subjects be so conveniently applied.

For there is this difficulty, that the primary notions which are presupposed for demonstrating geometrical matters, agreeing with the use of our senses, are easily admitted by any one at all. Hence there is in this case no difficulty, except in deducing the consequences correctly. But this can also be done by any one at all, even a less attentive person, if only he remembers what has gone before; and the minute distinction among the propositions has the purpose of bringing it about that they can be easily cited, and thus reduced to memory even by the unwilling.

In these metaphysical subjects, on the contrary, nothing gives more trouble than the clear and distinct perception of the primary notions. For although they themselves are by their nature no less known or even better known than those which are considered by geometers, yet since they are at enmity with many prejudices of sense to which we have been accustomed from our earliest years, they are perfectly known only by the really attentive and studious, who withdraw their minds as much as may be from corporeal things. And if they were set down by themselves, they would easily be denied by those desirous of contradicting.

That is the reason why I wrote meditations rather than disputations, like philosophers, or theorems and problems, like geometers: i.e., so that I might by this very fact testify that my business was only with those who did not refuse to consider the matter attentively with me and to meditate upon it. For by the very girding himself for the conflict of impeaching the truth, inasmuch as he withdraws himself from considering the reasons which persuade him of it to discover others which dissuade, a man is rendered less capable of perceiving truth itself.

Perhaps indeed some one will here object, that, while one should not, for the purpose of contradiction, seek any arguments when one knows the truth itself is before one, yet as long as this is doubtful, it is correct to examine all the arguments on both sides, that one may know which are stronger. On this view it would be unfair of me to wish to have my arguments admitted as true, before they were scrutinized, while prohibiting any consideration of others hostile to them.

This objection would indeed be justly made, if any of those things for which I desire an attentive and not unfriendly reader were such that they could withdraw him from the consideration of any matters in which there was even the slightest hope of finding more of truth than in mine. But among those things which I propose is the greatest doubt concerning all things, and I commend nothing more strongly than that each thing be most diligently examined, and that absolutely nothing be admitted which has not been so clearly and distinctly perceived, that we cannot refrain from assenting to it. And on the other hand there is nothing else from which I wish to withdraw the minds of readers, but those things which they have never sufficiently examined, and have drunk in not from any solid reason but from the senses only. So I do not think any one can believe he will be in greater danger of erring if he considers only those things which I propose to him, than he will be if he withdraws his mind from them, and turns it to other things, which are in some fashion opposed to them, and which pour darkness upon him (i.e. if he turns to the prejudices of the senses).

Therefore it is right that I desire singular attention in my readers, and I have chosen that fashion of writing before others, by which I thought this could be best achieved, and in which I am convinced readers will glean more that is of value than they themselves notice, while on the other hand from the synthetic fashion of writing they usually seem to themselves to have learned much more than they have really learned. But besides this I think it fair, to ignore utterly and despise as of no moment the judgments on my work of those who have been unwilling to meditate with me and have clung to their preconceived opinions.

But I know how difficult it will be, even for those who pay attention and seriously seek the truth, to perceive in one intuition the whole body of my *Meditations*, and at the same time to have distinct knowledge of each of its parts. Yet I think that both these things should be done at once, if the whole fruit of the work is to be captured. Therefore I append here some few propositions in that synthetic style, from which I hope my readers will get some profit. They should, however, notice, if you please, that I have not cared to include here as much as in the *Meditations*, since I should have to be much more prolix than in the *Meditations* themselves; nor shall I explain so accurately what I do include, partly because I seek brevity, and partly to prevent any one, because he thought this sufficient, from examining negligently the *Meditations* themselves, from which I am convinced much more that is of value can be perceived.

REASONS WHICH PROVE THE EXISTENCE OF GOD AND THE DISTINCTION OF MIND FROM BODY, ARRANGED IN GEOMETRICAL FASHION

DEFINITIONS

I. Under the name *thought* I include everything which is in us in such a way that we are immediately conscious of it. Thus all the operations of the will, intellect, imagination, and senses are thoughts. But I have added "immediately" in order to exclude those things which follow from them. Thus voluntary motion does indeed have thought for its principle, yet is not itself a thought.

II. By the name *idea* I understand that form of any thought, by the immediate perception of which I am conscious of that same thought; so that I can express nothing in words, understanding what I say, without its being certain from this very fact that there is in me an idea of what is signified by these words. And thus I call "ideas" not only the images depicted in the phantasy,—or rather I do not here call these ideas at all, in so far as they are in the corporeal phantasy, i.e. in so far as they are depicted in some part of the brain, but only in so far as they give form to the mind itself turned toward that part of the brain.

III. By the *objective reality of an idea* I understand the being (*entitatem*) of the thing represented by the idea, in so far as it is in the idea; and in the same way one can say "objective perfection," or objective artifice, etc. For whatever we perceive as in the objects of ideas, is in the ideas themselves objectively.

IV. The same things are said to be *formally* in the objects of ideas, when they are in them such as we perceive them; and *eminently*, when they are not indeed such as we perceive them; but are sufficient to be able to take the place of such characters as we perceive.

V. Everything in which there resides immediately, as in a subject, or through which there exists anything we perceive, i.e. any property or quality or attribute of which we have in us a real idea, is called *substance*. For we have no other idea of substance, accurately taken, than that it is a thing in which there exists either formally or eminently that something which we perceive, or which is objectively in some one of our ideas. For it is known by natural light, that nothing can be a real attribute to nothing.

VI. The substance, in which thought immediately resides, is called *mind*; moreover I speak here of mind (*mens*) rather than of spirit (*anima*), because the term spirit is equivocal and is often usurped for corporeal objects.

VII. The substance which is the immediate subject of local extension, and of the accidents which presuppose extension, such as figures, positions, local motions, etc., is called *body*. But whether it be one and the same substance that is called mind and body, or two different ones, will be inquired hereafter.

VIII. The substance, which we understand to be supremely perfect, and in which we conceive absolutely nothing which involves any defect or limitation of perfection, is called *God*.

IX. When we say that something is contained in the nature, or concept of any thing, it is the same as if we said that this is true of that thing, or can be affirmed of it.

X. Two substances are said to be really distinguished, when each of them can exist without the other.

POSTULATES

I request in the first place that my readers observe how weak are the reasons for which they have so far believed their senses, and how uncertain are all the judgments which they have erected upon them. And I request that they turn this over in their own minds so long and so often, that they finally acquire the habit of no longer trusting to their senses so much. For this I hold to be necessary for perceiving the certitude of metaphysical matters.

I request, secondly, that they consider their own mind, and all the attributes of it which they find they cannot doubt, even though they should suppose false everything they ever received from the senses. And I request them not to stop considering it until they have got for themselves the habit of perceiving it clearly and believing it easier to know than any corporeal object.

Thirdly, that they examine carefully those self-evident propositions which they find within them. Such are: that the same thing cannot at once be and not be; that nothing cannot be the efficient cause of anything, and the like. Thus they may exercise in its purity and freed from the perceptions of the senses that clearness of understanding which has been planted in them by nature, but which the perceptions of the senses are wont greatly to disturb and obscure. For in this way they will very easily be aware of the truth of the following Axioms.

Fourth, that they examine the ideas of those natures which contain a complex of many attributes at once, such as the nature of the triangle, the nature of the square, or of some other figure; and likewise the nature of mind, the nature of body, and above all the nature of God, or of the supremely perfect being. And I require them to observe that all those things which we perceive to be contained in these objects may truly be affirmed of them. Thus, because it is contained in the nature of a triangle that its three angles are equal to two right angles, and because divisibility is contained in the nature of body, or of the thing extended (for we conceive no extended thing so tiny that we cannot divide it at least in thought), it is true to say that the three angles of every triangle are equal to two right angles, and that every body is divisible.

Fifth, that they dwell long and much in contemplating the nature of the supremely perfect being; and that they consider, among other things, the fact that in the ideas of all other natures whatsoever there is contained possible existence; but in the idea of God, not only possible but absolutely necessary existence. For from this alone and without any discursive reasoning, they will know that God exists; and this will be no less self-evident to them, than that two is an even and three an uneven number, and the like. For some things are self-evident to some which are understood by others only through reasoning.

Sixth, that by examining all the examples of clear and distinct and likewise of obscure and confused perception, which I have considered in my *Meditations*, they accustom themselves to distinguishing what is clearly known from things obscure. For this is learned more easily by examples than by rules; and I think that I have there explained, or at least to some degree touched upon all examples of this matter.

Seventh and last, that, observing that they never seize on any falsity in what they clearly perceived; and that, on the contrary, they never, except by chance, find any truth in what they grasped but obscurely, they consider it to be wholly foreign to reason to call in doubt because of the prejudices of the senses alone, or because of hypotheses which contain something unknown, those matters which are clearly and distinctly perceived by the pure understanding. For thus they will easily admit the following Axioms as true and indubitable,—although to be sure several of them could have been better explained, and should have been propounded in the place of Theorems rather than Axioms, if I had wished to be more accurate.

AXIOMS OR COMMON NOTIONS

I. Nothing exists of which it cannot be inquired what is the cause for which it exists. For this can even be asked of God; not that there is need of any cause in order for him to exist, but because the very immensity of his nature is the cause or reason why there is no need of any cause of his existence.

II. The present time is not dependent on that which immediately precedes it; and for this reason, no less cause is needed to conserve a thing than to produce it at first.

III. Any thing or any perfection of a thing actually existent cannot have nothing, or a thing non-existent as the cause of its existence.

IV. Whatsoever of reality or perfection is in any thing is either formally or eminently in its first and adequate cause.

V. Hence it follows likewise, that the objective reality of our ideas requires a cause in which this same reality is contained, not simply objectively, but formally or eminently. And it is to be observed that this axiom must of necessity be admitted, as upon it alone depends the knowledge of all things, whether sensible or insensible. For whence do we know, for example, that the sky exists? Is it because we see it? But this vision does not affect the mind unless in so far as it is an idea, an idea, I say, inhering in the mind itself, but not an image depicted on the phantasy. Nor can we, by virtue of this idea, judge that the sky exists, except for the reason that every idea must have a cause of its objective reality which is really existent; and this cause we judge to be the sky itself, and so in other instances.

VI. There are diverse degrees of reality, that is, of being: for substance has more reality than accident or mode, and infinite substance than finite. Hence also there is more objective reality in the idea of substance than in that of accident, and in the idea of infinite than in the idea of finite substance.

VII. The will of a thinking being is carried, voluntarily indeed and freely, (for that is the essence of will), but nevertheless infallibly, to the good that is clearly known to it; and therefore, if it discover any perfections which it lacks, it will instantly confer them on itself if they are in its power.

VIII. That which can accomplish what is greater or more difficult can also accomplish what is less.

IX. It is a greater task to create or conserve a substance than the attributes or properties of a substance; but the creation of the same thing is not a greater task than its conservation, as has been already said.

X. In the idea or concept of a thing existence is contained, because we are unable to conceive anything except under the form of an existent; that is, possible or contingent existence is contained in the concept of a limited thing, but necessary and perfect existence in the concept of a supremely perfect being.

PROPOSITION I

The existence of God is known from the consideration of his nature alone.

DEMONSTRATION

To say that something is contained in the nature or in the concept of anything is the same as to say that this is true of that thing (by Definition IX). But necessary existence is contained in the nature or in the concept of God (by Axiom X).

Hence it is true to say of God that necessary existence is in him, or that God exists.

And this is the syllogism of which I made use in my reply to the sixth objection; and its conclusion may be self-evident to those who are free from all prejudices, as has been said in Postulate V. But because it is not so easy to reach so great perspicacity, we shall make the same inquiry by other methods.

PROPOSITION II

The existence of God is demonstrated, a posteriori, from this alone, that his idea is in us.

DEMONSTRATION

The objective reality of each of our ideas requires a cause in which this same reality may be contained, not simply objectively, but formally or eminently (by Axiom V). But we have in us the idea of God (by Definitions II and VIII), and the objective reality of this idea is not contained in us, either formally or eminently (by Axiom VI), nor can it be contained in anything else except in God himself (by Definition VIII). Therefore this idea of God which is in us requires God for its cause; and consequently God exists (by Axiom III).

PROPOSITION III

The existence of God is also demonstrated from this, that we ourselves, possessing the idea of him, exist.

DEMONSTRATION

If I possessed the power of conserving myself, so much the more would I have the power of conferring on myself all the perfections that are wanting to me (by Axioms VIII and IX), for these perfections are only attributes of substance whereas I myself am a substance. But I do not have the power of conferring on myself these perfections; for otherwise I should already possess them (by Axiom VII). Hence I do not have the power of conserving myself.

Further, I cannot exist without being conserved, so long as I exist, either by myself, supposing I have the power, or by another who has this power (by Axioms I and II). But I exist, and yet I have not the power of self-conservation, as has just been proved. Hence I am conserved by another.

Further, that by which I am conserved has in itself formally or eminently all that is in me (by Axiom IV). But there is in me the perception of many perfections that are wanting to me, and also the perception of the idea of God (by Definitions II and VIII). Hence the perception of these same perfections is in that by which I am conserved.

Finally, that same being cannot have the perception of any perfections that are wanting to him, that is to say, which he has not in himself formally or eminently (by Axiom VII). For since he has the power of conserving me, as has just been said, so much the more should he have the power of conferring these perfections on himself, if they were wanting to him (by Axioms VIII and IX). But he has the perception of all the perfections which I discover to be wanting to me, and which I conceive can be in God alone, as has just been proved. Therefore he has all these in himself, formally or eminently, and thus he is God.

COROLLARY

God has created the heaven and the earth and all that in them is; and besides this he can make all the things which we clearly perceive in the manner in which we perceive them.

DEMONSTRATION

All these things clearly follow from the preceding proposition. For in it it was proved that God exists, from its being necessary that some one should exist in whom are contained formally or eminently all the perfections of which there is in us any idea.

But we have in us the idea of a power so great, that by the being alone in whom it resides, the heaven and earth, etc., have been created, and also all the other things which are by me understood to be possible can be produced. Therefore at the same time with the existence of God from that very fact all these things have also been proved.

PROPOSITION IV

The mind and the body are really distinct.

DEMONSTRATION

All that we clearly perceive can be made by God in the manner in which we perceive it (by the preceding Corollary). But we clearly perceive mind, that is, thinking substance, without body, that is to say, without any extended substance (by Postulate II); and conversely, body without mind (as all readily admit). Hence at least by the divine power the mind can exist without the body, and the body without the mind.

Now, substances which can exist independently of one another are really distinct (by Definition X). But the mind and the body are substances (by Definitions V, VI, and VII) which can exist independently of one another (as has just been proved). Therefore the mind and the body are really distinct.

And it must be observed that I have here made use of divine power as a middle term, not that there is any need of any extraordinary power in order to separate mind from body, but because, since I have treated of God only in the foregoing propositions, I had nothing else I could use. Nor does it matter by what power two things are separated in order that we may know they are really distinct.

CHAPTER II

THOMAS HOBBES

Hobbes's long life stretches from the year of the Armada (when, as he says, "my mother bore twins, myself and fear") to 1679, just nine years before the accession of William and Mary. He was educated at Oxford, then became tutor in the Devonshire family. Politically he was a supporter of the Stuarts and, in fact, a personal friend of Charles II. When in 1640 he put into private circulation his first treatise on the body politic, Bishop Manwaring was jailed for preaching the doctrine there stated. His biographer Aubrey relates: "Then, thought Mr. Hobbes, it is time now for me to shift for myself, and so went into France, and resided at Paris." But when his political doctrines proved unpopular even with the Royalists, he returned to England and made his peace with Cromwell. During his youth classical literature had interested him more than the mathematics and traditional physics he heard at Oxford. His first published work was a translation of Thucydides (1628); and later he also translated Homer, made abstracts of Aristotle's *Rhetoric*, etc. On the other hand, he knew personally such men as Bacon and Galileo and in middle and later life was actively interested in the developments of the new science. He even waged pamphlet warfare on mathematical subjects, in which, for lack of training, he came off very badly. In 1675 he left London to spend his last four years in retirement in the country. Chief works: *De cive* (1647); *Of Human Nature, De corpore politico* (1650); *Leviathan* (1651); *De corpore* (1655); *De homine* (1657). Suggested readings: *English Works*, ed. Molesworth (London, 1839–45); *The Elements of Law*, ed. Tönnies (Cambridge, 1928) (*Of Human Nature* and *De corpore politico*). John Laird, *Hobbes* (London, 1934); Friedrich Lange, *History of Materialism* (London and New York, 1925); G. C. Robertson, *Hobbes* (Edinburgh and London, 1886); Sir Leslie Stephen, *Hobbes* (New York and London, 1904); Leo Strauss, *The Political Philosophy of Hobbes* (Oxford, 1936); A. E. Taylor, *Hobbes* (London, 1909).

ACCORDING to Hobbes, philosophy is ratiocination, or calculation by means of words, concerning the causes of phenomena. Such causal reasoning can take place in two directions: either we reason, in the synthetic method, from causes to effects, or, in the analytic method, from effects to causes. In the synthetic method, as Hobbes understands it, we start with certain terms arbitrarily defined; we follow out the consequences of our definitions and make constructions on the basis of them—as the geometrician, having defined a circle, proceeds to construct one. What the synthetic method gives us, then, is the result of our own definitions of words and our own constructions.

For Descartes clear and simple first principles must be really true of the world; and "synthetic" reasoning from them, if correct, gives us valid knowledge of real things. In Hobbes's synthetic method, on the contrary, the first principles are purely conventional: they are definitions of terms, not statements about reality; and reasoning or construction from them, similarly, produces an arbitrary language consistent in itself but without any necessary reference to an external world. It is by this method that Hobbes establishes, in the first three parts of the *De corpore*, a materialistic system in which body, substance, accident, etc., are defined but in which the whole structure is (like a system of mathematics) only hypothetically stated, not applied to the actual world. In the analytic method, on the other hand, we start with "effects" or "appearances"—notably with our own sensations—and reason hypothetically to their causes. In this procedure we use the system constructed by the synthetic method in order to "explain" actual appearances; and it is only here that we begin to talk about the actual world (as opposed to mere combinations of words). Even this actual world, however, is only "phenomenal." Our sensations show us only the appearances of bodies, not the bodies themselves; and it is only by applying the results of the synthetic method that we infer bodies in motion as their cause. By this combination of analytic and synthetic method, then, Hobbes completes his system. He has first established definitions of substance, body, accident, space, motion, etc., by the synthetic method. He then proceeds by the analytic method to fit the phenomena of sense into the causal framework of his defining system. Thus sense is defined as a "phantasm made by the reaction and endeavour outwards in the organ of sense, caused by an endeavour inwards from the object, remaining for some time more or less." Memory and imagination are defined as decaying sense; and men's feelings and actions are explained in terms of "endeavors" (i.e., tiny imperceptible motions of their bodies consequent on the movement of imagination). "Good" is whatever such endeavors move toward (i.e., whatever is the end of appetite or desire).[1]

Hobbes divided his philosophy into three parts: concerning body, man, and the state. We have seen how the philosophy of body and of man can be stated in terms of motion. But by analogy with the natural man, Hobbes tells us, we can go farther and indicate the character and origin of that great artificial man, the state, the huge leviathan of which natural men are members. In the individual man Hobbes distinguishes between natural powers—sense, imagination, and the movements following from them—and the artificial movements of ratiocination (artificial in that they depend for their existence on the invention of names). In like manner, always retaining the basic account in terms of the motion of bodies, one can contrast the natural motions of men toward and away from one another with the artificial relation they have entered into in the state. The basic natural motion of man is the endeavor to preserve himself ("endeavor" signifying, as in the definition of sense, imagination, etc., the tiny imperceptible motions of tiny parts of the body in response to impact from without or within). Hence the natural state of mankind consists in the endeavor of each to preserve himself (and the right of nature is the right of every man so to endeavor). But such a condition constitutes a war of all against all, in which all men are equal in the sense that each can equally destroy every other. So for the very end of self-preservation (i.e., for fear of self-destruction) it is essential to supplant the state of nature by an artificial device for the canceling of war and the preservation of peace. Such is the state. For the sake of peace, which preserves the existence endangered in the state of nature—and hence with the sole purpose of preserving life—men come together and, by a contract with one another, give over all their power to a sover-

[1] For the reason why Hobbes believes a materialistic language to be the *only* one we can intelligibly apply to phenomena see *Of Human Nature*, chap. ii, p. 193 below; also chaps. iv and v of the *Leviathan* (*Of Speech* and *Of Reason and Science*).

eign himself outside the contract who henceforth possesses absolutely the power thereby made over to him.

In such fashion Hobbes accounts for the motions of the complex body man in terms of the motions of simpler bodies and for the motions of the "artificial man" in terms of the motions of the natural man.

SELECTIONS FROM THE *DE CORPORE*[2]

PART I. COMPUTATION OR LOGIC

CHAPTER VI. OF METHOD

1. For the understanding of *method*, it will be necessary for me to repeat the definition of philosophy, delivered above (chap. I, art. 2,) in this manner, *Philosophy is the knowledge we acquire, by true ratiocination, of appearances, or apparent effects, from the knowledge we have of some possible production or generation of the same; and of such production, as has been or may be, from the knowledge we have of the effects.* METHOD, therefore, in the study of philosophy, *is the shortest way of finding out effects by their known causes, or of causes by their known effects.* But we are then said to know any effect, when we know *that there be causes of the same*, and *in what subject those causes are*, and *in what subject they produce that effect*, and *in what manner they work the same*. And this is the science of causes, or, as they call it, of the διότι. All other science, which is called the ὅτι, is either perception by sense, or the imagination, or memory remaining after such perception.

The first beginnings, therefore, of knowledge, are the phantasms of sense and imagination; and that there be such phantasms we know well enough by nature; but to know why they be, or from what causes they proceed, is the work of ratiocination; which consists (as is said above, in the 1st chapter, art. 2) in *composition*, and *division* or *resolution*. There is therefore no method, by which we find out the causes of things, but is either *compositive* or *resolutive*, or *partly compositive*, and *partly resolutive*. And the resolutive is commonly called *analytical* method, as the compositive is called *synthetical*.

[2] *English Works*, ed. Sir William Molesworth (London, 1839), I, 65 ff.

2. It is common to all sorts of method, to proceed from known things to unknown; and this is manifest from the cited definition of philosophy. But in knowledge by sense, the whole object is more known, than any part thereof; as when we see a man, the conception or whole idea of that man is first or more known, than the particular ideas of his being *figurate*, *animate*, and *rational*; that is, we first see the whole man, and take notice of his being, before we observe in him those other particulars. And therefore in any knowledge of the ὅτι, or that any thing *is*, the beginning of our search is from the whole idea; and contrarily, in our knowledge of the διότι, or of the causes of any thing, that is, in the sciences, we have more knowledge of the causes of the parts than of the whole. For the cause of the whole is compounded of the causes of the parts; but it is necessary that we know the things that are to be compounded, before we can know the whole compound. Now, by parts, I do not here mean parts of the thing itself, but parts of its nature; as, by the parts of man, I do not understand his head, his shoulders, his arms, &c. but his figure, quantity, motion, sense, reason, and the like; which accidents being compounded or put together, constitute the whole nature of man, but not the man himself. And this is the meaning of that common saying, namely, that some things are more known to us, others more known to nature; for I do not think that they, which so distinguish, mean that something is known to nature, which is known to no man; and therefore, by those things, that are more known to us, we are to understand things we take notice of by our senses, and, by more known to nature, those we acquire the knowledge of by reason; for in this sense it is, that the *whole*, that is, those things that have universal names, (which, for brevity's sake, I call *universal*) are more known to us than the *parts*, that is, such things as have names less universal, (which I therefore call *singular*); and the causes of the parts are more known to nature than the cause of the whole; that is, universals than singulars.

3. In the study of philosophy, men search after science either simply or indefinitely; that is, to know as much as they can, without propounding to themselves any limited question; or they enquire into the cause of some determined appearance, or endeavour to find out the certainty of something in question, as what is the cause of *light*, of *heat*, of *gravity*, of a *figure* propounded, and the

like; or in what *subject* any propounded *accident* is inherent; or
what may conduce most to the *generation* of some propounded
effect from many *accidents*; or in what manner particular causes
ought to be compounded for the production of some certain effect.
Now, according to this variety of things in question, sometimes the
analytical method is to be used, and sometimes the *synthetical*.

4. But to those that search after science indefinitely, which consists in the knowledge of the causes of all things, as far forth as it
may be attained, (and the causes of singular things are compounded
of the causes of universal or simple things) it is necessary that they
know the causes of universal things, or of such accidents as are
common to all bodies, that is, to all matter, before they can know
the causes of singular things, that is, of those accidents by which
one thing is distinguished from another. And, again, they must
know what those universal things are, before they can know their
causes. Moreover, seeing universal things are contained in the
nature of singular things, the knowledge of them is to be acquired
by reason, that is, by resolution. For example, if there be propounded a conception or *idea* of some singular thing, as of a
square, this square is to be resolved into a *plain, terminated with a
certain number of equal and straight lines and right angles*. For by
this resolution we have these things universal or agreeable to all
matter, namely, *line, plain*, (which contains *superficies*) *terminated, angle, straightness, rectitude*, and *equality;* and if we can find
out the causes of these, we may compound them altogether into
the cause of a square. Again, if any man propound to himself
the conception of *gold*, he may, by resolving, come to the ideas of
solid, visible, heavy, (that is, tending to the centre of the earth, or
downwards) and many other more universal than gold itself; and
these he may resolve again, till he come to such things as are most
universal. And in this manner, by resolving continually, we may
come to know what those things are, whose causes being first
known severally, and afterwards compounded, bring us to the
knowledge of singular things. I conclude, therefore, that the
method of attaining to the universal knowledge of things, is purely
analytical.

5. But the causes of universal things (of those, at least, that
have any cause) are manifest of themselves, or (as they say commonly) known to nature; so that they need no method at all; for

they have all but one universal cause, which is motion. For the variety of all figures arises out of the variety of those motions by which they are made; and motion cannot be understood to have any other cause besides motion; nor has the variety of those things we perceive by sense, as of *colours, sounds, savours,* &c. any other cause than motion, residing partly in the objects that work upon our senses, and partly in ourselves, in such manner, as that it is manifestly some kind of motion, though we cannot, without ratiocination, come to know what kind. For though many cannot understand till it be in some sort demonstrated to them, that all mutation consists in motion; yet this happens not from any obscurity in the thing itself, (for it is not intelligible that anything can depart either from rest, or from the motion it has, except by motion), but either by having their natural discourse corrupted with former opinions received from their masters, or else for this, that they do not at all bend their mind to the enquiring out of truth.

6. By the knowledge therefore of universals, and of their causes (which are the first principles by which we know the διότι of things) we have in the first place their definitions, (which are nothing but the explication of our simple conceptions.) For example, he that has a true conception of *place*, cannot be ignorant of this definition, *place is that space which is possessed or filled adequately by some body;* and so, he that conceives *motion* aright, cannot but know that *motion is the privation of one place, and the acquisition of another.* In the next place, we have their generations or descriptions; as (for example) that *a line is made by the motion of a point, superficies by the motion of a line,* and *one motion by another motion,* &c. It remains, that we enquire what motion begets such and such effects; as, what motion makes a straight line, and what a circular; what motion thrusts, what draws, and by what way; what makes a thing which is seen or heard, to be seen or heard sometimes in one manner, sometimes in another. Now the method of this kind of enquiry, is *compositive.* For first we are to observe what effect a body moved produceth, when we consider nothing in it besides its motion; and we see presently that this makes a line, or length; next, what the motion of a long body produces, which we find to be superficies; and so forwards, till we see what the effects of simple motion are; and then, in like manner, we are to observe what proceeds from the addition, multiplication, subtraction, and division,

of these motions, and what effects, what figures, and what properties, they produce; from which kind of contemplation sprung that
part of philosophy which is called *geometry*.

From this consideration of what is produced by simple motion,
we are to pass to the consideration of what effects one body moved
worketh upon another; and because there may be motion in all the
several parts of a body, yet so as that the whole body remain still
in the same place, we must enquire first, what motion causeth such
and such motion in the whole, that is, when one body invades
another body which is either at rest or in motion, what way, and
with what swiftness, the invaded body shall move; and, again,
what motion this second body will generate in a third, and so forwards. From which contemplation shall be drawn that part of
philosophy which treats of motion.

In the third place we must proceed to the enquiry of such effects
as are made by the motion of the parts of any body, as, how it
comes to pass, that things when they are the same, yet seem not
to be the same, but changed. And here the things we search after
are sensible qualities, such as *light, colour, transparency, opacity,
sound, odour, savour, heat, cold*, and the like; which because they
cannot be known till we know the causes of sense itself, therefore
the consideration of the causes of *seeing, hearing, smelling, tasting*,
and *touching*, belongs to this third place; and all those qualities
and changes, above mentioned, are to be referred to the fourth
place; which two considerations comprehend that part of philosophy which is called *physics*. And in these four parts is contained
whatsoever in natural philosophy may be explicated by demonstration, properly so called. For if a cause were to be rendered of
natural appearances in special, as, what are the motions and influences of the heavenly bodies, and of their parts, the reason
hereof must either be drawn from the parts of the sciences above
mentioned, or no reason at all will be given, but all left to uncertain
conjecture.

After *physics* we must come to *moral philosophy*; in which we
are to consider the motions of the mind, namely, *appetite, aversion,
love, benevolence, hope, fear, anger, emulation, envy, &c.*; what
causes they have, and of what they be causes. And the reason why
these are to be considered after *physics* is, that they have their
causes in sense and imagination, which are the subject of *physical*

contemplation. Also the reason, why all these things are to be searched after in the order above-said, is, that physics cannot be understood, except we know first what motions are in the smallest parts of bodies; nor such motion of parts, till we know what it is that makes another body move; nor this, till we know what simple motion will effect. And because all appearance of things to sense is determined, and made to be of such and such quality and quantity by compounded motions, every one of which has a certain degree of velocity, and a certain and determined way; therefore, in the first place, we are to search out the ways of motion simply (in which geometry consists); next the ways of such generated motions as are manifest; and, lastly, the ways of internal and invisible motions (which is the enquiry of natural philosophers). And, therefore, they that study natural philosophy, study in vain, except they begin at geometry; and such writers or disputers thereof, as are ignorant of geometry, do but make their readers and hearers lose their time.

7. *Civil* and *moral philosophy* do not so adhere to one another, but that they may be severed. For the causes of the motions of the mind are known, not only by ratiocination, but also by the experience of every man that takes the pains to observe those motions within himself. And, therefore, not only they that have attained the knowledge of the passions and perturbations of the mind, by the *synthetical method*, and from the very first principles of philosophy, may be proceeding in the same way, come to the causes and necessity of constituting commonwealths, and to get the knowledge of what is natural right, and what are civil duties; and, in every kind of government, what are the rights of the commonwealth, and all other knowledge appertaining to civil philosophy; for this reason, that the principles of the politics consist in the knowledge of the motions of the mind, and the knowledge of these motions from the knowledge of sense and imagination; but even they also that have not learned the first part of philosophy, namely, *geometry* and *physics*, may, notwithstanding, attain the principles of civil philosophy, by the *analytical method*. For if a question be propounded, as, *whether such an action be just or unjust*; if that *unjust* be resolved into *fact against law*, and that notion *law* into the *command* of him or them that have *coercive power*; and that *power* be derived from the *wills* of men that constitute such

power, to the end they may live in peace, they may at last come to this, that the appetites of men and the passions of their minds are such, that, unless they be restrained by some power, they will always be making war upon one another; which may be known to be so by any man's experience, that will but examine his own mind. And, therefore, from hence he may proceed, by compounding, to the determination of the justice or injustice of any propounded action. So that it is manifest, by what has been said, that the method of philosophy, to such as seek science simply, without propounding to themselves the solution of any particular question, is partly analytical, and partly synthetical; namely, that which proceeds from sense to the invention of principles, analytical; and the rest synthetical. . . . .

11. In the method of invention, the use of words consists in this, that they may serve for marks, by which whatsoever we have found out may be recalled to memory; for without this all our inventions perish, nor will it be possible for us to go on from principles beyond a syllogism or two, by reason of the weakness of memory. For example, if any man, by considering a triangle set before him should find that all its angles together taken are equal to two right angles, and that by thinking of the same tacitly, without any use of words either understood or expressed; and it should happen afterwards that another triangle, unlike the former, or the same in different situation, should be offered to his consideration, he would not know readily whether the same property were in this last or no, but would be forced, as often as a different triangle were brought before him (and the difference of triangles is infinite) to begin his contemplation anew; which he would have no need to do if he had the use of names, for every universal name denotes the conceptions we have of infinite singular things. Nevertheless, as I said above, they serve as *marks* for the help of our memory, whereby we register to ourselves our own inventions; but not as *signs* by which we declare the same to others; so that a man may be a philosopher alone by himself, without any master; Adam had this capacity. But to teach, that is, to demonstrate, supposes two at the least, and syllogistical speech.

12. And seeing teaching is nothing but leading the mind of him we teach, to the knowledge of our inventions, in that track by

which we attained the same with our own mind; therefore, the same method that served for our invention, will serve also for demonstration to others, saving that we omit the first part of method which proceeded from the sense of things to universal principles, which, because they are principles, cannot be demonstrated; and seeing they are known by nature, (as we said above in the 5th article) they need no demonstration, though they need explication. The whole method, therefore, of demonstration, is *synthetical*, consisting of that order of speech which begins from primary or most universal propositions, which are manifest of themselves, and proceeds by a perpetual composition of propositions into syllogisms, till at last the learner understand the truth of the conclusion sought after.

13. Now, such principles are nothing but definitions, whereof there are two sorts: one of names, that signify such things as have some conceivable cause, and another of such names as signify things of which we can conceive no cause at all. Names of the former kind are, *body*, or *matter*, *quantity*, or *extension*, *motion*, and whatsoever is common to all matter. Of the second kind, *are such a body*, *such and so great motion*, *so great magnitude*, *such figure*, and whatsoever we can distinguish one body from another by. And names of the former kind are well enough defined, when, by speech as short as may be, we raise in the mind of the hearer perfect and clear ideas or conceptions of the things named, as when we define motion to be *the leaving of one place, and the acquiring of another continually*; for though no thing moved, nor any cause of motion be in that definition, yet, at the hearing of that speech, there will come into the mind of the hearer an *idea* of motion clear enough. But definitions of things, which may be understood to have some cause, must consist of such names as express the cause or manner of their generation, as when we define a circle to be a figure made by the circumduction of a straight line in a plane, &c. Besides definitions, there is no other proposition that ought to be called primary, or (according to severe truth) be received into the number of principles. For those *axioms of Euclid*, seeing they may be demonstrated, are no principles of demonstration, though they have by the consent of all men gotten the authority of principles, because they need not be demonstrated. Also, those *petitions*, or *postulata*, (as they call them) though they be principles, yet they

are not principles of demonstration, but of construction only; that is, not of science, but of power; or (which is all one) not of *theorems*, which are speculations, but of *problems*, which belong to practice, or the doing of something. But as for those common received opinions, *Nature abhors vacuity*, *Nature doth nothing in vain*, and the like, which are neither evident in themselves, nor at all to be demonstrated, and which are oftener false than true, they are much less to be acknowledged for principles.

To return, therefore, to definitions; the reason why I say that the cause and generation of such things, as have any cause or generation, ought to enter into their definitions, is this. The end of science is the demonstration of the causes and generations of things; which if they be not in the definitions, they cannot be found in the conclusion of the first syllogism, that is made from those definitions; and if they be not in the first conclusion, they will not be found in any further conclusion deduced from that; and, therefore, by proceeding in this manner, we shall never come to science; which is against the scope and intention of demonstration.

14. Now, seeing definitions (as I have said) are principles, or primary propositions, they are therefore speeches; and seeing they are used for the raising of an *idea* of some thing in the mind of the learner, whensoever that thing has a name, the definition of it can be nothing but the explication of that name by speech; and if that name be given it for some compounded conception, the definition is nothing but a resolution of that name into its most universal parts. As when we define man, saying *man is a body animated, sentient, rational*, those names, *body animated, &c.* are parts of that whole name *man*; so that definitions of this kind always consist of *genus* and *difference*; the former names being all, till the last, *general*; and the last of all, *difference*. But if any name be the most universal in its kind, then the definition of it cannot consist of *genus* and *difference*, but is to be made by such circumlocution, as best explicateth the force of that name. Again, it is possible, and happens often, that the *genus* and *difference* are put together, and yet make no definition; as these words, *a straight line*, contain both the *genus* and *difference*; but are not a definition, unless we should think a straight line may be thus defined, *a straight line is a straight line*: and yet if there were added another name, consisting of different words, but signifying the same thing which these signify,

then these might be the definition of that name. From what has been said, it may be understood how a definition ought to be defined, namely, *that it is a proposition, whose predicate resolves the subject, when it may; and when it may not, it exemplifies the same.* . . . .

Part II. The First Grounds of Philosophy

Chapter VII. of place and time

1. In the teaching of natural philosophy, I cannot begin better (as I have already shewn) than from *privation;* that is, from feigning the world to be annihilated. But, if such annihilation of all things be supposed, it may perhaps be asked, what would remain for any man (whom only I except from this universal annihilation of things) to consider as the subject of philosophy, or at all to reason upon; or what to give names unto for ratiocination's sake.

I say, therefore, there would remain to that man ideas of the world, and of all such bodies as he had, before their annihilation, seen with his eyes, or perceived by any other sense; that is to say, the memory and imagination of magnitudes, motions, sounds, colours, &c. as also of their order and parts. All which things, though they be nothing but ideas and phantasms, happening internally to him that imagineth; yet they will appear as if they were external, and not at all depending upon any power of the mind. And these are the things to which he would give names, and subtract them from, and compound them with one another. For seeing, that after the destruction of all other things, I suppose man still remaining, and namely that he thinks, imagines, and remembers, there can be nothing for him to think of but what is past; nay, if we do but observe diligently what it is we do when we consider and reason, we shall find, that though all things be still remaining in the world, yet we compute nothing but our own phantasms. For when we calculate the magnitude and motions of heaven or earth, we do not ascend into heaven that we may divide it into parts, or measure the motions thereof, but we do it sitting still in our closets or in the dark. Now things may be considered, that is, be brought into account, either as internal accidents of our mind, in which manner we consider them when the question is about some faculty of the mind; or as species of external things, not as really existing, but appearing only to exist, or to have a being without us. And in this manner we are now to consider them.

2. If therefore we remember, or have a phantasm of any thing that was in the world before the supposed annihilation of the same; and consider, not that the thing was such or such, but only that it had a being without the mind, we have presently a conception of that we call *space*: an imaginary space indeed, because a mere phantasm, yet that very thing which all men call so. For no man calls it space for being already filled, but because it may be filled; nor does any man think bodies carry their places away with them, but that the same space contains sometimes one, sometimes another body; which could not be if space should always accompany the body which is once in it. And this is of itself so manifest, that I should not think it needed any explaining at all, but that I find space to be falsely defined by certain philosophers who infer from thence, one, that the world is infinite (for taking *space* to be the extension of bodies and thinking extension may encrease continually, he infers that bodies may be infinitely extended); and, another, from the same definition, concludes rashly, that it is impossible even to God himself to create more worlds than one; for, if another world were to be created, he says, that seeing there is nothing without this world, and therefore (according to his definition) no space, that new world must be placed in nothing; but in nothing nothing can be placed; which he affirms only, without showing any reason for the same; whereas the contrary is the truth: for more cannot be put into a space already filled, so much is empty space fitter than that, which is full, for the receiving of new bodies. Having therefore spoken thus much for these men's sakes, and for theirs that assent to them, I return to my purpose, and define *space* thus: SPACE *is the phantasm of a thing existing without the mind simply;* that is to say, that phantasm, in which we consider no other accident, but only that it appears without us.

3. As a body leaves a phantasm of its magnitude in the mind, so also a moved body leaves a phantasm of its motion, namely, an idea of that body passing out of one space into another by continual succession. And this idea, or phantasm, is that, which (without receding much from the common opinion, or from *Aristotle's* definition) I call *Time*. For seeing all men confess a year to be time, and yet do not think a year to be the accident or affection of any

body, they must needs confess it to be, not in the things without us, but only in the thought of the mind. So when they speak of the times of their predecessors, they do not think after their predecessors are gone, that their times can be any where else than in the memory of those that remember them. And as for those that say, days, years, and months are the motions of the sun and moon, seeing it is all one to say, motion *past* and motion *destroyed*, and that *future* motion is the same with motion which *is not yet begun*, they say that, which they do not mean, that there neither is, nor has been, nor shall be any time: for of whatsoever it may be said, *it has been* or *it shall* be, of the same also it might have been said heretofore, or may be said hereafter *it is*. What then can days, months, and years, be, but the names of such computations made in our mind? *Time* therefore is a phantasm, but a phantasm of motion, for if we would know by what moments time passes away, we make use of some motion or other, as of the sun, of a clock, of the sand in an hourglass, or we mark some line upon which we imagine something to be moved, there being no other means by which we can take notice of any time at all. And yet, when I say *time* is a phantasm of motion, I do not say this is sufficient to define it by; for this word *time* comprehends the notion of *former* and *latter*, or of succession in the motion of a body, in as much as it is first *here* then *there*. Wherefore a complete definition of *time* is such as this, TIME *is the phantasm of before and after in motion;* which agrees with this definition of *Aristotle, time is the number of motion according to former and latter;* for that numbering is an act of the mind; and therefore it is all one to say, *time is the number of motion according to former and latter;* and *time is a phantasm of motion numbered.* But that other definition, *time is the measure of motion,* is not so exact, for we measure time by motion and not motion by time. . . . .

CHAPTER VIII. OF BODY AND ACCIDENT

1. Having understood what imaginary space is, in which we supposed nothing remaining without us, but all those things to be destroyed, that, by existing heretofore, left images of themselves in our minds; let us now suppose some one of those things to be placed again in the world, or created anew. It is necessary, therefore, that this new-created or replaced thing do not only fill some part

of the space above mentioned, or be coincident and coextended with it, but also that it have no dependence upon our thought. And this is that which, for the extension of it, we commonly call *body;* and because it depends not upon our thought, we say is *a thing subsisting of itself;* as also *existing,* because without us; and, lastly, it is called the *subject,* because it is so placed in and *subjected* to imaginary space, that it may be understood by reason, as well as perceived by sense. The definition, therefore of *body* may be this, *a body is that, which having no dependence upon our thought, is coincident or coextended with some part of space.*

2. But what an *accident* is cannot so easily be explained by any definition, as by examples. Let us imagine, therefore, that a body fills any space, or is coextended with it; that coextension is not the coextended body, and, in like manner, let us imagine that the same body is removed out of its place; that removing is not the removed body: or let us think the same not removed; that not removing or rest is not the resting body. What, then, are these things? They are *accidents* of that body. But the thing in question is, *what is a accident?* which is an enquiry after that which we know already, and not that which we should enquire after. For who does not always and in the same manner understand him that says any thing is extended, or moved or not moved? But most men will have it be said that *an accident is something,* namely, some part of a natural thing, when, indeed, it is no part of the same. To satisfy these men, as well as may be, they answer best that define an *accident* to be *the manner by which any body is conceived;* which is all one as if they should say, *an accident is that faculty of any body, by which it works in us a conception of itself.* Which definition, though it be not an answer to the question propounded, yet it is an answer to that question which should have been propounded, namely, *whence does it happen that one part of any body appears here, another there?* For this is well answered thus: *it happens from the extension of that body,* Or, *how comes it to pass that the whole body, by succession, is seen now here, now there?* and the answer will be, *by reason of its motion.* Or, lastly, *whence is it that any body possesseth the same space for sometime?* and the answer will be, *because it is not moved.* For if concerning the name of a body, that is, concerning a concrete name, it be asked, *what is it?* the answer must be made by definition; for the question is concerning the

signification of the name. But if it be asked concerning an abstract name, *what is it?* the cause is demanded why a thing appears so or so. As if it be asked, *what is hard?* The answer will be, hard is that, whereof no part gives place, but when the whole gives place. But if it be demanded, *what is hardness?* a cause must be shewn why a part does not give place, except the whole give place. Wherefore, I define *an accident* to be *the manner of our conception of body.*

3. When an *accident* is said *to be in a body*, it is not so to be understood, as if any thing were contained in that body; as if, for example, redness were in blood, in the same manner, as blood is in a bloody cloth, that is, as a part in the whole; for so, an accident would be a body also. But, as magnitude, or rest, or motion, is in that which is great, or which resteth, or which is moved, (which, how it is to be understood, every man understands) so also, it is to be understood, that every other accident *is in* its subject. And this, also, is explicated by *Aristotle* no otherwise than negatively, namely, that *an accident is in its subject, not as any part thereof, but so as that it may be away, the subject still remaining;* which is right, saving that there are certain accidents which can never perish except the body perish also; for no body can be conceived to be without extension, or without figure. All other accidents, which are not common to all bodies, but peculiar to some only, as *to be at rest, to be moved, colour, hardness,* and the like, do perish continually, and are succeeded by others, yet so, as that the body never perisheth. And as for the opinion that some may have, that all other accidents are not in their bodies in the same manner that extension, motion, rest, or figure, are in the same; for example, that colour, heat, odour, virtue, vice, and the like, are otherwise in them, and, as they say, *inherent;* I desire they would suspend their judgment for the present, and expect a little, till it be found out by ratiocination, whether these very accidents are not also certain motions either of the mind of the perceiver, or of the bodies themselves which are perceived; for in the search of this, a great part of natural philosophy consists.

4. The *extension* of a body, is the same thing with the *magnitude* of it, or that which some call *real space.* But this *magnitude* does not depend upon our cogitation, as imaginary space doth; for this is an effect of our imagination, but *magnitude* is the cause of it;

this is an accident of the mind, that of a body existing out of the mind.

5. That space, by which word I here understand imaginary space, which is coincident with the magnitude of any body, is called the *place* of that body; and the body itself is that which we call the *thing placed*. Now *place*, and the *magnitude* of the *thing placed*, differ. First in this, that a body keeps always the same *magnitude*, both when it is at rest, and when it is moved; but when it is moved, it does not keep the same *place*. Secondly in this, that *place* is a phantasm of any body of such and such quantity and figure; but *magnitude* is the peculiar accident of every body; for one body may at several times have several places, but has always one and the same magnitude. Thirdly in this, that *place* is nothing out of the mind, nor magnitude any thing within it. And lastly, *place* is feigned extension, but *magnitude* true extension; and a placed body is not extension, but a thing extended. Besides, *place is immovable*; for, seeing that which is moved, is understood to be carried from place to place, if place were moved, it would also be carried from place to place, so that one place must have another place, and that place another place, and so on infinitely, which is ridiculous. And as for those, that, by making *place* to be of the same nature with *real space*, would from thence maintain it to be immovable, they also make place, though they do not perceive they make it so, to be a mere phantasm. For whilst one affirms that place is therefore said to be immovable, because space in general is considered there; if he had remembered that nothing is general or universal besides names or signs, he would easily have seen that that space, which he says is considered in general, is nothing but a phantasm, in the mind or the memory, of a body of such magnitude and such figure. And whilst another says: real space is made immovable by the understanding; as when, under the superficies of running water, we imagine other and other water to come by continual succession, that superficies fixed there by the understanding, is the *immovable place* of the river: what else does he make it to be but a phantasm, though he do it obscurely and in perplexed words? Lastly, the nature of place does not consist in the *superficies of the ambient*, but in *solid space*; for the whole placed body is coextended with its whole place, and every part of it with every answering part of the same place; but seeing every placed

body is a solid thing, it cannot be understood to be coextended with superficies. Besides, how can any whole body be moved, unless all its parts be moved together with it? Or how can the internal parts of it be moved, but by leaving their place. But the internal parts of a body cannot leave the superficies of an external part contiguous to it; and, therefore, it follows, that if place be the superficies of the ambient, then the parts of a body moved, that is, bodies moved, are not moved.

6. Space, or place, that is possessed by a body, is called *full*, and that which is not so possessed, is called *empty*.

7. *Here, there, in the country, in the city*, and other the like names, by which answer is made to the question *where is it?* are not properly names of place, nor do they of themselves bring into the mind the place that is sought; for *here* and *there* signify nothing, unless the thing be shewn at the same time with the finger or something else; but when the eye of him that seeks, is, by pointing or some other sign, directed to the thing sought, the place of it is not hereby defined by him that answers, but found out by him that asks the question. Now such shewings as are made by words only, as when we say, *in the country*, or *in the city*, are some of greater latitude than others, as when we say, *in the country, in the city, in such a street, in a house, in the chamber, in bed, &c.* For these do, by little and little, direct the seeker nearer to the proper place; and yet they do not determine the same, but only restrain it to a lesser space, and signify no more, than that the place of the thing is within a certain space designed by those words, as a part is in the whole. And all such names, by which answer is made to the question *where?* have, for the their *genus*, the name *somewhere*. From whence it may be understood, that whatsoever is somewhere, is in some place properly so called, which place is part of that greater space that is signified by some of these names, *in the country, in the city*, or the like.

8. A body, and the magnitude, and the place thereof, are divided by one and the same act of the mind; for, to divide an extended body, and the extension thereof, and the idea of that extension, which is place, is the same with dividing any one of them; because they are coincident, and it cannot be done but by the mind, that is by the division of space. From whence it is manifest, that neither two bodies can be together in the same place, nor one body be in two

places at the same time. Not two bodies in the same place; because when a body that fills its whole place is divided into two, the place itself is divided into two also, so that there will be two places. Not one body in two places; for the place that a body fills being divided into two, the placed body will be also divided into two; for, as I said, a place and the body that fills that place, are divided both together; and so there will be two bodies.

9. Two bodies are said to be *contiguous* to one another, and *continual*, in the same manner as spaces are; namely, *those are contiguous, between which there is no space.* Now, by space I understand, here as formerly, an idea or phantasm of a body. Wherefore, though between two bodies there be put no other body, and consequently no magnitude, or, as they call it, real space, yet if another body may be put between them, that is, if there intercede any imagined space which may receive another body, then those bodies are not contiguous. And this is so easy to be understood that I should wonder at some men, who being otherwise skilful enough in philosophy, are of a different opinion, but that I find that most of those that affect metaphysical subtleties wander from truth, as if they were led out of their way by an *ignis fatuus.* For can any man that has his natural senses, think that two bodies must therefore necessarily touch one another, because no other body is between them? Or that there can be no *vacuum,* because *vacuum* is nothing, or as they call it, *non ens?* Which is as childish, as if one should reason thus; no man can fast, because to fast is to eat nothing; but nothing cannot be eaten. *Continual, are any two bodies that have a common part; and more than two are continual, when every two, that are next to one another, are continual.*

10. MOTION *is a continual relinquishing of one place, and acquiring of another;* and that place which is relinquished is commonly called the *terminus a quo,* as that which is acquired is called the *terminus ad quem;* I say a continual relinquishing, because no body, how little soever, can totally and at once go out of its former place into another, so, but that some part of it will be in a part of a place which is common to both, namely, to the relinquished and the acquired places. For example, let any body be in the place *ACBD;* the same body cannot come into the place *BDEF,* but it

must first be in *GHIK*, whose part *GHBD* is common to both the places *ACBD*, and *GHIK*, and whose part *BDIK*, is common to both the places *GHIK*, and *BDEF*. Now it cannot be conceived

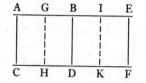

that any thing can be moved without time; for time is, by the definition of it, a phantasm, that is, a conception of motion; and, therefore, to conceive that any thing may be moved without time, were to conceive motion without motion, which is impossible. . . . .

PART IV. PHYSICS OR THE PHENOMENA OF NATURE

CHAPTER XXV.   OF SENSE AND ANIMAL MOTION

1. I have, in the first chapter, defined philosophy to be *knowledge of effects acquired by true ratiocination, from knowledge first had of their causes and generation; and of such causes or generations as may be, from former knowledge of their effects or appearances.* There are, therefore, two methods of philosophy; one, from the generation of things to their possible effects; and the other, from their effects or appearances to some possible generation of the same. In the former of these the truth of the first principles of our ratiocination, namely definitions, is made and constituted by ourselves, whilst we consent and agree about the appellations of things. And this part I have finished in the foregoing chapters; in which, if I am not deceived, I have affirmed nothing, saving the definitions themselves, which hath not good coherence with the definitions I have given; that is to say, which is not sufficiently demonstrated to all those, that agree with me in the use of words and appellations; for whose sake only I have written the same. I now enter upon the other part; which is the finding out by the appearances or effects of nature, which we know by sense, some ways and means by which they may be, I do not say they are, generated. The principles, therefore, upon which the following discourse depends, are not such as we ourselves make and pronounce

in general terms, as definitions; but such, as being placed in the things themselves by the Author of Nature, are by us observed in them; and we make use of them in single and particular, not universal propositions. Nor do they impose upon us any necessity of constituting theorems; their use being only, though not without such general propositions as have been already demonstrated, to show us the possibility of some production or generation. Seeing therefore, the science, which is here taught, hath its principles in the appearances of nature, and endeth in the attaining of some knowledge of natural causes, I have given to this part the title of PHYSICS, or the *Phenomena of Nature*. Now such things as appear, or are shown to us by nature, we call phenomena or appearances.

Of all the phenomena or appearances which are near us, the most admirable is apparition itself, τὸ φαίνεσθαι; namely, that some natural bodies have in themselves the patterns almost of all things, and others of none at all. So that if the appearances be the principles by which we know all other things, we must needs acknowledge sense to be the principle by which we know those principles, and that all the knowledge we have is derived from it. And as for the causes of sense, we cannot begin our search of them from any other phenomenon than that of sense itself. But you will say, by what sense shall we take notice of sense? I answer, by sense itself, namely, by the memory which for some time remains in us of things sensible, though they themselves pass away. For he that perceives that he hath perceived, remembers.

In the first place, therefore, the causes of our perception, that is, the causes of those ideas and phantasms which are perpetually generated within us whilst we make use of our senses, are to be enquired into; and in what manner their generation proceeds. To help which inquisition, we may observe first of all, that our phantasms or ideas are not always the same; but that new ones appear to us, and old ones vanish, according as we apply our organs of sense, now to one object, now to another. Wherefore they are generated, and perish. And from hence it is manifest, that they are some change or mutation in the sentient.

2. Now that all mutation or alteration is motion or endeavour (and endeavour also is motion) in the internal parts of the thing that is altered, hath been proved (in art. 9, chap. VIII) from this, that whilst even the least parts of any body remain in the same

situation in respect of one another, it cannot be said that any alteration, unless perhaps that the whole body together hath been moved, hath happened to it; but that it both appeareth and is the same it appeared and was before. Sense, therefore, in the sentient, can be nothing else but motion in some of the internal parts of the sentient; and the parts so moved are parts of the organs of sense. For the parts of our body, by which we perceive any thing, are those we commonly call the organs of sense. And so we find what is the subject of our sense, namely, that in which are the phantasms; and partly also we have discovered the nature of sense, namely, that it is some internal motion in the sentient.

I have shown besides (in chap. IX, art. 7) that no motion is generated but by a body contiguous and moved: from whence it is manifest, that the immediate cause of sense or perception consists in this, that the first organ of sense is touched and pressed. For when the uttermost part of the organ is pressed, it no sooner yields, but the part next within it is pressed also; and, in this manner, the pressure or motion is propagated through all the parts of the organ to the innermost. And thus also the pressure of the uttermost part proceeds from the pressure of some more remote body, and so continually, till we come to that from which, as from its fountain, we derive the phantasm or idea that is made in us by our sense. And this, whatsoever it be, is that we commonly call *the object*. Sense, therefore, is some internal motion in the sentient, generated by some internal motion of the parts of the object, and propagated through all the media to the innermost part of the organ. By which words I have almost defined what sense is.

Moreover, I have shown (art. 2, chap. XV) that all resistance is endeavour opposite to another endeavour, that is to say, reaction. Seeing, therefore, there is in the whole organ, by reason of its own internal natural motion, some resistance or reaction against the motion which is propagated from the object to the innermost part of the organ, there is also in the same organ an endeavour opposite to the endeavour which proceeds from the object; so that when that endeavour inwards is the last action in the act of sense, then from the reaction, how little soever the duration of it be, a phantasm or idea hath its being; which, by reason that the endeavour is now outwards, doth always appear as something situate without the organ. So that now I shall give you the whole definition of sense, as it is drawn from the explication of the causes thereof and the order of its generation, thus: SENSE *is a phantasm, made by the reaction and endeavour outwards in the organ of sense, caused by an endeavour inwards from the object, remaining for some time more or less.*

3. The *subject* of sense is the *sentient* itself, namely, some living creature; and we speak more correctly, when we say a living creature seeth, than when we say the eye seeth. The object is the thing received; and it is more accurately said, that we see the sun, than that we see the light. For light and colour, and heat and sound, and other qualities which are commonly called sensible, are not objects, but phantasms in the sentients. For a phantasm is the act of sense, and differs no otherwise from sense than *fieri*, that is, being a doing, differs from *factum esse*, that is, being done; which difference, in things that are done in an instant, is none at all; and a phantasm is made in an instant. For in all motion which proceeds by perpetual propagation, the first part being moved moves the second, the second the third, and so on to the last, and that to any distance, how great soever. And in what point of time the first or foremost part proceeded to the place of the second, which is thrust on, in the same point of time the last save one proceeded into the place of the last yielding part; which by reaction, in the same instant, if the reaction be strong enough, makes a phantasm; and a phantasm being made, perception is made together with it.

4. The *organs* of sense, which are in the sentient, are such parts thereof, that if they be hurt, the very generation of phantasms is thereby destroyed, though all the rest of the parts remain entire. Now these parts in the most of living creatures are found to be certain spirits and membranes, which, proceeding from the *pia mater*, involve the brain and all the nerves; also the brain itself, and the arteries which are in the brain; and such other parts, as being stirred, the heart also, which is the fountain of all sense, is stirred together with them. For whensoever the action of the object reacheth the body of the sentient, that action is by some nerve propagated to the brain; and if the nerve leading thither be so hurt or obstructed, that the motion can be propagated no further, no sense follows. Also if the motion be intercepted between the

brain and the heart by the defect of the organ by which the action is propagated, there will be no perception of the object.

5. But though all sense, as I have said, be made by reaction, nevertheless it is not necessary that every thing that reacteth should have sense. I know there have been philosophers, and those learned men, who have maintained that all bodies are endued with sense. Nor do I see how they can be refuted, if the nature of sense be placed in reaction only. And, though by the reaction of bodies inanimate a phantasm might be made, it would nevertheless cease, as soon as ever the object were removed. For unless those bodies had organs, as living creatures have, fit for the retaining of such motion as is made in them, their sense would be such, as that they should never remember the same. And therefore this hath nothing to do with that sense which is the subject of my discourse. For by sense, we commonly understand the judgment we make of objects by their phantasms; namely, by comparing and distinguishing those phantasms; which we could never do, if that motion in the organ, by which the phantasm is made, did not remain there for some time, and make the same phantasm return. Wherefore sense, as I here understand it, and which is commonly so called, hath necessarily some memory adhering to it, by which former and later phantasms may be compared together, and distinguished from one another.

Sense, therefore, properly so called, must necessarily have in it a perpetual variety of phantasms, that they may be discerned one from another. For if we should suppose a man to be made with clear eyes, and all the rest of his organs of sight well disposed, but endued with no other sense; and that he should look only upon one thing, which is always of the same colour and figure, without the least appearance of variety, he would seem to me, whatsoever others may say, to see, no more than I seem to myself to feel the bones of my own limbs by my organs of feeling; and yet those bones are always and on all sides touched by a most sensible membrane. I might perhaps say he were astonished, and looked upon it; but I should not say he saw it; it being almost all one for a man to be always sensible of one and the same thing, and not to be sensible at all of any thing.

6. And yet such as the nature of sense, that it does not permit a man to discern many things at once. For seeing the nature of

sense consists in motion; as long as the organs are employed about one object, they cannot be so moved by another at the same time, as to make by both their motions one sincere phantasm of each of them at once. And therefore two several phantasms will not be made by two objects working together, but only one phantasm compounded from the action of both.

Besides, as when we divide a body, we divide its place; and when we reckon many bodies, we must necessarily reckon as many places; and contrarily, as I have shown in the seventh chapter; so what number soever we say there be of times, we must understand the same number of motions also; and as oft as we count many motions, so oft we reckon many times. For though the object we look upon be of divers colours, yet with those divers colours it is but one varied object, and not variety of objects.

Moreover, whilst those organs which are common to all the senses, such as are those parts of every organ which proceed in men from the root of the nerves to the heart, are vehemently stirred by a strong action from some one object, they are, by reason of the contumacy which the motion, they have already, gives them against the reception of all other motion, made the less fit to receive any other impression from whatsoever other objects, to what sense soever those objects belong. And hence it is, that an earnest studying of one object, takes away the sense of all other objects for the present. For *study* is nothing else but a possession of the mind, that is to say, a vehement motion made by some one object in the organs of sense, which are stupid to all other motions as long as this lasteth; according to what was said by Terence, "*Populus studio stupidus in funambulo animum occuparat.*" For what is *stupor* but that which the Greeks call ἀναισθησία, that is, a cessation from the sense of other things? Wherefore at one and the same time, we cannot by sense perceive more than one single object; as in reading, we see the letters successively one by one, and not all together, though the whole page be presented to our eye; and though every several letter be distinctly written there, yet when we look upon the whole page at once, we read nothing.

From hence it is manifest, that every endeavour of the organ outwards, is not to be called sense, but that only, which at several times is by vehemence made stronger and more predominant than the rest; which deprives us of the sense of other phantasms, no otherwise than the sun deprives the rest of the stars of light, not by hindering their action, but by obscuring and hiding them with his excess of brightness.

7. But the motion of the organ, by which a phantasm is made, is not commonly called sense, except the object be present. And the phantasm remaining after the object is removed or past by, is called *fancy*, and in Latin *imaginatio;* which word, because all phantasms are not images, doth not fully answer the signification of the word *fancy* in its general acceptation. Nevertheless I may use it safely enough, by understanding it for the Greek φαντασία.

IMAGINATION therefore is nothing else but *sense decaying*, or *weakened*, by the absence of the object. But what may be the cause of this decay or weakening? Is the motion the weaker, because the object is taken away? If it were, then phantasms would always and necessarily be less clear in the imagination, than they are in sense; which is not true. For in dreams, which are the imaginations of those that sleep, they are no less clear than in sense itself. But the reason why in men waking the phantasms of things past are, more obscure than those of things present, is this, that their organs being at the same time moved by other present objects, those phantasms are the less predominant. Whereas in sleep, the passages being shut up, external action doth not at all disturb or hinder internal motion.

If this be true, the next thing to be considered, will be, whether any cause may be found out, from the supposition whereof it will follow, that the passage is shut up from the external objects of sense to the internal organ. I suppose, therefore, that by the continual action of objects, to which a reaction of the organ, and more especially of the spirits, is necessarily consequent, the organ is wearied, that is, its parts are no longer moved by the spirits without some pain; and consequently the nerves being abandoned and grown slack, they retire to their fountain, which is the cavity either of the brain or of the heart; by which means the action which proceeded by the nerves is necessarily intercepted. For action upon a patient, that retires from it, makes but little impression at the first; and at last, when the nerves are by little and little slackened, none at all. And therefore there is no more reaction, that is, no more sense, till the organ being refreshed by rest, and by a supply of new spirits recovering strength and motion, the sentient awaketh. And thus it seems to be always, unless some other preternatural cause intervene; as heat in the internal parts from lassitude, or from some disease stirring the spirits and other parts of the organ in some extraordinary manner.

8. Now it is not without cause, nor so casual a thing as many perhaps think it, that phantasms in this their great variety proceed from one another; and that the same phantasms sometimes bring into the mind other phantasms like themselves, and at other times extremely unlike. For in the motion of any continued body, one part follows another by cohesion; and therefore, whilst we turn our eyes and other organs successively to many objects, the motion which was made by every one of them remaining, the phantasms are renewed as often as any one of those motions comes to be predominant above the rest; and they become predominant in the same order in which at any time formerly they were generated by sense. So that when by length of time very many phantasms have been generated within us by sense, then almost any thought may arise from any other thought; insomuch that it may seem to be a thing indifferent and casual, which thought shall follow which. But for the most part this is not so uncertain a thing to waking as to sleeping men. For the thought or phantasm of the desired end brings in all the phantasms, that are means conducing to that end, and that in order backwards from the last to the first, and again forwards from the beginning to the end. But this supposes both appetite, and judgment to discern what means conduce to the end, which is gotten by experience; and experience is store of phantasms, arising from the sense of very many things. For φαντάζεσθαι and *meminisse, fancy* and *memory*, differ only in this, that memory supposeth the time past, which fancy doth not. In memory, the phantasms we consider are as if they were worn out with time; but in our fancy we consider them as they are; which distinction is not of the things themselves, but of the considerations of the sentient. For there is in memory something like that which happens in looking upon things at a great distance; in which as the small parts of the object are not discerned, by reason of their remoteness; so in memory, many accidents and places and parts of things, which were formerly perceived by sense, are by length of time decayed and lost.

The perpetual arising of phantasms, both in sense and imagination, is that which we commonly call discourse of the mind, and is common to men with other living creatures. For he that thinketh, compareth the phantasms that pass, that is, taketh notice of their likeness or unlikeness to one another. And as he that observes readily the likenesses of things of different natures, or that are very remote from one another, is said to have a good fancy; so he is said to have a good judgment, that finds out the unlikenesses or differences of things that are like one another. Now this observation of differences is not perception made by a common organ of sense, distinct from sense or perception properly so called, but is memory of the differences of particular phantasms remaining for some time; as the distinction between hot and lucid, is nothing else but the memory both of a heating, and of an enlightening object. . . . .

OF HUMAN NATURE, CHAPTER II[3]

Originally all *conceptions* proceed from the *action* of the thing itself, whereof it is the conception: now when the action is *present*, the conception it produceth is also called *sense;* and the thing by whose action the same is produced, is called the *object of the sense.*

By our several *organs* we have several *conceptions* of several qualities in the objects; for by *sight* we have a conception or image composed of *colour* and *figure*, which is all the notice and knowledge the object imparteth to us of its nature by the eye. By *hearing* we have a conception called *sound*, which is all the knowledge we have of the quality of the object from the ear. And so the rest of the senses are also conceptions of several qualities, or natures of their objects.

Because the *image* in vision consisting of *colour* and *shape* is the knowledge we have of the qualities of the object of that sense; it is no hard matter for a man to fall into this opinion, that the same *colour* and *shape* are the *very qualities themselves;* and for the same cause, that *sound* and *noise* are the *qualities of the bell*, or of the air. And this opinion hath been so long received, that the *contrary* must needs appear a great paradox; and yet the introduction of *species visible* and *intelligible* (which is necessary for the maintenance of that opinion) passing to and fro from the *object*,

[3] *Ibid.*, IV, 3 ff.

is *worse* than any paradox, as being a plain *impossibility*. I shall therefore endeavour to make plain these points:

That the subject wherein colour and image are inherent, is *not* the *object* or thing seen.

That there is nothing *without us* (really) which we call an *image* or colour.

That the said image or colour is but an *apparition* unto us of the *motion*, agitation, or alteration, which the *object* worketh in the *brain*, or spirits, or some internal substance of the head.

That as in *vision*, so also in conceptions that arise from the *other senses*, the subject of their *inherence* is not the *object*, but the *sentient*.

Every man hath so much experience as to have seen the *sun* and the other visible objects by reflection in the *water* and *glasses;* and this alone is sufficient for this conclusion, that *colour* and *image* may be there where the *thing seen* is *not*. But because it may be said that notwithstanding the *image* in the water be not in the object, but a thing merely *phantastical*, yet there may be *colour* really in the thing itself: I will urge further this experience, that divers times men see directly the *same* object *double*, as *two candles* for *one*, which may happen from distemper, or otherwise without distemper if a man will, the organs being either in their right temper, or equally distempered; the *colours* and *figures* in two such images of the same thing *cannot be inherent* therein, because the thing seen cannot be in *two places*.

One of these images therefore is *not inherent* in the object: but seeing the organs of the sight are then in equal temper or distemper, the *one* of them is no more inherent than the *other;* and consequently *neither* of them both are in the object; which is the first proposition, mentioned in the precedent number.

Secondly, that the image of any thing by *reflection* in a *glass* or *water* or the like, is *not* any thing *in* or *behind* the glass, or *in* or *under* the water, every man may grant to himself; which is the second proposition.

For the third, we are to consider, first that upon every *great agitation* or *concussion* of the *brain* (as it happeneth from a stroke, especially if the stroke be upon the *eye*) whereby the optic nerve suffereth any great violence, there *appeareth* before the *eyes* a certain light, which light is *nothing without*, but an apparition only, all that is real being the concussion or motion of the parts of that nerve; from which experience we may conclude, that *apparition of light is really nothing but motion* within. If therefore from *lucid bodies* there can be derived *motion*, so as to affect the optic nerve in such manner as is proper thereunto, there will follow an *image* of light somewhere in that line by which the motion was last derived to the eye; that is to say, in the object, if we look directly on it, and in the glass or water, when we look upon it in the line of reflection, which in effect is the third proposition; namely, that image and colour is but an apparition to us of that motion, agitation, or alteration which the object worketh in the brain or spirits, or some *internal* substance in the head.

But that *from all lucid*, shining and illuminate bodies, there is a *motion produced* to the eye, and, through the eye, to the *optic* nerve, and so into the *brain*, by which that apparition of *light* or *colour* is affected, is not hard to prove. And first, it is evident that the *fire*, the only lucid body here upon earth, worketh by *motion* equally every way; insomuch as the motion thereof *stopped* or inclosed, it is presently *extinguished*, and no more fire. And further, that that motion, whereby the fire worketh, is *dilation*, and *contraction* of itself *alternately*, commonly called *scintillation* or glowing, is manifest also by experience. From such *motion* in the fire must needs arise a *rejection* or casting from itself of that part of the *medium* which is *contiguous* to it, whereby that part also rejecteth the *next*, and so successively one part beateth back another to the very *eye;* and in the same manner the *exterior* part of the eye presseth the *interior*, (the laws of refraction still observed). Now the interior coat of the eye is nothing else but a piece of the *optic* nerve; and therefore the motion is still continued thereby into the *brain*, and by *resistance* or reaction of the brain, is also a *rebound* into the optic nerve again; which we *not conceiving* as motion or rebound from *within*, do think it is *without*, and call it light; as hath been already shewed by the experience of a stroke. We have no reason to doubt, that the fountain of light, the *sun*, worketh by any other ways than the *fire*, at least in this matter. And thus all *vision* hath its original from such *motion* as is here described: for where there is no light, there is no sight; and therefore *colour* also must be the same thing with *light*, as being the effect of the lucid bodies: their *difference* being only this, that when the light cometh *directly* from the fountain to the eye, or *indirectly* by reflection from *clean* and *polite* bodies, and such as have *not* any particular motion internal to alter it, we call it *light*; but when it cometh to the eye by reflection from *uneven*, *rough*, and coarse bodies, or such as are affected with internal motion of their own that may alter it, then we call it *colour*; colour and light differing only in this, that the one is *pure*, and the other *perturbed* light. By that which hath been said, not only the truth of the third proposition, but also the whole manner of producing light and colour, is apparent.

As colour is not inherent in the object, but an effect thereof upon us, caused by such motion in the object, as hath been described: so neither is *sound* in the thing we hear, but in ourselves. One manifest sign thereof is, that as a man may *see*, so also he may *hear double* or *treble*, by multiplication of *echoes*, which echoes are sounds as well as the original; and *not* being in one and the *same place*, cannot be *inherent* in the body that maketh them. Nothing can make anything which is not in itself: the *clapper* hath no *sound* in it, but *motion*, and maketh motion in the internal parts of the bell; so the *bell* hath motion, and not sound, that imparteth *motion* to the *air*; and the *air* hath motion, but not sound; the *air* imparteth motion by the *ear* and *nerve* unto the *brain*; and the brain hath motion but not sound; from the *brain*, it reboundeth back into the nerves *outward*, and thence it becometh an *apparition without*, which we call *sound*. And to proceed to the *rest* of the *senses*, it is apparent enough, that the *smell* and *taste* of the *same thing*, are *not* the *same* to *every man*; and therefore are not in the thing *smelt* or *tasted*, but in the men. So likewise the *heat* we feel from the fire is manifestly in *us*, and is quite *different* from the heat which is in the *fire:* for *our* heat is *pleasure* or *pain*, according as it is *great* or *moderate*; but in the *coal* there is no such thing. By this the fourth and last proposition is proved, *viz*, that as in vision, so also the conceptions that arise from *other* senses, the subject of their inherence is not in the object, but in the sentient.

And from hence also it followeth, that *whatsoever accidents* or qualities our senses make us think there be in the *world*, they be *not* there, but are *seeming* and *apparitions* only: the things that really *are* in the world without us, are those *motions* by which these seemings are caused. And this is the *great deception of sense*, which also is to be by sense *corrected:* for as sense telleth me, when I see *directly*, that the colour seemeth to *be* in the object; so also sense telleth me, when I see by *reflection*, that colour is not in the object.

SELECTIONS FROM THE *LEVIATHAN*[4]

THE INTRODUCTION

Nature, the art whereby God hath made and governs the world, is by the *art* of man, as in many other things, so in this also imitated, that it can make an artificial animal. For seeing life is but a motion of limbs, the beginning whereof is in some principal part within; why may we not say, that all *automata* (engines that move themselves by springs and wheels as doth a watch) have an artificial life? For what is the heart, but a *spring;* and the *nerves*, but so many *strings;* and the *joints*, but so many *wheels*, giving motion to the whole body, such as was intended by the artificer? *Art* goes yet further, imitating that rational and most excellent work of nature, *man*. For by art is created that great LEVIATHAN called a COMMONWEALTH, or STATE, in Latin CIVITAS, which is but an artificial man; though of greater stature and strength than the natural, for whose protection and defense it was intended; and in which the *sovereignty* is an artificial *soul*, as giving life and motion to the whole body; the *magistrates*, and other *officers* of judicature and execution, artificial *joints; reward* and *punishment*, by which fastened to the seat of the sovereignty every joint and member is moved to perform his duty, are the *nerves*, that do the same in the body natural; the *wealth* and *riches* of all the particular members, are the *strength; salus populi*, the *people's safety*, its *business; counsellors*, by whom all things needful for it to know are suggested unto it, are the *memory; equity*, and *laws*, an artificial *reason* and *will; concord*, health; *sedition*, sickness; *and civil war*, death. Lastly, the *pacts* and *covenants*, by which the parts of this body politic were at first made, set together, and united, resemble that *fiat*, or the *let us make man*, pronounced by God in the creation.

To describe the nature of this artificial man, I will consider First, the *matter* thereof, and the *artificer*; both which is *man*. Secondly, *how*, and by what *covenants* it is made; what are the

[4] *Ibid.*, III, ix ff.

rights and just *power* or *authority* of a *sovereign;* and what it is that *preserveth* or *dissolveth* it.

Thirdly, what is a *Christian commonwealth.*

Lastly, what is the *kingdom of darkness.*

Concerning the first, there is a saying much usurped of late, that *wisdom* is acquired, not by reading of *books,* but of men. Consequently whereunto, those persons, that for the most part can give no other proof of being wise, take great delight to show what they think they have read in men, by uncharitable censures of one another behind their backs. But there is another saying not of late understood, by which they might learn truly to read one another, if they would take the pains; that is, *nosce te ipsum, read thyself:* which was not meant, as it is now used, to countenance, either the barbarous state of men in power, towards their inferiors; or to encourage men of low degree, to a saucy behaviour towards their betters; but to teach us, that from the similitude of the thoughts and passions of one man, to the thoughts and passions of another, whosoever looketh into himself, and considereth what he doth, when he does *think, opine, reason, hope, fear,* &c. and upon what grounds; he shall thereby read and know, what are the thoughts and passions of all other men upon the like occasions. I say the similitude of *passions,* which are the same in all men, *desire, fear, hope,* &c.; not the similitude of the *objects* of the passions, which are the things *desired, feared, hoped,* &c.: for these the constitution individual, and particular education, do so vary, and they are so easy to be kept from our knowledge, that the characters of man's heart, blotted and confounded as they are with dissembling, lying, counterfeiting, and erroneous doctrines, are legible only to him that searcheth hearts. And though by men's actions we do discover their design sometimes; yet to do it without comparing them with our own, and distinguishing all circumstances, by which the case may come to be altered, is to decypher without a key, and be for the most part deceived, by too much trust, or by too much diffidence; as he that reads, is himself a good or evil man.

But let one man read another by his actions never so perfectly, it serves him only with his acquaintance, which are but few. He that is to govern a whole nation, must read in himself, not this or that particular man; but mankind: which though it be hard to do, harder than to learn any language or science; yet when I shall have set down my own reading orderly, and perspicuously, the pains left another, will be only to consider, if he also find not the same in himself. For this kind of doctrine admitteth no other demonstration.

PART I. OF MAN

CHAPTER I. OF SENSE

Concerning the thoughts of man, I will consider them first singly, and afterwards in train, or dependence upon one another. Singly, they are every one a *representation* or *appearance*, of some quality, or other accident of a body without us, which is commonly called an *object*. Which object worketh on the eyes, ears, and other parts of a man's body; and by diversity of working produceth diversity of appearances.

The original of them all, is that which we call SENSE, for there is no conception in a man's mind, which hath not at first, totally or by parts, been begotten upon the organs of sense. The rest are derived from that original.

To know the natural cause of sense, is not very necessary to the business now in hand; and I have elsewhere written of the same at large. Nevertheless, to fill each part of my present method, I will briefly deliver the same in this place.

The cause of sense, is the external body, or object, which presseth the organ proper to each sense, either immediately, as in the taste and touch; or mediately, as in seeing, hearing, and smelling; which pressure, by the mediation of the nerves, and other strings and membranes of the body, continued inwards to the brain and heart, causeth there a resistance, or counter-pressure, or endeavour of the heart to deliver itself, which endeavour, because *outward*, seemeth to be some matter without. And this *seeming*, or *fancy*, is that which men call *sense*; and consisteth, as to the eye, in a *light*, or *colour figured*; to the ear, in a *sound*; to the nostril, in an *odour*; to the tongue and palate, in a *savour*; and to the rest of the body, in *heat, cold, hardness, softness*, and such other qualities as we discern by *feeling*. All which qualities, called *sensible*, are in the object, that causeth them, but so many several motions of the matter, by which it presseth our organs diversely. Neither in us that are pressed, are they any thing else, but divers motions; for motion produceth nothing but motion. But their appearance to us is fancy, the same waking, that dreaming. And as pressing, rubbing, or striking the eye, makes us fancy a light; and pressing the ear, produceth a din; so do the bodies also we see, or hear, produce the same by their strong, though unobserved action. For if those colours and sounds were in the bodies, or objects that cause them, they could not be severed from them, as by glasses, and in echoes by reflection, we see they are; where we know the thing we see is in one place, the appearance in another. And though at some certain distance, the real and very object seem invested with the fancy it begets in us; yet still the object is one thing, the image or fancy is another. So that sense, in all cases, is nothing else but original fancy, caused, as I have said, by the pressure, that is, by the motion, of external things upon our eyes, ears, and other organs thereunto ordained.

But the philosophy-schools, through all the universities of Christendom, grounded upon certain texts of Aristotle, teach another doctrine, and say, for the cause of *vision*, that the thing seen, sendeth forth on every side a *visible species*, in English, *a visible show, apparition*, or *aspect*, or *a being seen;* the receiving whereof into the eye is *seeing*. And for the cause of *hearing*, that the thing heard, sendeth forth an *audible species*, that is an *audible aspect*, or *audible being seen;* which entering at the ear maketh *hearing*. Nay, for the cause of *understanding* also, they say the thing understood, sendeth forth an *intelligible species*, that is, an *intelligible being seen;* which, coming into the understanding, makes us understand. I say not this, as disproving the use of universities; but because I am to speak hereafter of their office in a commonwealth, I must let you see on all occasions by the way, what things would be amended in them; amongst which the frequency of insignificant speech is one.

CHAPTER II. OF IMAGINATION

That when a thing lies still, unless somewhat else stir it, it will lie still for ever, is a truth that no man doubts of. But that when a thing is in motion, it will eternally be in motion, unless somewhat else stay it, though the reason be the same, namely, that nothing can change itself, is not so easily assented to. For men measure, not only other men, but all other things, by themselves; and because they find themselves subject after motion, to pain, and lassitude, think everything else grows weary of motion, and seeks repose of its own accord; little considering, whether it be not some other motion, wherein that desire of rest they find in themselves, consisteth. From hence it is, that the schools say, heavy bodies fall downwards, out of an appetite to rest, and to conserve their nature in that place which is most proper for them; ascribing appetite, and knowledge of what is good for their conservation, which is more than man has, to things inanimate, absurdly.

When a body is once in motion, it moveth, unless something else hinder it, eternally; and whatsoever hindereth it cannot in an instant, but in time, and by degrees, quite extinguish it; and as we see in the water, though the wind cease, the waves give not over rolling for a long time after: so also it happeneth in that motion, which is made in the internal parts of a man, then, when he sees, dreams, &c. For after the object is removed, or the eye shut, we still retain an image of the thing seen, though more obscure than when we see it. And this is it, the Latins call *imagination*, from the image made in seeing; and apply the same, though improperly, to all the other senses. But the Greeks call it *fancy;* which signifies *appearance*, and is as proper to one sense, as to another. IMAGINATION therefore is nothing but *decaying sense;* and is found in men, and many other living creatures, as well sleeping, as waking.

The decay of sense in men waking, is not the decay of the motion made in sense; but an obscuring of it, in such manner as the light of the sun obscureth the light of the stars; which stars do no less exercise their virtue, by which they are visible, in the day than in the night. But because amongst many strokes, which our eyes, ears, and other organs receive from external bodies, the predominant only is sensible; therefore, the light of the sun being predominant, we are not affected with the action of the stars. And any object being removed from our eyes, though the impression it made in us remain, yet other objects more present succeeding, and working on us, the imagination of the past is obscured, and made weak, as the voice of a man is in the noise of the day. From whence it followeth, that the longer the time is, after the sight or sense of any object, the weaker is the imagination. For the continual change of man's body destroys in time the parts which in sense were moved: so that distance of time, and of place, hath one and the same effect in us. For as at a great distance of place, that which we look at appears dim, and without distinction of the smaller parts; and as voices grow weak, and inarticulate; so also, after great distance of time, our imagination of the past is weak; and we lose, for example, of cities we have seen, many particular streets, and of actions, many particular circumstances. This *decaying sense*, when we would express the thing itself, I mean *fancy* itself, we call *imagination*, as I said before: but when we would express the decay, and signify that the sense is fading, old, and past, it is called *memory*. So that imagination and memory are but one thing, which for divers considerations hath divers names.

Much memory, or memory of many things, is called *experience*. Again, imagination being only of those things which have been formerly perceived by sense, either all at once, or by parts at several times; the former, which is the imagining the whole object as it was presented to the sense, is *simple* imagination, as when one imagineth a man, or horse, which he hath seen before. The other is *compounded*; as when, from the sight of a man at one time, and of a horse at another, we conceive in our mind a Centaur. So when a man compoundeth the image of his own person with the image of the actions of another man, as when a man imagines himself a Hercules or an Alexander, which happeneth often to them that are much taken with reading of romances, it is a compound imagination, and properly but a fiction of the mind. There be also other imaginations that rise in men, though waking, from the great impression made in sense: as from gazing upon the sun, the impression leaves an image of the sun before our eyes a long time after; and from being long and vehemently attent upon geometrical figures, a man shall in the dark, though awake, have the images of lines and angles before his eyes; which kind of fancy hath no particular name, as being a thing that doth not commonly fall into men's discourse. . . . .

The imagination that is raised in man, or any other creature indued with the faculty of imagining, by words, or other voluntary signs, is that we generally call *understanding*; and is common to man and beast. For a dog by custom will understand the call, or the rating of his master; and so will many other beasts. That understanding which is peculiar to man, is the understanding not only his will, but his conceptions and thoughts, by the sequel and contexture of the names of things into affirmations, negations, and other forms of speech; and of this kind of understanding I shall speak hereafter.

CHAPTER III. OF THE CONSEQUENCE OR TRAIN OF IMAGINATIONS

By *Consequence*, or TRAIN of thoughts, I understand that succession of one thought to another, which is called, to distinguish it from discourse in words, *mental discourse*.

When a man thinketh on any thing whatsoever, his next thought after, is not altogether so casual as it seems to be. Not every thought to every thought succeeds indifferently. But as we have no imagination, whereof we have not formerly had sense, in whole, or in parts; so we have no transition from one imagination to another, whereof we never had the like before in our senses. The reason whereof is this. All fancies are motions within us, relics of those made in the sense: and those motions that immediately succeeded one another in the sense, continue also together after sense: insomuch as the former coming again to take place, and be predominant, the latter followeth, by coherence of the matter moved, in such manner, as water upon a plane table is drawn which way any one part of it is guided by the finger. But because in sense, to one and the same thing perceived, sometimes one thing, sometimes another succeedeth, it comes to pass in time, that in the imagining of any thing, there is no certainty what we shall imagine next; only this is certain, it shall be something that succeeded the same before, at one time or another.

This train of thoughts, or mental discourse, is of two sorts. The first is *unguided, without design*, and inconstant; wherein there is no passionate thought, to govern and direct those that follow, to itself, as the end and scope of some desire, or other passion: in which case the thoughts are said to wander, and seem impertinent one to another, as in a dream. Such are commonly the thoughts of men, that are not only without company, but also without care of anything; though even then their thoughts are as busy as at other times, but without harmony; as the sound which a lute out of tune would yield to any man; or in tune, to one that could not play. And yet in this wild ranging of the mind, a man may oft-times perceive the way of it, and the dependence of one thought upon another, For in a discourse of our present civil war, what could seem more impertinent, than to ask, as one did, what was the value of a Roman penny? Yet the coherence to me was manifest enough. For the thought of the war, introduced the thought of the delivering up the king to his enemies; the thought of that, brought in the thought of the delivering up of Christ; and that again the thought of the thirty pence, which was the price of that treason; and thence easily followed that malicious question, and all this in a moment of time; for thought is quick.

The second is more constant; as being *regulated* by some desire, and design. For the impression made by such things as we desire, or fear, is strong, and permanent, or, if it cease for a time, of quick return: so strong it is sometimes, as to hinder and break our sleep. From desire, ariseth the thought of some means we have seen produce the like of that which we aim at; and from the thought of that, the thought of means to that means; and so continually, till we come to some beginning within our own power. And because the end, by the greatness of the impression, comes often to mind, in case our thoughts begin to wander, they are quickly again reduced into the way: which observed by one of the seven wise men, made him give men this precept, which is now worn out, *Respice finem*; that is to say, in all your actions, look often upon what you would have, as the thing that directs all your thoughts in the way to attain it. . . . .

There is no other act of man's mind, that I can remember, naturally planted in him, so as to need no other thing, to the exercise of it, but to be born a man, and live with the use of his five senses. Those other faculties, of which I shall speak by and by, and which seem proper to man only, are acquired and increased by study and industry; and of most men learned by instruction, and discipline; and proceed all from the invention of words, and speech. For besides sense, and thoughts, and the train of thoughts, the mind of man has no other motion; though by the help of speech, and method, the same faculties may be improved to such a height, as to distinguish men from all other living creatures. . . . .

CHAPTER IV. OF SPEECH

The invention of *printing*, though ingenious, compared with the invention of *letters*, is no great matter. But who was the first that found the use of letters, is not known. He that first brought them into Greece, men say was Cadmus, the son of Agenor, king of Phoenicia. A profitable invention for continuing the memory of time passed, and the conjunction of mankind, dispersed into so many, and distant regions of the earth; and withal difficult, as proceeding from a watchful observation of the divers motions of the tongue, palate, lips, and other organs of speech; whereby to make as many differences of characters, to remember them. But the most noble and profitable invention of all other, was that of SPEECH, consisting of *names* or *appellations*, and their connexion; whereby men register their thoughts; recall them when they are past; and also declare them one to another for mutual utility and conversation; without which, there had been amongst men, neither commonwealth, nor society, nor contract, nor peace, no more than amongst lions, bears, and wolves. The first author of *speech* was God himself, that instructed Adam how to name such creatures as he presented to his sight; for the Scripture goeth no further in this matter. But this was sufficient to direct him to add more names,.as the experience and use of the creatures should give him occasion; and to join them in such manner by degrees, as to make himself understood; and so by succession of time, so much language might be gotten, as he had found use for; though not so copious, as an orator or philosopher has need of: for I do not find anything in the Scripture, out of which, directly or by consequence, can be gathered, that Adam was taught the names of all figures, numbers, measures, colours, sounds, fancies, relations; much less the names of words and speech, as *general, special, affirmative, negative, interrogative, optative, infinitive*, all which are useful; and least of all, of *entity, intentionality, quiddity*, and other insignificant words of the school.

But all this language gotten, and augmented by Adam and his posterity, was again lost at the Tower of Babel, when, by the hand of God, every man was stricken, for his rebellion, with an oblivion of his former language. And being hereby forced to disperse themselves into several parts of the world, it must needs be, that the diversity of tongues that now is, proceeded by degrees from them, in such manner, as need, the mother of all inventions, taught them; and in tract of time grew everywhere more copious.

The general use of speech, is to transfer our mental discourse, into verbal; or the train of our thoughts, into a train of words; and that for two commodities, whereof one is the registering of the consequences of our thoughts; which being apt to slip out of our memory and put us to a new labour, may again be recalled, by such words as they were marked by. So that the first use of names is to serve for *marks*, or *notes* of remembrance. Another is, when many use the same words, to signify, by their connexion and order, one to another, what they conceive, or think of each matter; and also what they desire, fear, or have any other passion for. And for this use they are called *signs*. Special uses of speech are these: first, to register, what by cogitation, we find to be the cause of anything, present or past; and what we find things present or past may produce, or effect; which in sum, is acquiring of arts. Secondly, to show to others that knowledge which we have attained, which is, to counsel and teach one another. Thirdly, to make known to others our wills and purposes, that we may have the mutual help of one another. Fourthly, to please and delight ourselves and others, by playing with our words, for pleasure or ornament, innocently.

To these uses, there are also four correspondent abuses. First, when men register their thoughts wrong, by the inconstancy of the signification of their words; by which they register for their conception, that which they never conceived, and so deceive themselves. Secondly, when they use words metaphorically; that is, in other sense than that they are ordained for; and thereby deceive others. Thirdly, by words, when they declare that to be their will, which is not. Fourthly, when they use them to grieve one another; for seeing nature hath armed living creatures, some with teeth, some with horns, and some with hands, to grieve an enemy, it is but an abuse of speech, to grieve him with the tongue, unless it be one whom we are obliged to govern; and then it is not to grieve, but to correct and amend.

The manner how speech serveth to the remembrance of the consequence of causes and effects, consisteth in the imposing of *names*, and the *connexion* of them.

Of names, some are *proper*, and singular to one only thing, as *Peter*, *John*, *this man*, *this tree;* and some are *common* to many things, as *man*, *horse*, *tree;* every of which, though but one name, is nevertheless the name of divers particular things; in respect of all which together, it is called an *universal;* there being nothing in the world universal but names; for the things named are every one of them individual and singular.

One universal name is imposed on many things, for their similitude in some quality, or other accident; and whereas a proper name bringeth to mind one thing only, universals recall any one of those many.

And of names universal, some are of more, and some of less extent; the larger comprehending the less large; and some again of equal extent, comprehending each other reciprocally. As for example: the name *body* is of larger signification than the word *man*, and comprehendeth it; and the names *man* and *rational*, are of equal extent, comprehending mutually one another. But here we must take notice, that by a name is not always understood, as in grammar, one only word; but sometimes, by circumlocution, many words together. For all these words, *he that in his actions observeth the laws of his country*, make but one name, equivalent to this one word, *just*.

By this imposition of names, some of larger, some of stricter signification, we turn the reckoning of the consequences of things imagined in the mind, into a reckoning of the consequences of appellations. For example: a man that hath no use of speech at all, such as is born and remains perfectly deaf and dumb, if he set before his eyes a triangle, and by it two right angles, such as are the corners of a square figure, he may, by meditation, compare and find, that the three angles of that triangle, are equal to those two right angles that stand by it. But if another triangle be shown him, different in shape from the former, he cannot know, without a new labour, whether the three angles of that also be equal to the same. But he that hath the use of words, when he observes, that such quality was consequent, not to the length of the sides, nor to any other particular thing in his triangle; but only to this, that the sides were straight, and the angles three; and that that was all, for which he named it a triangle; will boldly conclude universally, that such equality of angles is in all triangles whatsoever; and register his invention in these general terms, *every triangle hath its three angles equal to two right angles*. And thus the consequence found in one particular, comes to be registered and remembered, as a universal rule, and discharges our mental reckoning, of time and place, and delivers us from all labour of the mind, saving the first, and makes that which was found true *here*, and *now*, to be true in *all times* and *places*.

But the use of words in registering our thoughts is in nothing so evident as in numbering. A natural fool that could never learn by heart the order of numeral words, as *one*, *two*, and *three*, may observe every stroke of the clock, and nod to it, or say *one*, *one*, *one*, but can never know what hour it strikes. And it seems, there was a time when those names of number were not in use; and men were fain to apply their fingers of one or both hands, to those things they desired to keep account of; and that thence it proceeded, that now our numeral words are but ten, in any nation, and in some but five; and then they begin again. And he that can tell ten, if he recite them out of order, will lose himself, and not know when he has done. Much less will he be able to add, and subtract, and perform all other operations of arithmetic. So that without words there is no possibility of reckoning of numbers; much less of magnitudes, of swiftness, of force, and other things, the reckonings whereof are necessary to the being, or well-being of mankind.

When two names are joined together into a consequence, or affirmation, as thus, *a man is a living creature*; or thus, *if he be a man, he is a living creature*; if the latter name, *living creature*, signify all that the former name *man* signifieth, then the affirmation, or consequence, is *true*; otherwise *false*. For *true* and *false* are attributes of speech, not of things. And where speech is not, there is neither *truth* nor *falsehood*; *error* there may be, as when we expect that which shall not be, or suspect what has not been; but in neither case can a man be charged with untruth.

Seeing then that truth consisteth in the right ordering of names in our affirmations, a man that seeketh precise truth had need to remember what every name he uses stands for, and to place it accordingly, or else he will find himself entangled in words, as a bird in lime twigs, the more he struggles the more belimed. And therefore in geometry, which is the only science that it hath pleased God hitherto to bestow on mankind, men begin at settling the significations of their words; which settling of significations they call *definitions*, and place them in the beginning of their reckoning.

By this it appears how necessary it is for any man that aspires to true knowledge, to examine the definitions of former authors; and either to correct them, where they are negligently set down, or to make them himself. For the errors of definitions multiply themselves according as the reckoning proceeds, and lead men into absurdities, which at last they see, but cannot avoid, without reckoning anew from the beginning, in which lies the foundation of their errors. From whence it happens, that they which trust to books do as they that cast up many little sums into a greater, without considering whether those little sums were rightly cast up or not; and at last finding the error visible, and not mistrusting their first grounds, know not which way to clear themselves, but spend time in fluttering over their books; as birds that entering by the chimney, and finding themselves enclosed in a chamber, flutter at the false light of a glass window, for want of wit to consider which way they came in. So that in the right definition of names lies the first use of speech; which is the acquisition of science: and in wrong, or no definitions, lies the first abuse; from which proceed all false and senseless tenets; which make those men that take their instruction from the authority of books, and not from their own meditation, to be as much below the condition of ignorant men, as men endued with true science are above it. For between true science and erroneous doctrines, ignorance is in the middle. Natural sense and imagination are not subject to absurdity. Nature itself cannot err; and as men abound in copiousness of language, so they become more wise, or more mad than ordinary. Nor is it possible without letters for any man to become either excellently wise, or, unless his memory be hurt by disease or ill constitution of organs, excellently foolish. For words are wise men's counters, they do but reckon by them; but they are the money of fools, that value them by the authority of an Aristotle, a Cicero, or a Thomas, or any other doctor whatsoever, if but a man.

Subject to names, is whatsoever can enter into or be considered in an account, and be added one to another to make a sum, or subtracted one from another and leave a remainder. The Latins called accounts of money *rationes*, and accounting *ratiocinatio*; and that which we in bills or books of account call *items*, they call *nomina*, that is *names*; and thence it seems to proceed, that they extended the word *ratio* to the faculty of reckoning in all other things. The Greeks have but one word, λόγος for both *speech* and *reason*; not that they thought there was no speech without reason, but no reasoning without speech: and the act of reasoning they called *syllogism*, which signifieth summing up of the consequences of one saying to another. And because the same thing may enter into account for divers accidents, their names are, to show that diversity, diversely wrested and diversified. This diversity of names may be reduced to four general heads.

First, a thing may enter into account for *matter* or *body*; as *living, sensible, rational, hot, cold, moved, quiet*; with all which names the word *matter*, or *body*, is understood; all such being names of matter.

Secondly, it may enter into account, or be considered, for some accident or quality which we conceive to be in it; as for *being moved*, for *being so long*, for *being hot*, &c.; and then, of the name of the thing itself, by a little change or wresting, we make a name for that accident, which we consider; and for *living* put into the account *life*; for *moved, motion*; for *hot, heat*; for *long, length*; and the like: and all such names are the names of the accidents and properties by which one matter and body is distinguished from another. These are called *names abstract*, because severed, not from matter, but from the account of matter.

Thirdly, we bring into account the properties of our own bodies, whereby we make such distinction; as when anything is seen by us, we reckon not the thing itself, but the sight, the colour, the idea of it in the fancy: and when anything is heard, we reckon it not, but the hearing or sound only, which is our fancy or conception of it by the ear; and such are names of fancies.

Fourthly, we bring into account, consider, and give names, to *names* themselves, and to *speech:* for *general, universal, special, equivocal*, are names of names. And *affirmation, interrogation, commandment, narration, syllogism, sermon, oration*, and many other such, are names of speeches. And this is all the variety of names *positive;* which are put to mark somewhat which is in nature, or may be feigned by the mind of man, as bodies that are, or may be conceived to be; or of bodies, the properties that are, or may be feigned to be; or words and speech.

There be also other names, called *negative*, which are notes to signify that a word is not the name of the thing in question, as these words, *nothing, no man, infinite, indocible, three want four*, and the like; which are nevertheless of use in reckoning, or in correcting of reckoning, and call to mind our past cogitations, though they be not names of anything, because they make us refuse to admit of names not rightly used.

All other names are but insignificant sounds; and those of two sorts. One when they are new, and yet their meaning not explained by definition; whereof there have been abundance coined by schoolmen, and puzzled philosophers.

Another, when men make a name of two names, whose significations are contradictory and inconsistent; as this name, an *incorporeal body*, or, which is all one, an *incorporeal substance*, and a great number more. For whensoever any affirmation is false, the two names of which it is composed, put together and made one, signify nothing at all. For example, if it be a false affirmation to say *a quadrangle is round*, the word *round quadrangle* signifies nothing, but is a mere sound. So likewise, if it be false to say that virtue can be poured, or blown up and down, the words *impoured virtue, inblown virtue*, are as absurd and insignificant as a *round quadrangle*. And therefore you shall hardly meet with a senseless and insignificant word, that is not made up of some Latin or Greek names. A Frenchman seldom hears our Saviour called by the name of *parole*, but by the name of *verbe* often; yet *verbe* and *parole* differ no more, but that one is Latin and the other French.

When a man, upon the hearing of any speech, hath those thoughts which the words of that speech and their connexion were ordained and constituted to signify, then he is said to understand it; *understanding* being nothing else but conception caused by speech. And therefore if speech be peculiar to man, as for ought I know it is, then is understanding peculiar to him also. And therefore of absurd and false affirmations, in case they be universal, there can be no understanding; though many think they understand then, when they do but repeat the words softly, or con them in their mind.

What kinds of speeches signify the appetites, aversions, and passions of man's mind; and of their use and abuse, I shall speak when I have spoken of the passions.

The names of such things as affect us, that is, which please and displease us, because all men be not alike affected with the same thing, nor the same man at all times, are in the common discourses of men of *inconstant* signification. For seeing all names are imposed to signify our conceptions, and all our affections are but conceptions, when we conceive the same things differently, we can hardly avoid different naming of them. For though the nature of that we conceive, be the same; yet the diversity of our reception of it, in respect of different constitutions of body, and prejudices of opinion, gives every thing a tincture of our different passions. And therefore in reasoning a man must take heed of words; which besides the signification of what we imagine of their nature, have a signification also of the nature, disposition, and interest of the speaker; such as are the names of virtues and vices; for one man calleth *wisdom*, what another calleth *fear*; and one *cruelty*, what another *justice*; one *prodigality*, what another *magnanimity*; and one *gravity*, what another *stupidity*, &c. And therefore such names can never be true grounds of any ratiocination. No more can metaphors, and tropes of speech; but these are less dangerous, because they profess their inconstancy; which the other do not.

CHAPTER V. OF REASON AND SCIENCE

When a man *reasoneth*, he does nothing else but conceive a sum total, from *addition* of parcels; or conceive a remainder, from *subtraction* of one sum from another; which, if it be done by words, is conceiving of the consequence of the names of all the parts, to the name of the whole; or from the names of the whole and one part, to the name of the other part. And though in some things, as in numbers, besides adding and subtracting, men name other operations, as *multiplying* and *dividing*, yet they are the same; for multiplication, is but adding together of things equal; and division, but subtracting of one thing, as often as we can. These operations are not incident to numbers only, but to all manner of things that can be added together, and taken one out of another. For as arithmeticians teach to add and subtract in *numbers;* so the geometricians teach the same in *lines, figures,* solid and superficial, *angles, proportions, times,* degrees of *swiftness, force, power,* and the like;

the logicians teach the same in *consequences of words;* adding together two *names* to make an *affirmation,* and two *affirmations* to
make a *syllogism;* and *many syllogisms* to make a *demonstration;*
and from the *sum,* or *conclusion* of a *syllogism,* they subtract one
proposition to find the other. Writers of politics add together *pac-
tions* to find men's *duties;* and lawyers, *laws* and *facts,* to find what
is *right* and *wrong* in the actions of private men. In sum, in what
matter soever there is place for *addition* and *subtraction,* there also
is place for *reason;* and where these have no place, there *reason*
has nothing at all to do.

Out of all which we may define, that is to say determine, what
that is, which is meant by this word *reason,* when we reckon it
amongst the faculties of the mind. For REASON, in this sense, is
nothing but *reckoning,* that is adding and subtracting, of the consequences of general names agreed upon for the *marking* and *signifying* of our thoughts; I say *marking* them when we reckon by
ourselves, and *signifying,* when we demonstrate or approve our
reckonings to other men.

And, as in arithmetic, unpractised men must, and professors
themselves may often, err, and cast up false; so also in any other
subject of reasoning; the ablest, most attentive, and most practised
men may deceive themselves, and infer false conclusions; not but
that reason itself is always right reason, as well as arithmetic is a
certain and infallible art: but no one man's reason, nor the reason
of any one number of men, makes the certainty; no more than an
account is therefore well cast up, because a great many men have
unanimously approved it. And therefore, as when there is a controversy in an account, the parties must by their own accord, set
up, for right reason, the reason of some arbitrator, or judge, to
whose sentence they will both stand, or their controversy must
either come to blows, or be undecided, for want of a right reason
constituted by nature; so it is also in all debates of what kind soever. And when men that think themselves wiser than all others,
clamour and demand right reason for judge, yet seek no more, but
that things should be determined, by no other men's reason but
their own, it is as intolerable in the society of men, as it is in play
after trump is turned, to use for trump on every occasion, that
suite whereof they have most in their hand. For they do nothing
else, that will have every of their passions, as it comes to bear

sway in them, to be taken for right reason, and that in their own controversies: bewraying their want of right reason, by the claim they lay to it.

The use and end of reason, is not the finding of the sum and truth of one, or a few consequences, remote from the first definitions, and settled significations of names, but to begin at these, and proceed from one consequence to another. For there can be no certainty of the last conclusion, without a certainty of all those affirmations and negations, on which it was grounded and inferred. As when a master of a family, in taking an account, casteth up the sums of all the bills of expense into one sum, and not regarding how each bill is summed up, by those that give them in account; nor what it is he pays for; he advantages himself no more, than if he allowed the account in gross, trusting to every of the accountants' skill and honesty: so also in reasoning of all other things, he that takes up conclusions on the trust of authors, and doth not fetch them from the first items in every reckoning, which are the significations of names settled by definitions, loses his labour; and does not know anything, but only believeth.

When a man reckons without the use of words, which may be done in particular things, as when upon the sight of any one thing, we conjecture what was likely to have preceded, or is likely to follow upon it; if that which he thought likely to follow, follows not, or that which he thought likely to have preceded it, hath not preceded it, this is called *error;* to which even the most prudent men are subject. But when we reason in words of general signification, and fall upon a general inference which is false, though it be commonly called *error,* it is indeed an *absurdity,* or senseless speech. For error is but a deception, in presuming that somewhat is passed, or to come; of which, though it were not past, or not to come, yet there was no impossibility discoverable. But when we make a general assertion, unless it be a true one, the possibility of it is inconceivable. And words whereby we conceive nothing but the sound, are those we call *absurd, insignificant,* and *nonsense.* And therefore if a man should talk to me of a *round quadrangle;* or, *accidents of bread in cheese;* or *immaterial substances;* or of *a free subject; a free will;* or any *free,* but free from being hindered by opposition, I should not say he were in an error, but that his words were without meaning, that is to say, absurd.

I have said before, in the second chapter, that a man did excel all other animals in this faculty, that when he conceived any thing whatsoever, he was apt to enquire the consequences of it, and what effects he could do with it. And now I add this other degree of the same excellence, that he can by words reduce the consequences he finds to general rules, called *theorems*, or *aphorisms;* that is, he can reason, or reckon, not only in number, but in all other things, whereof one may be added unto, or subtracted from another.

But this privilege is allayed by another; and that is, by the privilege of absurdity; to which no living creature is subject, but man only. And of men, those are of all most subject to it, that profess philosophy. For it is most true that Cicero saith of them somewhere; that there can be nothing so absurd, but may be found in the books of philosophers. And the reason is manifest. For there is not one of them that begins his ratiocination from the definitions, or explications of the names they are to use; which is a method that hath been used only in geometry; whose conclusions have thereby been made indisputable.

I. The first cause of absurd conclusions I ascribe to the want of method; in that they begin not their ratiocination from definitions; that is, from settled significations of their words: as if they could cast account, without knowing the value of the numeral words, *one, two,* and *three.*

And whereas all bodies enter into account upon divers considerations, which I have mentioned in the precedent chapter; these considerations being diversely named, divers absurdities proceed from the confusion, and unfit connexion of their names into assertions. And therefore,

II. The second cause of absurd assertions, I ascribe to the giving of names of *bodies* to *accidents;* or of *accidents* to *bodies;* as they do, that say, *faith is infused,* or *inspired;* when nothing can be *poured,* or *breathed* into anything, but body; and that, *extension* is *body;* that *phantasms* are *spirits,* &c.

III. The third I ascribe to the giving of the names of the *accidents* of *bodies without us,* to the *accidents* of our *own bodies;* as they do that say, the *colour is in the body; the sound is in the air,* &c.

IV. The fourth, to the giving of the names of *bodies* to *names,* or *speeches;* as they do that say, that *there be things universal;* that *a living creature is genus,* or *a general thing,* &c.

v. The fifth, to the giving of the names of *accidents* to *names* and *speeches*; as they do that say, *the nature of a thing is its definition; a man's command is his will*; and the like.

vi. The sixth, to the use of metaphors, tropes, and other rhetorical figures, instead of words proper. For though it be lawful to say, for example, in common speech, *the way goeth, or leadeth hither, or thither; the proverb says this or that*, whereas ways cannot go, nor proverbs speak; yet in reckoning, and seeking of truth, such speeches are not to be admitted.

vii. The seventh, to names that signify nothing; but are taken up, and learned by rote from the schools, as *hypostatical, transubstantiate, consubstantiate, eternal-now*, and the like canting of schoolmen.

To him that can avoid these things it is not easy to fall into any absurdity, unless it be by the length of an account; wherein he may perhaps forget what went before. For all men by nature reason alike, and well, when they have good principles. For who is so stupid, as both to mistake in geometry, and also to persist in it, when another detects his error to him?

By this it appears that reason is not, as sense and memory, born with us; nor gotten by experience only, as prudence is; but attained by industry; first in apt imposing of names; and secondly by getting a good and orderly method in proceeding from the elements, which are names, to assertions made by connexion of one of them to another; and so to syllogisms, which are the connexions of one assertion to another, till we come to a knowledge of all the consequences of names appertaining to the subject in hand; and that is it, men call SCIENCE. And whereas sense and memory are but knowledge of fact, which is a thing past and irrevocable. *Science* is the knowledge of consequences, and dependence of one fact upon another: by which, out of that we can presently do, we know how to do something else when we will, or the like another time; because when we see how anything comes about, upon what causes, and by what manner; when the like causes come into our power, we see how to make it produce the like effects.

Children therefore are not endued with reason at all, till they have attained the use of speech; but are called reasonable creatures, for the possibility apparent of having the use of reason in time to come. And the most part of men, though they have the use of reasoning a little way, as in numbering to some degree; yet it serves them to little use in common life; in which they govern themselves, some better, some worse, according to their differences of experience, quickness of memory, and inclinations to several ends; but specially according to good or evil fortune, and the errors of one another. For as for *science*, or certain rules of their actions, they are so far from it, they know not what it is. Geometry they have thought conjuring; but for other sciences, they who have not been taught the beginnings and some progress in them, that they may see how they be acquired and generated, are in this point like children, that having no thought of generation, are made believe by the women that their brothers and sisters are not born, but found in the garden.

But yet they that have no *science*, are in better, and nobler condition, with their natural prudence; than men, that by mis-reasoning, or by trusting them that reason wrong, fall upon false and absurd general rules. For ignorance of causes, and of rules, does not set men so far out of their way, as relying on false rules, and taking for causes of what they aspire to, those that are not so, but rather causes of the contrary.

To conclude, the light of human minds is perspicuous words, but by exact definitions first snuffed, and purged from ambiguity; *reason* is the *pace*; increase of *science*, the *way*; and the benefit of mankind, the *end*. And, on the contrary, metaphors, and senseless and ambiguous words, are like *ignes fatui*; and reasoning upon them is wandering amongst innumerable absurdities; and their end, contention and sedition, or contempt. . . . .

CHAPTER VI. OF THE INTERIOR BEGINNINGS OF VOLUNTARY MOTIONS; COMMONLY CALLED THE PASSIONS; AND THE SPEECHES BY WHICH THEY ARE EXPRESSED

There be in animals, two sorts of *motions* peculiar to them: one called *vital*; begun in generation, and continued without interruption through their whole life; such as are the *course* of the *blood*, the *pulse*, the *breathing*, the *concoction*, *nutrition*, *excretion*, &c., to which motions there needs no help of imagination: the other is *animal motion*, otherwise called *voluntary motion*; as to *go*, to *speak*, to *move* any of our limbs, in such manner as is first fancied in our minds. That sense is motion in the organs and interior parts of man's body, caused by the action of the things we see, hear, &c.; and that fancy is but the relics of the same motion, remaining after sense, has been already said in the first and second chapters. And because *going, speaking,* and the like voluntary motions, depend always upon a precedent thought of *whither, which way,* and *what;* it is evident, that the imagination is the first internal beginning of all voluntary motion. And although unstudied men do not conceive any motion at all to be there, where the thing moved is invisible; or the space it is moved in is, for the shortness of it, insensible; yet that doth not hinder, but that such motions are. For let a space be never so little, that which is moved over a greater space, whereof that little one is part, must first be moved over that. These small beginnings of motion, within the body of man, before they appear in walking, speaking, striking, and other visible actions, are commonly called ENDEAVOUR.

This endeavour, when it is toward something which causes it, is called APPETITE, or DESIRE; the latter, being the general name; and the other oftentimes restrained to signify the desire of food, namely *hunger* and *thirst.* And when the endeavour is fromward something, it is generally called AVERSION. These words, *appetite* and *aversion,* we have from the Latins; and they both of them signify the motions, one of approaching, the other of retiring. So also do the Greek words for the same, which are ὁρμή and ἀφορμή. For nature itself does often press upon men those truths, which afterwards, when they look for somewhat beyond nature, they stumble at. For the Schools find in mere appetite to go, or move, no actual motion at all: but because some motion they must acknowledge, they call it metaphorical motion; which is but an absurd speech: for though words may be called metaphorical; bodies and motions can not.

That which men desire, they are also said to LOVE: and to HATE those things for which they have aversion. So that desire and love are the same thing; save that by desire, we always signify the absence of the object; by love, most commonly the presence of the same. So also by aversion, we signify the absence; and by hate, the presence of the object.

Of appetites and aversions, some are born with men; as appetite of food, appetite of excretion, and exoneration, which may also and more properly be called aversions, from somewhat they feel in their bodies; and some other appetites, not many. The rest, which are appetites of particular things, proceed from experience, and trial of their effects upon themselves or other men. For of things we know not at all, or believe not to be, we can have no further desire, than to taste and try. But aversion we have for things, not only which we know have hurt us, but also that we do not know whether they will hurt us, or not.

Those things which we neither desire, nor hate, we are said to *contemn;* CONTEMPT being nothing else but an immobility, or contumacy of the heart, in resisting the action of certain things; and proceeding from that the heart is already moved otherwise, by other more potent objects; or from want of experience of them.

And because the constitution of a man's body is in continual mutation, it is impossible that all the same things should always cause in him the same appetites, and aversions: much less can all men consent, in the desire of almost any one and the same object.

But whatsoever is the object of any man's appetite or desire, that is it which he for his part calleth *good:* and the object of his hate and aversion, evil; and of his contempt, *vile* and *inconsiderable*. For these words of good, evil, and contemptible, are ever used with relation to the person that useth them: there being nothing simply and absolutely so; nor any common rule of good and evil, to be taken from the nature of the objects themselves; but from the person of the man, where there is no commonwealth; or, in a commonwealth, from the person that representeth it; or from an arbitrator or judge, whom men disagreeing shall by consent set up, and make his sentence the rule thereof.

The Latin tongue has two words, whose significations approach to those of good and evil; but are not precisely the same; and those are *pulchrum* and *turpe*. Whereof the former signifies that, which by some apparent signs promiseth good; and the latter, that which promiseth evil. But in our tongue we have not so general names to express them by. But for *pulchrum* we say in some things, *fair;* in others, *beautiful*, or *handsome*, or *gallant*, or *honourable*, or *comely*, or *amiable;* and for *turpe, foul, deformed, ugly, base, nauseous*, and the like, as the subject shall require; all which words, in their proper places, signify nothing else but the *mien*, or countenance, that promiseth good and evil. So that of good there be three kinds; good in the promise, that is *pulchrum;* good in effect, as the end desired, which is called *jucundum, delightful;* and good as the means, which is called *utile, profitable;* and as many of evil: for *evil* in promise, is that they call *turpe;* evil in effect, and end, is *molestum, unpleasant, troublesome;* and evil in the means, *inutile, unprofitable, hurtful.*

As, in sense, that which is really within us, is, as I have said before, only motion, caused by the action of external objects, but in apparence; to the sight, light and colour; to the ear, sound; to the nostril, odour, &c.: so, when the action of the same object is continued from the eyes, ears, and other organs to the heart, the real effect there is nothing but motion, or endeavour; which consisteth in appetite, or aversion, to or from the object moving. But the apparence, or sense of that motion, is that we either call *delight,* or *trouble of mind.*

This motion, which is called appetite, and for the apparence of it *delight,* and *pleasure,* seemeth to be a corroboration of vital motion, and a help thereunto; and therefore such things as caused delight, were not improperly called *jucunda, a juvando,* from helping or fortifying; and the contrary, *molesta, offensive,* from hindering, and troubling the motion vital.

Pleasure therefore, or *delight,* is the apparence, or sense of good; and *molestation,* or *displeasure,* the apparence, or sense of evil. And consequently all appetite, desire, and love, is accompanied with some delight more or less; and all hatred and aversion, with more or less displeasure and offence.

Of pleasures or delights, some arise from the sense of an object present; and those may be called *pleasure of sense;* the word *sensual,* as it is used by those only that condemn them, having no place till there be laws. Of this kind are all onerations and exonerations of the body; as also all that is pleasant, in the *sight, hearing, smell, taste,* or *touch.* Others arise from the expectation, that proceeds from foresight of the end, or consequence of things; whether those things in the sense please or displease. And these are *pleasures of the mind* of him that draweth those consequences, and are generally called JOY. In the like manner, displeasures are some in the sense, and called PAIN; others in the expectation of consequences, and are called GRIEF.

These simple passions called *appetite, desire, love, aversion, hate, joy,* and *grief,* have their names for divers considerations diversified. As first, when they one succeed another, they are diversely called from the opinion men have of the likelihood of attaining what they desire. Secondly, from the object loved or hated. Thirdly, from the consideration of many of them together. Fourthly, from the alteration or succession itself.

For *appetite*, with an opinion of attaining, is called HOPE.

The same, without such opinion, DESPAIR.

Aversion, with opinion of HURT from the object, FEAR. . . . .

Fear of power invisible, feigned by the mind, or imagined from tales publicly allowed, RELIGION; not allowed, SUPERSTITION. And when the power imagined, is truly such as we imagine, TRUE RELIGION.

Fear, without the apprehension of why, or what, PANIC TERROR, called so from the fables, that make Pan the author of them; whereas, in truth, there is always in him that so feareth first, some apprehension of the cause, though the rest run away by example, every one supposing his fellow to know why. And therefore this passion happens to none but in a throng, or multitude of people.

Joy, from apprehension of novelty, ADMIRATION; proper to man, because it excites the appetite of knowing the cause.

Joy, arising from imagination of a man's own power and ability, is that exultation of the mind which is called GLORYING: which if grounded upon the experience of his own former actions, is the same with *confidence:* but if grounded on the flattery of others; or only supposed by himself, for delight in the consequences of it, is called VAIN-GLORY: which name is properly given; because a well grounded *confidence* begetteth attempt; whereas the supposing of power does not, and is therefore rightly called *vain*. . . . .

When in the mind of man, appetites, and aversions, hopes, and fears, concerning one and the same thing, arise alternately; and divers good and evil consequences of the doing, or omitting the thing propounded, come successively into our thoughts; so that sometimes we have an appetite to it; sometimes an aversion from it; sometimes hope to be able to do it; sometimes despair, or fear to attempt it; the whole sum of desires, aversions, hopes and fears continued till the thing be either done, or thought impossible, is that we call DELIBERATION.

Therefore of things past, there is no *deliberation;* because manifestly impossible to be changed: nor of things known to be impossible, or thought so; because men know, or think such deliberation vain. But of things impossible, which we think possible, we may deliberate; not knowing it is in vain.   And it is called *deliberation;* because it is a putting an end to the *liberty* we had of doing, or omitting, according to our own appetite, or aversion.

This alternate succession of appetites, aversions, hopes and fears, is no less in other living creatures than in man: and therefore beasts also deliberate.

Every *deliberation* is then said to *end,* when that whereof they deliberate, is either done, or thought impossible; because till then we retain the liberty of doing, or omitting; according to our appetite, or aversion.

In *deliberation,* the last appetite, or aversion, immediately adhering to the action, or to the omission thereof, is that we call the WILL; the act, not the faculty, of *willing.* And beasts that have *deliberation,* must necessarily also have *will.* The definition of the *will,* given commonly by the Schools, that it is a *rational appetite,* is not good. For if it were, then could there be no voluntary act against reason. For a *voluntary act* is that, which proceedeth from the *will,* and no other. But if instead of a rational appetite, we shall say an appetite resulting from a precedent deliberation, then the definition is the same that I have given here. *Will,* therefore, *is the last appetite in deliberating.* And though we say in common discourse, a man had a will once to do a thing, that nevertheless he forbore to do; yet that is properly but an inclination, which makes no action voluntary; because the action depends not of it, but of the last inclination, or appetite. For if the intervenient appetites, make any action voluntary; then by the same reason all intervenient aversions, should make the same action involuntary; and so one and the same action, should be both voluntary and involuntary.

By this it is manifest, that not only actions that have their beginning from covetousness, ambition, lust, or other appetites to the thing propounded; but also those that have their beginning from aversion, or fear of those consequences that follow the omission, are *voluntary actions.* . . . .

TABLE TO CHAPTER IX

SCIENCE, that is, knowledge of consequences; which is called also PHILOSOPHY

- **Consequences from the accidents of bodies natural; which is called NATURAL PHILOSOPHY**
  - Consequences from the accidents common to all bodies natural; which are *quantity*, and *motion*
    - Consequences from quantity, and motion *indeterminate*; which being the principles or first foundation of philosophy is called *Philosophia Prima* → **PHILOSOPHIA PRIMA**
    - Consequences from quantity and motion determined
      - *Mathematics*
        - By Figure → **GEOMETRY**
        - By Number → **ARITHMETIC**
    - Consequences from the motion, and quantity of bodies *in special*
      - Consequences from the motion and quantity of the greater parts of the world, as the *earth* and *stars* — *Cosmography* → **ASTRONOMY, GEOGRAPHY**
      - Consequences from the motions of special kinds, and figures of body — *Mechanics. Doctrine of weight* → *Science of* **ENGINEERS, ARCHITECTURE, NAVIGATION**
  - **PHYSICS or consequences from qualities**
    - Consequences from the qualities of bodies *transient*, such as some times appear, some times vanish, *Meteorology* → **METEOROLOGY**
    - Consequences from the qualities of bodies *permanent*
      - Consequences from the qualities of the stars
        - Consequences from the *light* of the stars. Out of this, and the motion of the sun, is made the science of... → **SCIOGRAPHY**
        - Consequences from the *influence* of the stars → **ASTROLOGY**
      - Consequences of the qualities from *liquid* bodies, that fill the space between the stars; such as are the air, or substances ethereal
      - Consequences from the qualities of *bodies terrestrial*
        - Consequences from the parts of the earth, that are *without sense*
          - Consequences from the qualities of *minerals*, as *stones, metals, &c.*
          - Consequences from the qualities of *vegetables*
        - Consequences from the qualities of *animals*
          - Consequences from the qualities of *animals in general*
            - Consequences from *vision* → **OPTICS**
            - Consequences from *sounds* → **MUSIC**
            - Consequences from the rest of the *senses*
          - Consequences from the qualities of *men in special*
            - Consequences from the *passions* of *men* → **ETHICS**
            - Consequences from *speech*
              - In *magnifying, vilifying, &c.* → **POETRY**
              - In *persuading* → **RHETORIC**
              - In *reasoning* → **LOGIC**
              - In *contracting* → **The *Science of* JUST AND UNJUST**
- **Consequences from the accidents of *politic* bodies; which is called POLITICS, and CIVIL PHILOSOPHY**
  1. Of consequences from the *institution* of COMMONWEALTHS, to the *rights* and *duties* of the *body politic* or *sovereign*
  2. Of consequences from the same, to the *duty* and *right* of the *subjects*

CHAPTER IX. OF THE SEVERAL SUBJECTS OF KNOWLEDGE

There are of KNOWLEDGE two kinds; whereof one is *knowledge of fact:* the other *knowledge of the consequence of one affirmation to another.* The former is nothing else, but sense and memory, and is *absolute knowledge;* as when we see a fact doing, or remember it done: and this is the knowledge required in a witness. The latter is called *science;* and is *conditional;* as when we know, that, *if the figure shown be a circle, then any straight line through the center shall divide it into two equal parts.* And this is the knowledge required in a philosopher; that is to say, of him that pretends to reasoning.

The register of *knowledge of fact* is called *history.* Whereof there be two sorts: one called *natural history;* which is the history of such facts, or effects of nature, as have no dependence on man's *will;* such as are the histories of *metals, plants, animals, regions,* and the like. The other, is *civil history;* which is the history of the voluntary actions of men in commonwealths.

The registers of science, are such *books* as contain the *demonstrations* of consequences of one affirmation, to another; and are commonly called *books of philosophy;* whereof the sorts are many, according to the diversity of the matter; and may be divided in such manner as I have divided them in the foregoing table.

CHAPTER X. OF POWER, WORTH, DIGNITY, HONOUR,
AND WORTHINESS

The POWER *of a man,* to take it universally, is his present means, to obtain some future apparent good; and is either *original* or *instrumental.*

Natural power, is the eminence of the faculties of body, or mind: as extraordinary strength, form, prudence, arts, eloquence, liberality, nobility. *Instrumental* are those powers, which acquired by these, or by fortune, are means and instruments to acquire more: as riches, reputation, friends, and the secret working of God, which men call good luck. For the nature of power, is in this point, like to fame, increasing as it proceeds; or like the motion of heavy bodies, which the further they go, make still the more haste.

The greatest of human powers, is that which is compounded of the powers of most men, united by consent, in one person, natural, or civil, that has the use of all their powers depending on his will; such as is the power of a commonwealth: or depending on the wills of each particular; such as is the power of a faction or of divers factions leagued. Therefore to have servants, is power; to have friends, is power: for they are strengths united.

Also riches joined with liberality, is power; because it procureth friends, and servants: without liberality, not so; because in this case they defend not; but expose men to envy, as a prey.

Reputation of power, is power; because it draweth with it the adherence of those that need protection.

So is reputation of love of a man's country, called popularity, for the same reason.

Also, what quality soever maketh a man beloved, or feared of many; or the reputation of such quality, is power; because it is a means to have the assistance, and service of many.

Good success is power; because it maketh reputation of wisdom, or good fortune; which makes men either fear him, or rely on him.

Affability of men already in power, is increase of power; because it gaineth love.

Reputation of prudence in the conduct of peace or war, is power; because to prudent men, we commit the government of ourselves, more willingly than to others.

Nobility is power, not in all places, but only in those commonwealths, where it has privileges: for in such privileges, consisteth their power.

Eloquence is power, because it is seeming prudence.

Form is power; because being a promise of good, it recommendeth men to the favour of women and strangers.

The sciences, are small power; because not eminent; and therefore, not acknowledged in any man; nor are at all, but in a few, and in them, but of a few things. For science is of that nature, as none can understand it to be, but such as in a good measure have attained it.

Arts of public use, as fortification, making of engines, and other instruments of war; because they confer to defence, and victory, are power: and though the true mother of them, be science, namely the mathematics; yet, because they are brought into the light, by the hand of the artificer, they be esteemed, the midwife passing with the vulgar for the mother, as his issue.

The *value*, or WORTH of a man, is as of all other things, his price; that is to say, so much as would be given for the use of his power: and therefore is not absolute; but a thing dependant on the need and judgment of another. An able conductor of soldiers, is of great price in time of war present, or imminent; but in peace not so. A learned and uncorrupt judge, is much worth in time of peace; but not so much in war. And as in other things, so in men, not the seller, but the buyer determines the price. For let a man, as most men do, rate themselves at the highest value they can; yet their true value is no more than it is esteemed by others.

The manifestation of the value we set on one another, is that which is commonly called honouring, and dishonouring. To value a man at a high rate, is to *honour* him; at a low rate, is to *dishonour* him. But high, and low, in this case, is to be understood by comparison to the rate that each man setteth on himself. . . . .

. . . . *Honourable* is whatsoever possession, action, or quality, is an argument and sign of power.

And therefore to be honoured, loved, or feared of many, is honourable; as arguments of power. To be honoured of few or none, *dishonourable.* . . . .

CHAPTER XI. OF THE DIFFERENCE OF MANNERS

By Manners, I mean not here, decency of behaviour; as how one should salute another, or how a man should wash his mouth, or pick his teeth before company, and such other points of the *small morals;* but those qualities of mankind, that concern their living together in peace, and unity. To which end we are to consider, that the felicity of this life, consisteth not in the repose of a mind satisfied. For there is no such *finis ultimus*, utmost aim, nor *summum bonum*, greatest good, as is spoken of in the books of the old moral philosophers. Nor can a man any more live, whose desires are at an end, than he, whose senses and imaginations are at a stand. Felicity is a continual progress of the desire, from one object to another; the attaining of the former, being still but the way to the latter. The cause whereof is, that the object of man's desire, is not to enjoy once only, and for one instant of time; but to assure for ever, the way of his future desire. And therefore the voluntary actions, and inclinations of all men, tend, not only to the procuring, but also to the assuring of a contented life; and differ only in the way: which ariseth partly from the diversity of passions, in divers men; and partly from the difference of the knowledge, or opinion each one has of the causes, which produce the effect desired.

So that in the first place, I put for a general inclination of all mankind, a perpetual and restless desire of power after power, that ceaseth only in death. And the cause of this, is not always that a man hopes for a more intensive delight, than he has already attained to; or that he cannot be content with a moderate power: but because he cannot assure the power and means to live well, which he hath present, without the acquisition of more. And from hence it is, that kings, whose power is greatest, turn their endeavours to the assuring it at home by laws, or abroad by wars: and when that is done, there succeedeth a new desire; in some, of fame from new conquest; in others, of ease and sensual pleasure; in others, of admiration, or being flattered for excellence in some art, or other ability of the mind.

Competition of riches, honour, command, or other power, inclineth to contention, enmity, and war: because the way of one competitor, to the attaining of his desire, is to kill, subdue, supplant, and repel the other. Particularly, competition of praise, inclineth to a reverence of antiquity. For men contend with the living, not with the dead; to these ascribing more than due, that they may obscure the glory of the other.

Desire of ease, and sensual delight, disposeth men to obey a common power: because by such desires, a man doth abandon the protection that might be hoped for from his own industry, and labour. Fear of death, and wounds, disposeth to the same; and for the same reason. On the contrary, needy men, and hardy, not contented with their present condition; as also, all men that are ambitious of military command, are inclined to continue the causes of war; and to stir up trouble and sedition; for there is no honour military but by war; nor any such hope to mend an ill game, as by causing a new shuffle.

Desire of knowledge, and arts of peace, inclineth men to obey a common power: for such desire, containeth a desire of leisure; and consequently protection from some other power than their own.

Desire of praise, disposeth to laudable actions, such as please them whose judgment they value; for of those men whome we contemn, we contemn also the praises. Desire of fame after death does the same. . . . .

To have received from one, to whom we think ourselves equal, greater benefits than there is hope to requite, disposeth to counterfeit love; but really secret hatred. . . . .

Vain-glorious men, such as without being conscious to themselves of great sufficiency, delight in supposing themselves gallant men, are inclined only to ostentation. . . . .

Vain-glorious men, such as estimate their sufficiency by the flattery of other men, or the fortune of some precedent action, without assured ground of hope from the true knowledge of themselves, are inclined to rash engaging; and in the approach of danger, or difficulty, to retire if they can: because not seeing the way of safety, they will rather hazard their honour, which may be salved with an excuse; than their lives, for which no salve is sufficient. . . . .

Eloquence, with flattery, disposeth men to confide in them that have it; because the former is seeming wisdom, the latter seeming kindness. Add to them military reputation, and it disposeth men to adhere, and subject themselves to them that have them. The two former having given them caution against danger from him; the latter gives them caution against danger from others. . . . .

Want of science, that is, ignorance of causes, disposeth, or rather constraineth a man to rely on the advice, and authority of others. . . . .

CHAPTER XIII. OF THE NATURAL CONDITION OF MANKIND AS CONCERNING THEIR FELICITY, AND MISERY

Nature hath made men so equal, in the faculties of the body, and mind; as that though there be found one man sometimes manifestly stronger in body, or of quicker mind that another; yet when all is reckoned together, the difference between man, and man, is not so considerable, as that one man can thereupon claim to himself any benefit, to which another may not pretend, as well as he.

For as to the strength of body, the weakest has strength enough to kill the strongest, either by secret machination, or by confederacy with others, that are in the same danger with himself.

And as to the faculties of the mind, setting aside the arts grounded upon words, and especially that skill of proceeding upon general, and infallible rules, called science; which very few have, and but in few things; as being not a native faculty, born with us; nor attained, as prudence, while we look after somewhat else, I find yet a greater equality amongst men, than that of strength. For prudence, is but experience; which equal time, equally bestows on all men, in those things they equally apply themselves unto. That which may perhaps make such equality incredible, is but a vain conceit of one's own wisdom, which almost all men think they have in a greater degree, than the vulgar; that is, than all men but themselves, and a few others, whom by fame, or for concurring with themselves, they approve. For such is the nature of men, that howsoever they may acknowledge many others to be more witty, or more eloquent, or more learned; yet they will hardly believe there be many so wise as themselves; for they see their own wit at hand, and other men's at a distance. But this proveth rather that men are in that point equal, than unequal. For there is not ordinarily a greater sign of the equal distribution of any thing, than that every man is contented with his share.

From this equality of ability, ariseth equality of hope in the attaining of our ends. And therefore if any two men desire the same thing, which nevertheless they cannot both enjoy, they become enemies; and in the way to their end, which is principally their own conservation, and sometimes their delectation only, endeavour to destroy, or subdue one another. And from hence it comes to pass, that where an invader hath no more to fear, than another man's single power; if one plant, sow, build, or possess a convenient seat, others may probably be expected to come prepared with forces united, to dispossess, and deprive him, not only of the fruit of his labour, but also of his life, or liberty. And the invader again is in the like danger of another.

And from this diffidence of one another, there is no way for any man to secure himself, so reasonable, as anticipation; that is, by force, or wiles, to master the persons of all men he can, so long, till he see no other power great enough to endanger him: and this is no more than his own conservation requireth, and is generally allowed. Also because there be some, that taking pleasure in contemplating their own power in the acts of conquest, which they pursue farther than their security requires; if others, that otherwise would be glad to be at ease within modest bounds, should not by invasion increase their power, they would not be able, long time, by standing only on their defence, to subsist. And by consequence, such augmentation of dominion over men being necessary to a man's conservation, it ought to be allowed him.

Again, men have no pleasure, but on the contrary a great deal of grief, in keeping company, where there is no power able to over-awe them all. For every man looketh that his companion should value him, at the same rate he sets upon himself: and upon all signs of contempt, or undervaluing, naturally endeavours, as far as he dares, (which amongst them that have no common power to keep them in quiet, is far enough to make them destroy each other), to extort a greater value from his contemners, by damage; and from others, by the example.

So that in the nature of man, we find three principal causes of quarrel. First, competition; second, diffidence; thirdly, glory.

The first, maketh men invade for gain; the second, for safety; and the third, for reputation. The first use violence, to make themselves masters of other men's persons, wives, children, and cattle; the second, to defend them; the third, for trifles, as a word, a smile, a different opinion, and any other sign of undervalue, either direct in their persons, or by reflection in their kindred, their friends, their nation, their profession, or their name.

Hereby it is manifest, that during the time men live without a common power to keep them all in awe, they are in that condition which is called war; and such a war, as is of every man, against every man. For WAR, consisteth not in battle only, or the act of fighting; but in a tract of time, wherein the will to contend by battle is sufficiently known: and therefore the notion of *time*, is to be considered in the nature of war; as it is in the nature of weather. For as the nature of foul weather, lieth not in a shower or two of rain; but in an inclination thereto of many days together: so the nature of war, consisteth not in actual fighting; but in the known disposition thereto, during all the time there is no assurance to the contrary. All other time is PEACE.

Whatsoever therefore is consequent to a time of war, where every man is enemy to every man; the same is consequent to the time, wherein men live without other security, than what their own strength, and their own invention shall furnish them withal. In such condition, there is no place for industry; because the fruit thereof is uncertain: and consequently no culture of the earth; no navigation, nor use of the commodities that may be imported by sea; no commodious building; no instruments of moving, and removing, such things as require much force; no knowledge of the face of the earth; no account of time; no arts; no letters; no society; and which is worst of all, continual fear, and danger of violent death; and the life of man, solitary, poor, nasty, brutish, and short.

It may seem strange to some man, that has not well weighed these things; that nature should thus dissociate, and render men apt to invade, and destroy one another: and he may therefore, not trusting to this inference, made from the passions, desire perhaps to have the same confirmed by experience. Let him therefore consider with himself, when taking a journey, he arms himself, and seeks to go well accompanied; when going to sleep, he locks his doors; when even in his house he locks his chests; and this when he knows there be laws, and public officers, armed, to revenge all injuries shall be done him; what opinion he has of his fellow-subjects, when he rides armed; of his fellow citizens, when he locks his doors; and of his children, and servants, when he locks his chests. Does he not there as much accuse mankind by his actions, as I do by my words? But neither of us accuse man's nature in it. The desires, and other passions of man, are in themselves no sin. No more are the actions, that proceed from those passions, till they know a law that forbids them: which till laws be made they cannot know: nor can any law be made, till they have agreed upon the person that shall make it.

It may peradventure be thought, there was never such a time, nor condition of war as this; and I believe it was never generally so, over all the world: but there are many places, where they live so now. For the savage people in many places of America, except the government of small families, the concord whereof dependeth on natural lust, have no government at all; and live at this day in that brutish manner, as I said before. Howsoever, it may be perceived what manner of life there would be, where there were no common power to fear, by the manner of life, which men that have formerly lived under a peaceful government, use to degenerate into, in a civil war.

But though there had never been any time, wherein particular men were in a condition of war one against another; yet in all times, kings, and persons of sovereign authority, because of their independency, are in continual jealousies, and in the state and posture of gladiators; having their weapons pointing, and their eyes fixed on one another; that is, their forts, garrisons, and guns upon the frontiers of their kingdoms; and continual spies upon their neighbours; which is a posture of war. But because they uphold thereby, the industry of their subjects; there does not follow from it, that misery, which accompanies the liberty of particular men.

To this war of every man, against every man, this also is consequent; that nothing can be unjust. The notions of right and wrong, justice and injustice have there no place. Where there is no common power, there is no law: where no law, no injustice. Force, and fraud, are in war the two cardinal virtues. Justice, and injustice are none of the faculties neither of the body, nor mind. If they were, they might be in a man that were alone in the world, as well as his senses, and passions. They are qualities, that relate to men in society, not in solitude. It is consequent also to the same condition, that there be no propriety, no dominion, no *mine*, and *thine* distinct; but only that to be every man's, that he can get; and for so long, as he can keep it. And thus much for the ill condition, which man by mere nature is actually placed in; though with a possibility to come out of it, consisting partly in the passions, partly in his reason.

The passions that incline men to peace, are fear of death; desire of such things as are necessary to commodious living; and a hope by their industry to obtain them. And reason suggesteth convenient articles of peace, upon which men may be drawn to agreement. These articles, are they, which otherwise are called the Laws of Nature: whereof I shall speak more particularly, in the two following chapters.

CHAPTER XIV.   OF THE FIRST AND SECOND NATURAL LAWS
AND OF CONTRACTS

The RIGHT OF NATURE, which writers commonly call *jus naturale*, is the liberty each man hath, to use his own power, as he will himself, for the preservation of his own nature; that is to say, of his own life; and consequently, of doing anything, which in his own judgment, and reason, he shall conceive to be the aptest means thereunto.

By LIBERTY, is understood, according to the proper signification of the word, the absence of external impediments: which impediments, may oft take away part of a man's power to do what he would; but cannot hinder him from using the power left him, according as his judgment, and reason shall dictate to him.

A LAW OF NATURE, *lex naturalis*, is a precept or general rule, found out by reason, by which a man is forbidden to do that, which is destructive of his life, or taketh away the means of preserving the same; and to omit that, by which he thinketh it may be best preserved. For though they that speak of this subject, use to confound *jus*, and *lex*, *right* and *law:* yet they ought to be distinguished; because RIGHT, consisteth in liberty to do, or to forbear; whereas LAW, determineth, and bindeth to one of them: so that law, and right, differ as much, as obligation, and liberty; which in one and the same matter are inconsistent.

And because the condition of man, as hath been declared in the precedent chapter, is a condition of war of every one against every one; in which case every one is governed by his own reason; and there is nothing he can make use of, that may not be a help unto him, in preserving his life against his enemies; it followeth, that in such a condition, every man has a right to every thing; even to one another's body. And therefore, as long as this natural right of every man to every thing endureth, there can be no security to any man, how strong or wise soever he be, of living out the time, which nature ordinarily alloweth men to live. And consequently it is a precept, or general rule of reason, *that every man, ought to endeavour peace, as far as he has hope of obtaining it; and when he cannot obtain it, that he may seek, and use, all helps, and advantages of war.* The first branch of which rule, containeth the first, and fundamental law of nature; which is, *to seek peace, and follow it.* The second, the sum of the right of nature; which is, *by all means we can, to defend ourselves.*

From this fundamental law of nature, by which men are commanded to endeavour peace, is derived this second law; *that a man be willing, when others are so too, as far forth, as for peace, and defence of himself he shall think it necessary, to lay down this right to all things; and be contented with so much liberty against other men, as he would allow other men against himself.* For as long as every man holdeth this right, of doing any thing he liketh; so long are all men in the condition of war. But if other men will not lay down their right, as well as he; then there is no reason for anyone, to divest himself of his: for that were to expose himself to prey, which no man is bound to, rather than to dispose himself to peace. This is that law of the Gospel; *whatsoever you require that others should do to you, that do ye to them.* And that law of all men, *quod tibi fieri non vis, alteri ne feceris.*

To *lay down* a man's *right* to any thing, is to *divest* himself of the *liberty*, of hindering another of the benefit of his own right to the same. For he that renounceth, or passeth away his right, giveth not to any other man a right which he had not before; because there is nothing to which every man had not right by nature: but only standeth out of his way, that he may enjoy his own original right, without hindrance from him; not without hindrance from another. So that the effect which redoundeth to one man, by another man's defect of right, is but so much diminution of impediments to the use of his own right original.

Right is laid aside, either by simply renouncing it; or by transferring it to another. By *simply* RENOUNCING; when he cares not to whom the benefit thereof redoundeth. By TRANSFERRING; when he intendeth the benefit thereof to some certain person, or persons. And when a man hath in either manner abandoned, or granted away his right; then is he said to be OBLIGED, or BOUND, not to hinder those, to whom such right is granted, or abandoned, from the benefit of it: and that he *ought*, and it is his DUTY, not to make void that voluntary act of his own: and that such hindrance is INJUSTICE, and INJURY, as being *sine jure;* the right being before renounced, or transferred. So that *injury*, or *injustice*, in the controversies of the world, is somewhat like to that, which in the disputations of scholars is called *absurdity.* For as it is there called an absurdity, to contradict what one maintained in the beginning: so in the world, it is called injustice, and injury, voluntarily to undo that, which from the beginning he had voluntarily done. The way by which a man either simply renounceth, or transferreth his right, is a declaration, or signification, by some voluntary and sufficient sign, or signs, that he doth so renounce, or transfer; or hath so renounced, or transferred the same, to him that accepteth it. And these signs are either words only, or actions only; or, as it happeneth most often, both words, and actions. And the same are the BONDS, by which men are bound, and obliged: bonds, that have their strength, not from their own nature, for nothing is more easily broken than a man's word, but from fear of some evil consequence upon the rupture.

Whensoever a man transferreth his right, or renounceth it; it is either in consideration of some right reciprocally transferred to himself; or for some other good he hopeth for thereby. For it is a voluntary act: and of the voluntary acts of every man, the object is some *good to himself*. And therefore there be some rights, which no man can be understood by any words, or other signs, to have abandoned, or transferred. As first a man cannot lay down the right of resisting them, that assault him by force, to take away his life; because he cannot be understood to aim thereby, at any good to himself. The same may be said of wounds, and chains, and imprisonment; both because there is no benefit consequent to such patience; as there is to the patience of suffering another to be wounded, or imprisoned: as also because a man cannot tell, when he seeth men proceed against him by violence, whether they intend his death or not. And lastly the motive, and end for which this renouncing, and transferring of right is introduced, is nothing else but the security of a man's person, in his life, and in the means of so preserving life, as not to be weary of it. And therefore if a man by words, or other signs, seem to despoil himself of the end, for which those signs were intended; he is not to be understood as if he meant it, or that it was his will; but that he was ignorant of how such words and actions were to be interpreted.

The mutual transferring of right, is that which men call CONTRACT.

There is difference between transferring of right to the thing; and transferring, or tradition, that is delivery of the thing itself. For the thing may be delivered together with translation of the right; as in buying and selling with ready-money; or exchange of goods, or lands: and it may be delivered some time after.

Again, one of the contractors, may deliver the thing contracted for on his part, and leave the other to perform his part at some determinate time after, and in the mean time be trusted; and then the contract on his part, is called PACT, or COVENANT: or both parts may contract now, to perform hereafter: in which cases, he that is to perform in time to come, being trusted, his performance is called *keeping of promise*, or faith; and the failing of performance, if it be voluntary, *violation of faith*. . . . .

CHAPTER XV. OF OTHER LAWS OF NATURE

From that law of nature, by which we are obliged to transfer to another, such rights, as being retained, hinder the peace of mankind, there followeth a third; which is this, *that men perform their covenants made:* without which, covenants are in vain, and but empty words; and the right of all men to all things remaining, we are still in the condition of war.

And in this law of nature, consisteth the fountain and original of JUSTICE. For where no covenant hath preceded, there hath no right been transferred, and every man has right to every thing; and consequently, no action can be unjust. But when a covenant is made, then to break it is *unjust:* and the definition of INJUSTICE, is no other than *the not performance of covenant.* And whatsoever is not unjust, is *just.*

But because covenants of mutual trust, where there is a fear of not performance on either part, as hath been said in the former chapter, are invalid; though the original of justice be the making of covenants; yet injustice actually there can be none, till the cause of such fear be taken away; which while men are in the natural condition of war, cannot be done. Therefore before the names of just, and unjust can have place, there must be some coercive power, to compel men equally to the performance of their covenants, by the terror of some punishment, greater than the benefit they expect by the breach of their covenant; and to make good that propriety, which by mutual contract men acquire, in recompense of the universal right they abandon: and such power there is none before the erection of a commonwealth. And this is also to be gathered out of the ordinary definition of justice in the Schools: for they say, that *justice is the constant will of giving to every man his own.* And therefore where there is no *own,* that is no propriety, there is no injustice; and where is no coercive power erected, that is, where there is no commonwealth, there is no propriety; all men having right to all things: therefore where there is no commonwealth, there nothing is unjust. So that the nature of justice, consisteth in keeping of valid covenants: but the validity of covenants begins not but with the constitution of a civil power, sufficient to compel men to keep them: and then it is also that propriety begins. . . . .

[*There follows the discussion of a group of subordinate laws of nature, all deducible from the first two.*]

. . . . These are the laws of nature, dictating peace, for a means of the conservation of men in multitudes; and which only concern the doctrine of civil society. There be other things tending to the destruction of particular men; as drunkenness, and all other parts of intemperance; which may therefore also be reckoned amongst those things which the law of nature hath forbidden; but are not necessary to be mentioned, nor are pertinent enough to this place.

And though this may seem too subtle a deduction of the laws of nature, to be taken notice of by all men; whereof the most part are too busy in getting food, and the rest too negligent to understand; yet to leave all men inexcusable, they have been contracted into one easy sum, intelligible even to the meanest capacity; and that is, *Do not that to another, which thou wouldst not have done to thyself;* which sheweth him, that he has no more to do in learning the laws of nature, but, when weighing the actions of other men with his own, they seem too heavy, to put them into the other part of the balance, and his own into their place, that his own passions, and self-love, may add nothing to the weight; and then there is none of these laws of nature that will not appear unto him very reasonable.

The laws of nature oblige *in foro interno;* that is to say, they bind to a desire they should take place: but *in foro externo;* that is, to the putting them in act, not always. For he that should be modest, and tractable, and perform all he promises, in such time, and place, where no man else should do so, should but make himself a prey to others, and procure his own certain ruin, contrary to the ground of all laws of nature, which tend to nature's preservation. And again, he that having sufficient security, that others shall observe the same laws towards him, observes them not himself, seeketh not peace, but war; and consequently the destruction of his nature by violence.

And whatsoever laws bind *in foro interno*, may be broken, not only by a fact contrary to the law, but also by a fact according to it, in case a man think it contrary. For though his action in this case, be according to the law; yet his purpose was against the law; which, where the obligation is *in foro interno*, is a breach.

The laws of nature are immutable and eternal; for injustice, ingratitude, arrogance, pride, iniquity, acception of persons, and the rest, can never be made lawful. For it can never be that war shall preserve life, and peace destroy it.

The same laws, because they oblige only to a desire, and endeavour, I mean an unfeigned and constant endeavour are easy to be observed. For in that they require nothing but endeavour, he that endeavoureth their performance, fulfilleth them, and he that fulfilleth the law, is just.

And the science of them, is the true and only moral philosophy. For moral philosophy is nothing else but the science of what is *good*, and *evil*, in the conversation and society of mankind. *Good*, and *evil*, are names that signify our appetites, and aversions; which in different tempers, customs, and doctrines of men, are different: and divers men, differ not only in their judgment, on the senses of what is pleasant, and unpleasant to the taste, smell, hearing, touch, and sight; but also of what is conformable, or disagreeable to reason, in the actions of common life. Nay, the same man, in divers times, differs from himself; and one time praiseth, that is, calleth good, what another time he dispraiseth, and calleth evil: from whence arise disputes, controversies, and at last war. And therefore so long as a man is in the condition of mere nature, which is a condition of war, his private appetite is the measure of good, and evil: and consequently all men agree on this, that peace is good, and therefore also the way, or means of peace, which, as I have shewed before, are *justice, gratitude, modesty, equity, mercy*, and the rest of the laws of nature, are good; that is to say; *moral virtues;* and their contrary *vices*, evil. Now the science of virtue and vice, is moral philosophy; and therefore the true doctrine of the laws of nature, is the true moral philosophy. But the writers of moral philosophy, though they acknowledge the same virtues and vices; yet not seeing wherein consisted their goodness; nor that they come to be praised, as the means of peaceable, sociable, and comfortable living, place them in a mediocrity of passions: as if not the cause, but the degree of daring, made fortitude; or not the cause, but the quantity of a gift, made liberality.

These dictates of reason, men used to call by the name of laws, but improperly: for they are but conclusions, or theorems concerning what conduceth to the conservation and defence of themselves; whereas law, properly, is the word of him, that by right hath command over others. But yet if we consider the same theorems, as delivered in the word of God, that by right commandeth all things; then are they properly called laws.

CHAPTER XVI. OF PERSONS, AUTHORS, AND THINGS PERSONATED

A person, is he, *whose words or actions are considered, either as his own, or as representing the words or actions of another man, or of any other thing, to whom they are attributed, whether truly or by fiction.*

When they are considered as his own, then is he called a *natural person:* and when they are considered as representing the words and actions of another, then is he a *feigned or artificial person.*

The word person is Latin: instead whereof the Greeks have πρόσωπον, which signifies the *face*, as *persona* in Latin signifies the *disguise*, or *outward appearance* of a man, counterfeited on the stage; and sometimes more particularly that part of it, which disguiseth the face, as a mask or vizard: and from the stage, hath been translated to any representer of speech and action, as well in tribunals, as theatres. So that a *person*, is the same that an *actor* is, both on the stage and in common conversation; and to *personate*, is to *act*, or *represent* himself, or another; and he that acteth another, is said to bear his person, or act in his name, in which sense Cicero useth it where he says, *Unus sustineo tres personas; mei, adversarii, et judicis:* I bear three persons; my own, my adversary's, and the judge's; and is called in divers occasions, diversely; as a *representer*, or *representative*, a *lieutenant*, a *vicar*, an *attorney*, a *deputy*, a *procurator*, an *actor*, and the like.

Of persons artificial, some have their words and actions *owned* by those whom they represent. And then the person is the *actor;* and he that owneth his words and actions, is the AUTHOR: in which case the actor acteth by authority. For that which in speaking of goods and possessions, is called an *owner*, and in Latin *dominus*, in Greek κύριος, speaking of actions, is called author. And as the right of possession, is called dominion; so the right of doing any action, is called AUTHORITY. So that by authority, is always understood a right of doing any act; and *done by authority*, done by commission, or licence from him whose right it is.

From hence it followeth, that when the actor maketh a covenant by authority, he bindeth thereby the author, no less than if he had made it himself; and no less subjecteth him to all the consequences of the same. And therefore all that hath been said formerly, (chap. xiv) of the nature of covenants between man and man in their natural capacity, is true also when they are made by their actors, representers, or procurators, that have authority from them, so far forth as is in their commission, but no further. . . . .

PART II. OF COMMONWEALTH

CHAPTER XVII. OF THE CAUSES, GENERATION, AND DEFINITION OF A COMMONWEALTH

The final cause, end, or design of men, who naturally love liberty, and dominion over others, in the introduction of that restraint upon themselves, in which we see them live in commonwealths, is the foresight of their own preservation, and of a more contented life thereby; that is to say, of getting themselves out from that miserable condition of war, which is necessarily consequent, as hath been shown in chapter xiii, to the natural passions of men, when there is no visible power to keep them in awe, and tie them by fear of punishment to the performance of their covenants, and observation of those laws of nature set down in the fourteenth and fifteenth chapters.

For the laws of nature, as *justice, equity, modesty, mercy*, and, in sum, *doing to others, as we would be done to*, of themselves, without the terror of some power, to cause them to be observed, are contrary to our natural passions, that carry us to partiality, pride, revenge, and the like. And covenants, without the sword, are but words, and of no strength to secure a man at all. Therefore notwithstanding the laws of nature, which every one hath then kept, when he has the will to keep them, when he can do it safely, if there be no power erected, or not great enough for our security; every man will, and may lawfully rely on his own strength and art, for caution against all other men. And in all places, where men have lived by small families, to rob and spoil one another, has been a trade, and so far from being reputed against the law of nature, that the greater spoils they gained, the greater was their honour; and men observed no other laws therein, but the laws of honour; that is, to abstain from cruelty, leaving to men their lives, and instruments of husbandry. And as small families did then; so now do cities and kingdoms which are but greater families, for their own security, enlarge their dominions, upon all pretences of danger, and fear of invasion, or assistance that may be given to invaders, and endeavour as much as they can, to subdue, or weaken their neighbours, by open force, and secret arts, for want of other caution, justly; and are remembered for it in after ages with honour.

Nor is it the joining together of a small number of men, that gives them this security; because in small numbers, small additions on the one side or the other, make the advantage of strength so great, as is sufficient to carry the victory; and therefore gives encouragement to an invasion. The multitude sufficient to confide in for our security, is not determined by any certain number, but by comparison with the enemy we fear; and is then sufficient, when the odds of the enemy is not of so visible and conspicuous moment, to determine the event of war, as to move him to attempt.

And be there never so great a multitude; yet if their actions be directed according to their particular judgments, and particular appetites, they can expect thereby no defence, nor protection, neither against a common enemy, nor against the injuries of one another. For being distracted in opinions concerning the best use and application of their strength, they do not help but hinder one another; and reduce their strength by mutual opposition to nothing: whereby they are easily, not only subdued by a very few that agree together; but also when there is no common enemy, they make war upon each other, for their particular interests. For if we could suppose a great multitude of men to consent in the observation of justice, and other laws of nature, without a common power to keep them all in awe; we might as well suppose all mankind to do the same; and then there neither would be, nor need to be any civil government, or commonwealth at all; because there would be peace without subjection.

Nor is it enough for the security, which men desire should last all the time of their life, that they be governed, and directed by one judgment, for a limited time; as in one battle, or one war. For though they obtain a victory by their unanimous endeavour against a foreign enemy; yet afterwards, when either they have no common enemy, or he that by one part is held for an enemy, is by another part held for a friend, they must needs by the difference of their interests dissolve, and fall again into a war amongst themselves.

It is true, that certain living creatures, as bees and ants, live sociably one with another, which are therefore by Aristotle numbered amongst political creatures; and yet have no other direction, than their particular judgments and appetites; nor speech, whereby one of them can signify to another, what he thinks expedient for the common benefit: and therefore some man may perhaps desire to know, why mankind cannot do the same. To which I answer,

First, that men are continually in competition for honour and dignity, which these creatures are not; and consequently amongst men there ariseth on that ground, envy and hatred, and finally war; but amongst these not so.

Secondly, that amongst these creatures, the common good differeth not from the private; and being by nature inclined to their private, they procure thereby the common benefit. But man, whose joy consisteth in comparing himself with other men, can relish nothing but what is eminent.

Thirdly, that these creatures, having not, as man, the use of reason, do not see, nor think they see any fault, in the administration of their common business; whereas amongst men, there are very many, that think themselves wiser, and able to govern the public, better than the rest; and these strive to reform and innovate, one this way, another that way; and thereby bring it into distraction and civil war.

Fourthly, that these creatures, though they have some use of voice, in making known to one another their desires, and other affections; yet they want that art of words, by which some men can represent to others, that which is good, in the likeness of evil; and evil, in the likness of good; and augment, or diminish the apparent greatness of good and evil; discontenting men, and troubling their peace at their pleasure.

Fifthly, irrational creatures cannot distinguish between *injury*, and *damage;* and therefore as long as they be at ease, they are not offended with their fellows: whereas man is then most troublesome, when he is most at ease: for then it is that he loves to shew his wisdom, and control the actions of them that govern the commonwealth.

Lastly, the agreement of these creatures is natural; that of men, is by covenant only, which is artificial: and therefore it is no wonder if there be somewhat else required, besides covenant, to make their agreement constant and lasting; which is a common power, to keep them in awe, and to direct their actions to the common benefit.

The only way to erect such a common power, as may be able to defend them from the invasion of foreigners, and the injuries of one another, and thereby to secure them in such sort, as that by their own industry, and by the fruits of the earth, they may nourish themselves and live contentedly; is, to confer all their power and strength upon one man, or upon one assembly of men, that may reduce all their wills, by plurality of voices, unto one will: which is as much as to say, to appoint one man, or assembly of men, to bear their person; and every one to own, and acknowledge himself to be author of whatsoever he that so beareth their person, shall act, or cause to be acted, in those things which concern the common peace and safety; and therein to submit their wills, every one to his will, and their judgments, to his judgment. This is more than consent, or concord; it is a real unity of them all, in one and the same person, made by covenant of every man with every man, in such manner, as if every man should say to every man, *I authorize and give up my right of governing myself, to this man, or to this assembly of men, on this condition, that thou give up thy right to him, and authorize all his actions in like manner.* This done, the multitude so united in one person, is called a COMMONWEALTH, in Latin CIVITAS. This is the generation of that great LEVIATHAN, or rather, to speak more reverently, of that *mortal god*, to which we owe under the *immortal God*, our peace and defence. For by this authority, given him by every particular man in the commonwealth, he hath the use of so much power and strength conferred on him, that by terror thereof, he is enabled to perform the wills of them all, to peace at home, and mutual aid against their enemies abroad. And in him consisteth the essence of the commonwealth; which, to define it, is *one person, of whose acts a great multitude, by mutual covenants one with another, have made themselves every one the author, to the end he may use the strength and means of them all, as he shall think expedient, for their peace and common defence.*

And he that carrieth this person, is called SOVEREIGN, and said to have *sovereign power;* and every one besides, his SUBJECT.

The attaining to this sovereign power, is by two ways. One, by natural force; as when a man maketh his children, to submit themselves, and their children, to his government, as being able to destroy them if they refuse; or by war subdueth his enemies to his will, giving them their lives on that condition. The other, is when men agree amongst themselves, to submit to some man, or assembly of men, voluntarily, on confidence to be protected by him against all others. This latter, may be called a political commonwealth, or commonwealth by *institution;* and the former, a commonwealth by *acquisition.* And first, I shall speak of a commonwealth by institution.

CHAPTER XVIII. OF THE RIGHTS OF SOVEREIGNS BY INSTITUTION

A *commonwealth* is said to be *instituted,* when a *multitude* of men do agree, and *covenant, every one, with every one,* that to whatsoever *man,* or *assembly of men,* shall be given by the major part, the *right* to *present* the person of them all, that is to say, to be their *representative;* every one, as well he that *voted for it,* as he that *voted against it,* shall *authorize* all the actions and judgments, of that man, or assembly of men, in the same manner, as if they were his own, to the end, to live peaceably amongst themselves, and be protected against other men.

From this institution of a commonwealth are derived all the *rights,* and *faculties* of him, or them, on whom sovereign power is conferred by the consent of the people assembled.

First, because they covenant, it is to be understood, they are not obliged by former covenant to anything repugnant hereunto. And consequently they that have already instituted a commonwealth, being thereby bound by covenant, to own the actions, and judgments of one, cannot lawfully make a new covenant, amongst themselves, to be obedient to any other, in any thing whatsoever, without his permission. And therefore, they that are subject to a monarch, cannot without his leave cast off monarchy, and return to the confusion of a disunited multitude; nor transfer their person from him that beareth it, to another man, or other assembly of men: for they are bound, every man to every man, to own, and be reputed author of all, that he that already is their sovereign, shall do, and judge fit to be done: so that any one man dissenting, all the rest should break their covenant made to that man, which is injustice: and they have also every man given the sovereignty to him that beareth their person; and therefore if they depose him, they take from him that which is his own, and so again it is injustice. Besides, if he that attempteth to depose his sovereign, be killed, or punished by him for such attempt, he is author of his own punishment, as being by the institution, author of all his sovereign shall do: and because it is injustice for a man to do anything, for which he may be punished by his own authority, he is also upon that title, unjust. And whereas some men have pretended for their disobedience to their sovereign, a new covenant, made, not with men, but with God; this also is unjust: for there is no covenant with God, but by mediation of somebody that representeth God's person; which none doth but God's lieutenant, who hath the sovereignty under God. But this pretence of covenant with God, is so evident a lie, even in the pretenders' own consciences, that it is not only an act of an unjust, but also of a vile and unmanly disposition.

Secondly, because the right of bearing the person of them all, is given to him they make sovereign, by covenant only of one to another, and not of him to any of them; there can happen no breach of covenant on the part of the sovereign; and consequently none of his subjects, by any pretence of forfeiture, can be freed from his subjection. That he which is made sovereign maketh no covenant with his subjects beforehand, is manifest; because either he must make it with the whole multitude, as one party to the covenant; or he must make a several covenant with every man. With the whole, as one party, it is impossible; because as yet they are not one person: and if he make so many several covenants as there be men, those covenants after he hath the sovereignty are void; because what act soever can be pretended by any one of them for breach thereof, is the act both of himself, and of all the rest, because done in the person, and by the right of every one of them in particular. Besides, if any one, or more of them, pretend a breach of the covenant made by the sovereign at his institution; and others, or one other of his subjects, or himself alone, pretend there was no such breach, there is in this case, no judge to decide the controversy; it returns therefore to the sword again; and every man recovereth the right of protecting himself by his own strength, contrary to the design they had in the institution. It is therefore vain to grant sovereignty by way of precedent covenant. The opinion that any monarch receiveth his power by covenant, that is to say, on condition, proceedeth from want of understanding this easy truth, that covenants being but words and breath, have no force to oblige, contain, constrain, or protect any man, but what it has from the public sword; that is, from the untied hands of that man, or assembly of men that hath the sovereignty, and whose actions are avouched by them all, and performed by the strength of them all, in him united. But when an assembly of men is made sovereign; then no man imagineth any such covenant to have passed in the institution; for no man is so dull as to say, for example, the people of Rome made a covenant with the Romans, to hold the sovereignty on such or such conditions; which not performed, the Romans might lawfully depose the Roman people. That men see not the reason to be alike in a monarchy, and in a popular government, proceedeth from the ambition of some, that are kinder to the government of an assembly, whereof they may hope to participate, than of monarchy, which they despair to enjoy.

Thirdly, because the major part hath by consenting voices declared a sovereign; he that dissented must now consent with the rest; that is, be contented to avow all the actions he shall do, or else justly be destroyed by the rest. For if he voluntarily entered into the congregation of them that were assembled, he sufficiently declared thereby his will, and therefore tacitly covenanted, to stand to what the major part should ordain: and therefore if he refuse to stand thereto, or make protestation against any of their decrees, he does contrary to his covenant, and therefore unjustly. And whether he be of the congregation, or not; and whether his consent be asked, or not, he must either submit to their decrees, or be left in the condition of war he was in before; wherein he might without injustice be destroyed by any man whatsoever.

Fourthly, because every subject is by this institution author of all the actions, and judgments of the sovereign instituted; it follows, that whatsoever he doth, it can be no injury to any of his subjects; nor ought he to be by any of them accused of injustice. For he that doth anything by authority from another, doth therein no injury to him by whose authority he acteth: but by this institution of a commonwealth, every particular man is author of all the sovereign doth: and consequently he that complaineth of injury from his sovereign, complaineth of that whereof he himself is author; and therefore ought not to accuse any man but himself; no nor himself of injury; because to do injury to one's self, is impossible. It is true that they that have sovereign power may commit iniquity, but not injustice, or injury in the proper signification.

Fifthly, and consequently to that which was said last, no man that hath sovereign power can justly be put to death, or otherwise in any manner by his subjects punished. For seeing every subject is author of the actions of his sovereign; he punisheth another for the actions committed by himself.

And because the end of this institution, is the peace and defence of them all; and whosoever has right to the end, has right to the means; it belongeth of right, to whatsoever man, or assembly that hath the sovereignty, to be judge both of the means of peace and defence, and also of the hindrances, and disturbances of the same; and to do whatsoever he shall think necessary to be done, both beforehand, for the preserving of peace and security, by prevention of discord at home, and hostility from abroad; and, when peace and security are lost, for the recovery of the same. And therefore,

Sixthly, it is annexed to the sovereignty, to be judge of what opinions and doctrines are averse, and what conducing to peace; and consequently, on what occasions, how far, and what men are to be trusted withal, in speaking to multitudes of people; and who shall examine the doctrines of all books before they be published. For the actions of men proceed from their opinions; and in the well-governing of opinions, consisteth the well-governing of men's actions, in order to their peace, and concord. And though in matter of doctrine, nothing ought to be regarded but the truth; yet this is not repugnant to regulating the same by peace. For doctrine repugnant to peace, can no more be true, than peace and concord can be against the law of nature. It is true, that in a commonwealth, where by the negligence, or unskilfulness of governors, and teachers, false doctrines are by time generally received; the contrary truths may be generally offensive. Yet the most sudden, and rough bursting in of a new truth, that can be, does never break the peace, but only sometimes awake the war. For those men that are so remissly governed, that they dare take up arms to defend, or introduce an opinion, are still in war; and their condition not peace, but only a cessation of arms for fear of one another; and they live, as it were, in the precincts of battle continually. It belongeth therefore to him that hath the sovereign power, to be judge, or constitute all judges of opinions and doctrines, as a thing necessary to peace; thereby to prevent discord and civil war.

Seventhly, is annexed to the sovereignty, the whole power of prescribing the rules, whereby every man may know, what goods he may enjoy, and what actions he may do, without being molested by any of his fellow-subjects; and this is it men call *propriety*. For before constitution of sovereign power, as hath already been shown, all men had right to all things; which necessarily causeth war: and therefore this propriety, being necessary to peace, and depending on sovereign power, is the act of that power, in order to the public peace. These rules of propriety, or *meum* and *tuum*, and of *good*, *evil*, *lawful*, and *unlawful* in the actions of subjects, are the civil laws; that is to say, the laws of each commonwealth in particular; though the name of civil law be now restrained to the ancient civil laws of the city of Rome; which being the head of a great part of the world, her laws at that time were in these parts the civil law.

Eighthly, is annexed to the sovereignty, the right of judicature; that is to say, of hearing and deciding all controversies, which may arise concerning law, either civil, or natural; or concerning fact. For without the decision of controversies, there is no protection of one subject, against the injuries of another; the laws concerning *meum* and *tuum* are in vain; and to every man remaineth, from the natural and necessary appetite of his own conservation, the right of protecting himself by his private strength, which is the condition of war, and contrary to the end for which every commonwealth is instituted.

Ninthly, is annexed to the sovereignty, the right of making war and peace with other nations, and commonwealths; that is to say, of judging when it is for the public good, and how great forces are to be assembled, armed, and paid for that end; and to levy money upon the subjects, to defray the expenses thereof. For the power by which the people are to be defended, consisteth in their armies; and the strength of an army, in the union of their strength under one command; which command the sovereign instituted, therefore hath; because the command of the *militia*, without other institution, maketh him that hath it sovereign. And therefore whosoever is made general of an army, he that hath the sovereign power is always generalissimo.

Tenthly, is annexed to the sovereignty, the choosing of all counsellors, ministers, magistrates, and officers, both in peace and war. For seeing the sovereign is charged with the end, which is the common peace and defense, he is understood to have power to use such means, as he shall think most fit for his discharge.

Eleventhly, to the sovereign is committed the power of rewarding with riches, or honour, and of punishing with corporal or pecuniary punishment, or with ignominy, every subject according to the law he hath formerly made; of if there be no law made, according as he shall judge most to conduce to the encouraging of men to serve the commonwealth, or deterring of them from doing disservice to the same.

Lastly, considering what value men are naturally apt to set upon themselves; what respect they look for from others; and how little they value other men; from whence continually arise amongst them, emulation, quarrels, factions, and at last war, to the destroying of one another, and diminution of their strength against a common enemy; it is necessary that there be laws of honour, and a public rate of the worth of such men as have deserved, or are able to deserve well of the commonwealth; and that there be force in the hands of some or other, to put those laws in execution. But it hath already been shown, that not only the whole *militia*, or forces of the commonwealth; but also the judicature of all controversies, is annexed to the sovereignty. To the sovereign therefore it belongeth also to give titles of honour; and to appoint what order of place, and dignity, each man shall hold; and what signs of respect, in public or private meetings, they shall give to one another.

These are the rights, which make the essence of sovereignty; and which are the marks, whereby a man may discern in what man, or assembly of men, the sovereign power is placed, and resideth. For these are incommunicable, and inseparable. The power to coin money; to dispose of the estate and persons of infant heirs; to have præemption in markets; and all other statute prerogatives, may be transferred by the sovereign; and yet the power to protect his subjects be retained. But if he transfer the *militia*, he retains the judicature in vain, for want of execution of the laws: or if he grant away the power of raising money; the *militia* is in vain; or if he give away the government of doctrines, men will be frighted into rebellion with the fear of spirits. And so if we consider any one of the said rights, we shall presently see, that the holding of all the rest will produce no effect, in the conservation of peace and justice, the end for which all commonwealths are instituted. And this division is it, whereof it is said, a *kingdom divided in itself cannot stand:* for unless this division precede, division into opposite armies can never happen. If there had not first been an opinion received of the greatest part of England, that these powers were divided between the King, and the Lords, and the House of Commons, the people had never been divided and fallen into this civil war; first between those that disagreed in politics; and after between the dissenters about the liberty of religion; which have so instructed men in this point of sovereign right, and there be few now in England that do not see, that these rights are inseparable, and will be so generally acknowledged at the next return of peace; and so continue, till their miseries are forgotten; and no longer, except the vulgar be better taught than they have hitherto been.

And because they are essential and inseparable rights, it follows necessarily, that in whatsoever words any of them seem to be granted away, yet if the sovereign power itself be not in direct terms renounced, and the name of sovereign no more given by the grantees to him that grants them, the grant is void: for when he has granted all he can, if we grant back the sovereignty, all is restored, as inseparably annexed thereunto.

This great authority being indivisible, and inseparably annexed to the sovereignty, there is little ground for the opinion of them, that say of sovereign kings, though they be *singulis majores*, of greater power than every one of their subjects, yet they be *universis minores*, of less power than them all together. For if by *all together*, they mean not the collective body as one person, then *all together*, and *every one*, signify the same; and the speech is absurd. But if by *all together*, they understand them as one person, which person the sovereign bears, then the power of all together, is the same with the sovereign's power; and so again the speech is absurd: which absurdity they see well enough, when the sovereignty is in an assembly of the people; but in a monarch they see it not; and yet the power of sovereignty is the same in whomsoever it be placed.

And as the power, so also the honour of the sovereign, ought to be greater, than that of any, or all the subjects. For in the sovereignty is the fountain of honour. The dignities of lord, earl, duke, and prince are his creatures. As in the presence of the master, the servants are equal, and without any honour at all; so are the subjects, in the presence of the sovereign. And though they shine some more, some less, when they are out of his sight; yet in his presence, they shine no more than the stars in the presence of the sun.

But a man may here object, that the condition of subjects is very miserable; as being obnoxious to the lusts, and other irregular passions of him, or them that have so unlimited a power in their hands. And commonly they that live under a monarch, think it the fault of monarchy; and they that live under the government of democracy, or other sovereign assembly, attribute all the inconvenience to that form of commonwealth; whereas the power in all forms, if they be perfect enough to protect them, is the same: not considering that the state of man can never be without some incommodity or other; and that the greatest, that in any form of government can possibly happen to the people in general, is scarce sensible, in respect to the miseries, and horrible calamities, that accompany a civil war, or that dissolute condition of masterless men, without subjection to laws, and a coercive power to tie their hands from rapine and revenge: nor considering that the greatest pressure of sovereign governors, proceedeth not from any delight, or profit they can expect in the damage or weakening of their subjects, in whose vigour, consisteth their own strength and glory;

but in the restiveness of themselves, that unwillingly contributing to their own defence, make it necessary for their governors to draw from them what they can in time of peace, that they may have means on any emergent occasion, or sudden need, to resist, or take advantage on their enemies. For all men are by nature provided of notable multiplying glasses, that is their passions and self-love, through which, every little payment appeareth a great grievance; but are destitute of those prospective glasses, namely moral and civil science, to see afar off the miseries that hang over them, and cannot without such payment be avoided.

CHAPTER XIX. OF THE SEVERAL KINDS OF COMMONWEALTH BY INSTITUTION, AND OF SUCCESSION TO THE SOVEREIGN POWER

The difference of commonwealths, consisteth in the difference of the sovereign, or the person representative of all and every one of the multitude. And because the sovereignty is either in one man, or in an assembly of more than one; and into that assembly either every man hath right to enter, or not every one, but certain men distinguished from the rest; it is manifest, there can be but three kinds of commonwealth. For the representative must needs be one man, or more: and if more, then it is the assembly of all, or but of a part. When the representative is one man, then is the commonwealth a MONARCHY: when an assembly of all that will come together, then it is a DEMOCRACY, or popular commonwealth: when an assembly of a part only, then it is called an ARISTOCRACY. Other kind of commonwealth there can be none: for either one, or more, or all, must have the sovereign power, which I have shown· to be indivisible, entire.

There be other names of government, in the histories, and books of policy; as *tyranny*, and *oligarchy:* but they are not the names of other forms of government, but of the same forms misliked. For they that are discontented under *monarchy*, call it *tyranny;* and they that are displeased with *aristocracy*, call it *oligarchy:* so also, they which find themselves grieved under a *democracy*, call it *anarchy*, which signifies want of government; and yet I think no man believes, that want of government, is any new kind of government: nor by the same reason ought they to believe, that the government is of one kind, when they like it, and other, when they mislike it, or are oppressed by the governors. . . . .

CHAPTER **XX**. OF DOMINION PATERNAL, AND DESPOTICAL

A commonwealth *by acquisition*, is that, where the sovereign power is acquired by force; and it is acquired by force, when men singly, or many together by plurality of voices, for fear of death, or bonds, do authorize all the actions of that man, or assembly, that hath their lives and liberty in his power.

And this kind of dominion, or sovereignty, differeth from sovereignty by institution, only in this, that men who choose their sovereign, do it for fear of one another, and not of him whom they institute: but in this case, they subject themselves, to him they are afraid of. In both cases they do it for fear: which is to be noted by them, that hold all such covenants, as proceed from fear of death or violence, void: which if it were true, no man, in any kind of commonwealth, could be obliged to obedience. It is true, that in a commonwealth once instituted, or acquired, promises proceeding from fear of death or violence, are no covenants, nor obliging, when the thing promised is contrary to the laws; but the reason is not, because it was made upon fear, but because he that promiseth, hath no right in the thing promised. Also, when he may lawfully perform, and doth not, it is not the invalidity of the covenant, that absolveth him, but the sentence of the sovereign. Otherwise, whensoever a man lawfully promiseth, he unlawfully breaketh: but when the sovereign, who is the actor, acquitteth him, then he is acquitted by him that extorted the promise, as by the author of such absolution.

But the rights, and consequences of sovereignty, are the same in both. His power cannot, without his consent, be transferred to another: he cannot forfeit it: he cannot be accused by any of his subjects, of injury: he cannot be punished by them: he is judge of what is necessary for peace; and judge of doctrines: he is sole legislator; and supreme judge of controversies; and of the times, and occasions of war, and peace: to him it belongeth to choose magistrates, counsellors, commanders, and all other officers, and ministers; and to determine of rewards, and punishments, honour, and order. The reasons whereof, are the same which are alleged in the precedent chapter, for the same rights, and consequences of sovereignty by institution.

Dominion is acquired two ways; by generation, and by conquest. The right of dominion by generation, is that, which the parent hath over his children; and is called PATERNAL. And is not so derived from the generation, as if therefore the parent had dominion over his child because he begat him; but from the child's consent, either express, or by other sufficient arguments declared. . . . .

Dominion acquired by conquest, or victory in war, is that which some writers call DESPOTICAL, from Δεσπότης, which signifieth a *lord*, or *master;* and is the dominion of the master over his servant. And this dominion is then acquired to the victor, when the vanquished, to avoid the present stroke of death, covenanteth either in express words, or by other sufficient signs of the will, that so long as his life, and the liberty of his body is allowed him, the victor shall have the use thereof, at his pleasure. . . . .

. . . . The rights and consequences of both *paternal* and *despotical* dominion, are the very same with those of a sovereign by institution. . . . . So that for a man that is monarch of divers nations, whereof he hath, in one the sovereignty by institution of the people assembled, and in another by conquest, that is by the submission of each particular, to avoid death or bonds; to demand of one nation more than of the other, from the title of conquest, as being a conquered nation, is an act of ignorance of the rights of sovereignty; for the sovereign is absolute over both alike; or else there is no sovereignty at all; and so every man may lawfully protect himself, if he can, with his own sword, which is the condition of war. . . . .

So that it appeareth plainly, to my understanding, both from reason, and Scripture, that the sovereign power, whether placed in one man, as in monarchy, or in one assembly of men, as in popular, and aristocratical commonwealths, is as great, as possibly men can be imagined to make it. And though of so unlimited a power, men may fancy many evil consequences, yet the consequences of the want of it, which is perpetual war of every man against his neighbour, are much worse. The condition of man in this life shall never be without inconveniences; but there happeneth in no commonwealth any great inconvenience, but what proceeds from the subject's disobedience, and breach of those covenants, from which the commonwealth hath its being. And whosoever thinking sovereign power too great, will seek to make it less, must subject himself, to the power, that can limit it; that is to say, to a greater.

The greatest objection is, that of the practice; when men ask, where, and when, such power has by subjects been acknowledged. But one may ask them again, when, or where there has been a kingdom long free from sedition and civil war. In those nations, whose commonwealths have been long-lived, and not been destroyed by some foreign war, the subjects never did dispute of the sovereign power. But howsoever, an argument from the practice of men, that have not sifted to the bottom, and with exact reason weighed the causes, and nature of commonwealths, and suffer daily those miseries, that proceed from the ignorance thereof, is invalid. For though in all places of the world, men should lay the foundation of their houses on the sand, it could not thence be inferred, that so it ought to be. The skill of making, and maintaining commonwealths, consisteth in certain rules, as doth arithmetic and geometry; not, as tennis-play, on practice only: which rules, neither poor men have the leisure, nor men that have had the leisure, have hitherto had the curiosity, or the method to find out.

CHAPTER XXI. OF THE LIBERTY OF SUBJECTS

LIBERTY, OR FREEDOM, signifieth, properly, the absence of opposition; by opposition, I mean external impediments of motion; and may be applied no less to irrational, and inanimate creatures, than to rational. For whatsoever is so tied, or environed, as it cannot move but within a certain space, which space is determined by the opposition of some external body, we say it hath not liberty to go further. And so of all living creatures, whilst they are imprisoned, or restrained, with walls, or chains; and of the water whilst it is kept in by banks, or vessels, that otherwise would spread itself into a larger space, we use to say, they are not at liberty, to move in such manner, as without those external impediments they would. But when the impediment of motion, is in the constitution of the thing itself, we use not to say; it wants the liberty; but the power to move; as when a stone lieth still, or a man is fastened to his bed by sickness.

And according to this proper, and generally received meaning of the word, a FREEMAN, *is he, that in those things, which by his strength and wit he is able to do, is not hindered to do what he has a will to.* But when the words *free*, and *liberty*, are applied to any thing but bodies, they are abused; for that which is not subject to motion is not subject to impediment: and therefore, when it is said, for example, the way is free, no liberty of the way is signified, but of those that walk in it without stop. And when we say a gift is free, there is not meant any liberty of the gift, but of the giver, that was not bound by any law or covenant to give it. So when we *speak freely*, it is not the liberty of voice, or pronunciation, but of the man, whom no law hath obliged to speak otherwise than he did. Lastly, from the use of the word *free-will*, no liberty can be inferred of the will, desire, or inclination, but the liberty of the man; which consisteth in this, that he finds no stop, in doing what he has the will, desire, or inclination to do.

Fear and liberty are consistent; as when a man throweth his goods into the sea for *fear* the ship should sink, he doth it nevertheless very willingly, and may refuse to do it if he will; it is therefore the action of one that was *free:* so a man sometimes pays his debt, only for *fear* of imprisonment, which because nobody hindered him from detaining, was the action of a man at *liberty*. And generally all actions which men do in commonwealths, for *fear* of the law, are actions, which the doers had *liberty* to omit.

Liberty, and *necessity* are consistent: as in the water, that hath not only *liberty*, but a *necessity* of descending by the channel; so likewise in the actions which men voluntarily do: which, because they proceed from their will, proceed from *liberty;* and yet, because every act of man's will, and every desire, and inclination proceedeth from some cause, and that from another cause, in a continual chain, whose first link is in the hand of God the first of all causes, proceed from *necessity.* So that to him that could see the connexion of those causes, the *necessity* of all men's voluntary actions, would appear manifest. And therefore God, that seeth, and disposeth all things, seeth also that the liberty of man in doing what he will, is accompanied with the *necessity* of doing that which God will, and no more, nor less. For though men may do many things, which God does not command, nor is therefore author of them; yet they can have no passion, nor appetite to anything, of which appetite God's will is not the cause. And did not his will assure the *necessity* of man's will, and consequently of all that on man's will dependeth, the *liberty* of men would be a contradiction, and impediment to the omnipotence and *liberty* of God. And this shall suffice, as to the matter in hand, of that natural *liberty*, which only is properly called *liberty*.

But as men, for the attaining of peace, and conservation of themselves thereby, have made an artificial man, which we call a commonwealth; so also have they made artificial chains, called *civil laws*, which they themselves, by mutual covenants, have fastened at one end, to the lips of that man, or assembly, to whom they have given the sovereign power; and at the other end to their own ears. These bonds, in their own nature but weak, may nevertheless be made to hold, by the danger, though not by the difficulty of breaking them.

In relation to these bonds only it is, that I am to speak now, of the *liberty* of *subjects*. For seeing there is no commonwealth in the world, wherein there be rules enough set down, for the regulating of all the actions, and words of men; as being a thing impossible: it followeth necessarily, that in all kinds of actions by the laws praetermitted, men have the liberty, of doing what their own reasons shall suggest, for the most profitable to themselves. For if we take liberty in the proper sense, for corporal liberty; that is to say, freedom from chains and prison; it were very absurd for men to clamour as they do, for the liberty they so manifestly enjoy. Again, if we take liberty, for an exemption from laws, it is no less absurd, for men to demand as they do, that liberty, by which all other men may be masters of their lives. And yet, as absurd as it is, this is it they demand; not knowing that the laws are of no power to protect them, without a sword in the hands of a man, or men, to cause those laws to be put in execution. The liberty of a subject, lieth therefore only in those things, which in regulating their actions, the sovereign hath praetermitted: such as is the liberty to buy, and sell, and otherwise contract with one another; to choose their own abode, their own diet, their own trade of life, and institute their children as they themselves think fit; and the like.

Nevertheless we are not to understand, that by such liberty, the sovereign power of life and death, is either abolished, or limited. For it has been already shown, that nothing the sovereign representative can do to a subject, on what pretence soever, can properly be called injustice, or injury; because every subject is author of every act the sovereign doth; so that he never wanteth right to anything, otherwise, than as he himself is the subject of God, and bound thereby to observe the laws of nature. And therefore it may, and doth often happen in commonwealths, that a subject may be put to death, by the command of the sovereign power; and yet neither do the other wrong; as when Jephtha caused his daughter to be sacrificed: in which, and the like cases, he that so dieth, had liberty to do the action, for which he is nevertheless, without injury put to death. And the same holdeth also in a sovereign prince, that putteth to death an innocent subject. For though the action be against the law of nature, as being contrary to equity, as was the killing of Uriah, by David; yet it was not an injury to Uriah, but to God. Not to Uriah, because the right to do what he pleased was given him by Uriah himself: and yet to God, because David was God's subject, and prohibited all iniquity by the law of nature: which distinction, David himself, when he repented the fact, evidently confirmed, saying, *To thee only have I sinned.* In the same manner, the people of Athens, when they banished the most potent of their commonwealth for ten years, thought they committed no injustice; and yet they never questioned what crime he had done; but what hurt he would do: nay they commanded the banishment of they knew not whom; and every citizen bringing his oystershell into the market place, written with the name of him he desired should be banished, without actually accusing him, sometimes banished an Aristides, for his reputation of justice; and sometimes a scurrilous jester, as Hyperbolus, to make a jest of it. And yet a man cannot say, the sovereign people of Athens wanted right to banish them; or an Athenian the liberty to jest, or to be just. . . . .

But it is an easy thing, for men to be deceived, by the specious name of liberty; and for want of judgment to distinguish, mistake that for their private inheritance, and birth-right, which is the right of the public only. And when the same error is confirmed by the authority of men in reputation for their writings on this subject, it is no wonder if it produce sedition, and change of government. In these western parts of the world, we are made to receive our opinions concerning the institution, and rights of commonwealths, from Aristotle, Cicero, and other men, Greeks and Romans, that living under popular states, derived those rights, not from the principles of nature, but transcribed them into their books, out of the practice of their own commonwealths, which were popular; as the grammarians describe the rules of language, out of the practice of the time; or the rules of poetry, out of the poems of Homer and Virgil. And because the Athenians were taught, to keep them from desire of changing their government, that they were freemen, and all that lived under monarchy were slaves; therefore Aristotle puts it down in his *Politics*, (*lib. 6. cap.* ii.) *In democracy*, LIBERTY *is to be supposed: for it is commonly held, that no man is* FREE *in any other government.* And as Aristotle; so Cicero, and other writers have grounded their civil doctrine, on the opinions of the Romans, who were taught to hate monarchy, at first, by them that having deposed their sovereign, shared amongst them the sovereignty of Rome; and afterwards by their successors. And by reading of these Greek, and Latin authors, men from their childhood have gotten a habit, under a false show of liberty, of favouring tumults, and of licentious controlling the actions of their sovereigns, and again of controlling those controllers; with the effusion of so much blood, as I think I may truly say, there was never any thing so dearly bought, as these western parts have bought the learning of the Greek and Latin tongues.

To come now to the particulars of the true liberty of a subject; that is to say, what are the things, which though commanded by the sovereign, he may nevertheless, without injustice, refuse to do; we are to consider, what rights we pass away, when we make a commonwealth; or, which is all one, what liberty we deny ourselves, by owning all the actions, without exception, of the man, or assembly, we make our sovereign. For in the act of our *submission*, consisteth both our *obligation*, and our *liberty;* which must therefore be inferred by arguments taken from thence; there being no obligation on any man, which ariseth not from some act of his own; for all men equally, are by nature free. And because such arguments, must either be drawn from the express words, *I authorize all his actions*, or from the intention of him that submitteth himself to his power, which intention is to be understood by the end for which he so submitteth; the obligation, and liberty of the subject, is to be derived, either from those words, or others equivalent; or else from the end of the institution of sovereignty, namely, the peace of the subjects within themselves, and their defence against a common enemy.

First therefore, seeing sovereignty by institution, is by covenant of every one to every one; and sovereignty by acquisition, by covenants of the vanquished to the victor, or child to the parent; it is manifest, that every subject has liberty in all those things, the right whereof cannot by covenant be transferred. I have shewn before in the 14th chapter, that covenants, not to defend a man's own body, are void. Therefore,

If the sovereign command a man, though justly condemned, to kill, wound, or maim himself; or not to resist those that assault him; or to abstain from the use of food, air, medicine, or any other thing, without which he cannot live; yet hath that man the liberty to disobey.

If a man be interrogated by the sovereign, or his authority, concerning a crime done by himself, he is not bound, without assurance of pardon, to confess it; because no man, as I have shown in the same chapter, can be obliged by covenant to accuse himself.

Again, the consent of a subject to sovereign power, is contained in these words, *I authorize, or take upon me, all his actions;* in which there is no restriction at all, of his own former natural liberty: for by allowing him to *kill me,* I am not bound to kill myself when he commands me. It is one thing to say, *kill me, or my fellow, if you please;* another thing to say, *I will kill myself, or my fellow.* It followeth therefore, that

No man is bound by the words themselves, either to kill himself, or any other man; and consequently, that the obligation a man may sometimes have, upon the command of the sovereign to execute any dangerous, or dishonourable office, dependeth not on the words of our submission; but on the intention, which is to be understood by the end thereof. When therefore our refusal to obey, frustrates the end for which the sovereignty was ordained; then there is no liberty to refuse: otherwise there is.

Upon this ground, a man that is commanded as a soldier to fight against the enemy, though his sovereign have right enough to punish his refusal with death, may nevertheless in many cases refuse, without injustice; as when he substituteth a sufficient soldier in his place: for in this case he deserteth not the service of the commonwealth. And there is allowance to be made for natural timorousness; not only to women, of whom no such dangerous duty is expected, but also to men of feminine courage. When armies fight, there is on one side, or both, a running away; yet when they do it not out of treachery, but fear, they are not esteemed to do it unjustly, but dishonourably. For the same reason, to avoid battle, is not injustice, but cowardice. But he that inrolleth himself a soldier, or taketh imprest money, taketh away the excuse of a timorous nature; and is obliged, not only to go to the battle, but also not to run from it, without his captain's leave. And when the defence of the commonwealth, requireth at once the help of all that are able to bear arms, every one is obliged; because otherwise the institution of the commonwealth, which they have not the purpose, or courage to preserve, was in vain.

To resist the sword of the commonwealth, in defence of another man, guilty, or innocent, no man hath liberty; because such liberty, takes away from the sovereign, the means of protecting us; and is therefore destructive of the very essence of government. But in case a great many men together, have already resisted the sovereign power unjustly, or committed some capital crime, for which every one of them expecteth death, whether have they not the liberty then to join together, and assist, and defend one another? Certainly they have: for they but defend their lives, which the guilty man may as well do, as the innocent. There was indeed injustice in the first breach of their duty; their bearing of arms subsequent to it, though it be to maintain what they have done, is no new unjust act. And if it be only to defend their persons, it is not unjust at all. But the offer of pardon taketh from them, to whom it is offered, the plea of self-defence, and maketh their perseverance in assisting, or defending the rest, unlawful.

As for other liberties, they depend on the silence of the law. In cases where the sovereign has prescribed no rule, there the subject hath the liberty to do, or forbear, according to his own discretion. And therefore such liberty is in some places more, and in some less; and in some times more, in other times less, according as they that have the sovereignty shall think most convenient. As for example, there was a time, when in England a man might enter into his own land, and dispossess such as wrongfully possessed it, by force. But in after times, that liberty of forcible entry, was taken away by a statute made, by the king, in parliament. And in some places of the world, men have the liberty of many wives: in other places, such liberty is not allowed. . . . .

The obligation of subjects to the sovereign, is understood to last as long, and no longer, than the power lasteth, by which he is able to protect them. For the right men have by nature to protect themselves, when none else can protect them, can by no covenant be relinquished. The sovereignty is the soul of the commonwealth; which once departed from the body, the members do no more receive their motion from it. The end of obedience is protection; which, wheresoever a man seeth it, either in his own, or in another's sword, nature applieth his obedience to it, and his endeavour to maintain it. And though sovereignty, in the intention of them that make it, be immortal; yet it is in its own nature, not only subject to violent death, by foreign war; but also through the ignorance, and passions of men, it hath in it, from the very institution, many seeds of a natural mortality, by intestine discord. . . . .

CHAPTER XXIX. OF THOSE THINGS THAT WEAKEN, OR TEND TO THE DISSOLUTION OF A COMMONWEALTH

Though nothing can be immortal, which mortals make; yet, if men had the use of reason they pretend to, their commonwealths might be secured, at least from perishing by internal diseases. For by the nature of their institution, they are designed to live, as long as mankind, or as the laws of nature, or as justice itself, which gives them life. Therefore when they come to be dissolved, not by external violence, but intestine disorder, the fault is not in men, as they are the *matter*; but as they are the *makers*, and orderers of them. For men, as they become at last weary of irregular jostling, and hewing one another, and desire with all their hearts, to conform themselves into one firm and lasting edifice: so for want, both of the art of making fit laws, to square their actions by, and also of humility, and patience, to suffer the rude and cumbersome points of their present greatness to be taken off, they cannot without the help of a very able architect, be compiled into any other than a crazy building, such as hardly lasting out their own time, must assuredly fall upon the heads of their posterity.

Amongst the *infirmities* therefore of a commonwealth, I will reckon in the first place, those that arise from an imperfect institution, and resemble the diseases of a natural body, which proceed from a defectuous procreation.

Of which, this is one, *that a man to obtain a kingdom, is some-*

times content with less power, than to the peace, and defence of the commonwealth is necessarily required. From whence it cometh to pass, that when the exercise of the power laid by, is for the public safety to be resumed, it hath the resemblance of an unjust act; which disposeth great numbers of men, when occasion is presented to rebel; in the same manner as the bodies of children, gotten by diseased parents, are subject either to untimely death, or to purge the ill quality, derived from their vicious conception, by breaking out into biles and scabs. And when kings deny themselves some such necessary power, it is not always, though sometimes, out of ignorance of what is necessary to the office they undertake; but many times out of a hope to recover the same again at their pleasure. Wherein they reason not well; because such as will hold them to their promises, shall be maintained against them by foreign commonwealths; who in order to the good of their own subjects let slip few occasions to *weaken* the estate of their neighbours. So was Thomas Becket, Archbishop of Canterbury, supported against Henry the Second, by the Pope; the subjection of ecclesiastics to the commonwealth, having been dispensed with by William the Conqueror at his reception, when he took an oath, not to infringe the liberty of the church. And so were the barons, whose power was by William Rufus, to have their help in transferring the succession from his elder brother to himself, increased to a degree inconsistent with the sovereign power, maintained in their rebellion against king John, by the French.

Nor does this happen in monarchy only. For whereas the style of the ancient Roman commonwealth was, *the senate and people of Rome;* neither senate, nor people pretended to the whole power; which first caused the seditions, of Tiberius Gracchus, Caius Gracchus, Lucius Saturninus, and others; and afterwards the wars between the senate and the people, under Marius and Sylla; and again under Pompey and Caesar, to the extinction of their democracy, and the setting up of monarchy.

The people of Athens bound themselves but from one only action; which was, that no man on pain of death should propound the renewing of the war for the island of Salamis; and yet thereby, if Solon had not caused to be given out he was mad, and afterwards in gesture and habit of a madman, and in verse, propounded it to the people that flocked about him, they had had an enemy perpetually in readiness, even at the gates of their city; such damage, or shifts, are all commonwealths forced to, that have their power never so little limited.

In the second place, I observe the *diseases* of a commonwealth, that proceed from the poison of seditious doctrines, whereof one is, *That every private man is judge of good and evil actions*. This is true in the condition of mere nature, where there are no civil laws; and also under civil government, in such cases as are not determined by the law. But otherwise, it is manifest, that the measure of good and evil actions, is the civil law; and the judge the legislator, who is always representative of the commonwealth. From this false doctrine, men are disposed to debate with themselves, and dispute the commands of the commonwealth; and afterwards to obey, or disobey them, as in their private judgments they shall think fit; whereby the commonwealth is distracted and *weakened*.

Another doctrine repugnant to civil society, is, that *whatsoever a man does against his conscience, is sin;* and it dependeth on the presumption of making himself judge of good and evil. For a man's conscience, and his judgment is the same thing, and as the judgment, so also the conscience may be erroneous. Therefore, though he that is subject to no civil law, sinneth in all he does against his conscience, because he has no other rule to follow but his own reason; yet it is not so with him that lives in a commonwealth; because the law is the public conscience, by which he hath already undertaken to be guided. Otherwise in such diversity, as there is of private consciences, which are but private opinions, the commonwealth must needs be distracted, and no man dare to obey the sovereign power, further than it shall seem good in his own eyes.

It hath also been commonly taught, *that faith and sanctity, are not to be attained by study and reason, but by supernatural inspiration, or infusion*. Which granted, I see not why any man should render a reason of his faith; or why every Christian should not be also a prophet; or why any man should take the law of his country, rather than his own inspiration, for the rule of his action. And thus we fall again in the fault of taking upon us to judge of good and evil; or to make judges of it, such private men as pretend to be supernaturally inspired, to the dissolution of all civil government.

Faith comes by hearing, and hearing by those accidents, which guide us into the presence of them that speak to us; which accidents are all contrived by God Almighty; and yet are not supernatural, but only, for the great number of them that concur to every effect, unobservable. Faith and sanctity, are indeed not very frequent; but yet they are not miracles, but brought to pass by education, discipline, correction, and other natural ways, by which God worketh them in his elect, at such times as he thinketh fit. And these three opinions, pernicious to peace and government, have in this part of the world, proceeded chiefly from the tongues, and pens of unlearned divines, who joining the words of Holy Scripture together, otherwise than is agreeable to reason, do what they can, to make men think, that sanctity and natural reason, cannot stand together.

A fourth opinion, repugnant to the nature of a commonwealth, is that, *that he that hath the sovereign power is subject to the civil laws*. It is true, that sovereigns are all subject to the laws of nature; because such laws be divine, and cannot by any man, or commonwealth be abrogated. But to those laws which the sovereign himself, that is, which the commonwealth maketh, he is not subject. For to be subject to laws, is to be subject to the commonwealth, that is to the sovereign representative, that is to himself; which is not subjection, but freedom from the laws. Which error, because it setteth the laws above the sovereign, setteth also a judge above him, and a power to punish him; which is to make a new sovereign; and again for the same reason a third, to punish the second; and so continually without end, to the confusion and dissolution of the commonwealth.

A fifth doctrine, that tendeth to the dissolution of a commonwealth, is, *that every private man has an absolute propriety in his goods; such, as excludeth the right of the sovereign*. Every man has indeed a propriety that excludes the right of every other subject: and he has it only from the sovereign power; without the protection whereof, every other man should have equal right to the same. But if the right of the sovereign also be excluded, he cannot perform the office they have put him into; which is, to defend them both from foreign enemies, and from the injuries of one another; and consequently there is no longer a commonwealth.

And if the propriety of subjects, exclude not the right of the sovereign representative to their goods; much less to their offices of judicature, or execution, in which they represent the sovereign himself.

There is a sixth doctrine, plainly, and directly against the essence of a commonwealth; and it is this, *that the sovereign power may be divided*. For what is it to divide the power of a commonwealth, but to dissolve it; for powers divided mutually destroy each other. And for these doctrines, men are chiefly beholding to some of those, that making profession of the laws, endeavour to make them depend upon their own learning, and not upon the legislative power.

And as false doctrine, so also oftentimes the example of different government in a neighbouring nation, disposeth men to alteration of the form already settled. So the people of the Jews were stirred up to reject God, and to call upon the prophet Samuel, for a king after the manner of the nations: so also the lesser cities of Greece, were continually disturbed, with seditions of the aristocratical, and democratical factions; one part of almost every commonwealth, desiring to imitate the Lacedemonians; the other, the Athenians. And I doubt not, but many men have been contented to see the late troubles in England, out of an imitation of the Low Countries; supposing there needed no more to grow rich, than to change, as they had done, the form of their government. For the constitution of man's nature, is of itself subject to desire novelty. When therefore they are provoked to the same, by the neighbourhood also of those that have been enriched by it, it is almost impossible for them, not to be content with those that solicit them to change; and love the first beginnings, though they be grieved with the continuance of disorder; like hot bloods, that having gotten the itch, tear themselves with their own nails, till they can endure the smart no longer.

And as to rebellion in particular against monarchy; one of the most frequent causes of it, is the reading of the books of policy, and histories of the ancient Greeks, and Romans; from which, young men, and all others that are unprovided of the antidote of solid reason, receiving a strong, and delightful impression, of the great exploits of war, achieved by the conductors of their armies, receive withal a pleasing idea, of all they have done besides; and imagine their great prosperity, not to have proceeded from the emulation of particular men, but from the virtue of their popular form of government: not considering the frequent seditions, and civil wars, produced by the imperfection of their policy. From the reading, I say, of such books, men have undertaken to kill their kings, because the Greek and Latin writers, in their books, and discourses of policy, make it lawful, and laudable, for any man so to do; provided, before he do it, he call him tyrant. For they say not *regicide*, that is, killing a king, but *tyrannicide*, that is, killing of a tyrant is lawful. From the same books, they that live under a monarch conceive an opinion, that the subjects in a popular commonwealth enjoy liberty; but that in a monarchy they are all slaves. I say, they that live under a monarchy conceive such an opinion; not that they live under a popular government: for they find no such matter. In sum, I cannot imagine, how anything can be more prejudicial to a monarchy, than the allowing of such books to be publicly read, without present applying such correctives of discreet masters, as are fit to take away their venom: which venom I will not doubt to compare to the biting of a mad dog, which is a disease the physicians call *hydrophobia*, or *fear of water*. For as he that is so bitten, has a continual torment of thirst, and yet abhorreth water; and is in such an estate, as if the poison endeavoured to convert him into a dog: so when a monarchy is once bitten to the quick, by those democratical writers, that continually snarl at that estate; it wanteth nothing more than a strong monarch, which nevertheless out of a certain *tyrannophobia*, or fear of being strongly governed, when they have him, they abhor.

As there have been doctors, that hold there be three souls in a man; so there be also that think there may be more souls, that is, more sovereigns, than one, in a commonwealth; and set up a *supremacy* against the *sovereignty; canons* against *laws;* and a *ghostly authority* against the *civil;* working on men's minds, with words and distinctions, that of themselves signify nothing, but bewray by their obscurity; that there walketh, as some think, invisibly another kingdom, as it were a kingdom of fairies, in the dark. Now seeing it is manifest, that the civil power, and the power of the commonwealth is the same thing; and that supremacy, and the power of making canons, and granting faculties, implieth a commonwealth; it followeth, that where one is sovereign, another supreme; where one can make laws, and another make canons;

there must needs be two commonwealths, of one and the same subjects; which is a kingdom divided in itself, and cannot stand.....

Sometimes also in the merely civil government, there be more than one soul; as when the power of levying money, which is the nutritive faculty, has depended on a general assembly; the power of conduct and command, which is the motive faculty, on one man; and the power of making laws, which is the rational faculty, on the accidental consent, not only of those two, but also of a third; this endangereth the commonwealth, sometimes for want of consent to good laws: but most often for want of such nourishment, as is necessary to life, and motion. For although few perceive, that such government, is not government, but division of the commonwealth into three factions, and call it mixed monarchy; yet the truth is, that it is not one independent commonwealth, but three independent factions; nor one representative person, but three. . . . .

Hitherto I have named such diseases of a commonwealth, as are of the greatest, and most present danger. There be other not so great; which nevertheless are not unfit to be observed. As first, the difficulty of raising money. . . . . Again, ... when the treasure of the commonwealth, flowing out of its due course, is gathered together in too much abundance, in one, or a few private men, by monopolies, or by farms of the public revenues. . . . . Also the popularity of a potent subject, unless the commonwealth have very good caution of his fidelity, is a dangerous disease. . . . . Another infirmity of a commonwealth, is the immoderate greatness of a town, when it is able to furnish out of its own circuit, the number, and expense of a great army. . . . . To which may be added, the liberty of disputing against absolute power, by pretenders to political prudence; which though bred for the most part in the lees of the people, yet animated by false doctrines, are perpetually meddling with the fundamental laws, to the molestation of the commonwealth; like the little worms, which physicians call *ascarides*. . . . . We may further add, the insatiable appetite, or βουλιμια, of enlarging dominion. . . . .

Lastly, when in a war, foreign or intestine, the enemies get a final victory; so as, the forces of the commonwealth keeping the field no longer, there is no further protection of the subjects in their loyalty; then is the commonwealth DISSOLVED, and every man at liberty to protect himself by such courses as his own discretion shall suggest unto him. For the sovereign is the public soul, giving life and motion to the commonwealth; which expiring, the members are governed by it no more, than the carcase of a man, by his departed, though immortal, soul. For though the right of a sovereign monarch cannot be extinguished by the act of another; yet the obligation of the members may. For he that wants protection, may seek it any where; and when he hath it, is obliged, without fraudulent pretence of having submitted himself out of fear, to protect his protection as long as he is able. But when the power of an assembly is once suppressed, the right of the same perisheth utterly; because the assembly is itself extinct; and consequently, there is no possibility for the sovereignty to re-enter.

CHAPTER III

BENEDICTUS DE SPINOZA

Baruch or Benedict Spinoza (born 1632) was during his youth a member of the Spanish and Portuguese Jewish community in Amsterdam. Here he received a thorough training in Hebrew literature and Jewish philosophy; but his zeal for study led him further to explore the literature of the "priests' language," Latin. It was probably through his Latin teacher that he first met the new physical science and the writings of Descartes. For these explorations and for his more and more heretical opinions, Spinoza was publicly excommunicated in 1656. Henceforth he lived in various quiet villages in the Netherlands, and finally in the Hague, devoting himself to philosophic study and living by the trade of lens-grinding, which he had learned in accordance with Jewish custom. He maintained an extensive correspondence on philosophical subjects with men like Oldenburg and Tschirnhausen, and in 1665 he interrupted his work on the *Ethics* to write an impassioned defense of free speech (*Theological Political Treatise* [1670]) in support of the liberal party headed by his good friend Jan De Witt. In 1673 Spinoza rejected the offer of the professorship of philosophy at Heidelberg, finding himself unwilling to relinquish his retirement for the claims of teaching and fearful of the restrictions on freedom of speech involved in such a position. So he lived on quietly in The Hague until his death from consumption in 1677. Chief works: Completed: *Principles of Descartes' Philosophy* and *Metaphysical Thoughts* (1663); *Theological Political Treatise* (1670); *Ethics* (first published in 1677); *Short Treatise concerning God, Man and His Well-Being* (first published in 1862); Fragments: *On the Improvement of the Understanding, Political Treatise, Hebrew Grammar* (all published in 1677). Suggested readings: *Chief Works*, trans. Elwes (London, 1887–91, 1906–8); *Selections*, ed. Wild (New York and Chicago, 1930); *Correspondence*, trans. A. Wolf (New York, 1928); *Principles of Descartes' Philosophy* (Chicago, 1905). Samuel Alexander, *Spinoza and Time* (London, 1921); H. H. Joachim, *A Study in the Ethics of Spinoza* (Oxford, 1901); A. O. Lovejoy, *The Dialectic of Bruno and Spinoza* ("University of California Publications," Vol. I [Berkeley, 1904]); J. M. Lucas, *Oldest Biography of Spinoza*, ed. Wolf (New York, 1927); R. P. McKeon, *The Philosophy of Spinoza* (New York, 1927), and "Causation and the Geometric Method in the Philosophy of Spinoza," *Philosophical Review*, XXXIX (1930), 178 and 275; J. Martineau, *A Study of Spinoza* (London, 1895); Sir Frederick Pollock, *Spinoza: His Life and Philosophy* (London, 1880); H. A. Wolfson, *The Philosophy of Spinoza* (2 vols.; Cambridge, Mass., 1934).

IN HIS correspondence with Oldenburg, as we have noticed above, Spinoza insisted on the importance for science of the rational understanding of principles as opposed to the imaginative grasp of particulars in observation. That insistence, like the desideratum of a "universal mathematics" in Descartes, forms the keystone of Spinoza's thought. But Spinoza carried out more rigidly than Descartes had done the consequences of this fundamental principle.[1] For Descartes, all the mind clearly and distinctly apprehends is true: that belief is the cardinal principle of his philosophy. It expresses the faith that human reasoning inevitably indicates the real structure of the world. If that is so, however, the world itself must be a logical system, in which events follow from laws as conclusions from premises. Yet Descartes does not complete the inference which his own principle suggests. In the first place, he cannot quite bring himself consistently to maintain the rationalistic principle as ultimate. A knowledge of God's goodness has to guarantee our faith in clear and distinct ideas against the possibility of a *deus deceptor*. And that means, in the second place, that the causal structure of the world depends finally on the inscrutable purposes of God, to which human logic cannot apply. In Descartes's universe, in other words, final cause is more basic than formal. Even the mechanical causes which we study in physics, moreover, depend for their efficacy upon the continually repeated intervention of God. Each moment of time, according to Descartes, is independent of the preceding; and God, again out of his inscrutable goodness, must recreate the world at every moment to keep it running. Thus efficient as well as final or formal cause enters into the Cartesian world-scheme, but efficient like formal cause is dependent upon the purposes of a beneficent creator. Here again, however, Spinoza sets aside Descartes's hesitancy to carry out the inference from his own premises. Spinoza denies altogether the existence of final causes, attributing the use of such concepts to superstition and ignorance. Efficient cause he likewise subordinates to formal. He describes the world, indeed, as a huge concatenation of determined causes and effects. If understood in its entirety, however, this chain of

[1] Although Spinoza is presented here in comparison with Descartes, it should be remembered that he formulated his views through careful amplification and refutation of many of his earlier predecessors as well. The vast wealth of medieval material that forms the foundation for the structure of the *Ethics* is examined by Professor Wolfson in his *Philosophy of Spinoza* (Cambridge, Mass., 1934).

mechanically determined events loses the aspects of a temporal succession. It appears as a timeless, logical system, in which the only causal relation is the logical one of ground and consequent. To know nature, for Spinoza, is to know it "under the aspect of eternity," that is, under the aspect of logic, as a huge theory, in which every tiniest event follows rigorously as a conclusion from the totality of all events as its premise.

Again, Descartes established three substances in his world: two finite substances, thinking and extended; and one infinite thinking substance, God. But in defining substance in the *Replies to Objections* he admits that the term cannot be applied univocally to God and to created substance. Substance is what exists independently; but ultimately only God has independent existence. It seems to follow, then, that, although we call both finite and infinite beings "substance," the name really belongs only to the infinite substance, God. That, at least, was the conclusion drawn by Spinoza. For him there is only one, infinite substance, of which finite things are modifications. The one substance, moreover, has infinite attributes, of which we know two: thought and extension. We may consider nature (or God) as a thinking substance, modified in an infinite set of modifications; or as an extended substance, modified in an infinite set of modifications. The "modes" (i.e., modifications or affections) by which either attribute is modified—i.e., the modes which follow from either attribute are immediate infinite modes, mediate infinite modes, and finite modes. The immediate infinite mode of extension is motion and rest, of thought the absolutely infinite intellect. The only mediate infinite mode Spinoza explicitly mentions is "the face of the whole universe," and he does not state definitely whether this mode belongs to one attribute or both. Particular things, finally, are finite modes. Thus my mind, for example, is a finite modification of God, considered under the attribute of thought; and my body is the very same modification of God, considered under the attribute of extension. Spinoza calls the mind the *idea* of the body; and, conversely, the body is the correlate, under extension, of the mind. But that is only to say that mind and body are the same thing viewed under two different aspects, and both are modifications of the one substance, God.

It is on this foundation that Spinoza builds his ideal of human happiness. For him, as for the Stoics, it is only "accordance with reason" that can afford freedom to man. A man's mind is the sum total of his ideas, each of which is a modification of substance under the attribute of thought—each of which, that is, is contained in substance as thinking, in the mind of God. To each such idea corresponds the same modification considered as an affection of the body—considered under the attribute of extension, or as a modification of God in so far as he is extended substance. Now the series of ideas throughout nature (like the series of bodily affections) have infinite concatenations with one another. Therefore, most of the ideas in an individual mind are contained in God's mind (i.e., in the totality of nature as thinking substance) in intimate connection with many ideas beyond the content of that particular finite mind, just as the affections of which they are ideas are expressed in God in his character of extended substance in connection with other bodily modifications. Or, as Spinoza puts it, such ideas are contained in God's mind, not in so far as he forms the essence of the human mind alone, but of other minds as well. They are therefore said by Spinoza to be in the human mind *inadequate*, that is, insufficient or incomplete. For instance, if a body A strikes a body B, then the idea of A-striking-B will be contained in God's mind is so far as his mind contains the ideas of bodies A and B, that is (since the mind is the idea of the body), in so far as he forms the essence of the minds of A and B. But A's mind is the idea only of body A, not of B. Therefore the idea of A-striking-B is contained in A's mind only partially or inadequately in comparison with the total idea as contained in the mind of God. Such is the situation with regard to most of our ideas. If, however, one can find some ideas corresponding to bodily modifications which are complete in the smallest part of every body, then a mind containing the ideas of those modifications will contain them completely, or, in other words, they will be contained in God's mind in so far as he forms the essence of the human mind alone; or they will be in the human mind complete or adequate. The adequate ideas mentioned by Spinoza are extension, rest, and motion. The human mind conceives its adequate ideas, then, completely, not partially or in dependence on ideas beyond itself. In so far as it contains such ideas, therefore, the human mind is self-sufficient, independent, *free*. In so far as we have inadequate ideas, Spinoza says, we suffer and are the slaves of desire;[2] in so far as we have adequate ideas, our emotions are correspondingly rational, and we may be said to act. But the completeness with which the human mind conceives adequate ideas is the very same completeness—the same truth—with which they are conceived in God's mind. And thus the human mind in understanding adequate ideas understands God—understands, in other words, one aspect of the whole rational system which is God or nature. By inadequate ideas we see things as beyond one another, stretched out incompletely, in duration. But in adequate knowledge we conceive ideas as they actually are in God's mind: in their place in an eternal, rational system. By such vision, therefore, the individual sees his own place as a finite modification in the totality of nature and at the same time understands the character of that totality itself. By such vision man achieves freedom for himself and with it his highest happiness: the intellectual love of God.

The same contrast between the bondage of desire and the freedom of reason marks Spinoza's political philosophy.

[2] Thus that part of the *Ethics* in which Spinoza discusses the passions is called "Of Human Bondage." Spinoza, like Hobbes, explains the passions in terms of the "endeavor" of each individual thing to maintain itself throughout an indefinite duration. He considers the fundamental passions to be three: desire, joy, and sorrow.

Thus in the *Politico-Theological Tractate* his aim is to defend freedom of thought and speech—to show that it is not only harmless but in the long run actually indispensable to government. But this he does, oddly enough, on the basis of a view of natural right and of the powers of constituted authority strikingly like that of Hobbes. As for Hobbes, in the first place, right is for Spinoza more basic than law—at least than law in the sense of standard or obligation. The right of any being in its natural state is simply coextensive with its power. It endeavors in its own way to preserve itself, and its right so to do is unlimited, or limited only by its capacity to make its aim effective. The "law" it follows in this course, moreover, is not an obligation which, like a civil law, it may or may not obey. It is simply the actual way the being in question naturally operates, involving no question of good or bad, ought or ought not. Now, of course, men living in this forthright natural state, governed by the desire to continue living, and exercising now and then some glimmering of reason, observe that their state would be more secure if, for their own mutual advantage, they formed a civil body. This they do, in Hobbesian fashion, by giving over their rights absolutely to a supreme authority—although for Spinoza the democratic form, as resigning least of natural right, is the most desirable kind of government. In every form of state, however, the power of the supreme authority is, as for Hobbes, indivisible and absolute. There is no right and wrong in nature; such concepts are only introduced by the institution of the contractual relation in the state. Therefore justice is identical with legality; the sovereign laws cannot be wrong, since right *means* legal. Even sin is in this sense a matter for law to settle; so external forms of religious worship are to be determined by the state. So far Spinoza goes with Hobbes. But, both agree, the rights of sovereigns have one limit— their power. If a sovereign body does *not* actually preserve life and peace to some degree, the civil state dissolves and a state of nature reinsues. So a sovereign body can exercise its

right only while or in so far as it has power; where its effec-
tiveness ceases, it dies. But where, actually, does such effec-
tiveness cease? For Hobbes, to judge from some at least of
his statements, it would seem that a tyrant may be just as
effective as a more moderate ruler, once he educates his people to the proper sense that right is always his. Against this,
Spinoza insists on three definite limits to the sovereign power,
and hence to sovereign right (not of course limits for any
moral reason, but limits, he thinks, in actual fact). First, he
says in the *Political Treatise*, just as in the case of individuals,
so in civil matters, the state ruled by reason is the strongest
state. Secondly, the state cannot sanely command what cannot be induced: for example, there is no sense in commanding
people to believe the part greater than the whole—for they
simply won't believe it. Thirdly, the state cannot, without
signing its own death warrant, command what causes great
indignation in many quarters, and so conspiracy, and revolution. But now it appears, by virtue of these three factual
limitations on supreme political power, that, despite the
moral absoluteness of such power, liberty of thought and
speech are saved. By the second, we see that men's thoughts
cannot be commanded; by the third, that their speech, for
practical reasons, should not be. And by the first (the one
really un-Hobbesian principle), we understand that the
flourishing of the life of reason, which is the life of intellectual freedom, is after all the real keynote to the power
and independence of a state.

SELECTIONS FROM THE TREATISE *ON THE IM-PROVEMENT OF THE UNDERSTANDING*[3]

After experience has taught me that all the usual surroundings
of social life are vain and futile; seeing that none of the objects of
my fears contained in themselves anything either good or bad, except in so far as the mind is affected by them, I finally resolved to

[3] *The Chief Works of Benedict de Spinoza*, trans. from the Latin by R. H. M.
Elwes (London, 1887), II, 1 ff.

inquire whether there might be some real good having power to communicate itself, which would affect the mind singly, to the exclusion of all else; whether, in fact, there might be anything of which the discovery and attainment would enable me to enjoy continuous, supreme, and unending happiness. I say "I FINALLY resolved," for at first sight it seemed unwise willingly to lose hold on what was sure for the sake of something then uncertain. I could see the benefits which are acquired through fame and riches, and that I should be obliged to abandon the quest of such objects, if I seriously devoted myself to the search for something different and new. I perceived that if true happiness chanced to be placed in the former I should necessarily miss it; while if, on the other hand, it were not so placed, and I gave them my whole attention, I should equally fail.

I therefore debated whether it would not be possible to arrive at the new principle, or at any rate at a certainty concerning its existence, without changing the conduct and usual plan of my life; with this end in view I made many efforts, but in vain. For the ordinary surroundings of life which are esteemed by men (as their actions testify) to be the highest good, may be classed under the three heads—Riches, Fame, and the Pleasures of Sense: with these three the mind is so absorbed that it has little power to reflect on any different good. By sensual pleasure the mind is enthralled to the extent of quiescence, as if the supreme good were actually attained, so that it is quite incapable of thinking of any other object; when such pleasure has been gratified it is followed by extreme melancholy, whereby the mind, though not enthralled, is disturbed and dulled.

The pursuit of honors and riches is likewise very absorbing, especially if such objects be sought simply for their own sake, inasmuch as they are then supposed to constitute the highest good. In the case of fame the mind is still more absorbed, for fame is conceived as always good for its own sake, and as the ultimate end to which all actions are directed. Further, the attainment of riches and fame is not followed as in the case of sensual pleasures by repentance, but, the more we acquire, the greater is our delight, and, consequently, the more we are incited to increase both the one and the other; on the other hand, if our hopes happen to be frustrated we are plunged into the deepest sadness. Fame has the further drawback that it compels its votaries to order their lives according to the opinions of their fellow-men, shunning what they usually shun, and seeking what they usually seek.

When I saw that all these ordinary objects of desire would be obstacles in the way of a search for something different and new—nay, that they were so opposed thereto, that either they or it would have to be abandoned, I was forced to inquire which would prove the most useful to me: for, as I say, I seemed to be willingly losing hold on a sure good for the sake of something uncertain. However, after I had reflected on the matter, I came in the first place to the conclusion that by abandoning the ordinary objects of pursuit, and betaking myself to a new quest, I should be leaving a good, uncertain by reason of its own nature, as may be gathered from what has been said, for the sake of a good not uncertain in its nature (for I sought for a fixed good), but only in the possibility of its attainment.

Further reflection convinced me, that if I could really get to the root of the matter, I should be leaving certain evils for a certain good. I thus perceived that I was in a state of great peril, and I compelled myself to seek with all my strength for a remedy, however uncertain it might be; as a sick man struggling with a deadly disease, when he sees that death will surely be upon him unless a remedy be found, is compelled to seek such a remedy with all his strength, inasmuch as his whole hope lies therein. All the objects pursued by the multitude, not only bring no remedy that tends to preserve our being, but even act as hindrances, causing the death not seldom of those who possess them, and always of those who are possessed by them. There are many examples of men who have suffered persecution even to death for the sake of their riches, and of men who in pursuit of wealth have exposed themselves to so many dangers, that they have paid away their life as a penalty for their folly. Examples are no less numerous of men, who have endured the utmost wretchedness for the sake of gaining or preserving their reputation. Lastly, there are innumerable cases of men, who have hastened their death through over-indulgences in sensual pleasure. All these evils seem to have arisen from the fact, that happiness or unhappiness is made wholly to depend on the quality of the object which we love. When a thing is not loved, no quarrels will arise concerning it—no sadness will be felt if it perishes—no envy if it is possessed by another—no fear, no hatred, in short no disturbances of the mind. All these arise from the love of what is perishable, such as the objects already mentioned. But love toward a thing eternal and infinite feeds the mind wholly with joy, and is itself unmingled with any sadness, wherefore it is greatly to be desired and sought for with all our strength. Yet it was not at random that I used the words, "If I could go to the root of the matter," for, though what I have urged was perfectly clear to my mind, I could not forthwith lay aside all love of riches, sensual enjoyment, and fame. One thing was evident, namely, that while my mind was employed with these thoughts it turned away from its former objects of desire, and seriously considered the search for a new principle; this state of things was a great comfort to me, for I perceived that the evils were not such as to resist all remedies. Although these intervals were at first rare, and of very short duration, yet afterward, as the true good became more and more discernible to me, they became more frequent and more lasting; especially after I had recognized that the acquisition of wealth, sensual pleasure, or fame, is only a hindrance, so long as they are sought as ends not as means; if they be sought as means they will be under restraint, and, far from being hindrances, will further not a little the end for which they are sought, as I will show in due time.

I will here only briefly state what I mean by true good, and also what is the nature of the highest good. In order that this may be rightly understood, we must bear in mind that the terms good and evil are only applied relatively, so that the same thing may be called both good and bad, according to the relations in view, in the same way as it may be called perfect or imperfect. Nothing regarded in its own nature can be called perfect or imperfect; especially when we are aware that all things which come to pass, come to pass according to the eternal order and fixed laws of nature. However, human weakness cannot attain to this order in its own thoughts, but meanwhile man conceives a human character much more stable than his own, and sees that there is no reason why he should not himself acquire such a character. Thus he is led to seek for means which will bring him to this pitch of perfection, and calls everything which will serve as such means a true good. The chief good is that he should arrive, together with other individuals if possible, at the possession of the aforesaid character. What that character is we shall show in due time, namely, that it is the knowledge of the union existing between the mind and the whole of nature. This, then, is the end for which I strive, to attain to such a character myself, and to endeavor that many should attain to it with me. In other words, it is part of my happiness to lend a helping hand, that many others may understand even as I do, so that their understanding and desire may entirely agree with my own. In order to bring this about, it is necessary to understand as much of nature as will enable us to attain to the aforesaid character, and also to form a social order such as is most conducive to the attainment of this character by the greatest number with the least difficulty and danger. We must seek the assistance of Moral Philosophy[4] and the Theory of Education; further, as health is no insignificant means for attaining our end, we must also include the whole science of Medicine, and, as many difficult things are by contrivance rendered easy, and we can in this way gain much time and convenience, the science of Mechanics must in no way be despised. But, before all things, a means must be devised for improving the understanding and purifying it, as far as may be at the outset, so that it may apprehend things without error, and in the best possible way.

Thus it is apparent to every one that I wish to direct all sciences to one end and aim, so that we may attain to the supreme human perfection which we have named; and, therefore, whatsoever in the sciences does not serve to promote our object will have to be rejected as useless. To sum up the matter in a word, all our actions and thoughts must be directed to this one end. Yet, as it is necessary that while we are endeavoring to attain our purpose, and bring the understanding into the right path, we should carry on our life, we are compelled first of all to lay down certain rules of life as provisionally good, to wit, the following:

I. To speak in a manner intelligible to the multitude, and to comply with every general custom that does not hinder the attainment of our purpose. For we can gain from the multitude no small advantages, provided that we strive to accommodate ourselves to

---

[4] I do no more here than enumerate the sciences necessary for our purpose; I lay no stress on their order.

its understanding as far as possible: moreover, we shall in this way gain a friendly audience for the reception of the truth.

II. To indulge ourselves with pleasures only in so far as they are necessary for preserving health.

III. Lastly, to endeavor to obtain only sufficient money or other commodities to enable us to preserve our life and health, and to follow such general customs as are consistent with our purpose.

Having laid down these preliminary rules, I will betake myself to the first and most important task, namely, the amendment of the understanding, and the rendering it capable of understanding things in the manner necessary for attaining our end.

In order to bring this about, the natural order demands that I should here recapitulate all the modes of perception, which I have hitherto employed for affirming or denying anything with certainty, so that I may choose the best, and at the same time begin to know my own powers and the nature which I wish to perfect.

Reflection shows that all modes of perception or knowledge may be reduced to four:

I. Perception arising from hearsay or from some sign which everyone may name as he pleases.

II. Perception arising from mere experience—that is, from experience not yet classified by the intellect, and only so called because the given event has happened to take place, and we have no contradictory fact to set against it, so that it therefore remains unassailed in our mind.

III. Perception arising when the essence of one thing is inferred from another thing, but not adequately; this comes when from some effect we gather its cause, or when it is inferred from some general proposition that some property is always present.

IV. Lastly, there is the perception arising when a thing is perceived solely through its essence, or through the knowledge of its proximate cause.

All these kinds of perception I will illustrate by examples. By hearsay I know the day of my birth, my parentage, and other matters about which I have never felt any doubt. By mere experience I know that I shall die, for this I can affirm from having seen that others like myself have died, though all did not live for the same period, or die by the same disease. I know by mere experience that oil has the property of feeding fire, and water of extinguishing it. In the same way I know that a dog is a barking animal, man a rational animal, and in fact nearly all the practical knowledge of life.

We deduce one thing from another as follows: when we clearly perceive that we feel a certain body and no other, we thence clearly infer that the mind is united to the body, and that their union is the cause of the given sensation; but we cannot thence absolutely understand the nature of the sensation and the union. Or, after I have become acquainted with the nature of vision, and know that it has the property of making one and the same thing appear smaller when far off than when near, I can infer that the sun is larger than it appears, and can draw other conclusions of the same kind.

Lastly, a thing may be perceived solely through its essence; when, from the fact of knowing something, I know what it is to know that thing, or when, from knowing the essence of the mind, I know that it is united to the body. By the same kind of knowledge we know that two and three make five, or that two lines each parallel to a third, are parallel to one another, etc. The things which I have been able to know by this kind of knowledge are as yet very few.

In order that the whole matter may be put in a clearer light, I will make use of a single illustration as follows: Three numbers are given—it is required to find a fourth, which shall be to the third as the second is to the first. Tradesmen will at once tell us that they know what is required to find the fourth number, for they have not yet forgotten the rule which was given to them arbitrarily without proof by their masters; others construct a universal axiom from their experience with simple numbers, where the fourth number is self-evident, as in the case of 2, 4, 3, 6; here it is evident that if the second number be multiplied by the third, and the product divided by the first, the quotient is 6; when they see that by this process the number is produced which they knew beforehand to be the proportional, they infer that the process always holds good for finding a fourth number proportional. Mathematicians, however, know by the proof of the nineteenth proposition of the seventh book of Euclid, what numbers are proportionals, namely, from the nature and property of proportion it follows that the product of the first and fourth will be equal to the product of the second and third: still they do not see the adequate proportionality of the given numbers or, if they do see it, they see it not by virtue of Euclid's proposition, but intuitively, without going through any process.

In order that from these modes of perception the best may be selected, it is well that we should briefly enumerate the means necessary for attaining our end.

I. To have an exact knowledge of our nature which we desire to perfect, and to know as much as is needful of nature in general.

II. To collect in this way the differences, the agreements, and the oppositions of things.

III. To learn thus exactly how far they can or cannot be modified.

IV. To compare this result with the nature and power of man. We shall thus discern the highest degree of perfection to which man is capable of attaining. We shall then be in a position to see which mode of perception we ought to choose.

As to the first mode, it is evident that from hearsay our knowledge must always be uncertain, and, moreover, can give us no insight into the essence of a thing, as is manifest in our illustration; now one can only arrive at knowledge of a thing through knowledge of its essence, as will hereafter appear. We may, therefore, clearly conclude that the certainty arising from hearsay cannot be scientific in its character. For simple hearsay cannot affect anyone whose understanding does not, so to speak, meet it half way.

The second mode of perception[5] cannot be said to give us the idea of the proportion of which we are in search. Moreover its results are very uncertain and indefinite, for we shall never discover anything in natural phenomena by its means, except accidental properties, which are never clearly understood, unless the essence of the things in question be known first. Wherefore this mode also must be rejected.

On the third mode of perception we may say in a manner that it gives us the idea of the thing sought, and that it enables us to draw conclusions without risk of error; yet it is not by itself sufficient to put us in possession of the perfection we aim at.

The fourth mode alone apprehends the adequate essence of a

[5] I shall here treat a little more in detail of experience, and shall examine the method adopted by the Empirics, and by recent philosophers.

thing without danger of error. This mode, therefore, must be the one which we chiefly employ. How, then, should we avail ourselves of it so as to gain the fourth kind of knowledge with the least delay concerning things previously unknown? I will proceed to explain.

Now that we know what kind of knowledge is necessary for us, we must indicate the way and the method whereby we may gain the said knowledge concerning the things needful to be known. In order to accomplish this, we must first take care not to commit ourselves to a search, going back to infinity—that is, in order to discover the best method for finding out the truth, there is no need of another method to discover such method; nor of a third method for discovering the second, and so on to infinity. By such proceedings, we should never arrive at the knowledge of the truth, or, indeed, at any knowledge at all. The matter stands on the same footing as the making of material tools, which might be argued about in a similar way. For, in order to work iron, a hammer is needed, and the hammer cannot be forthcoming unless it has been made; but, in order to make it, there was need of another hammer and other tools, and so on to infinity. We might thus vainly endeavor to prove that men have no power of working iron. But as men at first made use of the instruments supplied by nature to accomplish very easy pieces of workmanship, laboriously and imperfectly, and then, when these were finished, wrought other things more difficult with less labor and greater perfection; and so gradually mounted from the simplest operations to the making of tools, and from the making of tools to the making of more complex tools, and fresh feats of workmanship, till they arrived at making, with small expenditure of labor, the vast number of complicated mechanisms, which they now possess. So, in like manner, the intellect, by its native strength,[6] makes for itself intellectual instruments, whereby it acquires strength for performing other intellectual operations, and from these operations gets again fresh instruments, or the power of pushing its investigations further, and thus gradually proceeds till it reaches the summit of wisdom.

That this is the path pursued by the understanding may be readily seen, when we understand the nature of the method for

[6] By native strength, I mean that not bestowed on us by external causes, as I shall afterwards explain in my philosophy.

finding out the truth, and of the natural instruments so necessary for the construction of more complex instruments, and for the progress of investigation. I thus proceed with my demonstration.

A true idea (for we possess a true idea) is something different from its correlate (*ideatum*); thus a circle is different from the idea of a circle. The idea of a circle is not something having a circumference and a centre, as a circle has; nor is the idea of a body that body itself. Now, as it is something different from its correlate, it is capable of being understood through itself; in other words, the idea, in so far as its actual essence (*essentia formalis*) is concerned, may be the subject of another objective essence (*essentia objectiva*). And, again, this second objective essence will, regarded in itself, be something real, and capable of being understood; and so on, indefinitely. For instance, the man Peter is something real; the true idea of Peter is the reality of Peter represented objectively, and is in itself something real, and quite distinct from the actual Peter. Now, as this true idea of Peter is in itself something real, and has its own individual existence, it will also be capable of being understood—that is, of being the subject of another idea, which will contain by representation (*objective*) all that the idea of Peter contains actually (*formaliter*). And, again, this idea of the idea of Peter has its own individuality, which may become the subject of yet another idea; and so on, indefinitely. This every one may make trial of for himself, by reflecting that he knows what Peter is, and also knows that he knows, and further knows that he knows that he knows, etc. Hence it is plain that, in order to understand the actual Peter, it is not necessary first to understand the idea of Peter, and still less the idea of the idea of Peter. This is the same as saying that, in order to know, there is no need to know that we know, much less to know that we know that we know. This is no more necessary than to know the nature of a circle before knowing the nature of a triangle. But, with these ideas, the contrary is the case: for, in order to know that I know, I must first know. Hence it is clear that certainty is nothing else than the objective essence of a thing: in other words, the mode in which we perceive an acual reality is certainty. Further, it is also evident that, for the certitude of truth, no further sign is necessary beyond the possession of a true idea: for, as I have shown, it is not necessary to know that we know that we know. Hence, again, it is clear that no one can know the nature of the highest certainty, unless he possesses an adequate idea, or the subjective essence of a thing: for certainty is identical with such subjective essence. Thus, as the truth needs no sign—it being sufficient to possess the objective essence of things, or, in other words, the ideas of them, in order that all doubts may be removed—it follows that the true method does not consist in seeking for the signs of truth after the acquisition of the idea, but that the true method teaches us the order in which we should seek for truth itself, or the subjective essences of things, or ideas, for all these expressions are synonymous. Again, method must necessarily be concerned with reasoning or understanding—I mean, method is not identical with reasoning in the search for causes, still less is it the comprehension of the causes of things: it is the discernment of a true idea, by distinguishing it from other perceptions and by investigating its nature in order that we may thus know our power of understanding, and may so train our mind that it may, by a given standard, comprehend whatsoever is intelligible, by laying down certain rules as aids, and by avoiding useless mental exertion.

Whence we may gather that method is nothing else than reflective knowledge, or the idea of an idea; and that as there can be no idea of an idea—unless an idea exists previously—there can be no method without a pre-existent idea. Therefore, that will be a good method which shows us how the mind should be directed, according to the standard of the given true idea.

Again, seeing that the ratio existing between two ideas is the same as the ratio between the actual realities corresponding to those ideas, it follows that the reflective knowledge which has for its object the most perfect being is more excellent than reflective knowledge concerning other objects—in other words, that method will be most perfect which affords the standard of the given idea of the most perfect being whereby we may direct our mind. We thus easily understand how, in proportion as it acquires new ideas, the mind simultaneously acquires fresh instruments for pursuing its inquiries further. For we may gather from what has been said, that a true idea must necessarily first of all exist in us as a natural instrument; and that when this idea is apprehended by the mind, it enables us to understand the difference existing between itself and all other perceptions. In this, one part of the method consists.

Now it is clear that the mind apprehends itself better in proportion as it understands a greater number of natural objects; it follows, therefore, that this portion of the method will be more perfect in proportion as the mind attains to the comprehension of a greater number of objects, and that it will be absolutely perfect when the mind gains a knowledge of the absolutely perfect being or becomes conscious thereof. Again, the more things the mind knows, the better does it understand its own strength and the order of nature; by increased self-knowledge it can direct itself more easily, and lay down rules for its own guidance; and, by increased knowledge of nature, it can more easily avoid what is useless.

And this is the sum total of method, as we have already stated. We may add that the idea in the world of thought is in the same case as its correlate in the world of reality. If, therefore, there be anything in nature which is without connection with any other thing, and if we assign to it an objective essence, which would in every way correspond to the formal reality, the objective essence would have no connection with any other ideas—in other words, we could not draw any conclusion with regard to it. On the other hand, those things which are connected with others— as all things that exist in nature—will be understood by the mind, and their objective essences will maintain the same mutual relations as their formal realities—that is to say, we shall infer from these ideas other ideas, which will in turn be connected with others, and thus our instruments for proceeding with our investigation will increase. This is what we are endeavoring to prove. Further, from what has just been said—namely, that an idea must, in all respects, correspond to its correlate in the world of reality (*essentia formalis*)—it is evident that, in order to reproduce in every respect the faithful image of nature, our mind must deduce all its ideas from the idea which represents the origin and source of the whole of nature, so that it may itself become the source of other ideas. . . . .

As regards that which constitutes the reality of truth, it is certain that a true idea is distinguished from a false one, not so much by its extrinsic object as by its intrinsic nature. If an architect conceives a building properly constructed, though such a building may never have existed, and may never exist, nevertheless the idea is true; and the idea remains the same, whether it be put into execution or not. On the other hand, if any one asserts, for instance, that Peter exists, without knowing whether Peter really exists or not, the assertion, as far as its asserter is concerned, is false, or not true, even though Peter actually does exist. The assertion that Peter exists is true only with regard to him who knows for certain that Peter does exist. Whence it follows that there is in ideas something real, whereby the true are distinguished from the false. This in reality must be inquired into, if we are to find the best standard of truth (we have said that we ought to determine our thoughts by the given standard of a true idea, and that method is reflective knowledge), and to know the properties of our understanding. Neither must we say that the difference between true and false arises from the fact that true knowledge consists in knowing things through their primary causes, wherein it is totally different from false knowledge, as I have just explained it: for thought is said to be true, if it involves objectively the essence of any principle which has no cause, and is known through itself and in itself. Wherefore the reality (*forma*) of true thought must exist in the thought itself, without reference to other thoughts; it does not acknowledge the object as its cause, but must depend on the actual power and nature of the understanding. For, if we suppose that the understanding has perceived some new entity which has never existed, as some conceive the understanding of God before He created things (a perception which certainly could not arise from any object), and has legitimately deduced other thoughts from the said perception, all such thoughts would be true, without being determined by any external object; they would depend solely on the power and nature of the understanding. Thus, that which constitutes the reality of a true thought must be sought in the thought itself and deduced from the nature of the understanding. In order to pursue our investigation, let us confront ourselves with some TRUE idea, whose object we know for certain to be dependent on our power of thinking, and to have nothing corresponding to it in nature. With an idea of this kind before us, we shall, as appears from what has just been said, be more easily able to carry on the research we have in view. For instance, in order to form the conception of a sphere, I invent a cause at my pleasure—namely, a semicircle revolving round its centre, and thus producing a sphere.

This is indisputably a true idea; and, although we know that no sphere in nature has ever actually been so formed, the perception remains true, and is the easiest manner of conceiving a sphere. We must observe that this perception asserts the rotation of a semicircle—which assertion would be false, if it were not associated with the conception of a sphere, or of a cause determining a motion of the kind, or absolutely, if the assertion were isolated. The mind would then only tend to the affirmation of the sole motion of a semicircle which is not contained in the conception of a semicircle, and does not arise from the conception of any cause capable of producing such motion.

Thus FALSITY consists only in this, that something is affirmed of a thing, which is not contained in the conception we have formed of that thing, as motion or rest of a semicircle. Whence it follows that simple ideas cannot be other than TRUE—e.g., the simple idea of a semicircle, of motion, of rest, of quantity, etc. . . . . .

Now, in order at length to pass on to the second part of this method, I shall first set forth the object aimed at, and next the means for its attainment. The object aimed at is the acquisition of clear and distinct ideas, such as are produced by the pure intellect, and not by chance physical motions. In order that all ideas may be reduced to unity, we shall endeavor so to associate and arrange them that our mind may, as far as possible, reflect objectively the reality of nature, both as a whole and as parts.

As for the first point, it is necessary (as we have said) for our purpose that everything should be conceived, either SOLELY THROUGH ITS ESSENCE, OR THROUGH ITS PROXIMATE CAUSE. If the thing be self-existent, or as is commonly said, the cause of itself, it must be understood through its essence only; if it be not self-existent, but requires a cause for its existence, it must be understood through its proximate cause. For, in reality, the knowledge of an effect is nothing else than the acquisition of more perfect knowledge of its cause. Therefore, we may never, while we are concerned with inquiries into actual things, draw any conclusions from abstractions; we shall be extremely careful not to confound that which is only in the understanding with that which is in the thing itself. The best basis for drawing a conclusion will be either some particular affirmative essence, or a true and legitimate definition. For the understanding can not descend from universal axioms by themselves to particular things, since axioms are of infinite extent, and do not determine the understanding to contemplate one particular thing more than another. Thus the true method of discovery is to form thoughts from some given definition. This process will be the more fruitful and easy in proportion as the thing given be better defined. Wherefore, the cardinal point of all this second part of method consists in the knowledge of the conditions of good definition, and the means of finding them. I will first treat of the conditions of definition.

A definition, if it is to be called perfect, must explain the inmost essence of a thing, and must take care not to substitute for this any of its properties. In order to illustrate my meaning, without taking an example which would seem to show a desire to expose other people's errors, I will choose the case of something abstract, the definition of which is of little moment. Such is a circle. If a circle be defined as a figure, such that all straight lines drawn from the center to the circumference are equal, every one can see that such a definition does not in the least explain the essence of a circle, but solely one of its properties. Though, as I have said, this is of no importance in the case of figures and other abstractions, it is of great importance in the case of physical beings and realities: for the properties of things are not understood so long as their essences are unknown. If the latter be passed over, there is necessarily a perversion of the succession of ideas which should reflect the succession of nature, and we go far astray from our object.

In order to be free from this fault, the following rules should be observed in definition:

I. If the thing in question be created, the definition must (as we have said) comprehend the proximate cause. For instance, a circle should, according to this rule, be defined as follows: the figure described by any line whereof one end is fixed and the other free. This definition clearly comprehends the proximate cause.

II. A conception or definition of a thing should be such that all the properties of that thing, in so far as it is considered by itself, and not in conjunction with other things, can be deduced from it, as may be seen in the definition given of a circle: for from that it clearly follows that all straight lines drawn from the center to the circumference are equal. That this is a necessary characteristic of a definition is so clear to any one, who reflects on the matter, that there is no need to spend time in proving it, or in showing that, owing to this second condition, every definition should be affirmative. I speak of intellectual affirmation, giving little thought to verbal affirmations which, owing to the poverty of the language, must sometimes, perhaps, be expressed negatively, though the idea contained is affirmative.

The rules for the definition of an uncreated thing are as follows:

I. The exclusion of all idea of cause—that is, the thing must not need explanation by anything outside itself.

II. When the definition of the thing has been given, there must be no room for doubt as to whether the thing exists or not.

III. It must contain, as far as the mind is concerned, no substantives which could be put into an adjectival form; in other words, the object defined must not be explained through abstractions.

IV. Lastly, though this is not absolutely necessary, it should be possible to deduce from the definition all the properties of the thing defined.

All these rules become obvious to any one giving strict attention to the matter.

I have also stated that the best basis for drawing a conclusion is a particular affirmative essence. The more specialized the idea is, the more is it distinct, and therefore clear. Wherefore a knowledge of particular things should be sought for as diligently as possible.

As regards the order of our perceptions, and the manner in which they should be arranged and united, it is necessary that as soon as is possible and rational, we should inquire whether there be any being (and, if so, what being) that is the cause of all things, so that its essence, represented in thought (*essentia objectiva*), may be the cause of all our ideas, and then our mind will to the utmost possible extent reflect nature. For it will possess, objectively, nature's essence, order, and union. Thus we can see that it is before all things necessary for us to deduce all our ideas from physical things—that is, from real entities proceeding, as far as may be, according to the series of causes, from one real entity to another real entity, never passing to universals and abstractions, either for the purpose of deducing some real entity from them, or deducing them from some real entity. Either of these processes interrupts the true progress of the understanding. But it must be observed that, by the series of causes and real entities, I do not here mean the series of particular and mutable things, but only the series of fixed and eternal things. It would be impossible for human infirmity to follow up the series of particular mutable things, both on account of their multitude, surpassing all calculation, and on account of the infinitely diverse circumstances surrounding one and the same thing, any one of which may be the cause for its existence or non-existence. Indeed, their existence has no connection with their essence, or (as we have said already) is not an eternal truth. Neither is there any need that we should understand their series, for the essences of particular mutable things are not to be gathered from their series or order of existence, which would furnish us with nothing beyond their extrinsic denominations, their relations, or, at most, their circumstances, all of which are very different from their inmost essence. This inmost essence must be sought solely from fixed and eternal things, and from the laws, inscribed (so to speak) in those things as in their true codes, according to which all particular things take place and are arranged; nay, these mutable particular things depend so intimately and essentially (so to phrase it) upon the fixed things, that they cannot either be or be conceived without them.

Whence these fixed and eternal things, though they are themselves particular, will nevertheless, owing to their presence and power everywhere, be to us as universals, or genera of definitions of particular mutable things, and as the proximate causes of all things.

But, though this be so, there seems to be no small difficulty in arriving at the knowledge of these particular things, for to conceive them all at once would far surpass the powers of the human understanding. The arrangement whereby one thing is understood before another, as we have stated, should not be sought from their series of existence, nor from eternal things. For the latter are all by nature simultaneous. Other aids are therefore needed besides those employed for understanding eternal things and their laws; however, this is not the place to recount such aids, nor is there any need to do so, until we have acquired a sufficient knowledge of eternal things and their infallible laws, and until the nature of our senses has become plain to us. . . . .

If, as I stated in the first part, it belongs to the nature of thought to form true ideas, we must here inquire what is meant by the faculties and power of the understanding. The chief part of our method is to understand as well as possible the powers of the intellect, and its nature; we are, therefore, compelled (by the considerations advanced in the second part of the method (necessarily to draw these conclusions from the definition itself of thought and understanding. But, so far, we have not got any rules for finding definitions, and, as we cannot set forth such rules without a previous knowledge of nature, that is without a definition of the understanding and its power, it follows either that the definition of the understanding must be clear in itself, or that we can understand nothing. Nevertheless this definition is not absolutely clear in itself; however, since its properties, like all things that we possess through the understanding, cannot be known clearly and distinctly, unless its nature be known previously, the definition of the understanding makes itself manifest, if we pay attention to its properties, which we know clearly and distinctly. Let us, then, enumerate here the properties of the understanding, let us examine them, and begin by discussing the instruments for research which we find innate in us.

The properties of the understanding which I have chiefly remarked, and which I clearly understand, are the following:—

I. It involves certainty—in other words, it knows that a thing exists in reality as it is reflected objectively.

II. That it perceives certain things, or forms some ideas absolutely, some ideas from others. Thus it forms the idea of quantity absolutely, without reference to any other thoughts; but ideas of motion it only forms after taking into consideration the idea of quantity.

III. Those ideas which the understanding forms absolutely express infinity; determinate ideas are derived from other ideas. Thus in the idea of quantity, perceived by means of a cause, the quantity is determined, as when a body is perceived to be formed by the motion of a plane, a plane by the motion of a line, or, again, a line by the motion of a point. All these are perceptions which do not serve toward understanding quantity, but only toward determining it. This is proved by the fact that we conceive them as formed as it were by motion, yet this motion is not perceived unless the quantity be perceived also; we can even prolong the motion so as to form an infinite line, which we certainly could not do unless we had an idea of infinite quantity.

IV. The understanding forms positive ideas before forming negative ideas.

V. It perceives things not so much under the condition of duration as under a certain form of eternity, and in an infinite number; or rather in perceiving things it does not consider either their number or duration, whereas, in imagining them, it perceives them in a determinate number, duration, and quantity.

VI. The ideas which we form as clear and distinct, seem so to follow from the sole necessity of our nature, that they appear to depend absolutely on our sole power; with confused ideas the contrary is the case. They are often formed against our will.

VII. The mind can determine in many ways the ideas of things, which the understanding forms from other ideas: thus, for instance, in order to define the plane of an ellipse, it supposes a point adhering to a cord to be moved round two centres, or, again, it conceives an infinity of points, always in the same fixed relation to a given straight line, or a cone cut in an oblique plane, so that the angle of inclination is greater than the angle of the vertex of the cone, or in an infinity of other ways.

VIII. The more ideas express perfection of any object, the more perfect are they themselves; for we do not admire the architect who has planned a chapel so much as the architect who has planned a splendid temple.

I do not stop to consider the rest of what is referred to thought, such as love, joy, etc. They are nothing to our present purpose, and cannot even be conceived unless the understanding be perceived previously. When perception is removed, all these go with it.

False and fictitious ideas have nothing positive about them (as we have abundantly shown) which causes them to be called false or fictitious; they are only considered as such through the defectiveness of knowledge. Therefore, false and fictitious ideas as such can teach us nothing concerning the essence of thought; this must be sought from the positive properties just enumerated; in other words, we must lay down some common basis from which these properties necessarily follow, so that when this is given, the properties are necessarily given also, and when it is removed, they too vanish with it.

. . . .

[*The fragment ends here*]

ETHICS, PART I[7]

Of God

DEFINITIONS

I. By CAUSE of itself, I understand that, whose essence involves existence; or that, whose nature cannot be conceived unless existing.

II. That thing is called finite in its own kind (*in suo genere*) which can be limited by another thing of the same nature. For example, a body is called finite, because we always conceive another which is greater. So a thought is limited by another thought; but a body is not limited by a thought, nor a thought by a body.

III. By substance, I understand that which is in itself and is conceived through itself; in other words, that, the conception of which does not need the conception of another thing from which it must be formed.

IV. By attribute, I understand that which the intellect perceives of substance, as if constituting its essence.

V. By mode, I understand the affections of substance, or that which is in another thing through which also it is conceived.

VI. By God, I understand Being absolutely infinite, that is to say, substance consisting of infinite attributes, each one of which expresses eternal and infinite essence.

Explanation.—I say absolutely infinite but not infinite in its own kind (*in suo genere*); for of whatever is infinite only in its own kind (*in suo genere*), we can deny infinite attributes; but to the essence of that which is absolutely infinite pertains whatever expresses essence and involves no negation.

VII. That thing is called free which exists from the necessity of its own nature alone, and is determined to action by itself alone.

[7] *Ethic Demonstrated in Geometrical Order and Divided into Five Parts*, trans. from the Latin by William Hall White (London: Trübner & Co., 1883), Part I: *Of God*.

That thing, on the other hand, is called necessary, or rather compelled, which by another is determined to existence and action in a fixed and prescribed manner.

VIII. By eternity, I understand existence itself, so far as it is conceived necessarily to follow from the definition alone of the eternal thing.

Explanation.—For such existence, like the essence of the thing, is conceived as an eternal truth. It cannot therefore be explained by duration or time, even if the duration be conceived without beginning or end.

AXIOMS

I. Everything which is, is either in itself or in another.

II. That which cannot be conceived through another must be conceived through itself.

III. From a given determinate cause an effect necessarily follows; and, on the other hand, if no determinate cause be given, it is impossible that an effect can follow.

IV. The knowledge (*cognitio*) of an effect depends upon and involves the knowledge of the cause.

V. Those things which have nothing mutually in common with one another cannot through one another be mutually understood, that is to say, the conception of the one does not involve the conception of the other.

VI. A true idea must agree with that of which it is the idea (*cum suo ideato*).

VII. The essence of that thing which can be conceived as not existing does not involve existence.

PROP. I.—*Substance is by its nature prior to its affections.*

Demonst.—This is evident from Defs. 3 and 5.

PROP. II.—*Two substances having different attributes have nothing in common with one another.*

Demonst.—This is also evident from Def. 3. For each substance must be in itself and must be conceived through itself, that is to say, the conception of one does not involve the conception of the other.—Q.E.D.

PROP. III.—*If two things have nothing in common with one another, one cannot be the cause of the other.*

Demonst.—If they have nothing mutually in common with one another, they cannot (Ax. 5) through one another be mutually understood, and therefore (Ax. 4) one cannot be the cause of the other.—Q.E.D.

PROP. IV.—*Two or more distinct things are distinguished from one another, either by the difference of the attributes of the substances, or by the difference of their affections.*

Demonst.—Everything which is, is either in itself or in another (Ax. 1), that is to say (Defs. 3 and 5), outside the intellect there is nothing but substances and their affections. There is nothing therefore outside the intellect by which a number of things can be distinguished one from another, but substances or (which is the same thing by Def. 4) their attributes and their affections.—Q.E.D.

PROP. V.—*In nature there cannot be two or more substances of the same nature or attribute.*

Demonst.—If there were two or more distinct substances, they must be distinguished one from the other by difference of attributes or difference of affections (Prop. 4). If they are distinguished only by difference of attributes, it will be granted that there is but one substance of the same attribute. But if they are distinguished by difference of affections, since substance is prior by nature to its affections (Prop. 1), the affections therefore being placed on one side, and the substance being considered in itself, or, in other words (Def. 3 and Ax. 6), truly considered, it cannot be conceived as distinguished from another substance, that is to say (Prop. 4), there cannot be two or more substances, but only one possessing the same nature or attribute.—Q.E.D.

PROP. VI.—*One substance cannot be produced by another substance.*

Demonst.—There cannot in nature be two substances of the same attribute (Prop. 5), that is to say (Prop. 2), two which have anything in common with one another. And therefore (Prop. 3) one cannot be the cause of the other, that is to say, one cannot be produced by the other.—Q.E.D.

Corol.—Hence it follows that there is nothing by which substance can be produced, for in nature there is nothing but substances and their affections (as is evident from Ax. 1 and Defs. 3 and 5). But substance cannot be produced by substance (Prop. 6). Therefore

absolutely there is nothing by which substance can be produced.—
Q.E.D.

Another Demonst.—This corollary is demonstrated more easily by
the *reductio ad absurdum*. For if there were anything by which
substance could be produced, the knowledge of substance would
be dependent upon the knowledge of its cause (Ax. 4), and therefore (Def. 3) it would not be substance.

PROP. VII.—*It pertains to the nature of substance to exist.*

Demonst.—There is nothing by which substance can be produced (Corol. Prop. 6). It will therefore be the cause of itself, that
is to say (Def. 1), its essence necessarily involves existence, or in
in other words it pertains to its nature to exist.—Q.E.D.

PROP. VIII.—*Every substance is necessarily infinite.*

Demonst.—Substance which has only one attribute cannot exist
except as one substance (Prop. 5), and to the nature of this one
substance it pertains to exist (Prop. 7). It must therefore from its
nature exist as finite or infinite. But it cannot exist as finite substance, for (Def. 2) it must (if finite) be limited by another substance of the same nature, which also must necessarily exist
(Prop. 7), and therefore there would be two substances of the
same attribute, which is absurd (Prop. 5). It exists therefore as
infinite substance.—Q.E.D.

Schol. 1.—Since finiteness is in truth partly negation, and infinitude absolute affirmation of existence of some kind, it follows
from Prop. 7 alone that all substance must be infinite.

Schol. 2.—I fully expect that those who judge things confusedly,
and who have not been accustomed to cognise things through their
first causes, will find it difficult to comprehend the demonstration
of the 7th Proposition, since they do not distinguish between the
modifications of substances and substances themselves, and are
ignorant of the manner in which things are produced. Hence it
comes to pass that they erroneously ascribe to substances a beginning like that which they see belongs to natural things; for
those who are ignorant of the true causes of things confound every
thing, and without any mental repugnance represent trees speaking
like men, or imagine that men are made out of stones as well as
begotten from seed, and that all forms can be changed the one into

the other. So also those who confound human nature with the divine, readily attribute to God human affects,[8] especially so long as they are ignorant of the manner in which affects are produced in the mind. But if men would attend to the nature of substance, they could not entertain a single doubt of the truth of Proposition 7; indeed this proposition would be considered by all to be axiomatic, and reckoned amongst common notions. For by "substance" would be understood that which is in itself and is conceived through itself, or, in other words, that, the knowledge of which does not need the knowledge of another thing. But by "modifications" would be understood those things which are in another thing—those things, the conception of which is formed from the conception of the thing in which they are. Hence we can have true ideas of non-existent modifications, since although they may not actually exist outside the intellect, their essence nevertheless is so comprehended in something else, that they may be conceived through it. But the truth of substances is not outside the intellect unless in the substances themselves, because they are conceived through themselves. If any one, therefore, were to say that he possessed a clear and distinct, that is to say, a true idea of substance, and that he nevertheless doubted whether such a substance exists, he would forsooth be in the same position as if he were to say that he had a true idea and nevertheless doubted whether or not it was false (as is evident to any one who pays a little attention). Similarly if any one were to affirm that substance is created, he would affirm at the same time that a false idea had become true, and this is a greater absurdity than can be conceived. It is therefore necessary to admit that the existence of substance, like its essence, is an eternal truth. Hence a demonstration (which I have thought worth while to append) by a different method is possible, showing that there are not two substances possessing the same nature. But in order to prove this methodically it is to be noted: 1. That the true definition of any one thing neither involves nor expresses anything except the nature of the thing defined. From which it follows, 2. That a definition does not involve or express

[8] *Affectus* is translated by "affect" and *affectio* by "affection." There seems to be no other way in the English language of marking the relationship of the two words and preserving their exact meaning. *Affectus* has sometimes been translated "passion," but Spinoza uses *passio* for passion, and means something different from *affectus*. See Def. III, part 3. [Tr.]

any certain number of individuals, since it expresses nothing but the nature of the thing defined. For example, the definition of a triangle expresses nothing but the simple nature of a triangle, and not any certain number of triangles. 3. It is to be observed that of every existing thing there is some certain cause by reason of which it exists. 4. Finally, it is to be observed that this cause, by reason of which a thing exists, must either be contained in the nature itself and definition of the existing thing (simply because it pertains to the nature of the thing to exist), or it must exist outside the thing. This being granted, it follows that if a certain number of individuals exist in nature, there must necessarily be a cause why those individuals, and neither more nor fewer, exist. If, for example, there are twenty men in existence (whom, for the sake of greater clearness, I suppose existing at the same time, and that no others existed before them), it will not be sufficient, in order that we may give a reason why twenty men exist, to give a cause for human nature generally; but it will be necessary, in addition, to give a reason why neither more nor fewer than twenty exist, since, as we have already observed under the third head, there must necessarily be a cause why each exists. But this cause (as we have shown under the second and third heads) cannot be contained in human nature itself, since the true definition of a man does not involve the number twenty, and therefore (by the fourth head) the cause why these twenty men exist, and consequently the cause why each exists, must necessarily lie outside each one; and therefore we must conclude generally that whenever it is possible for several individuals of the same nature to exist, there must necessarily be an external cause for their existence.

Since now it pertains to the nature of substance to exist (as we have shown in this scholium), its definition must involve necessary existence, and consequently from its definition alone its existence must be concluded. But from its definition (as we have already shown under the second and third heads) the existence of more substances than one cannot be deduced. It follows, therefore, from this definition necessarily that there cannot be two substances possessing the same nature.

PROP. IX.—*The more reality or being a thing possesses, the more attributes belong to it.*

Demonst.—This is evident from Def. 4.

PROP. X.—*Each attribute of a substance must be conceived through itself.*

Demonst.—For an attribute is that which the intellect perceives of substance, as if constituting its essence (Def. 4), and therefore (Def. 3) it must be conceived through itself.—Q.E.D.

Schol.—From this it is apparent that although two attributes may be conceived as really distinct—that is to say, one without the assistance of the other—we cannot nevertheless thence conclude that they constitute two beings or two different substances; for this is the nature of substance, that each of its attributes is conceived through itself, since all the attributes which substance possesses were always in it together, nor could one be produced by another; but each expresses the reality or being of substance. It is very far from being absurd, therefore, to ascribe to one substance a number of attributes, since nothing in nature is clearer than that each being must be conceived under some attribute, and the more reality or being it has, the more attributes it possesses expressing necessity or eternity and infinity. Nothing consequently is clearer than that Being absolutely infinite is necessarily defined, as we have shown (Def. 6), as Being which consists of infinite attributes, each one of which expresses a certain essence, eternal and infinite. But if any one now asks by what sign, therefore, we may distinguish between substances, let him read the following propositions, which show that in nature only one substance exists, and that it is absolutely infinite. For this reason that sign would be sought for in vain.

PROP. XI.—*God, or substance consisting of infinite attributes, each one of which expresses eternal and infinite essence, necessarily exists.*

Demonst.—If this be denied, conceive, if it be possible, that God does not exist. Then it follows (Ax. 7) that His essence does not involve existence. But this (Prop. 7) is absurd. Therefore God necessarily exists.—Q.E.D.

Another proof.—For the existence or non-existence of everything there must be a reason or cause. For example, if a triangle exists, there must be a reason or cause why it exists; and if it does not exist, there must be a reason or cause which hinders its existence or which negates it. But this reason or cause must either be contained in the nature of the thing or lie outside it. For example, the nature of the thing itself shows the reason why a square circle does not exist, the reason being that a square circle involves a contradiction. And the reason, on the other hand, why substance exists follows from its nature alone, which involves existence (see Prop. 7). But the reason why a circle or triangle exists or does not exist is not drawn from their nature, but from the order of corporeal nature generally; for from that it must follow, either that a triangle necessarily exists, or that it is impossible for it to exist. But this is self-evident. Therefore it follows that if there be no cause nor reason which hinders a thing from existing, it exists necessarily. If, therefore, there be no reason nor cause which hinders God from existing, or which negates His existence, we must conclude absolutely that He necessarily exists. But if there be such a reason or cause, it must be either in the nature itself of God or must lie outside it, that is to say, in another substance of another nature. For if the reason lay in a substance of the same nature, the existence of God would be by this very fact admitted. But substance possessing another nature could have nothing in common with God (Prop. 2), and therefore could not give Him existence nor negate it. Since, therefore, the reason or cause which could negate the divine existence cannot be outside the divine nature, it will necessarily, supposing that the divine nature does not exist, be in His Nature itself, which would therefore involve a contradiction. But to affirm this of the Being absolutely infinite and consummately perfect is absurd. Therefore neither in God nor outside God is there any cause or reason which can negate His existence, and therefore God necessarily exists.—Q.E.D.

Another proof.—Inability to exist is impotence, and, on the other hand, ability to exist is power, as is self-evident. If, therefore, there is nothing which necessarily exists excepting things finite, it follows that things finite are more powerful than the absolutely infinite Being, and this (as is self-evident) is absurd; therefore either nothing exists or Being absolutely infinite also necessarily exists. But we ourselves exist, either in ourselves or in something else which necessarily exists (Ax. 1 and Prop. 7). Therefore the Being absolutely infinite, that is to say (Def. 6), God, necessarily exists.—Q.E.D.

Schol.—In this last demonstration I wished to prove the existence of God *a posteriori*, in order that the demonstration might be the more easily understood, and not because the existence of God does not follow *a priori* from the same grounds. For since ability to exist is power, it follows that the more reality belongs to the nature of anything, the greater is the power for existence it derives from itself; and it also follows, therefore, that the Being absolutely infinite, or God, has from Himself an absolutely infinite power of existence, and that He therefore necessarily exists. Many persons, nevertheless, will perhaps not be able easily to see the force of this demonstration, because they have been accustomed to contemplate those things alone which flow from external causes, and they see also that those things which are quickly produced from these causes, that is to say, which easily exist, easily perish, whilst, on the other hand, they adjudge those things to be more difficult to produce, that is to say, not so easy to bring into existence, to which they conceive more properties pertain. In order that these prejudices may be removed, I do not need here to show in what respect this saying, "What is quickly made quickly perishes," is true, nor to inquire whether, looking at the whole of nature, all things are or are not equally easy. But this only it will be sufficient for me to observe, that I do not speak of things which are produced by external causes, but that I speak of substances alone which (Prop. 6) can be produced by no external cause. For whatever perfection or reality those things may have which are produced by external causes, whether they consist of many parts or of few, they owe it all to the virtue of an external cause, and therefore their existence springs from the perfection of an external cause alone and not from their own. On the other hand, whatever perfection substance has is due to no external cause. Therefore its existence must follow from its nature alone, and is therefore nothing else than its essence. Perfection consequently does not prevent the existence of a thing, but establishes it; imperfection, on the other hand, prevents existence, and so of no existence can we be more sure than of the existence of the Being absolutely infinite or perfect, that is to say, God. For since His essence shuts out all imperfection and involves absolute perfection, for this very reason all cause of doubt concerning His existence is taken away, and the highest certainty concerning it is given,—a truth which I trust will be evident to any one who bestows only moderate attention.

PROP. XII.—*No attribute of substance can be truly conceived from which it follows that substance can be divided.*

Demonst.—For the parts into which substance thus conceived would be divided will or will not retain the nature of substance. If they retain it, then (Prop. 8) each part will be infinite, and (Prop. 6) the cause of itself, and will consist of an attribute differing from that of any other part (Prop. 5), so that from one substance more substances could be formed, which (Prop. 6) is absurd. Moreover the parts (Prop. 2) would have nothing in common with their whole, and the whole (Def. 4 and Prop. 10) could be, and could be conceived without its parts, which no one will doubt to be an absurdity. But if the second case be supposed, namely, that the parts will not retain the nature of substance, then, since the whole substance might be divided into equal parts, it would lose the nature of substance and cease to be, which (Prop. 7) is absurd.

PROP. XIII.—*Substance absolutely infinite is indivisible.*

Demonst.—For if it were divisible, the parts into which it would be divided will or will not retain the nature of substance absolutely infinite. If they retain it, there will be a plurality of substances possessing the same nature, which (Prop. 5) is absurd. If the second case be supposed, then (as above), substance absolutely infinite can cease to be, which (Prop. 11) is also absurd.

Corol.—Hence it follows that no substance, and consequently no bodily substance in so far as it is substance, is divisible.

Schol.—That substance is indivisible is more easily to be understood from this consideration alone, that the nature of substance cannot be conceived unless as infinite, and that by a part of substance nothing else can be understood than finite substance, which (Prop. 8) involves a manifest contradiction.

PROP. XIV.—*Besides God, no substance can be nor can be conceived.*

Demonst.—Since God is Being absolutely infinite, of whom no attribute can be denied which expresses the essence of substance (Def. 6), and since He necessarily exists (Prop. 11), it follows that if there were any substance besides God, it would have to be explained by some attribute of God, and thus two substances would exist possessing the same attribute, which (Prop. 5) is absurd; and therefore there cannot be any substance excepting God, and consequently none other can be conceived. For if any other could be conceived, it would necessarily be conceived as existing, and this (by the first part of this demonstration) is absurd. Therefore besides God no substance can be, nor can be conceived.—Q.E.D.

Corol. 1.—Hence it follows with the greatest clearness, firstly, that God is one, that is to say (Def. 6), in nature there is but one substance, and it is absolutely infinite, as (Schol. Prop. 10) we have already intimated.

Corol. 2.—It follows, secondly, that the thing extended (*rem extensam*) and the thing thinking (*rem cogitantem*) are either attributes of God or (Ax. 1) affections of the attributes of God.

PROP. XV.—*Whatever is, is in God, and nothing can either be or be conceived without God.*

Demonst.—Besides God there is no substance, nor can any be conceived (Prop. 14), that is to say (Def. 3), nothing which is in itself and is conceived through itself. But modes (Def. 5) can neither be nor be conceived without substance; therefore in the divine nature only can they be, and through it alone can they be conceived. But besides substances and modes nothing is assumed (Ax. 1). Therefore nothing can be or be conceived without God.—Q.E.D.

Schol.—There are those who imagine God to be like a man, composed of body and soul and subject to passions; but it is clear enough from what has already been demonstrated how far off men who believe this are from the true knowledge of God. But these I dismiss, for all men who have in any way looked into the divine nature deny that God is corporeal. That He cannot be so they conclusively prove by showing that by "body" we understand a certain quantity possessing length, breadth, and depth, limited by some fixed form; and that to attribute these to God, a being absolutely infinite, is the greatest absurdity. But yet at the same time, from other arguments by which they endeavour to confirm their proof, they clearly show that they remove altogether from the divine nature substance itself corporeal or extended, affirming that it was created by God. By what divine power, however, it could have been created they are altogether ignorant, so that it is clear they do not understand what they themselves say. But I have demonstrated, at least in my own opinion, with sufficient

clearness (see Corol. Prop. 6 and Schol. 2, Prop. 8), that no substance can be produced or created by another being (*ab alio*).
Moreover (Prop. 14), we have shown that besides God no substance
can be nor can be conceived; and hence we have concluded that
extended substance is one of the infinite attributes of God. But
for the sake of a fuller explanation, I will refute my adversaries'
arguments, which, taken altogether, come to this. First, that corporeal substance, in so far as it is substance, consists, as they
suppose, of parts, and therefore they deny that it can be infinite,
and consequently that it can pertain to God. This they illustrate
by many examples, one or two of which I will adduce. If corporeal
substance, they say, be infinite, let us conceive it to be divided into
two parts; each part, therefore, will be either finite or infinite.

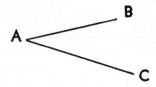

If each part be finite, then the infinite is composed of two finite
parts, which is absurd. If each part be infinite, there is then an
infinite twice as great as another infinite, which is also absurd.
Again, if infinite quantity be measured by equal parts of a foot
each, it must contain an infinite number of such parts, and similarly if it be measured by equal parts of an inch each; and therefore one infinite number will be twelve times greater than another
infinite number. Lastly, if from one point of any infinite quantity
it be imagined that two lines, *AB*, *AC*, which at first are at a certain and determinate distance from one another, be infinitely extended, it is plain that the distance between *B* and *C* will be continually increased, and at length from being determinate will be
indeterminable. Since therefore these absurdities follow, as they
think, from supposing quantity to be infinite, they conclude that
corporeal substance must be finite, and consequently cannot pertain to the essence of God. A second argument is assumed from
the absolute perfection of God. For God, they say, since He is a
being absolutely perfect, cannot suffer; but corporeal substance,
since it is divisible, can suffer: it follows, therefore, that it does
not pertain to God's essence. These are the arguments which I

find in authors, by which they endeavour to show that corporeal substance is unworthy of the divine nature, and cannot pertain to it. But any one who will properly attend will discover that I have already answered these arguments, since the sole foundation of them is the supposition that bodily substance consists of parts, a supposition which (Prop. 12 and Corol. Prop. 13) I have shown to be absurd. Moreover, if any one will rightly consider the matter, he will see that all these absurdities (supposing that they are all absurdities, a point which I will now take for granted), from which these authors attempt to draw the conclusion that substance extended is finite, do not by any means follow from the supposition that quantity is infinite, but from the supposition that infinite quantity is measurable, and that it is made up of finite parts. Therefore, from the absurdities to which this leads nothing can be concluded, excepting that infinite quantity is not measurable, and that it cannot be composed of finite parts. But this is what we have already demonstrated (Prop. 12, &c.), and the shaft therefore which is aimed at us turns against those who cast it. If, therefore, from these absurdities any one should attempt to conclude that substance extended must be finite, he would, forsooth, be in the position of the man who supposes a circle to have the properties of a square, and then concludes that it has no centre, such that all the lines drawn from it to the circumference are equal. For corporeal substance, which cannot be conceived except as infinite, one and indivisible (Props. 8, 5, and 12), is conceived by those against whom I argue to be composed of finite parts, and to be multiplex and divisible, in order that they may prove it finite. Just in the same way others, after they have imagined a line to consist of points, know how to discover many arguments, by which they show that a line cannot be divided *ad infinitum;* and indeed it is not less absurd to suppose that corporeal substance is composed of bodies or parts than to suppose that a body is composed of surfaces, surfaces of lines, and that lines, finally, are composed of points. Every one who knows that clear reason is infallible ought to admit this, and especially those who deny that a vacuum can exist. For if corporeal substance could be so divided that its parts could be really distinct, why could not one part be annihilated, the rest remaining, as before, connected with one another? And why must all be so fitted together that there can be no vacuum? For of things which are really distinct the one from the other, one can be and remain in its own position without the other. Since, therefore, it is supposed that there is no vacuum in nature (about which I will speak at another time), but that all the parts must be united, so that no vacuum can exist, it follows that they cannot be really separated; that is to say, that corporeal substance, in so far as it is substance, cannot be divided. If, nevertheless, any one should now ask why there is a natural tendency to consider quantity as capable of division, I reply that quantity is conceived by us in two ways: either abstractly or superficially; that is to say, as we imagine it, or else as substance, in which way it is conceived by the intellect alone. If, therefore, we regard quantity (as we do very often and easily) as it exists in the imagination, we find it to be finite, divisible, and composed of parts; but if we regard it as it exists in the intellect, and conceive it in so far as it is substance, which is very difficult, then, as we have already sufficiently demonstrated, we find it to be infinite, one, and indivisible. This will be plain enough to all who know how to distinguish between the imagination and the intellect, and more especially if we remember that matter is everywhere the same, and that, except in so far as we regard it as affected in different ways, parts are not distinguished in it; that is to say, they are distinguished with regard to mode, but not with regard to reality. For example, we conceive water as being divided, in so far as it is water, and that its parts are separated from one another; but in so far as it is corporeal substance we cannot thus conceive it, for as such it is neither separated nor divided. Moreover, water, in so far as it is water, is originated and destroyed; but in so far as it is substance, it is neither originated nor destroyed. By this reasoning I think that I have also answered the second argument, since that too is based upon the assumption that matter, considered as substance, is divisible and composed of parts. And even if what I have urged were not true, I do not know why matter should be unworthy of the divine nature, since (Prop. 14) outside God no substance can exist from which the divine nature could suffer. All things, I say, are in God, and everything which takes place takes place by the laws alone of the infinite nature of God, and follows (as I shall presently show) from the necessity of His essence. Therefore in no way whatever can it be asserted that God suffers from anything, or that substance extended, even if it be supposed divisible, is unworthy of the divine nature, provided only it be allowed that it is eternal and infinite. But enough on this point for the present.

PROP. XVI.—*From the necessity of the divine nature infinite numbers of things in infinite ways (that is to say, all things which can be conceived by the infinite intellect) must follow.*

Demonst.—This proposition must be plain to every one who considers that from the given definition of anything a number of properties necessarily following from it (that is to say, following from the essence of the thing itself) are inferred by the intellect, and just in proportion as the definition of the thing expresses a greater reality, that is to say, just in proportion as the essence of the thing defined involves a greater reality, will more properties be inferred. But the divine nature possesses absolutely infinite attributes (Def. 6), each one of which expresses infinite essence in its own kind (*in suo genere*), and therefore, from the necessity of the divine nature, infinite numbers of things in infinite ways (that is to say, all things which can be conceived by the infinite intellect) must necessarily follow.—Q.E.D.

Corol. 1.—Hence it follows that God is the efficient cause of all things which can fall under the infinite intellect.

Corol. 2.—It follows, secondly, that God is cause through Himself, and not through that which is contingent (*per accidens*).

Corol. 3.—It follows, thirdly, that God is absolutely the first cause.

PROP. XVII.—*God acts from the laws of His own nature only, and is compelled by no one.*

Demonst.—We have just shown (Prop. 16) that from the necessity, or (which is the same thing) from the laws only of the divine nature, infinite numbers of things absolutely follow; and we have demonstrated (Prop. 15) that nothing can be, nor can be conceived, without God, but that all things are in God. Therefore, outside Himself, there can be nothing by which He may be determined or compelled to act; and therefore He acts from the laws of His own nature only, and is compelled by no one.—Q.E.D.

Corol. 1.—Hence it follows, firstly, that there is no cause, either external to God or within Him, which can excite Him to act except the perfection of His own nature.

Corol. 2.—It follows, secondly, that God alone is a free cause; for God alone exists from the necessity alone of His own nature (Prop. 11, and Corol. 1, Prop. 14), and acts from the necessity alone of His own nature (Prop. 17). Therefore (Def. 7) He alone is a free cause.—Q.E.D.

Schol.—There are some who think that God is a free cause because He can, as they think, bring about that those things which we have said follow from His nature—that is to say, those things which are in His power—should not be, or should not be produced by Him. But this is simply saying that God could bring about that it should not follow from the nature of a triangle that its three angles should be equal to two right angles, or that from a given cause an effect should not follow, which is absurd. But I shall show farther on, without the help of this proposition, that neither intellect nor will pertain to the nature of God.

I know, indeed, that there are many who think themselves able to demonstrate that intellect of the highest order and freedom of will both pertain to the nature of God, for they say that they know nothing more perfect which they can attribute to Him than that which is the chief perfection in ourselves. But although they conceive God as actually possessing the highest intellect, they nevertheless do not believe that He can bring about that all those things should exist which are actually in His intellect, for they think that by such a supposition they would destroy His power. If He had created, they say, all things which are in His intellect, He could have created nothing more, and this, they believe, does not accord with God's omnipotence so then they prefer to consider God as indifferent to all things, and creating nothing excepting that which He has decreed to create by a certain absolute will. But I think that I have shown with sufficient clearness (Prop. 16) that from the supreme power of God, or from His infinite nature, infinite things in infinite ways, that is to say, all things, have necessarily flowed, or continually follow by the same necessity, in the same way as it follows from the nature of a triangle, from eternity and to eternity, that its three angles are equal to two right angles. The omnipotence of God has therefore been actual from eternity, and in the same actuality will remain to eternity. In this way the omnipotence of God, in my opinion, is far more firmly established. My adversaries, indeed (if I may be permitted to speak plainly), seem to deny the omnipotence of God, inasmuch as they are forced to admit that He has in His mind an infinite number of things which might be created, but which, nevertheless, He will never be able to create, for if He were to create all things which He has in His mind, He would, according to them, exhaust His omnipotence and make Himself imperfect. Therefore, in order to make a perfect God, they are compelled to make Him incapable of doing all those things to which His power extends, and anything more absurd than this, or more opposed to God's omnipotence, I do not think can be imagined. Moreover—to say a word, too, here about the intellect and will which we commonly attribute to God—if intellect and will pertain to His eternal essence, these attributes cannot be understood in the sense in which men generally use them, for the intellect and will which could constitute His essence would have to differ entirely from our intellect and will, and could resemble ours in nothing except in name. There could be no further likeness than that between the celestial constellation of the Dog and the animal which barks. This I will demonstrate as follows. If intellect pertains to the divine nature, it cannot, like our intellect, follow the things which are its object (as many suppose), nor can it be simultaneous in its nature with them, since God is prior to all things in causality (Corol. 1, Prop. 16); but, on the contrary, the truth and formal essence of things is what it is, because as such it exists objectively in God's intellect. Therefore the intellect of God, in so far as it is conceived to constitute His essence, is in truth the cause of things, both of their essence and of their existence,—a truth which seems to have been understood by those who have maintained that God's intellect, will, and power are one and the same thing. Since, therefore, God's intellect is the sole cause of things, both of their essence and of their existence (as we have already shown), it must necessarily differ from them with regard both to its essence and existence; for an effect differs from its cause precisely in that which it has from its cause. For example, one man is the cause of the existence but not of the essence of another, for the essence is an eternal truth; and therefore with regard to essence the two men may exactly resemble one another, but with regard to existence they must differ. Consequently if the existence of one should perish, that of the other will not therefore perish; but if the essence of one could be destroyed and become false, the essence of the other would be likewise destroyed. Therefore a thing which is the cause both of the essence and of the existence of any effect must differ from that effect both with regard to its essence and with regard to its existence. But the intellect of God is the cause both of the essence and existence of our intellect; therefore the intellect of God, so far as it is conceived to constitute the divine essence, differs from our intellect both with regard to its essence and its existence, nor can it coincide with our intellect in anything except the name, which is what we essayed to prove. The same demonstration may be applied to the will, as anyone may easily see for himself.

PROP. XVIII.—*God is the immanent, and not the transitive*[9] *cause of all things.*

Demonst.—All things which are, are in God and must be conceived through Him (Prop. 15), and therefore (Corol. 1, Prop. 16) He is the cause of the things which are in Himself. This is the first thing which was to be proved. Moreover, outside God there can be no substance (Prop. 14), that is to say (Def. 3), outside Him nothing can exist which is in itself. This was the second thing to be proved. God, therefore, is the immanent, but not the transitive cause of all things.—Q.E.D.

PROP. XIX.—*God is eternal, or, in other words, all His attributes are eternal.*

Demonst.—For God (Def. 6) is substance, which (Prop. 11) necessarily exists, that is to say (Prop. 7), a substance to whose nature it pertains to exist, or (which is the same thing) a substance from the definition of which it follows that it exists, and therefore (Def. 8) He is eternal. Again, by the attributes of God is to be understood that which (Def. 4) expresses the essence of the divine substance, that is to say, that which pertains to substance. It is this, I say, which the attributes themselves must involve. But eternity pertains to the nature of substance (Prop. 7). Therefore each of the attributes must involve eternity, and therefore all are eternal.—Q.E.D.

Schol.—This proposition is as clear as possible, too, from the manner in which (Prop. 11) I have demonstrated the existence of God. From that demonstration I say it is plain that the existence

---

[9] *Transiens*, passing over and into from the outside. [Tr.]

of God, like His essence, is an eternal truth. Moreover (Prop. 19 of the "Principles of the Cartesian Philosophy"), I have demonstrated by another method the eternity of God, and there is no need to repeat the demonstration here.

PROP. XX.—*The existence of God and His essence are one and the same thing.*

God (Prop. 19) and all His attributes are eternal, that is to say (Def. 8), each one of His attributes expresses existence. The same attributes of God, therefore, which (Def. 4) manifest the eternal essence of God, at the same time manifest His eternal existence; that is to say, the very same thing which constitutes the essence of God constitutes at the same time His existence, and therefore His existence and His essence are one and the same thing.—Q.E.D.

Corol. 1.—Hence it follows, 1. That the existence of God, like His essence, is an eternal truth.

Corol. 2.—It follows, 2. That God is immutable, or (which is the same thing) all His attributes are immutable; for if they were changed as regards their existence, they must be changed also as regards their essence (Prop. 20); that is to say (as is self-evident), from being true, they would become false, which is absurd.

PROP. XXI.—*All things which follow from the absolute nature of any attribute of God must for ever exist, and must be infinite; that is to say, through that same attribute they are eternal and infinite.*

Demonst.—Conceive, if possible (supposing that the truth of the proposition is denied), that in some attribute of God something which is finite and has a determinate existence or duration follows from the absolute nature of that attribute; for example, an idea of God in thought.[10] But thought, since it is admitted to be an attribute of God, is necessarily (Prop. 11) in its nature infinite. But so far as it has the idea of God it is by supposition finite. But (Def. 2) it cannot be conceived as finite unless it be determined by thought itself. But it cannot be determined by thought itself so far as it constitutes the idea of God, for so far by supposition it is finite. Therefore it must be determined by thought so far as it does not constitute the idea of God, but which, nevertheless (Prop. 11), necessarily exists. Thought, therefore, exists which does not

[10] Not the idea which man forms of God, but rather one of God's ideas. [TR.]

form the idea of God, and therefore from its nature, in so far as it is absolute thought, the idea of God does not necessarily follow (for it is conceived as forming and as not forming the idea of God), which is contrary to the hypothesis. Therefore, if an idea of God in thought, or anything else in any attribute of God, follow from the necessity of the absolute nature of that attribute (for the demonstration being universal will apply in every case), that thing must necessarily be infinite, which was the first thing to be proved.

Again, that which thus follows from the necessity of the nature of any attribute cannot have a determinate duration. For, if the truth of this be denied, let it be supposed that in some attribute of God a thing exists which follows from the necessity of the nature of the attribute—for example, an idea of God in thought—and let it be supposed that at some time it has either not existed or will not exist. But since thought is supposed to be an attribute of God, it must exist both necessarily and unchangeably (Prop. 11, and Corol. 2, Prop. 20). Therefore, beyond the limits of the duration of the idea of God (for it is supposed that at some time it has either not existed or will not exist), thought must exist without the idea of God; but this is contrary to hypothesis, for the supposition is that thought being given, the idea of God necessarily follows. Therefore neither an idea of God in thought, nor anything else which necessarily follows from the absolute nature of any attribute of God, can have a determinate duration, but through the same attribute is eternal; which was the second thing to be proved. Observe that what we have affirmed here is true of everything which in any attribute of God necessarily follows from the absolute nature of God.

PROP. XXII.—*Whatever follows from any attribute of God, in so far as it is modified by a modification which through the same attribute exists necessarily and infinitely, must also exist necessarily and infinitely.*

Demonst.—This proposition is demonstrated in the same manner as the preceding proposition.

PROP. XXIII.—*Every mode which exists necessarily and infinitely must necessarily follow either from the absolute nature of some attribute of God, or from some attribute modified by a modification which exists necessarily and infinitely.*

Demonst.—Mode is that which is in something else through which it must be conceived (Def. 5), that is to say (Prop. 15), it is in God alone and through God alone can be conceived. If a mode, therefore, be conceived to exist necessarily and to be infinite, its necessary existence and infinitude must be concluded from some attribute of God or perceived through it, in so far as it is conceived to express infinitude and necessity of existence, that is to say (Def. 8), eternity, or, in other words (Def. 6 and Prop. 19), in so far as it is considered absolutely. A mode, therefore, which exists necessarily and infinitely must follow from the absolute nature of some attribute of God, either immediately (Prop. 21), or mediately through some modification following from His absolute nature, that is to say (Prop. 22), a modification which necessarily and infinitely exists.—Q.E.D.[11]

PROP. XXIV.—*The essence of things produced by God does not involve existence.*

This is evident from the first Definition; for that thing whose nature (considered, that is to say, in itself) involves existence, is the cause of itself and exists from the necessity of its own nature alone.

Corol.—Hence it follows that God is not only the cause of the commencement of the existence of things, but also of their continuance in existence, or, in other words (to use scholastic phraseology), God is the *causa essendi rerum*. For if we consider the essence of things, whether existing or non-existing, we discover that it neither involves existence nor duration, and therefore the essence of existing things cannot be the cause of their existence nor of their duration, but God only is the cause, to whose nature alone existence pertains (Corol. 1, Prop. 14).

PROP. XXV.—*God is not only the efficient cause of the existence of things, but also of their essence.*

[11] [On the infinite modes, of which Spinoza has been treating in the last three propositions see Letter LXIV, to Schuller, where Spinoza mentions examples (1) of immediate infinite modes and (2) of mediate infinite modes: "Lastly, the examples for which you ask are, of the first kind, in Thought, absolutely infinite understanding, but in Extension, motion and rest; of the second kind, the face of the whole Universe, which, although it varies in infinite modes, yet remains always the same." (*The Correspondence of Spinoza*, trans. A. Wolf [Garden City, N.Y.: Dial Press, 1928]). By permission of the publishers.—EDITORS.]

Demonst.—Suppose that God is not the cause of the essence of things; then (Ax. 4) the essence of things can be conceived without God, which (Prop. 15) is absurd. Therefore God is the cause of the essence of things.—Q.E.D.

Schol.—This proposition more clearly follows from Prop. 16. For from this proposition it follows that, from the existence of the divine nature, both the essence of things and their existence must necessarily be concluded, or, in a word, in the same sense in which God is said to be the cause of Himself He must be called the cause of all things. This will appear still more clearly from the following corollary.

Corol.—Individual things are nothing but affections or modes of God's attributes, expressing those attributes in a certain and determinate manner. This is evident from Prop. 15 and Def. 5.

PROP. XXVI.—*A thing which has been determined to any action was necessarily so determined by God, and that which has not been thus determined by God cannot determine itself to action.*

Demonst.—That by which things are said to be determined to any action is necessarily something positive (as is self-evident); and therefore God, from the necessity of His nature, is the efficient cause both of its essence and of its existence (Props. 25 and 16), which was the first thing to be proved. From this also the second part of the proposition follows most clearly. For if a thing which has not been determined by God could determine itself, the first part of the proposition would be false, and to suppose this possible is an absurdity, as we have shown.

PROP. XXVII.—*A thing which has been determined by God to any action cannot render itself indeterminate.*

Demonst.—This proposition is evident from the third Axiom.

PROP. XXVIII.—*An individual thing, or a thing which is finite and which has a determinate existence, cannot exist nor be determined to action unless it be determined to existence and action by another cause which is also finite and has a determinate existence; and again, this cause cannot exist nor be determined to action unless by another cause which is also finite and determined to existence and action, and so on* ad infinitum.

Demonst.—Whatever is determined to existence and action is thus determined by God (Prop. 26 and Corol. Prop. 24). But that which is finite and which has a determinate existence could not be produced by the absolute nature of any attribute of God, for whatever follows from the absolute nature of any attribute of God is infinite and eternal (Prop. 21). The finite and determinate must therefore follow from God, or from some attribute of God, in so far as the latter is considered to be affected by some mode, for besides substance and modes nothing exists (Ax. 1, and Defs. 3 and 5), and modes (Corol. Prop. 25) are nothing but affections of God's attributes. But the finite and determinate could not follow from God, or from any one of His attributes, so far as that attribute is affected with a modification which is eternal and infinite (Prop. 22). It must, therefore, follow or be determined to existence and action by God, or by some attribute of God, in so far as the attribute is modified by a modification which is finite, and which has a determinate existence. This was the first thing to be proved. Again, this cause or this mode (by the same reasoning by which we have already demonstrated the first part of this proposition) must be determined by another cause, which is also finite, and which has a determinate existence, and this last cause (by the same reasoning) must, in its turn, be determined by another cause, and so on continually (by the same reasoning) *ad infinitum.*

Schol.—Since certain things must have been immediately produced by God, that is to say, those which necessarily follow from His absolute nature; these primary products being the mediating cause for those things which, nevertheless, without God can neither be nor can be conceived; it follows, firstly, that of things immediately produced by God He is the proximate cause absolutely, and not in their own kind (*in suo genere*), as we say; for effects of God can neither be nor be conceived without their cause (Prop. 15, and Corol. Prop. 24).

It follows, secondly, that God cannot be properly called the remote cause of individual things, unless for the sake of distinguishing them from the things which He has immediately produced, or rather which follow from His absolute nature. For by a remote cause we understand that which is in no way joined to its effect. But all things which are, are in God, and so depend upon Him that without Him they can neither be nor be conceived.

PROP. XXIX.—*In nature there is nothing contingent, but all things are determined from the necessity of the divine nature to exist and act in a certain manner.*

Demonst.—Whatever is, is in God (Prop. 15); but God cannot be called a contingent thing, for (Prop. 11) He exists necessarily and not contingently. Moreover, the modes of the divine nature have followed from it necessarily and not contingently (Prop. 16), and that, too, whether it be considered absolutely (Prop. 21), or as determined to action in a certain manner (Prop. 27). But God is the cause of these modes, not only in so far as they simply exist (Corol. Prop. 24), but also (Prop. 26) in so far as they are considered as determined to any action. And if they are not determined by God (by the same proposition), it is an impossibility and not a contingency that they should determine themselves; and, on the other hand (Prop. 27), if they are determined by God, it is an impossibility and not a contingency that they should render themselves indeterminate. Wherefore all things are determined from a necessity of the divine nature, not only to exist, but to exist and act in a certain manner, and there is nothing contingent.—Q.E.D.

Schol.—Before I go any farther, I wish here to explain, or rather to recall to recollection, what we mean by *natura naturans* and what by *natura naturata*. For, from what has gone before, I think it is plain that by *natura naturans* we are to understand that which is in itself and is conceived through itself, or those attributes of substance which express eternal and infinite essence, that is to say (Corol. 1, Prop. 14, and Corol. 2, Prop. 17), God in so far as He is considered as a free cause. But by *natura naturata* I understand everything which follows from the necessity of the nature of God, or of any one of God's attributes, that is to say, all the modes of God's attributes in so far as they are considered as things which are in God, and which without God can neither be nor can be conceived.

PROP. XXX.—*The actual intellect, whether finite or infinite, must comprehend the attributes of God and the affections of God, and nothing else.*

Demonst.—A true idea must agree with that of which it is the idea (Ax. 6), that is to say (as is self-evident), that which is objectively contained in the intellect must necessarily exist in nature.

But in nature (Corol. 1, Prop. 14) only one substance exists, namely, God, and no affections (Prop. 15) excepting those which are in God, and which (by the same proposition) can neither be nor be conceived without God. Therefore the actual intellect, whether finite or infinite, must comprehend the attributes of God and the affections of God, and nothing else.—Q.E.D.

PROP. XXXI.—*The actual intellect, whether it be finite or infinite, together with the will, desire, love, &c., must be referred to the* natura naturata *and not to the* natura naturans.

Demonst.—For by the intellect (as is self-evident) we do not understand absolute thought, but only a certain mode of thought, which mode differs from other modes, such as desire, love, &c., and therefore (Def. 5) must be conceived through absolute thought, that is to say (Prop. 15 and Def. 6), it must be conceived through some attribute of God which expresses the eternal and infinite essence of thought in such a manner that without that attribute it can neither be nor can be conceived. Therefore (Schol. Prop. 29) the actual intellect, &c., must be referred to the *natura naturata*, and not to the *natura naturans*, in the same manner as all other modes of thought.—Q.E.D.

Schol.—I do not here speak of the *actual* intellect because I admit that any intellect *potentially* exists, but because I wish, in order that there may be no confusion, to speak of nothing excepting of that which we perceive with the utmost clearness, that is to say, the understanding itself, which we perceive as clearly as we perceive anything. For we can understand nothing through the intellect which does not lead to a more perfect knowledge of the understanding.

PROP. XXXII.—*The will cannot be called a free cause, but can only be called necessary.*

Demonst.—The will is only a certain mode of thought, like the intellect, and therefore (Prop. 28) no volition can exist or be determined to action unless it be determined by another cause, and this again by another, and so on *ad infinitum*. And if the will be supposed infinite, it must be determined to existence and action by God, not in so far as He is substance absolutely infinite, but in so far as He possesses an attribute which expresses the infinite and eternal essence of thought (Prop. 23). In whatever way, therefore, the will be conceived, whether as finite or infinite, it requires a cause by which it may be determined to existence and action, and therefore (Def. 7) it cannot be called a free cause but only necessary or compelled.—Q.E.D.

Corol. 1.—Hence it follows, firstly, that God does not act from freedom of the will.

Corol. 2.—It follows, secondly, that will and intellect are related to the nature of God as motion and rest, and absolutely as all natural things, which (Prop. 29) must be determined by God to existence and action in a certain manner. For the will, like all other things, needs a cause by which it may be determined to existence and action in a certain manner, and although from a given will or intellect infinite things may follow, God cannot on this account be said to act from freedom of will, any more than He can be said to act from freedom of motion and rest by reason of the things which follow from motion and rest (for from motion and rest infinite numbers of things follow). Therefore, will does not appertain to the nature of God more than other natural things, but is related to it as motion and rest and all other things are related to it; these all following, as we have shown, from the necessity of the divine nature, and being determined to existence and action in a certain manner.

Prop. XXXIII.—*Things could have been produced by God in no other manner and in no other order than that in which they have been produced.*

Demonst.—All things have necessarily followed from the given nature of God (Prop. 16), and from the necessity of His nature have been determined to existence and action in a certain manner (Prop. 29). If, therefore, things could have been of another nature, or could have been determined in another manner to action, so that the order of nature would have been different, the nature of God might then be different to that which it now is, and hence (Prop. 11) that different nature would necessarily exist, and there might consequently be two or more Gods, which (Corol. 1, Prop. 14) is absurd. Therefore, things could be produced by God in no other manner and in no other order than that in which they have been produced.—Q.E.D.

Schol. 1.—Since I have thus shown, with greater clearness than that of noonday light, that in things there is absolutely nothing by virtue of which they can be called contingent, I wish now to explain in a few words what is to be understood by *contingent*, but firstly, what is to be understood by *necessary* and *impossible*. A thing is called necessary either in reference to its essence or its cause. For the existence of a thing necessarily follows either from the essence and definition of the thing itself, or from a given efficient cause. In the same way a thing is said to be impossible either because the essence of the thing itself or its definition involves a contradiction, or because no external cause exists determinate to the production of such a thing. But a thing cannot be called contingent unless with reference to a deficiency in our knowledge. For if we do not know that the essence of a thing involves a contradiction, or if we actually know that it involves no contradiction, and nevertheless we can affirm nothing with certainty about its existence because the order of causes is concealed from us, that thing can never appear to us either as necessary or impossible, and therefore we call it either contingent or possible.

Schol. 2.—From what has gone before it clearly follows that things have been produced by God in the highest degree of perfection, since they have necessarily followed from the existence of a most perfect nature. Nor does this doctrine accuse God of any imperfection, but, on the contrary, His perfection has compelled us to affirm it. Indeed, from its contrary would clearly follow, as I have shown above, that God is not absolutely perfect, since, if things had been produced in any other fashion another nature would have had to be assigned to Him, different from that which the consideration of the most perfect Being compels us to assign to Him. I do not doubt that many will reject this opinion as ridiculous, nor will they care to apply themselves to its consideration, and this from no other reason than that they have been in the habit of assigning to God another liberty widely different from that absolute will which (Def. 7) we have taught. On the other hand, I do not doubt, if they were willing to study the matter and properly to consider the series of our demonstrations, that they would altogether reject this liberty which they now assign to God, not only as of no value, but as a great obstacle to knowledge. Neither is there any need that I should here repeat those things which are said in the scholium to Prop. 17. But for the sake of those who differ from me, I will here show that although it be granted that will pertains to God's essence, it follows nevertheless from His perfection that things could be created in no other mode or order by Him. This it will be easy to show if we first consider that which my opponents themselves admit, that it depends upon the decree and will of God alone that each thing should be what it is, for otherwise God would not be the cause of all things. It is also admitted that all God's decrees were decreed by God Himself from all eternity, for otherwise imperfection and inconstancy would be proved against Him. But since in eternity there is no *when* nor *before* nor *after*, it follows from the perfection of God alone that He neither can decree nor could ever have decreed anything else than that which He has decreed; that is to say, God has not existed before His decrees, and can never exist without them. But it is said that although it be supposed that God had made the nature of things different from that which it is, or that from eternity He had decreed something else about nature and her order, it would not thence follow that any imperfection exists in God. But if this be said, it must at the same time be allowed that God can change His decrees. For if God had decreed something about nature and her order other than that which He has decreed—that is to say, if He had willed and conceived something else about nature—He would necessarily have had an intellect and a will different from those which He now has. And if it be allowed to assign to God another intellect and another will without any change of His essence and of His perfections, what is the reason why He cannot now change His decrees about creation and nevertheless remain equally perfect? For His intellect and will regarding created things and their order remain the same in relationship to His essence and perfection in whatever manner His intellect and will are conceived. Moreover, all the philosophers whom I have seen admit that there is no such thing as an intellect existing potentially in God, but only an intellect existing actually. But since His intellect and His will are not distinguishable from His essence, as all admit, it follows from this also that if God had had another intellect actually and another will, His essence would have been necessarily different, and hence, as I showed at the beginning, if things had been produced by God in a manner different from that in which they now exist, God's intellect and will, that is to say, His essence (as has been granted), must have been different, which is absurd.

Since, therefore, things could have been produced by God in no other manner or order, this being a truth which follows from His absolute perfection, there is no sound reasoning which can persuade us to believe that God was unwilling to create all things which are in His intellect with the same perfection as that in which they exist in His intellect. But we shall be told that there is no perfection nor imperfection in things, but that that which is in them by reason of which they are perfect or imperfect and are said to be good or evil depends upon the will of God alone, and therefore if God had willed He could have effected that that which is now perfection should have been the extreme of imperfection, and *vice versa*. But what else would this be than openly to affirm that God, who necessarily understands what He wills, is able by His will to understand things in a manner different from that in which He understands them, which, as I have just shown, is a great absurdity? I can therefore turn the argument on my opponents in this way. All things depend upon the power of God. In order that things may be differently constituted, it would be necessary that God's will should be differently constituted; but God's will cannot be other than it is, as we have lately most clearly deduced from His perfection. Things therefore cannot be differently constituted. I confess that this opinion, which subjects all things to a certain indifferent God's will, and affirms that all things depend upon God's good pleasure, is at a less distance from the truth than the opinion of those who affirm that God does everything for the sake of the Good. For these seem to place something outside of God which is independent of Him, to which He looks while He is at work as to a model, or at which He aims as if at a certain mark. This is indeed nothing else than to subject God to fate, the most absurd thing which can be affirmed of Him whom we have shown to be the first and only free cause of the essence of all things as well as of their existence. Therefore it is not worth while that I should waste time in refuting this absurdity.

PROP. XXXIV.—*The power of God is His essence itself.*

Demonst.—From the necessity alone of the essence of God it follows that God is the cause of Himself (Prop. 11), and (Prop. 16

and its Corol.) the cause of all things. Therefore the power of God, by which He Himself and all things are and act, is His essence itself.—Q.E.D.

PROP. XXXV.—*Whatever we conceive to be in God's power necessarily exists.*

Demonst.—For whatever is in God's power must (Prop. 34) be so comprehended in His essence that it necessarily follows from it, and consequently exists necessarily.—Q.E.D.

PROP. XXXVI.—*Nothing exists from whose nature an effect does not follow.*

Demonst.—Whatever exists expresses the nature or the essence of God in a certain and determinate manner (Corol. Prop. 25); that is to say (Prop. 34), whatever exists expresses the power of God, which is the cause of all things, in a certain and determinate manner, and therefore (Prop. 16) some effect must follow from it.

APPENDIX

I have now explained the nature of God and its properties. I have shown that He necessarily exists; that He is one God; that from the necessity alone of His own nature He is and acts; that He is, and in what way He is, the free cause of all things; that all things are in Him, and so depend upon Him that without Him they can neither be nor can be conceived; and, finally, that all things have been predetermined by Him, not indeed from freedom of will or from absolute good pleasure, but from His absolute nature or infinite power.

Moreover, wherever an opportunity was afforded, I have endeavoured to remove prejudices which might hinder the perception of the truth of what I have demonstrated; but because not a few still remain which have been and are now sufficient to prove a very great hindrance to the comprehension of the connection of things in the manner in which I have explained it, I have thought it worth while to call them up to be examined by reason. But all these prejudices which I here undertake to point out depend upon this solely: that it is commonly supposed that all things in nature, like men, work to some end; and indeed it is thought to be certain that God Himself directs all things to some sure end, for it is said that God has made all things for man, and man that he may worship God. This, therefore, I will first investigate by inquiring, firstly, why so many rest in this prejudice, and why all are so naturally inclined to embrace it? I shall then show its falsity, and, finally, the manner in which there have arisen from it prejudices concerning *good* and *evil*, *merit* and *sin*, *praise* and *blame*, *order* and *disorder*, *beauty* and *deformity*, and so forth. This, however, is not the place to deduce these things from the nature of the human mind. It will be sufficient if I here take as an axiom that which no one ought to dispute, namely, that man is born ignorant of the causes of things, and that he has a desire, of which he is conscious, to seek that which is profitable to him. From this it follows, firstly, that he thinks himself free because he is conscious of his wishes and appetites, whilst at the same time he is ignorant of the causes by which he is led to wish and desire, not dreaming what they are; and, secondly, it follows that man does everything for an end, namely, for that which is profitable to him, which is what he seeks. Hence it happens that he attempts to discover merely the final causes of that which has happened; and when he has heard them he is satisfied, because there is no longer any cause for further uncertainty. But if he cannot hear from another what these final causes are, nothing remains but to turn to himself and reflect upon the ends which usually determine him to the like actions, and thus by his own mind he necessarily judges that of another. Moreover, since he discovers, both within and without himself, a multitude of means which contribute not a little to the attainment of what is profitable to himself—for example, the eyes, which are useful for seeing, the teeth for mastication, plants and animals for nourishment, the sun for giving light, the sea for feeding fish, &c.—it comes to pass that all natural objects are considered as means for obtaining what is profitable. These too being evidently discovered and not created by man, hence he has a cause for believing that some other person exists, who has prepared them for man's use. For having considered them as means it was impossible to believe that they had created themselves, and so he was obliged to infer from the means which he was in the habit of providing for himself that some ruler or rulers of nature exist, endowed with human liberty, who have taken care of all things for him, and have made all things for his use. Since he never heard anything about the mind of these rulers, he was compelled to judge of it from his own, and hence he affirmed that the gods direct everything for his advantage, in order that he may be bound to them and hold them in the highest honour. This is the reason why each man has devised for himself, out of his own brain, a different mode of worshipping God, so that God might love him above others, and direct all nature to the service of his blind cupidity and insatiable avarice.

Thus has this prejudice been turned into a superstition and has driven deep roots into the mind—a prejudice which was the reason why every one has so eagerly tried to discover and explain the final causes of things. The attempt, however, to show that nature does nothing in vain (that is to say, nothing which is not profitable to man), seems to end in showing that nature, the gods, and man are alike mad.

Do but see, I pray, to what all this has led. Amidst so much in nature that is beneficial, not a few things must have been observed which are injurious, such as storms, earthquakes, diseases, and it was affirmed that these things happened either because the gods were angry because of wrongs which had been inflicted on them by man, or because of sins committed in the method of worshipping them; and although experience daily contradicted this, and showed by an infinity of examples that both the beneficial and the injurious were indiscriminately bestowed on the pious and the impious, the inveterate prejudices on this point have not therefore been abandoned. For it was much easier for a man to place these things aside with others of the use of which he was ignorant, and thus retain his present and inborn state of ignorance, than to destroy the whole superstructure and think out a new one. Hence it was looked upon as indisputable that the judgments of the gods far surpass our comprehension; and this opinion alone would have been sufficient to keep the human race in darkness to all eternity, if mathematics, which does not deal with ends, but with the essences and properties of forms, had not placed before us another rule of truth. In addition to mathematics, other causes also might be assigned, which it is superfluous here to enumerate, tending to make men reflect upon these universal prejudices, and leading them to a true knowledge of things.

I have thus sufficiently explained what I promised in the first place to explain. There will now be no need of many words to show that nature has set no end before herself, and that all final causes are nothing but human fictions. For I believe that this is sufficiently evident both from the foundations and causes of this prejudice, and from Prop. 16 and Corol. Prop. 32, as well as from all those propositions in which I have shown that all things are begotten by a certain eternal necessity of nature and in absolute perfection. Thus much, nevertheless, I will add, that this doctrine concerning an end altogether overturns nature. For that which is in truth the cause it considers as the effect, and *vice versa*. Again, that which is first in nature it puts last; and, finally, that which is supreme and most perfect it makes the most imperfect. For (passing by the first two assertions as self-evident) it is plain from Props. 21, 22, and 23, that that effect is the most perfect which is immediately produced by God, and in proportion as intermediate causes are necessary for the production of a thing is it imperfect. But if things which are immediately produced by God were made in order that He might obtain the end He had in view, then the last things for the sake of which the first exist, must be the most perfect of all. Again, this doctrine does away with God's perfection. For if God works to obtain an end, He necessarily seeks something of which he stands in need. And although theologians and metaphysicians distinguish between the end of want and the end of assimilation (*finem indegentiæ et finem assimilationis*), they confess that God has done all things for His own sake, and not for the sake of the things to be created, because before the creation they can assign nothing excepting God for the sake of which God could do anything; and therefore they are necessarily compelled to admit that God stood in need of and desired those things for which He determined to prepare means. This is self-evident. Nor is it here to be overlooked that the adherents of this doctrine, who have found a pleasure in displaying their ingenuity in assigning the ends of things, have introduced a new species of argument, not the *reductio ad impossible*, but the *reductio ad ignorantiam*, to prove their position, which shows that it had no other method of defence left. For, by way of example, if a stone has fallen from some roof on somebody's head and killed him, they will demonstrate in this manner that the stone has fallen in order to kill the man. For if it did not fall for that purpose by the will of God, how could so many circumstances concur through chance (and a number often simultaneously do concur)? You will answer, perhaps, that the event happened because the wind blew and the man was passing that way. But, they will urge, why did the wind blow at that time, and why did the man pass that way precisely at the same moment? If you again reply that the wind rose then because the sea on the preceding day began to be stormy, the weather hitherto having been calm, and that the man had been invited by a friend, they will urge again—because there is no end of questioning—But why was the sea agitated? why was the man invited at that time? And so they will not cease from asking the causes of causes, until at last you fly to the will of God, the refuge for ignorance.

So, also, when they behold the structure of the human body, they are amazed; and because they are ignorant of the causes of such art, they conclude that the body was made not by mechanical but by a supernatural or divine art, and has been formed in such a way so that the one part may not injure the other. Hence it happens that the man who endeavours to find out the true causes of miracles, and who desires as a wise man to understand nature, and not to gape at it like a fool, is generally considered and proclaimed to be a heretic and impious by those whom the vulgar worship as the interpreters both of nature and the gods. For these know that if ignorance be removed, amazed stupidity, the sole ground on which they rely in arguing or in defending their authority, is taken away also. But these things I leave and pass on to that which I determined to do in the third place.

After man has persuaded himself that all things which exist are made for him, he must in everything adjudge that to be of the greatest importance which is most useful to him, and he must esteem that to be of surpassing worth by which he is most beneficially affected. In this way he is compelled to form those notions by which he explains nature; such, for instance, as *good*, *evil*, *order*, *confusion*, *heat*, *cold*, *beauty*, and *deformity*, &c.; and because he supposes himself to be free, notions like those of *praise* and *blame*, *sin* and *merit*, have arisen. These latter I shall hereafter explain when I have treated of human nature; the former I will here briefly unfold.

It is to be observed that man has given the name *good* to every thing which leads to health and the worship of God; on the contrary, everything which does not lead thereto he calls *evil*. But because those who do not understand nature affirm nothing about things themselves, but only imagine them, and take the imagination to be understanding, they therefore, ignorant of things and their nature, firmly believe an *order* to be in things; for when things are so placed that, if they are represented to us through the senses, we can easily imagine them, and consequently easily remember them, we call them well arranged; but if they are not placed so that we can imagine and remember them, we call them badly arranged or *confused*. Moreover, since those things are more especially pleasing to us which we can easily imagine, men therefore prefer order to confusion, as if order were something in nature apart from our own imagination; and they say that God has created everything in order, and in this manner they ignorantly attribute imagination to God, unless they mean perhaps that God, out of consideration for the human imagination, has disposed things in the manner in which they can most easily be imagined. No hesitation either seems to be caused by the fact that an infinite number of things are discovered which far surpass our imagination, and very many which confound it through its weakness. But enough of this. The other notions which I have mentioned are nothing but modes in which the imagination is affected in different ways, and nevertheless they are regarded by the ignorant as being specially attributes of things, because, as we have remarked, men consider all things as made for themselves, and call the nature of a thing good, evil, sound, putrid, or corrupt, just as they are affected by it. For example if the motion by which the nerves are affected by means of objects represented to the eye conduces to well-being, the objects by which it is caused are called *beautiful*; while those exciting a contrary motion are called *deformed*. Those things, too, which stimulate the senses through the nostrils are called sweet-smelling or stinking; those which act through the taste are called sweet or bitter, full-flavoured or insipid; those which act through the touch, hard or soft, heavy or light; those, lastly, which act through the ears are said to make a noise, sound, or harmony, the last having caused men to lose their senses to such a degree that they have believed that God even is delighted with it. Indeed, philosophers may be found who have persuaded themselves that the celestial motions beget a harmony. All these things sufficiently show that every one judges things by the constitution of his brain, or rather accepts the affections of his imagination in the place of things. It is not, therefore, to be wondered at, as we may observe in passing, that all those controversies which we see have arisen amongst men, so that at last scepticism has been the result. For although human bodies agree in many things, they differ in more, and therefore that which to one person is good will appear to another evil, that which to one is well arranged to another is confused, that which pleases one will displease another, and so on in other cases which I pass by both because we cannot notice them at length here, and because they are within the experience of every one. For every one has heard the expressions: So many heads, so many ways of thinking; Every one is satisfied with his own way of thinking; Differences of brains are not less common than differences of taste;—all which maxims show that men decide upon matters according to the constitution of their brains, and imagine rather than understand things. If men understood things, they would, as mathematics prove, at least be all alike convinced if they were not all alike attracted. We see, therefore, that all those methods by which the common people are in the habit of explaining nature are only different sorts of imaginations, and do not reveal the nature of anything in itself, but only the constitution of the imagination; and because they have names as if they were entities existing apart from the imagination, I call them entities not of the reason but of the imagination. All argument, therefore, urged against us based upon such notions can be easily refuted. Many people, for instance, are accustomed to argue thus:—If all things have followed from the necessity of the most perfect nature of God, how is it that so many imperfections have arisen in nature—corruption, for instance, of things till they stink; deformity, exciting disgust; confusion, evil, crime, &c.? But, as I have just observed, all this is easily answered. For the perfection of things is to be judged by their nature and power alone; nor are they more or less perfect because they delight or offend the human senses, or because they are beneficial or prejudicial to human nature. But to those who ask why God has not created all men in such a manner that they might be controlled by the dictates of reason alone, I give but this answer: Because to Him material was not wanting for the creation of everything, from the highest down to the very lowest grade of perfection; or, to speak more properly, because the laws of His nature were so ample that they sufficed for the production of everything which can be conceived by an infinite intellect, as I have demonstrated in Prop. 16.

These are the prejudices which I undertook to notice here. If any others of a similar character remain, they can easily be rectified with a little thought by any one.

LETTER XXXII (IN PART)[12]

TO THE VERY NOBLE AND LEARNED MR. HENRY OLDENBURG

MOST NOBLE SIR,

I thank you and the very Noble Mr. Boyle very much for kindly encouraging me to go on with my Philosophy. I do indeed proceed with it, as far as my slender powers allow, not doubting meanwhile of your help and goodwill.

When you ask me what I think about the question which turns on *the Knowledge how each part of Nature accords with the whole of it, and in what way it is connected with the other parts,* I think you mean to ask for the reasons on the strength of which we believe that each part of Nature accords with the whole of it, and is connected with the other parts. For I said in my preceding letter that I do not know how the parts are really interconnected, and how each part accords with the whole; for to know this it would be necessary to know the whole of Nature and all its Parts.

I shall therefore try to show the reason which compels me to make this assertion; but I should like first to warn you that I do not attribute to Nature beauty or ugliness, order or confusion. For things cannot, except with respect to our imagination, be called beautiful, or ugly, ordered or confused.

By connection of the parts, then, I mean nothing else than that the laws, or nature, of one part adapt themselves to the laws, or nature, of another part in such a way as to produce the least possible opposition. With regard to whole and parts, I consider things as parts of some whole, in so far as their natures are mutually adapted so that they are in accord among themselves, as far as possible; but in so far as things differ among themselves, each produces an idea in our mind, which is distinct from the others, and is therefore considered to be a whole, not a part. For

[12] *The Correspondence of Spinoza,* trans. A. Wolf (Garden City: Dial Press, 1928). By permission of the publishers.

instance, since the motions of the particles of lymph, chyle, etc., are so mutually adapted in respect of magnitude and figure that they clearly agree among themselves, and all together constitute one fluid, to that extent only, chyle, lymph, etc., are considered to be parts of the blood: but in so far as we conceive the lymph particles as differing in respect of figure and motion from the particles of chyle, to that extent we consider them to be a whole, not a part.

Let us now, if you please, imagine that a small worm lives in the blood, whose sight is keen enough to distinguish the particles of blood, lymph, etc., and his reason to observe how each part on collision with another either rebounds, or communicates a part of its own motion, etc. That worm would live in this blood as we live in this part of the universe, and he would consider each particle of blood to be a whole, and not a part. And he could not know how all the parts are controlled by the universal nature of blood, and are forced, as the universal nature of blood demands, to adapt themselves to one another, so as to harmonize with one another in a certain way. For if we imagine that there are no causes outside the blood to communicate new motions to the blood, and that outside the blood there is no space, and no other bodies, to which the particles of blood could transfer their motion, it is certain that the blood would remain always in its state, and its particles would suffer no changes other than those which can be conceived from the given relation of the motion of the blood to the lymph and chyle, etc., and so blood would have to be considered always to be a whole and not a part. But, since there are very many other causes which in a certain way control the laws of the nature of blood, and are in turn controlled by the blood, hence it comes about that other motions and other changes take place in the blood, which result not only from the mere relation of the motion of its parts to one another, but from the relation of the motion of the blood and also of the external causes to one another: in this way the blood has the character of a part and not of a whole. I have only spoken of whole and part.

Now, all the bodies of nature can and should be conceived in the same way as we have here conceived the blood: for all bodies are surrounded by others, and are mutually determined to exist and to act in a definite and determined manner, while there is preserved in all together, that is, in the whole universe, the same proportion of motion and rest. Hence it follows that every body, in so far as it exists modified in a certain way, must be considered to be a part of the whole universe, to be in accord with the whole of it, and to be connected with the other parts. And since the nature of the universe is not limited, like the nature of the blood, but absolutely infinite, its parts are controlled by the nature of this infinite power in infinite ways, and are compelled to suffer infinite changes. But I conceive that with regard to substance each part has a closer union with its whole. For as I endeavoured to show in my first letter, which I wrote to you when I was still living at Rhynsburg, since it is of the nature of substance to be infinite, it follows that each part belongs to the nature of corporeal substance, and can neither exist nor be conceived without it.

You see, then, in what way and why I think that the human Body is a part of Nature. As regards the human Mind I think it too is a part of Nature: since I state that there exists in Nature an infinite power of thought, which in so far as it is infinite, contains in itself objectively the whole of Nature, and its thoughts proceed in the same way as Nature, which, to be sure, is its ideatum.

Then I declare that the human mind is this same power, not in so far as it is infinite, and perceives the whole of Nature, but in so far as it is finite and perceives only the human Body, and in this way I declare that the human Mind is a part of a certain infinite intellect. . . . .

Of the rest on another occasion. Now I can say no more than that I ask you to give a hearty greeting from me to the very Noble Mr. Boyle, and to remember me who am

In all affection yours
B. DE SPINOZA.

VOORBURG, *20 November 1665.*

CHAPTER IV

GOTTFRIED WILHELM LEIBNIZ

Leibniz was born at Leipzig in 1646, studied there and at Jena, took his degree at Altorf, and then entered the service of the Elector of Mainz at Frankfurt. In 1672 he traveled to Paris and London, lived at Paris until 1677, and before his return to Germany visited Spinoza at The Hague. He then went to Hanover as librarian and historian to the House of Brunswick. Later he lived at the court of the Prussian Queen Sophie Charlotte in Berlin (where he directed the founding of the Academy) and after that in Vienna. He died in Hanover in 1716. In all these places he had been active as philosopher, mathematician, historian, political theorist, and jurist; and sometimes these various activities even coincided—as when he tried to demonstrate logically the proper choice for the Polish succession, or as in all his efforts to advance religious peace by the philosophic reconciliation of Catholic and Protestant theologies. Chief works (most of Leibniz' philosophic statements are contained in brief expositions or even fragments, comparatively few of which were published during his lifetime; a few of the better-known works are mentioned here, but for a fuller bibliography see Latta's *Monadology*): *Meditations on Knowledge, Truth and Ideas* (1684); *Correspondence with Arnauld* (1686–90); *Whether the Essence of Body Consists in Extension* (1691 and 1693); *New System of Nature* (1695); *New Essays on Human Understanding* (1704); *Theodicy* (1710); *The Principles of Nature and of Grace* (1714); *Monadology* (1714); *Correspondence with Clark* (1715–16). Suggested readings: *Philosophical Works*, ed. Duncan (New Haven, 1890, 1908); *Philosophical Writings*, ed. Morris (London and Toronto, 1934); *Discourse on Metaphysics, Correspondence with Arnauld, and Monadology* (Chicago, 1931); *New Essays*, trans. Langley (Chicago, 1916); *The Monadology and Other Philosophical Writings*, ed. Latta (Oxford, 1898, 1925). H. W. Carr, *Leibniz* (London, 1929); Latta's ed. of *Monadology, etc.*; Bertrand Russell, *A Critical Exposition of the Philosophy of Leibniz* (Cambridge, 1900).

INVENTOR of the infinitesimal calculus, Leibniz hoped also to invent a logical calculus and a universal logical language, by means of which men might attain that universal agreement in scientific matters which he as well as Descartes and Spinoza thought possible. With these instruments at their disposal, he thought, two philosophers who disagreed about a particular point could, instead of arguing fruitlessly and endlessly, take out their pencils, sit down amicably at their desks, and say, "Let us calculate." Thus the whole of human knowledge would be one vast multiplication table with which any normal person could work, once he had learned the rules. But this hope for logic is not only a hope for the success of new mechanical equipment in the shape of certain easily applicable symbols and formulas: it is a belief closely allied to Leibniz' basic premise with regard to the nature of truth—a premise from which in turn some of his chief metaphysical views follow. A true proposition, according to Leibniz, is always one in which the predicate is contained in the subject, hence from any subject it should be possible by certain calculations to elicit any predicate applicable to it. Thus all true statements are ultimately reducible to statements of the form A is A; for saying that A is B, if B is already contained in A, is only another way of saying that A is A. Now except for the manner of statement this view seems not so very different from Spinoza's—where all the world and all true knowledge of it is thought of as one great logical system within which any particular fact is already included in its proper place. For Spinoza, however, this logical rigor means, metaphysically, the elimination of free will and of final causes from the universe; the strictly necessary relation of ground and consequent is the one causal relation basic to reality as well as to truth. For Leibniz, in contrast, almost the greatest merit of his discovery that truth consists basically in identities, is the fashion in which it serves not to destroy but to rescue the principle of freedom.

All truths, Leibniz holds, are either explicitly or implicitly expressions of identities. This is most evident in the case of mathematical propositions, where with the help of definitions any statement can actually be proved by reduction to an identical statement. There are other propositions, however, where the possibility of such reduction is not so evident. Such are all the propositions that deal with special conditions in space and time, instead of referring to abstract universal objects like those of mathematics. Propositions like those of logic and mathematics, for which we can actually show by reduction that the predicate is contained in the subject, Leibniz calls *necessary* propositions; and they hold, he says, for all possible worlds. That is to say, they are true universally, simply in consequence of the principle that A is A (to which, after all, they are all equivalent) and without any reference to any conditions of space, time, or existence. Those other propositions in which the reducibility to an identical proposition is not apparent, Leibniz calls *contingent;* they hold only for certain existential conditions, not in abstraction from all existence. Even the more universal of them, like the law of gravity, for example, though they hold, short of miracles, for everything in this world, hold only for *this* world, not for all possible ones—and so even they are limited by the condition that this world, not another, should be the one that exists. These propositions, by virtue of the special conditions attached to them, seem to be incapable of demonstration in the sense in which necessary propositions are demonstrable; for the existential conditions involved cannot, by us at least, be elicited from the mere concept of the subject. (So for instance from the mere concept of the sun we cannot deduce that it shone yesterday, is shining today, or will shine tomorrow.) But is truth, then, after all, always a matter of the inclusion of predicate in subject, or are these contingent propositions an exception? Here the ways part between philosophers like Hume and Kant, on the one hand, and Leibniz, on the other. *All* true propositions are, for Leibniz, at least implicitly identities; the point is that in contingent propositions the reduction takes infinite steps and cannot be performed by imperfect, human minds. All men can do toward understanding contingent propositions as truths is to affirm a second principle which follows from the first one we have stated. In every truth, Leibniz says, the predicate is contained in the subject. But then there must be in every subject of a proposition something that involves and accounts for each predicate applied to it. On the one hand, in other words, every substance, as possible subject of a proposition, contains within it every predicate that will ever be applied to it—or all its accidents past, present, and future;

and, conversely, every predicate of a subject, or every accident of a substance, has a Sufficient Reason in the nature of
the subject or substance to which it belongs. This is Leibniz'
second great principle: the Principle of Sufficient Reason.
For contingent propositions, he declares, it is true we cannot
demonstrate, that is, reduce to identities; but we can at least
assert that the predicate must be really contained in the
subject even though we cannot show how it is so contained.
For, were it not so contained, there would be no sufficient
reason for the affirmation of the predicate; but that would
contradict the principle of Sufficient Reason, which is absurd.
So, we see, for contingent truths, the predicate is contained
in the subject, and we declare it so contained by reference
to the Law of Sufficient Reason. The actual reduction, however, is infinitely long and exceeds our powers; we can only
supplement logical methods here by the evidence of experience—which however will never give us demonstration or
complete knowledge. In fact, as opposed to our mere assertion of the general principle, the actual Sufficient Reason for
a given contingent fact is perfectly understood only by God,
who has the immediate perception we lack of the identity
involved. That is, only he understands the actual reason for
his choice of this contingent rather than another.

So much for the difference between necessary and contingent truths in terms of our knowledge of them. But the distinction can be enlarged to metaphysical scope. Setting the
laws of logic and mathematics, true for all possible worlds,
against contingent propositions, true for this world only, we
may say that the former are ruled by the Principle of Identity, to which they are all reducible, while the others demand
likewise a Principle of Sufficient Reason. So we get two basic
principles which involve with them several important metaphysical tenets. By both principles, we know already that
every predicate of a subject, or accident of a substance, is
contained in its very nature. But every individual substance
bears some intrinsic relation to every other, for a relation

between any two can always be stated; and every proposition which states a relation, since its subject contains its predicate, states an intrinsic relation. Therefore every subject contains, in a way, all other subjects—or the whole universe. At the same time, no subject is extrinsically affected—since all its predicates are contained in itself; and so, although all substances are related to one another, there can be no direct influence of one substance on another. Thus it is only by a Pre-established Harmony that various substances appear to be working on one another. They are actually going on, each, in its own way, reflecting the whole universe from within itself, but working in harmony with all other substances by an initial decree of their Creator. And this notion fits, again, with the Principle of Sufficient Reason; for if we look at the two most perplexing substances in this respect, a human mind and its body, we see that, as against the way of "direct influence" or of "occasional cause," the most orderly and economic way to arrange their co-operation is by just such a Pre-established Harmony of independent entities. Moreover, as to the nature of body itself, we see that there is no *reason* to stop subdividing a body at any particular point—and so, by the principle of Sufficient Reason, we declare bodies infinitely divisible, and each body full of infinite smaller bodies. And, further, we find that, against the Cartesians, body cannot be merely extension. For in that case there might be parts of bodies and bodies exactly alike except in number (if they were exactly alike in extension, which is conceivable); and that is impossible, since there would then be no sufficient reason to distinguish the two. So "bodies" must contain some non-corporeal principle or form which is the real substance of them and the reason for the predicates they assume. Thus "bodies" as well as minds are really souls, not bodies; the only difference is that some souls perceive more clearly than others and are called rational.

But we have yet to see how this distinction of Leibniz' contributes to the definition of freedom as a metaphysical principle. On the contrary, if every predicate is implied by its subject, if the concept of Brutus involves killing Caesar, and the concept of Judas involves betraying his Lord, it looks as if necessity rather than freedom were supreme. Leibniz insists, however, that it is not, as in the case of mathematical propositions, *metaphysical* necessity by which such predicates are contained in their subjects. It is only a *hypothetical* necessity—dependent on God's choice of *this* world, not inevitable for any possible universe. True, when God chooses this world, he chooses with it Caesar, who is such that he will choose to be a tyrant, and Brutus, who is such that he will choose to kill him. But the choice, both for God and for these his rational creatures, is free. God contemplates all possible worlds—the sphere of Identity—and, in accordance with the Law of Sufficient Reason, though inscrutably for us, chooses the best. Caesar and Brutus, in their imperfect way, likewise choose what seems to them best—and the choice is equally free. True, God foresees and even in a sense foreordains their choice; but he foresees it *as* a free choice—not as he foresees the eternal operation of metaphysically necessary laws or even the long-continued working of the fundamental physical laws of this chosen universe. So the distinction between necessary and contingent truths, again distinguished, furnishes for Leibniz the key to the difficulty of free substances. Necessary truths depend on the Principle of Identity alone and are universal and absolute in their necessity. Contingent truths involve the Law of Sufficient Reason and their necessity is hypothetical, depending always on God's choice, in accordance with that principle, of this best of all possible worlds. But again within that world, with its created substances and its hypothetically and physically necessary sequence of events, there are some substances which are one step farther from the metaphysical necessity of the eternal truths. Granted this world, and no miracles, some physical events can be pretty well predicted. But the choices of rational agents can never be predicted—they are free as God's acts are free; and the identity involved in affirmations about their acts is even more remote from demonstration, if that be possible, than are the identities implicit in ordinary contingent truths.

FIRST TRUTHS[1]

First *truths* are those which make a self-identical statement in themselves or deny the opposite statement by the very fact of its being opposite. As: A is A, or A is not non-A. If it is true that A is B, it is false that A is not B or that A is non-B. Again, anything whatsoever is such as it is. Anything whatsoever is similar to itself or equal to itself. Nothing is greater or less than itself. These and other propositions of this kind, which may indeed themselves have their grades of priority, can nevertheless be all included under the one name of *identical* propositions.

Moreover, all remaining truths are reduced to the first by the help of definitions, or by the resolution of concepts which constitutes *proof a priori*, independent of experience. I shall give an example. This proposition, received among the axioms by Mathematicians as well as by all others: that the whole is greater than its part, or the part less than the whole, is very easily demonstrated from the definition of less or greater, with the addition of a primitive or identical axiom. For *Less* is what is equal to a part of another (*greater*). Surely this definition is very easy for the understanding, and in conformity with the practice of mankind, when they compare things with one another, and by withdrawing the excess from the greater find it equal to the less. Hence one may reason thus: The part is equal to the part of the whole (for by an identical axiom, anything whatsoever is equal to itself). But that which is equal to a part of the whole, is less than the whole (by the definition of less). Therefore the part is less than the whole.

Therefore the predicate or consequence is always present in the subject or antecedent. And it is in this very fact that the nature of truth as a whole, or the connection among the terms of an enunciation, consists, as Aristotle has also observed. And in identities that connection and comprehension of the predicate in the

[1] Translated from *Opuscules et fragments inédits de Leibniz*, ed. Louis Couturat (Paris: Félix Alcan, 1903), pp. 518–23. By permission of the publishers.

subject is in fact expressed; in all remaining propositions it is implicit, or to be shown by the analysis of concepts, on which demonstration a priori is based.

This is true, moreover, in every affirmative truth whether universal or singular, necessary or contingent, and as well in those called intrinsic as extrinsic. And here there is hidden a marvellous secret in which is contained the nature of contingency or the essential distinction between necessary and contingent truths, and by which also the difficulty concerning the fated necessity of free things is removed.

From these things, insufficiently considered because of their too great simplicity, many matters of great moment follow. For from this source springs immediately the received axiom that nothing is without a reason, or that no effect is without a cause. Otherwise there might be a truth which could not be proved a priori, or which would not be resolved into identical truths; but that is contrary to the nature of truth, which is always, either expressly or implicitly, identical. It follows also that when everything in the data is in the same condition on the one hand as on the other, then in the same way also in what is sought or in the consequences everything will be in the same condition on both sides. This is because no reason for diversity (which must in all events be sought for in the data) can be produced. And a corollary or rather example of this is the postulate of Archimedes relating to things originally equiponderable, that when the arms of the scale and the weights placed on either side are equal, they are all in equilibrium. Hence *also a reason is given for eternal things:* if the world were feigned to have been from eternity, and only globes to have been in it, a reason would have to be produced why globes rather than cubes.

Hence also it follows that *two individual things differing only in number cannot exist in nature.* For surely it should be possible to produce a reason why they are different—which reason must be sought for from some difference in the things themselves. So what St. Thomas acknowledged concerning separated intelligences, which he declared never differed in number alone, must also be said of other things. Nor are two eggs or two leaves or blades of grass in a garden ever found perfectly similar to one another. And perfect similarity therefore finds a place only in incomplete and abstract concepts, where things come into account not wholly but according to a certain fashion of considering them. Thus when we consider figures only, we neglect the material figured, and so two triangles are rightly considered similar in geometry, even though two perfectly similar material triangles are never found. And gold and other metals, salts too, and many fluids may be held to be homogeneous bodies; but. this can be admitted only with respect to the senses, and not even so is it exactly true.

It follows also *that there are no purely extrinsic denominations*, which have absolutely no foundation in the thing itself denominated. For the concept of the subject denominated must involve the concept of the predicate. Hence as often as the denomination of the thing is changed, some variation must occur in the thing itself.

A complete or perfect concept of an individual substance involves all its predicates past, present and future. For in all events it is true even now that a future predicate is future, and so it is contained in the concept of the thing. And therefore in the perfect individual notion of Peter or Judas, considered under the form of possibility, by abstracting the mind from the divine decree of creating him, there are present and seen by GOD all the things that will happen to them, necessary as well as free. And thus it is manifest that GOD chooses from infinite possible individuals those which he considers more congenial to the supreme and secret ends of his wisdom,— not, if one is to speak exactly, that he decides that Peter should sin, or Judas be damned, but only that he decides that in preference to other possibilities, Peter who will sin (not indeed, necessarily but freely), and Judas who will undergo damnation, should come into existence. That is, he decides that a possible concept should be made actual. And although the future salvation of Peter is also contained in the eternal possible concept of him, still it is not so contained without the concourse of grace,—for in that perfect concept of this possible Peter, the aids of divine grace to be brought him are also contained under the concept of possibility.

Every individual substance involves in its perfect concept the whole universe, and all existences in it past, present and future. For there is nothing, on which some true denomination cannot be imposed from some other thing, at least by way of comparison or relation. Moreover, there is no purely extrinsic denomination. The same thing is shown by me in many other ways agreeing together.

Indeed *all individual created substances are different expressions of the same universe,* and of the same universal cause, that is, GOD; but the expressions vary in perfection like different representations or drawings in perspective of the same town seen from different points.

Every individual created substance exercises physical action and passion on all others. For when a change is made in one, some responding change follows in all others, since the denomination is altered. And this is in conformity with our experiences of nature: for we see that in a vessel full of fluid (and the whole universe is like a vessel) a motion made in the center is propagated to the extremes, even though it may be rendered more and more imperceptible, as it recedes farther from its origin.

In strictness it can be said that *no created substance exercises metaphysical action or influence on another.* For, not to mention the impossibility of explaining how anything would pass over from one thing into the substance of another, it has already been shown that from the concept of anything whatsoever all its future states already follow. And what we call causes are, (in metaphysical rigor), only required as concomitants. This same fact is illustrated by our very experiences of nature; for bodies do indeed recede from other bodies by the force of their own elasticity (*Elastrum*), not by a foreign force, even though another body has been required in order that the elasticity (which originates from something intrinsic to the body itself) might act.

Hence, if the difference of soul and body is granted, their union can be explained, without the vulgar hypothesis of influence, which cannot be understood, and without the hypothesis of the occasional cause, which calls on a GOD from the machine. For GOD has from the beginning so fashioned soul as well as body, with so much wisdom and so much artifice, that from the first constitution or concept itself of either one, everything that happens in the one corresponds perfectly to everything that happens in the other. This I call the *hypothesis of concomitance.* This is true in all substances of the whole universe, but is not perceptible in all, as it is in the case of soul and body.[2]

[2] Cf. "A Letter of Leibnitz on His Philosophical Hypothesis and the Curious Problem Proposed by His Friends to the Mathematicians" (1696) (from *The*

There is no vacuum. For the different parts of empty space would be perfectly similar and congruous with one another, nor

---

Philosophical Works of Leibnitz, trans. George Martin Duncan [New Haven: Tuttle, Morehouse & Taylor, 1890], No. XV, pp. 92–93):

"Some wise and penetrating friends, having considered my novel hypothesis concerning the great question of the union of soul and body, and having found it of importance have besought me to give some explanations of the difficulties which have been raised and which come from the fact that it has not been well understood.

"I have thought that the matter might be rendered intelligible for every sort of mind by the following comparison:

"Imagine two clocks or two watches which agree perfectly. Now this may happen in *three ways*. The first consists in the mutual influence of one clock on the other; the second, in the care of a man who attends thereto; the third, in their own accuracy.

"The *first way*, which is that of influence, has been experimented on by the late M. Huygens, to his great astonishment. He had two large pendulums attached to the same piece of wood; the continual vibrations of these pendulums communicated similar vibrations to the particles of wood; but these different vibrations not being able to subsist very well in their order and without hindering each other, unless the pendulums agreed, it happened by a kind of marvel that even when their beats had been purposely disturbed they soon came again to beat together, almost like two chords which are in unison.

"The *second way* of making two clocks, even although poor, always accord, would be to have a skillful workman who should see to it that they are kept in constant agreement. This is what I call the way of assistance.

"Finally, the *third way* would be to make in the first place these two clocks with so much art and accuracy that we might be assured of their future accordance. This is the way of the pre-established agreement.

"Put now the soul and the body in the place of these two clocks. Their harmony or sympathy will take place by one of these three methods. The way of *influence* is that of common philosophy; but as we cannot conceive of material particles or properties, or immaterial qualities, which can pass from one of these substances into the other, we are obliged to abandon this view. The way of *assistance* is that of the system of occasional causes; but I hold that this is making a *Deus ex Machina* intervene in a natural and ordinary matter, when, according to reason, he ought not to intervene except in the manner in which he cooperates in all the other affairs of nature.

"Thus, there remains only my hypothesis; that is, the way of a harmony pre-established by a prevenient divine contrivance, which from the beginning has formed each of these substances in a way so perfect and regulated with so much accuracy that merely by following laws of its own, received with its being, it nevertheless agrees with the other, just as if there were mutual influence, or as if God in addition to his general cooperation constantly put his hand thereto.

"After this I do not think I need to prove anything, unless it be that you wish me to prove that God has everything necessary to making use of this prevenient contrivance, examples of which we see even among men, according to their skill. And supposing that he can do it you see well that this is the most admirable way and the one most worthy of him.

"It is true that I have yet other proofs but they are more profound, and it is not necessary to state them here."

could they be distinguished from one another, and so they would differ only in number, which is absurd. In the same way as space, time is also proven not to be a thing.[3]

There is no atom, rather there is no body so tiny that it may not be actually subdivided. By the very nature of the case while it suffers from all other things of the whole universe, it both receives from all some effect, which ought to effect a variation in the body, and at the same time it has preserved all its past impressions and is storing up its future ones. And if any one should say that the effect is contained in the motions impressed on the atom, which might bring about an effect without its division, the reply can be made to him, that not only must the effects result in the atom from all the impressions of the universe, but also conversely the state of the whole universe must be inferred from the atom, and the cause from the effect—but indeed from the figure and motion of the atom alone it cannot be inferred by a regress by what impressions it has come to this state; since the same motion can be obtained by different impressions; not to mention that no reason can be produced, why bodies of a certain smallness should be no further divisible.

Hence it follows that *a world of infinite creatures is contained in every particle of the universe*. But the continuum is not divided into points, nor is it divided in all possible ways; not into points, since points are not parts, but termini; not in all possible ways, since it is not all creatures that are contained in the same one, but only the certain progression of them to infinity. Thus he who should suppose the right angle and again its part bisected, would set up other divisions than one who should suppose it trisected.

There is no determinate figure in actual things, for none can satisfy the infinite impressions. Thus neither the circle nor ellipse nor any other line is definable by us except by the intellect, either before the lines are drawn or before the parts are separated.[4]

---

[3] Omitted by Leibniz: *"There is no corporeal substance which contains nothing but extension and magnitude, figure and the variation of these.* For thus there could exist two corporeal substances perfectly similar to one another, which is absurd. Hence it follows that there is something in corporeal substances analogous to soul, which they call form."

[4] Omitted by Leibniz: Space and extension and motion are not things, but ways of considering which have a foundation.

Extension and motion, and bodies themselves in so far as they are lodged only in these, are not substances, but really phenomena like rainbows and mock suns (parhelia). For figures are not from the side of the thing, and bodies if they are considered to be only extension are not one substance but many.

For the substance of bodies there is required something free from extension, otherwise there will be no principle of the reality of phenomena or of their true unity. Thus bodies are always considered many, never one, and so in truth not many. Cordemoius proved atoms by a similar argument; and when these are excluded, there remains something lacking extension, analogous to the soul, which they formerly called form or Species.

A corporeal substance can neither arise nor perish except by creation or annihilation. For if it should once endure, it will always endure; for there is neither any reason for a difference, nor do the dissolutions of the parts of the body have anything in common with the destruction of the body itself. Therefore *ensouled beings do not arise or perish, they are only transformed.*

NECESSARY AND CONTINGENT TRUTHS[5]

A true affirmation is one, the predicate of which is present in the subject. Thus in every true affirmative proposition, necessary or contingent, universal or singular, the concept of the predicate is in some way contained in the concept of the subject, so that he who perfectly understood each concept as GOD understands it, would by that very fact perceive that the predicate is present in the subject. Hence it follows that all the knowledge of propositions which is in GOD, whether it be of simple understanding about the essences of things, or of vision about the existences of things, or mediate knowledge about conditioned existences, results immediately from the perfect intellection of each term, which can be subject or predicate of any proposition; or that the a priori knowledge of complex things springs from the understanding of those that are incomplex.

An absolutely necessary proposition is one which can be resolved into identical propositions, or the opposite of which implies a con-

[5] Translated from *Opuscules et fragments inédits de Leibniz*, ed. Couturat (Paris: Félix Alcan, 1903), pp. 16–22. By permission of the publishers. (The concluding portion is omitted.)

tradiction. Let me show this by an example in numbers. I shall call binary every number which can be exactly divided by two, and ternary or quaternary—every one that can be exactly divided by three or four, and so on. For we understand every number to be resolved into those which exactly divide it. I say therefore that this proposition: that a duodenary number is quaternary, is absolutely necessary, since it can be resolved into identical propositions in the following way. A duodenary number is binary-senary (by definition); senary is binary ternary (by definition). Therefore a duodenary number is binary binary ternary. Further binary binary is quaternary (by definition). Therefore a duodenary number is quaternary ternary. Therefore a duodenary number is quaternary. Q.E.D. But even if other definitions had been given, it could always have been shown that it comes to the same thing. Therefore I call this necessity metaphysical or geometrical. What lacks such necessity, I call contingent; but what implies a contradiction, or that the opposite of which is necessary, is called *impossible*. Other things are called *possible*. In contingent truth, even though the predicate is really present in the subject, nevertheless by whatever resolution you please of either term, indefinitely continued, you will never arrive at demonstration or identity. And it is for GOD alone, comprehending the infinite all at once, to perceive how one is present in the other, and to understand a priori the perfect reason of contingency, which in creatures is furnished (*a posteriori*) by experience. Thus contingent truths are related to necessary as surd roots, i.e. the roots of incommensurable numbers, to the expressible roots of commensurable numbers. For just as it can be shown that a small number is present in another greater number, by reducing both to the greatest common measure, so too essential propositions or truths are demonstrated: i.e., a resolution is carried on until it arrives at terms which it is established by the definitions are common to either term. But as a greater number contains a certain other incommensurable number, and let whatever resolution you please be continued to infinity, it never arrives at a common measure—so in contingent truth, it never arrives at demonstration however much you may resolve the concepts. There is only this difference, that in surd roots we can nevertheless carry out demonstrations, by showing that the error is less than any assignable number, but in contingent truths not even this is conceded to a created mind. And so I consider that I have unfolded something secret, which has long perplexed even myself—while I did not understand how the predicate could be in the subject, and yet the proposition not be necessary. But the knowledge of things geometrical and the analysis of infinities kindled this light for me, so that I understood that concepts too are resoluble to infinity.

Hence we now learn that propositions which pertain to the essences and those which pertain to the existences of things are different. Essential surely are those which can be demonstrated from the resolution of terms, that is, which are necessary, or virtually identical, and the opposite of which, moreover, is impossible or virtually contradictory. And these are the eternal truths. They did not obtain only while the world existed, but they would also obtain if GOD had created a world with a different plan. But from these, existential or contingent truths differ entirely. Their truth is understood a priori by the infinite mind alone, and they cannot be demonstrated by any resolution. They are of the sort that are true at a certain time, and they do not only express what pertains to the possibility of things, but also what actually does exist, or would exist contingently if certain things were supposed. For example, take the proposition, I am now living, the sun is shining. For suppose I say that the sun is shining in our hemisphere at this hour, because up to now its motion has been such that, granted its continuation, this certainly follows. Even then (not to mention the non-necessary obligation of its continuing) that its motion even before this was so much and of this kind is similarly a contingent truth, for which again the reason should be inquired—nor could it be fully produced except from the perfect knowledge of all parts of the universe. This, however, exceeds all created powers. For there is no portion of matter, which is not actually subdivided into other parts; hence the parts of any body whatsoever are actually infinite. Thus neither the sun nor any other body can be perfectly known by a creature. Much less can we arrive at the end of the analysis if we search for the mover causing the motion of any body whatsoever and again for the mover of this; for we shall always arrive at smaller bodies without end. But GOD is not in need of that transition from one contingent to another earlier or simpler contingent,—a transition which can never have an end (as also one contingent is in fact not the cause of another, even though it may seem so to us). But he perceives in any individual substance from its very concept the truth of all its accidents, calling in nothing extrinsic, since any one at all involves in its way all the others and the whole universe. Hence into all propositions into which existence and time enter, by that very fact the whole series of things enters, nor can the now or here be understood except in relation to other things. For this reason such propositions do not allow of a demonstration or terminable resolution by which their truth might appear. And the same holds of all accidents of individual created substances. Indeed even though some one were able to know the whole series of the universe, he still could not state the reason of it, except by having undertaken the comparison of it with all other possible universes. From this it is clear why a demonstration of no contingent proposition can be found, however far the resolution of concepts be continued.

It must not be thought, however, that only singular propositions are contingent, for there are (and can be inferred by induction) some propositions true for the most part; and there are also propositions almost always true at least naturally, so that an exception is ascribed to a miracle. Indeed, I think there are certain propositions most universally true in this series of things, and certainly never to be violated even by miracle, not that they could not be violated by GOD, but that when he himself chose this series of things, by that very fact he decided to observe them (as the specific properties of this very series chosen). And through these propositions set up once for all by the force of the divine decree, it is possible to state the reason for other universal propositions and also for many contingent propositions which can be observed in this universe. For from the first essential laws of the series, true without exception, which contain the whole aim of GOD in choosing the universe, and even include miracles as well, subaltern laws of nature can be derived, which have only physical necessity, and which are not modified except by miracle, by reason of an intuition of some more powerful final cause. And from these finally are inferred others the universality of which is still less; and GOD can also reveal to creatures this kind of demonstration of intermediate universals from one another, a part of which makes up physical science. But one could never by any analysis come to the most universal laws nor to the perfect reasons for individual things; for this knowledge is necessarily appropriate only to GOD. Nor indeed should it disturb any one, that I have said there are certain laws essential to this series of things, since we have nevertheless said above that these very laws are not necessary and essential, but contingent and existential. For since the fact that the series itself exists is contingent, and depends on a free decree of GOD, its laws too, considered absolutely, will be contingent; hypothetically, however, if the series is supposed, they are necessary and so far essential.

These things will now be of advantage to us in distinguishing free substances from others. The accidents of every individual substance if they are predicated of it constitute a contingent proposition, which does not have metaphysical necessity. And the fact that this stone tends downward when its support is removed, is not a necessary but a contingent proposition; nor can such an event be demonstrated from the concept of this stone with the help of the universal concepts which enter into it; and so GOD alone perceives this perfectly. For he alone knows, whether he himself is not going to suspend by a miracle that subaltern law of nature by which heavy things are driven downward. Nor do others understand the most universal laws, nor can they go through the infinite analysis which is necessary to connect the concept of this stone with the concept of the whole universe or with the most universal laws. However this at least can be foreknown from the subaltern laws of nature, that unless the law of gravity is suspended by a miracle, descent follows. But free or intelligent substances have in fact something greater and more marvellous in the direction of a certain imitation of GOD; so that they are bound by no definite subaltern laws of nature, but (as if it were a privation by a certain miracle), they act from the spontaneity of their own power alone, and by an intuition of some final cause they break the nexus and course of efficient causes according to their will. And so true is this, that there is no creature knowing of hearts, who could predict with certainty what another mind will choose according to the laws of nature,—as it can be predicted in another case, at least by an angel, how some body will act if the course of nature be not interrupted. For as the course of the universe is changed by the free will of GOD, so by the free will of the mind the course of its thoughts is changed; so that no subaltern universal laws sufficient for predicting their choice can be found in minds as they are in bodies. This does not, however, at all prevent the future actions of the mind, like his own future actions, from being fixed for GOD, as they are also fixed for the series of things which he chooses. And surely he knows perfectly the strength of his own decree, and also understands at the same time what is contained in the concept of this mind which he himself has admitted into the number of things that are to exist—in so much as it involves this very series of things and its most universal laws. And although this one thing is most true, that the mind never chooses what now appears worse, still it does not always choose what now appears better; since it can put off and suspend judgment till further deliberation and turn its attention to thinking of other things. As to the question whether this will be done, it is not sufficiently determined by any evidence or definite law; certainly not in those minds, which are not sufficiently confirmed in good or evil. For in the case of the blessed another statement must be made.

Hence also it can be understood, what that indifference is which attends liberty. Surely as contingency is opposed to metaphysical necessity, so indifference excludes not only metaphysical, but also physical necessity. It is, in a way, a matter of physical necessity, that GOD should do all things as well as possible (although it is not in the power of any creature to apply this universal rule to individuals, and thus to draw any certain consequences from the divine free actions). It is also a matter of physical necessity that those confirmed in good, angels or blessed, should act from virtue (in such a way, in fact, that it can be predicted with certainty even by a creature, how they will act). It is a matter of physical necessity, that what is heavy strives downward, that the angles of incidence and of reflection are equal, and other things of that kind. But it is not a matter of physical necessity that men should in this life choose some particular good, howsoever specious and apparent it may be, although that is sometimes emphatically to be presumed. For although it may never be possible for that complete metaphysical indifference to exist, such that the mind should be disposed in quite the same way to either one of two contradictories and, again, that anything should be in equilibrium as it were with all its nature, (for we have already observed that even a future predicate is really already present in the concept of the subject, and that therefore mind is not, metaphysically speaking, indifferent, since GOD from the perfect concept of it which he has already perceives all its future accidents, and since mind is not now indifferent to its everlasting concept), still the physical indifference of mind is great enough so that it is certainly not under physical necessity (nor yet metaphysical, i.e. so that no universal reason or law of nature is assignable from which any Creature, however perfect and learned in the state of this mind, can infer with certainty, what the mind, at least naturally (without the extraordinary concourse of GOD) will choose. . . . . [6]

[6] Cf. Leibniz' correspondence with Clarke, Leibniz' fifth paper, pars. 1–9 (*Philosophical Works of Leibnitz*, ed. Duncan [New Haven: Tuttle, Morehouse & Taylor, 1890], pp. 254–56):

"1. I shall at this time make a *larger* answer; to clear the difficulties; and to try whether the author be willing to hearken to reason, and to show that he is a lover of truth; or whether he will only cavil, without clearing anything.

"2. He often endeavors to impute to me *necessity and fatality;* though perhaps no one has better and more fully explained, than I have done in my *Theodicaea,* the true difference between *liberty, contingency, spontaneity,* on the one side; and absolute *necessity, chance, coaction,* on the other. I know not yet, whether the author does this, because he *will* do it, whatever I may say; or whether he does it (supposing him sincere in those imputations,) because he has *not yet* duly *considered* my opinions. I shall soon find what I am to think of it, and I shall take my measures accordingly.

"3. It is true, that *reason* in the *mind* of a wise being, and *motives* in any mind whatsoever, do that which answers to the effect produced by *weights* in a *balance.* The author objects, that this notion leads to *necessity* and *fatality.* But he says so, without proving it, and without taking notice of the explications I have formerly given, in order to remove the difficulties that may be raised upon that head.

"4. He seems also to play with *equivocal* terms. There are *necessities,* which ought to be admitted. For we must distinguish between an *absolute* and an *hypothetical* necessity. We must also distinguish between a *necessity,* which takes place because the opposite implies a contradiction; (which necessity is called *logical, metaphysical,* or *mathematical;*) and a *necessity* which is *moral,* whereby a wise being chooses the best, and every mind follows the strongest inclination.

"5. *Hypothetical necessity* is that, which the supposition or *hypothesis* of God's *foresight* and *pre-ordination* lays upon *future contingents.* And this must needs be admitted, unless we deny, as the *Socinians* do, God's *foreknowledge of future contingents,* and his *providence* which regulates and governs every particular thing.

"6. But neither that *foreknowledge,* nor that *pre-ordination,* derogate from *liberty.* For God, being moved by his supreme reason to choose, among many series of things or worlds possible, that, in which free creatures should take such or such resolutions, though not without his concourse; has thereby rendered every event certain and determined once for all; without derogating thereby from the liberty of those creatures: that simple decree of choice, not at all changing, but only *actualizing* their free natures, which he saw in his ideas.

"7. As for *moral* necessity, this also does not derogate from *liberty.* For when a

CONCERNING THE UNIVERSAL SYNTHESIS AND ANALYSIS OR THE ART OF DISCOVERY AND JUDGMENT[7]

When I was learning logic as a boy, and used, even then, to inquire more deeply into the grounds of those things which were proposed to me, I made this objection to my masters: just as there are predicaments of incomplex terms, to which concepts are ordered, why could not predicaments of complex terms, to which truths would be ordered, be formed in the same way? For indeed I was ignorant of the fact that geometers do this very thing, when they demonstrate and arrange propositions according as they depend on one another. Moreover it seemed to me that the scheme would be universally valid, if there were already true predicaments of simple terms and something new were established for asserting them, like an alphabet of thought, or a catalogue of highest genera (or of genera adopted as highest), such as a, b, c, d, e, f, from the combination of which subordinate concepts would be formed. For one must realize that genera reciprocally present differentiae to one another; and that every differentia can be conceived as a genus and every genus as a differentia, and so "rational animal"

---

wise being, and especially God, who has supreme wisdom, chooses what is best, he is not the less free upon that account: on the contrary, it is the most perfect liberty, not to be hindered from acting in the best manner. And when any other chooses according to the most apparent and the most strongly inclining good, he imitates therein the liberty of a truly wise being, in proportion to his disposition. Without this, the choice would be a blind chance.

"8. But good, either true, or apparent; in a word, the motive, inclines without necessitating; that is, without imposing an *absolute necessity*. For when God (for instance,) chooses the best; what he does not choose, and is inferior in perfection, is nevertheless possible. But if what he chooses, was absolutely necessary; any other way would be impossible; which is against the hypothesis. For God chooses among possibles, that is, among many ways, none of which implies a contradiction.

"9. But to say, that God can only choose what is *best*; and to infer from thence, that what he does not choose, is impossible; that, I say, is confounding of terms: 'tis blending *power* and *will*, *metaphysical necessity* and *moral necessity*, *essences* and *existences*. For what is necessary, is so by its essence, since the opposite implies a contradiction; but a contingent which exists, owes its existence to *the principle of what is best*, which is a *sufficient reason* for the existence of things. And therefore I say, that motives incline without necessitating; and that there is a certainty and infallibility, but not an absolute necessity in contingent things."

[7] Translated from *Die philosophischen Schriften von Gottfried Wilhelm Leibniz*, ed. C. J. Gerhardt (Berlin, 1875-90), VII, 292-98.

is as correctly said as, if a fiction is permitted, "animal rational."
And if indeed the vulgar genera do not exhibit species by their
combination, I concluded that they were not correctly constituted.
And in fact the genera next below the highest would be binions,
as *ab*, *ac*, *bd*, *cf*; the genera of the third grade would be ternions,
as *abc*, *bdf*, and so on. But if the highest genera or those adopted
as highest were infinite, as in numbers (in which case prime numbers can be adopted for the highest genera, for all even numbers
can be called binaries, all those divisible by three can be called
ternaries, and so on, and a derivative number can be expressed
through the primary numbers as genera; thus every senary number
is binary ternary) at least the order of the highest genera would be
established as in numbers, and so the order would also appear in
the lower genera. And whatever species is proposed, one can enumerate in order the propositions demonstrable of it or the predicates, broader as well as convertible, from which the more memo-
rable ones could be selected. For if there is a species *y*, whose
concept is *abcd*, and *l* is substituted for *ab*, *m* for *ac*, *n* for *ad*, *p* for
bc, *q* for *bd*, *r* for *cd*, which are binions; and again for the ternions, *s*
for *abc*, *v* for *abd*, *w* for *acd*, *x* for *bcd*, those are to be sure all predicates of that same *y*, but the convertible predicates of *y* will be only
these: *ax*, *bw*, *cv*, *ds*; *lr*, *mq*, *np*. Of these matters I have spoken at
greater length in the *Short Dissertation on the Combinatory Art*, which
I brought out when I had scarcely reached young manhood, when
Kircher's long promised work of the same title had not yet appeared
(a work in which I hoped some such device would be established,
but afterward when it appeared I saw it was only Lullian and similar matters that were renewed there, but that the true analysis of
human thoughts had not entered the author's mind even in dreams,
just as it had not in the case of others who nevertheless thought of
restoring philosophy). The first concepts from the combination of
which others are formed are either distinct or confused. Those
are distinct which are understood through themselves, like the concept of being. Those are confused (and yet clear) which are perceived through themselves, like the colored, which we cannot explain to another except by pointing. For even though its nature is
resoluble, since it has a cause, nevertheless there are no separately
explicable marks by which it can be described and sufficiently
known by us. But it is known only confusedly and so it does not

have a *nominal definition.* A nominal definition consists in the enumeration of marks or requisites for sufficiently distinguishing the thing in question from all others, where if the requisites of requisites are always sought for, one will finally come to primary concepts which either have no requisites at all or have none sufficiently explicable by us. This is the art of treating distinct concepts. But it belongs to the art of treating confused concepts to mark the distinct concepts, or those understood through themselves or at least resoluble, which accompany those confused concepts; with their aid, we can sometimes arrive at the cause or at some resolution of the confused concepts.

Further all derived concepts originate from the combinations of primary ones, and those further compounded from the combination of the compounded; but care must be taken, lest useless combinations be made by joining together things that are incompatible with one another,—a matter which can be judged only by experiments or by resolution into distinct simple concepts. Indeed this must be carefully observed in constructing real definitions, so that it may be determined that they are possible, and that the concepts from which they are determined can be joined together. Hence even though every convertible property of a thing can be considered as a nominal definition, since all the other attributes of the thing can always be demonstrated from it, still it is not always appropriate for a real definition. For I have noticed that there are certain properties which I call paradoxes, of which one can doubt whether they are possible, for example one can doubt whether there is a curve, every point of every segment of which subtends the two extremes of its segment by the same angle. For let us suppose, that we adjust the points of a curve in this way for one segment, we cannot yet foresee whether what can be seen to follow by some happy chance in one place only, will always hold, i.e., whether the same points occurring in another segment would again satisfy, for they are already determined and can no longer be freely chosen. And yet we know that this is the nature of the circle; and so even if some one could give a name to the curve having that property, he would nevertheless not determine whether it was possible, nor, therefore, whether the definition was real. But the concept of the circle proposed by Euclid, that it is a figure described by the motion of a straight line in a plane around a fixed end-point, furnishes a real definition, for it is evident that such a figure is possible. Thus it is useful to have definitions involving the generation of the thing, or at least, if that is wanting, its constitution, that is, the manner in which it appears to be producible or at least possible. It was this observation that I formerly used in examining the imperfect demonstration of the existence of GOD, which Descartes put forward, about which I have often disputed, even in writing, with the most learned Cartesians. For Descartes argues thus: whatever can be demonstrated from the definition of a thing, can also be predicated of it. But from the definition of GOD (that he is being most perfect, or as certain scholastics used to put it, than which nothing greater can be thought) existence follows (for existence is a perfection, and that thing which by itself further involves existence, would certainly be greater or more perfect); therefore existence can be predicated of GOD or GOD exists. This argument, renewed by Descartes, was defended by a certain one of the old scholastics in his own book (entitled *Against the Fool*), but Thomas, after the rest, has replied, that this is to suppose that GOD is, or, as I interpret it, has an essence, at least such as is the essence of the rose in winter, or that such a concept is possible. This is the privilege of the most perfect being, that supposing it to be possible, it forthwith exists, or that from its essence or possible concept existence follows. But if this demonstration was to be rigorous, possibility must first be demonstrated. Surely we cannot without anxiety weave demonstrations for any concept, unless we know it to be possible. For with impossibles or things involving contradictories their contradictories too can be demonstrated, which is the a priori reason why possibility is required for a real definition. Hence also Hobbes's difficulty is satisfied; to wit: Hobbes, since he saw that all truths can be demonstrated from definitions, and also believed all definitions to be arbitrary and nominal, since it is a matter of arbitrary choice to impose names on things, wanted truths too to consist in names and to be arbitrary. But one must realize that concepts cannot be conjoined at will, but that a possible concept should be formed from them, in order that one may get a real definition. From this it is clear that every real definition contains some affirmation at least of possibility. Hence even though names are arbitrary, still once they are supposed, the consequences are necessary and certain truths arise which even though they depend on imposed characters are nevertheless real. For example, the proof of the divisibility of a number by nine through the addition of the digits depends on the imposed characters of the decimal progression, and yet it contains real truth. Further to construct an hypothesis or to explain the way of producing a thing, is nothing else than demonstrating the possibility of the thing, which is useful even though the thing in question is not generated in such fashion. For the same ellipse can be understood either as described in a plane with the help of two foci and a string drawn round them, or cut from a cone or a cylinder; and when one hypothesis or mode of generation has been found we have a real definition, from which still others can be drawn; and from these are chosen those which are most in keeping with other circumstances, when the method by which the thing is actually produced is sought. Further among real definitions those are most perfect, which are common to all hypotheses and modes of generation, and involve the proximate cause, in short those from which the possibility of the thing is immediately evident, that is, those which presuppose no experience or demonstration of the possibility of another thing. This is the case when the thing is resolved into nothing but primary concepts understood through themselves. Such knowledge I usually call adequate or intuitive; for thus if there were any inconsistency, it would appear at once, since there is no room for further resolution.

From these ideas or definitions, further, all truths can be demonstrated, except identical propositions, which it is clear are by their nature indemonstrable, and can truly be called axioms. For vulgar axioms are (by the resolution either of the subject or the predicate or both) reduced to identical axioms or demonstrated, so that if one supposes the contrary the same thing seems at once to be and not to be. From this it is clear that ostensive and apagogic demonstration coincide in the last analysis, and that it was also observed correctly by the scholastics, that all axioms when their terms are understood are reduced to the principle of contradiction. And so a reason can be given for any truth whatsoever, for the connection of the predicate with the subject is either evident in itself, as in identical propositions, or it must be explained, which is done by the resolution of the terms. And this is the single and highest criterion of truth, namely in abstract matters not depending on experience, that it is either identical or reducible to identities. And from this the elements of eternal truth and the method of proceeding in all things, if only they are understood, can be drawn just as demonstrably as in geometry. In this way all things are understood by GOD a priori and in the manner of eternal verity, since he does not need experience; and indeed by him all things are known adequately, by us scarcely any adequately, few a priori, and many by experience, in which last other principles and other criteria must be employed. In matters of fact, therefore, or contingent things, which depend not on reason but observation or experiment, first truths (in relation to us) are whatever we perceive immediately within ourselves, or whatever we are conscious of in ourselves concerning ourselves; for these things it is impossible to test by other experiences nearer to us and more intrinsic. Moreover, I perceive within me not only myself who think, but also many differentiations in my thoughts, some of which I infer to be outside myself, and little by little I gain faith in the senses and attack the Sceptics; for in such things as are not matters of metaphysical necessity, that agreement of phenomena among themselves, which is not rashly made but has a cause, must be by us considered as truth. Certainly we do not distinguish sleep from waking except by this agreement of phenomena, nor do we predict that the sun will rise tomorrow except because he has so often kept his word. The great force of authority and of public testimony makes for this, since it is not credible that many should conspire to deceive, to which can be added what St. Augustine has said of the utility of believing. The history of phenomena is already constituted and is to be constructed by the authority of the senses and of other witnesses; and if truths abstracted from experience are joined to these, mixed sciences are thus formed. Moreover there is need of a peculiar art both for making and ordering and conjoining expressions, so that from them useful inductions may be made and causes found, and aphorisms and preconceptions formed. But the negligence of men is to be wondered at, who have leisure for trifles but are neglectful of those things by which they could provide for their soundness and health, though perchance they have in their power the remedies for a great part of their troubles, if they would correctly use the observations of this century, available in such large numbers, and the true method of analysis. Now man's knowledge of nature seems to me like a shop, very well fitted out in all kinds of goods but lacking in order and a catalogue.

Further, it also appears from these things, what the distinction is between synthesis and analysis. Synthesis takes place when beginning from principles and running through truths in order we apprehend certain progressions and construct, as it were, tables or sometimes also general formulae, in which afterward a given thing can be found. Analysis goes back from the cause of a single given problem toward principles, just as if nothing had ever been discovered before by us or others. It is more important to construct a synthesis, since that labor is forever valid, while by instituting an analysis because of particular problems we often do what has been done already. But to use a synthesis constructed by others and theorems invented by others belongs to a lesser art than, by practising analysis, to be able to accomplish everything oneself, especially since the discoveries of others or even our very own are not always present or at hand. Analysis is twofold, one common kind, moving through leaps and bounds, which is used in algebra, another peculiar one which I call reductive, which is much more elegant but little known. Analysis is more necessary in practice, in order that we may solve given problems; but he who wishes to indulge in theory, content up to now to practise analysis so that he has the analytic art in his power, prefers for the rest to follow synthesis, nor does he readily touch on questions other than those to which the order itself leads him. For thus he always proceeds joyfully and easily, and never feels any difficulty or is disappointed of success; and in a short time he ascends to much greater things than he himself ever hoped at the start. The crowd, however, corrupt the fruit of meditation by making haste, when they strain by leaps and bounds toward more difficult questions and with great labor accomplish nothing. For we must realize that that and only that method of inquiry is perfect, by which we can foresee whether it will lead us to an issue. But they are mistaken who think that one is writing analytically when the source of discovery is revealed, synthetically when it is suppressed. I have often observed that minds capable of discovery are some more analytic, some more combinatory. It is more combinatory or synthetic to find the use and application of something, as, given a magnetic needle, to think of its application to the compass; it is more analytic, on the other hand, given the title of a discovery or supposing an end to discover the means. Pure analysis, however, is rare; for often in seeking the means we light on devices formerly discovered by others or by ourselves, whether by chance or reasoning, which we apprehend either in our memory or in the statements of others as in a table or catalogue, and apply to this purpose. But this is synthetic. For the rest, the combinatory art is to me in particular that science (which can also be called, generally, characteristic or *specious*) which treats of the forms or formulae of things in general, that is of *quality* in general or of similar and dissimilar, according as different formulae arise from *a*, *b*, *c*, etc. combined among themselves (whether they represent quantities or anything else). It is distinguished from algebra which deals with formulae applied to *quantity*, or with the equal and unequal. And so algebra is subordinated to the combinatory art, and continually uses its rules, which however are much more general, nor do they find a place in algebra only but also in the art of deciphering, in various kinds of games, in geometry itself treated as linear according to the fashion of the ancients, and finally in all things where the form of similarity occurs.

THE PRINCIPLES OF NATURE AND OF GRACE[8]

1. *Substance* is being, capable of action. It is simple or compound. *Simple substance* is that which has no parts. *Compound* substance is a collection of simple substances or *monads*. *Monas* is a Greek word which signifies unity, or that which is one.

Compounds, or bodies, are multitudes; and simple substances, lives, souls, spirits are unities. And there must be simple substances everywhere, because without simple substances there would be no compounds; and consequently all nature is full of life.

2. Monads, having no parts, cannot be formed or decomposed. They cannot begin or end naturally; and consequently last as long as the universe, which will indeed be changed but will not be destroyed. They cannot have shapes; otherwise they would have parts. And consequently a monad, in itself and at a given moment, could not be distinguished from another except by its internal qualities and actions, which can be nothing else than its *perceptions*

(that is, representations of the compound, or of what is external, in the simple), and its *appetitions* (that is, its tendencies from one perception to another), which are the principles of change. For the simplicity of substance does not prevent multiplicity of modifications, which must be found together in this same simple substance, and must consist in the variety of relations to things which are external. Just as in a centre or point, altogether simple as it is, there is found an infinity of angles formed by lines which there meet.

3. Everything in nature is full. There are everywhere simple substances, separated in reality from each other by activities of their own which continually change their relations; and each simple substance, or monad, which forms the centre of a compound substance (as, for example, of an animal) and the principle of its unity, is surrounded by a mass composed of an infinity of other monads, which constitute the body proper of this central monad; and in accordance with the affections of this it represents, as a *centre*, the things which are outside of itself. And this *body* is *organic*, when it forms a sort of automaton or natural machine; which is a machine not only in its entirety, but also in its smallest perceptible parts. And as, because of the plenitude of the world, everything is connected and each body acts upon every other body, more or less according to the distance, and by reaction is itself affected thereby; it follows that each monad is a mirror, living or endowed with internal activity, representative according to its point of view of the universe, and as regulated as the universe itself. And perceptions in the monad spring one from the other, by the law of appetites or by the *final causes of good and evil*, which consist in visible, regulated or unregulated perceptions; just as the changes of bodies and external phenomena spring one from another, by the laws of *efficient causes*, that is, of movements. Thus there is perfect *harmony* between the perceptions of the monad and the movements of bodies, established at the beginning between the system of efficient causes and that of final causes. And in this consists the accord and physical union of the soul and body, although neither one can change the laws of the other.

4. Each monad, with a particular body, makes a living substance. Thus there is not only life everywhere, provided with members or organs, but also there is an infinity of degrees in monads, some dominating more or less over the others. But when the monad

has organs so adjusted that by means of them there is clearness and distinctness in the impressions which it receives and consequently in the perceptions which represent them (as, for example, when by means of the shape of the humors of the eyes, the rays of light are concentrated and act with more force); this can extend even to *feeling* (*sentiment*), that is, even to a perception accompanied by *memory*, that is, one a certain echo of which remains a long time to make itself heard upon occasion; and such a living being is called an *animal*, as its monad is called a soul. And when this soul is elevated to *reason* it is something more sublime and is reckoned among spirits, as will soon be explained.

It is true that animals are sometimes in the condition of simple living beings, and their souls in the condition of simple monads, namely, when their perceptions are not sufficiently distinct to be remembered, as happens in a profound, dreamless sleep, or in a swoon. But perceptions which have become entirely confused must be re-developed in animals, for reasons which I shall shortly (§ 12) enumerate. Therefore it is well to make a distinction between the *perception*, which is the internal condition of the monad representing external things, and *apperception*, which is consciousness or the reflective knowledge of this internal state; the latter not being given to all souls, nor at all times to the same soul. And it is for want of this distinction that the Cartesians have failed, taking no account of the perceptions of which we are not conscious as people take no account of imperceptible bodies. It is this also which made the same Cartesians believe that only spirits are monads, that there is no soul of brutes, and still less other *principles of life*.

And as they shocked too much the common opinion of men by refusing feeling to brutes, they have, on the other hand, accommodated themselves too much to the prejudices of the multitude, by confounding a *long swoon*, caused by a great confusion of perceptions, with *death strictly speaking*, where all perception would cease. This confirmed the ill-founded belief in the destruction of some souls, and the bad opinion of some so-called strong minds, who have contended against the immortality of the soul.

5. There is a continuity in the perceptions of animals which bears some resemblance to reason; but it is only founded in the memory of *facts*, and not at all in the knowledge of *causes*. Thus a dog shuns the stick with which it has been beaten, because mem-

ory represents to it the pain which the stick has caused it. And men in so far as they are empirics, that is to say, in three-fourths of their actions, act simply as brutes. For example, we expect that there will be daylight to-morrow, because we have always had the experience; only an astronomer foresees it by reason, and even this prediction will finally fail when the cause of day, which is not eternal, shall cease. But *true reasoning* depends upon necessary or eternal truths, such as those of logic, numbers, geometry, which establish an indubitable connection of ideas and unfailing consequences. The animals in which these consequences are not noticed, are called *brutes;* but those which know these necessary truths are properly those which are called *rational animals*, and their souls are called *spirits*. These souls are capable of performing acts of reflection, and of considering that which is called the *ego, substance, monad, soul, spirit*, in a word, immaterial things and truths. It is this which renders us capable of the sciences and of demonstrative knowledge.

6. Modern researches have taught us, and reason approves of it, that living beings whose organs are known to us, that is to say, plants and animals, do not come from putrefaction or from chaos, as the ancients believed, but from *pre-formed* seeds, and consequently by the transformation of pre-existing living beings. There are animalcules in the seeds of large animals, which by means of conception assume a new dress which they make their own and by means of which they can nourish themselves and increase their size, in order to pass to a larger theatre and to accomplish the propagation of the large animal. It is true that the souls of spermatic human animals are not rational and do not become so until conception determines these animals to the human nature. And as generally animals are not born altogether in conception or *generation*, neither do they perish altogether in what we call *death;* for it is reasonable that what does not begin naturally, should not end either in the order of nature. Therefore, quitting their mask or their rags, they merely return to a more subtile theatre where they can, nevertheless, be just as sensitive and just as well regulated as in the larger. And what we have just said of large animals, takes place also in the generation and death of smaller spermatic animals, in comparison with which the former may pass for large; for everything extends *ad infinitum* in nature.

Thus not only souls, but also animals, are ingenerable and imperishable: they are only developed, unfolded, reclothed, unclothed, transformed: souls never quit their entire body and do not pass from one body into another which is entirely new to them.

There is therefore no *metempsychosis*, but there is *metamorphosis;* animals change, take and leave only parts: the same thing which happens little by little and by small invisible particles but continually in nutrition, and suddenly, visibly but rarely in conception or death, which cause a gain or loss of everything at one time.

7. Up to this time we have spoken as simple *physicists:* now we must advance to *metaphysics* by making use of the *great principle*, little employed in general, which teaches that *nothing happens without a sufficient reason;* that is to say, that nothing happens without its being possible for him who should sufficiently understand things, to give a reason sufficient to determine why it is so and not otherwise. This principle laid down, the first question which should rightly be asked, would be, *Why is there something rather than nothing?* For nothing is simpler and easier than something. Further, suppose that things must exist, we must be able to give a reason *why they must exist so* and not otherwise.[9]

8. Now this sufficient reason for the existence of the universe could not be found *in the series of contingent things*, that is, of bodies and of their representations in souls; for matter being indifferent in itself to motion and to rest and to this or another

---

9 Cf. Leibniz' second paper to Clarke (Duncan, p. 239): ".... The great foundation of *mathematics* is the *principle of contradiction or identity*, that is, that a proposition cannot be true and false at the same time; and that therefore *A* is *A*, and cannot be *not A*. This single principle is sufficient to demonstrate every part of arithmetic and geometry, that is, all *mathematical* principles. But in order to proceed from *mathematics* to *natural philosophy*, another principle is requisite, as I have observed in my *Theordicaea:* I mean, *the principle of a sufficient reason, viz.:* that nothing happens without a *reason* why it should be *so*, rather than *otherwise*. And therefore *Archimedes* being desirous to proceed from *mathematics* to *natural philosophy*, in his book *De Aequilibrio*, was obliged to make use of a particular case of the great principle of *a sufficient reason*. He takes it for granted, that if there be a *balance*, in which every thing is alike on both sides, and if equal weights are hung on the two ends of that balance, the whole will be at rest. 'Tis because no *reason* can be given, why one side should weigh down, rather than the other. Now, by that single principle, *viz.:* that *there ought to be a sufficient reason why things should be so, and not otherwise*, one may demonstrate the being of a God, and all the other parts of *metaphysics* or *natural theology;* and even, in some measure, those principles of *natural philosophy*, that are independent upon *mathematics:* I mean, the *dynamic* principles, or the *principles of force.*"

motion, we could not find the reason of motion in it, and still less of a certain motion. And although the present motion which is in matter, comes from the preceding motion, and that from still another preceding, yet in this way we should never make any progress, go as far as we might; for the same question would always remain.

Therefore it must be that the sufficient reason which has no need of another reason, be outside this series of contingent things and be found in a substance which is its cause, or which is a necessary being, carrying the reason of its existence within itself; otherwise we should still not have a sufficient reason in which we could rest. And this final reason of things is called *God*.

9. This simple primitive substance must contain in itself eminently the perfections contained in the derivative substances which are its effects; thus it will have perfect power, knowledge and will: that is, it will have omnipotence and sovereign goodness. And as *justice*, taken generally, is only goodness conformed to wisdom, there must too be sovereign justice in God. The reason which has caused things to exist by him, makes them still dependent upon him in existing and in working: and they are continually receiving from him that which gives them some perfection; but the imperfection which remains in them, comes from the essential and original limitation of the creature.

10. It follows from the supreme perfection of God, that in creating the universe he has chosen the best possible plan, in which there is the greatest variety together with the greatest order; the best arranged ground, place, time; the most results produced in the most simple ways; the most of power, knowledge, happiness and goodness in the creatures that the universe could permit. For since all the possibles in the understanding of God laid claim to existence in proportion to their perfections, the actual world, as the resultant of all these claims, must be the most perfect possible. And without this it would not be possible to give a reason why things have turned out so rather than otherwise.

11. The supreme wisdom of God compelled him to choose the *laws of movement* best adjusted and most suited to abstract or metaphysical reasons. He preserves there the same quantity of total and absolute force, or of actions; the same quantity of respective force or of reaction; lastly the same quantity of directive force.

Farther, action is always equal to reaction, and the whole effect is always equivalent to the full cause. And it is not surprising that we could not by the mere consideration of the *efficient causes* or of matter, account for those laws of movement which have been discovered in our time, and a part of which have been discovered by myself. For I have found that it was necessary to have recourse to *final causes*, and that these laws do not depend upon the *principle of necessity*, like logical, arithmetical and geometrical truths, but upon the *principle of fitness*, that is, upon the choice of wisdom. And this is one of the most efficacious and evident proofs of the existence of God, to those who can examine these matters thoroughly.[10]

[10] Cf. Leibniz' fourth paper to Clarke (Duncan, pp. 253–54):

"P.S. All those who maintain a *vacuum*, are more influenced by imagination than by reason. When I was a young man, I also gave in to the notion of a *vacuum* and *atoms*; but reason brought me into the right way. It was a pleasing imagination. Men carry their inquiries no farther than those two things: they (as it were) nail down their thoughts to them: they fancy, they have found out the first elements of things, a *non plus ultra*. We would have nature to go no farther; and to be finite, as our minds are: but this is being ignorant of the greatness and majesty of the author of things. The least corpuscle is actually subdivided *in infinitum*, and contains a world of other creatures, which would be wanting in the universe, if that corpuscle was an *atom*, that is, a body of one entire piece without subdivision. In like manner, to admit a *vacuum* in nature, is ascribing to God a very imperfect work: 'tis violating the grand principle of the necessity of a *sufficient reason;* which many have talked of, without understanding its true meaning; as I have lately shown, in proving, by that principle, that *space* is only an *order* of things, as *time* also is, and not at all an absolute being. To omit many other arguments against a vacuum and atoms, I shall here mention those which I ground upon *God's perfection*, and upon the *necessity of a sufficient reason*. I lay it down as a principle, that every perfection, which God *could* impart to things without derogating from their other perfections, has actually been imparted to them. Now, let us fancy a *space* wholly empty. God *could* have placed some matter in it, without derogating in any respect from all other things: therefore he hath actually placed some matter in that space: therefore, there is no space *wholly* empty: therefore all is full. The same argument proves that there is no corpuscle, but what is subdivided. I shall add another argument, grounded upon the necessity of a *sufficient reason*. 'Tis *impossible* there should be any principle to determine what proportion of matter there ought to be, out of all the possible degrees from a *plenum* to a *vacuum*, or from a *vacuum* to a *plenum*. Perhaps it will be said, that the one should be equal to the other: but, because matter is more perfect than a *vacuum*, reason requires that a geometrical proportion should be observed, and that there should be as much more matter than *vacuum*, as the former deserved to have the preference before the latter. But then there must be no *vacuum* at all; for the perfection of matter is to that of a *vacuum*, as *something* to *nothing*. And the case is the same with *atoms:* What reason can any one assign for *confining* nature in the progression of subdivision? These are fictions merely arbitrary, and unworthy of true philosophy. The reasons alleged for a *vacuum*, are mere sophisms."

12. It follows, farther, from the perfection of the supreme author, that not only is the order of the entire universe the most perfect possible, but also that each living mirror representing the universe in accordance with its point of view, that is to say, that each *monad*, each *substantial centre*, must have its perceptions and its desires as well regulated as is compatible with all the rest. Whence it follows, still farther, that *souls*, that is, the most dominating monads, or rather, animals, cannot fail to awaken from the state of stupor in which death or some other accident may put them.

13. For everything in things is regulated once for all with as much order and harmony as is possible, supreme wisdom and goodness not being able to act except with perfect harmony. The present is big with the future, the future could be read in the past, the distant is expressed in the near. One could become acquainted with the beauty of the universe in each soul, if one could unfold all its folds, which only develop visibly in time. But as each distinct perception of the soul includes innumerable confused perceptions which comprise the whole universe, the soul itself knows the things of which it has perception only so far as it has distinct and clear perceptions of them.

Each soul knows the infinite, knows all, but confusedly. As in walking on the sea-shore and hearing the great noise which it makes, I hear the individual sounds of each wave, of which the total sound is composed, but without distinguishing them; so our confused perceptions are the result of the impressions which the whole universe makes upon us. It is the same with each monad. God alone has a distinct consciousness of everything, for he is the source of all. It has been well said that he is as centre everywhere, but that his circumference is nowhere, since without any withdrawal from this centre, everything is immediately present to him.

14. As regards the rational soul, or *spirit*, there is something in it more than in the monads, or even in simple souls. It is not only a mirror of the universe of creatures, but also an image of the Divinity. The *spirit* has not only a perception of the works of God, but it is even capable of producing something which resembles them, although in miniature. For, to say nothing of the marvels of dreams where we invent without trouble, and even involuntarily things which when awake we should have to think a long time in order to hit upon, our soul is architectonic in its

voluntary actions also, and, discovering the sciences according to which God has regulated things (*pondere, mensura, numero,* etc.), it imitates, in its department and in the little world where it is permitted to exercise itself, what God does in the large world.

15. This is why all spirits, whether of men or of genii, entering by virtue of reason and of the eternal truths into a sort of society with God, are members of the City of God, that is to say, of the most perfect state, formed and governed by the greatest and best of monarchs; where there is no crime without punishment, no good actions without proportionate recompense; and finally as much virtue and happiness as is possible; and this is not by a derangement of nature, as if what God prepares for souls disturbed the laws of bodies, but by the very order of natural things, in virtue of the harmony pre-established for all time between the *realms of nature and of grace*, between God as Architect and God as Monarch; so that *nature* leads to grace and *grace*, while making use of nature, perfects it.

16. Thus although reason cannot teach us the details, reserved to Revelation, of the great future, we can be assured by this same reason that things are made in a manner surpassing our desires. God also being the most perfect and most happy, and consequently, the most lovable of substances, and truly pure love consisting in the state which finds pleasure in the perfections and happiness of the loved object, this love ought to give us the greatest pleasure of which we are capable, when God is its object.

17. And it is easy to love him as we ought, if we know him as I have just described. For although God is not visible to our external senses, he does not cease to be very lovable and to give very great pleasure. We see how much pleasure honors give men, although they do not at all consist in the qualities of the external senses.

Martyrs and fanatics (although the affection of the latter is ill-regulated), show what pleasure of the spirit can accomplish; and what is more, even sensuous pleasures are reduced to confusedly known intellectual pleasures.

Music charms us, although its beauty only consists in the harmony of numbers and in the reckoning of the beats or vibrations of sounding bodies, which meet at certain intervals, of which we are not conscious and which the soul does not cease to make.

The pleasures which sight finds in proportions are of the same nature; and those caused by the other senses amount to almost the same things, although we cannot explain it so clearly.

18. It may be said that even from the present time on, the *love of God* makes us enjoy a foretaste of future felicity. And although it is distinterested, it itself constitutes our greatest good and interest even if we should not seek it therein and should consider only the pleasure which it gives, without regard to the utility it produces; for it gives us perfect confidence in the goodness of our author and master, producing a true tranquillity of mind; not like the Stoics who force themselves to patience, but by a present content which assures us of future happiness. And besides the present pleasure, nothing can be more useful for the future; for the love of God fulfills our hopes, too, and leads us in the road of supreme happiness, because by virtue of the perfect order established in the universe, everything is done in the best possible way, as much for the general good as for the greatest individual good of those who are convinced of this and are content with the divine government; this conviction cannot be wanting to those who know how to love the source of all good. It is true that supreme felicity, by whatever *beatific vision* or knowledge of God it be accompanied, can never be full; because, since God is infinite, he cannot be wholly known. Therefore our happiness will never, and ought not, consist in full joy, where there would be nothing farther to desire, rendering our mind stupid; but in a perpetual progress to new pleasures and to new perfections.

CHAPTER V

ISAAC NEWTON[1]

Newton was born in Lincolnshire in 1642, became subsizar of Trinity College, Cambridge in 1661, scholar in 1664, fellow in 1667, and Lucasian Professor of Mathematics in 1669. He was elected fellow of the Royal Society in 1672, when his lectures on optics were presented to that body. His most celebrated work, the *Mathematical Principles of Natural Philosophy*, was written mostly in 1685 and 1686 and published in 1687. From 1703 until his death in 1727 he was president of the Royal Society.

SELECTIONS FROM THE *MATHEMATICAL PRINCIPLES OF NATURAL PHILOSOPHY*[2]

FROM THE AUTHOR'S PREFACE[3]

SINCE the ancients (as we are told by *Pappus*), made great account of the science of mechanics in the investigation of natural things, and the moderns, laying aside substantial forms and occult qualities, have endeavoured to subject the phaenomena of nature to the laws of mathematics, I have in this treatise cultivated mathematics so far as it regards philosophy. The ancients considered mechanics in a twofold respect; as rational philosophy, which proceeds accurately by demonstration, and as practical. To practical mechanics belong all the manual arts, from which mechanics took its name. But as artificers do not work with perfect accuracy, it comes to pass that mechanics is so distinguished from geometry, that what is perfectly accurate is called geometrical; what is less so, is called mechanical. The errors, however, are not in the art, but in the artificers. He that works with less accuracy is an imperfect mechanic; and if any could work with perfect accuracy, he would be the most perfect mechanic of all;

---

[1] Reference has been made in chap. ii above to Newton's central place among the exponents of the "new mechanical philosophy." Brief selections from Newton's *Principia* are now included here, in their appropriate place chronologically.

[2] From *Newton's Principia: The Mathematical Principles of Natural Philosophy* by Sir Isaac Newton, trans. Andrew Motte (New York: 1846), with some slight modifications in the translation.

[3] Motte, pp. lxvii–lxviii.

for the description of right lines and circles, upon which geometry is founded, belongs to mechanics. Geometry does not teach us to draw these lines, but requires them to be drawn; for it requires that the learner should first be taught to describe these accurately, before he enters upon geometry; then it shows how by these operations problems may be solved. To describe right lines and circles are problems, but not geometrical problems. The solution of these problems is required from mechanics; and by geometry the use of them, when so solved, is shown; and it is the glory of geometry that from those few principles, brought from without, it is able to produce so many things. Therefore geometry is founded in mechanical practice, and is nothing but that part of universal mechanics which accurately proposes and demonstrates the art of measuring. But since the manual arts are chiefly conversant in the moving of bodies, it comes to pass that geometry is commonly referred to their magnitudes, and mechanics to their motion. In this sense rational mechanics will be the science of motions resulting from any forces whatsoever, and of the forces required to produce any motions, accurately proposed and demonstrated. This part of mechanics was cultivated by the ancients in the five powers which relate to manual arts; they considered gravity (it not being a manual power), no otherwise than as it moved weights by those powers. Our design not respecting arts, but philosophy, and our subject not manual but natural powers, we consider chiefly those things which relate to gravity, levity, elastic force, the resistance of fluids, and the like forces, whether attractive or impulsive; and therefore we offer this work as the mathematical principles of philosophy; for all the difficulty of philosophy seems to consist in this—from the phaenomena of motions to investigate the forces of nature, and then from these forces to demonstrate the other phaenomena; and to this end the general propositions in the first and second book are directed. In the third book we give an example of this in the explication of the System of the World; for by the propositions mathematically demonstrated in the former books, we in the third derive from the celestial phaenomena the forces of gravity with which bodies tend to the sun and several planets. Then from these forces, by other propositions which are also mathematical, we deduce the motions of the planets, the comets, the moon, and the sea. I wish we could derive the rest of the phaenomena of nature by the same kind of reasoning from mechanical principles; for I am induced by many reasons to suspect that they may all depend upon certain forces by which the particles of bodies, by some causes hitherto unknown, are either mutually impelled towards each other, and cohere in regular figures, or are repelled and recede from each other; which forces being unknown, philosophers have hitherto attempted the search of nature in vain; but I hope the principles here laid down will afford some light either to this or some truer method of philosophy. . . . .

RULES OF REASONING IN PHILOSOPHY[4]

Rules of Reasoning in Philosophy.—Rule I. We are to admit no more causes of natural things than such as are both true and sufficient to explain their appearances.

To this purpose the philosophers say that Nature does nothing in vain, and more is in vain when less will serve; for Nature is pleased with simplicity, and affects not the pomp of superfluous causes.

Rule II. Therefore to the same natural effects we must, as far as possible, assign the same causes.

As to respiration in a man and in a beast; the descent of stones in Europe and in America; the light of our culinary fire and of the sun; the reflection of light in the earth, and in the planets.

Rule III. The qualities of bodies, which admit neither intension nor remission of degrees, and which are found to belong to all bodies within the reach of our experiments, are to be esteemed the universal qualities of all bodies whatsoever.

For since the qualities of bodies are only known to us by experiments, we are to hold for universal all such as universally agree with experiments; and such as are not liable to diminution can never be quite taken away. We are certainly not to relinquish the evidence of experiments for the sake of dreams and vain fictions of our own devising; nor are we to recede from the analogy of Nature, which uses to be simple, and always consonant to itself. We no other way know the extension of bodies than by our senses, nor do these reach it in all bodies; but because we perceive extension in all that are sensible, therefore, we ascribe it universally to all others also. The abundance of bodies are hard, we learn

4 From Book III of the *Principia* (Motte, pp. 384–85).

by experience; and because the hardness of the whole arises from the hardness of the parts, we therefore justly infer the hardness of the undivided particles not only of the bodies we feel but of all others. That all bodies are impenetrable, we gather not from reason, but from sensation. The bodies which we handle we find impenetrable, and thence conclude impenetrability to be an universal property of all bodies whatsoever. That all bodies are moveable, and endowed with certain powers (which we call the vires inertiae) of persevering in their motion, or in their rest, we only infer from the like properties observed in the bodies which we have seen. The extension, hardness, impenetrability, mobility, and *vires inertiae* of the whole, result from the extension, hardness, impenetrability, mobility, and *vires inertiae* of the parts; and thence we conclude the least particles of all bodies to be also all extended, and hard and impenetrable, and moveable, and endowed with their proper *vires inertiae*. And this is the foundation of all philosophy. Moreover, that the divided but contiguous particles of bodies may be separated from one another is matter of observation; and, in the particles that remain undivided, our minds are able to distinguish yet lesser parts, as is mathematically demonstrated. But whether the parts so distinguished, and not yet divided, may, by the powers of Nature, be actually divided and separated from one another, we cannot certainly determine. Yet, had we the proof of but one experiment that any undivided particle, in breaking a hard and solid body, suffered a division, we might by virtue of this rule, conclude that the undivided as well as the divided particles may be divided and actually separated to infinity.

Lastly, if it universally appears, by experiments and astronomical observations, that all bodies about the earth gravitate towards the earth, and that in proportion to the quantity of matter which they severally contain; that the moon likewise according to the quantity of its matter, gravitates towards the earth; that, on the other hand, our sea gravitates towards the moon; and all the planets mutually one towards another; and the comets in like manner towards the sun; we must, in consequence of this rule, universally allow that all bodies whatsoever are endowed with a principle of mutual gravitation. For the argument from the appearances concludes with more force for the universal gravitation of all bodies than for their impenetrability; of which, among those in the celestial regions, we have no experiments, nor any manner of observation. Not that I affirm gravity to be essential to bodies: by their *vis insita* I mean nothing but their *vis inertiae*. This is immutable. Their gravity is diminished as they recede from the earth.

Rule IV. In experimental philosophy we are to look upon propositions collected by general induction from phaenomena as accurately or very nearly true, notwithstanding any contrary hypotheses that may be imagined, till such time as other phaenomena occur, by which they may either be made more accurate, or liable to exceptions.

This rule we must follow, that the argument of induction may not be evaded by hypotheses. . . . .[5]

BOOK I. SCHOLIUM TO THE DEFINITIONS[6]

I. Absolute, true, and mathematical time, of itself, and from its own nature flows equably without regard to anything external; and by another name is called duration; relative, apparent, and

[5] Cf. close of Book III (Motte, pp. 506–7):

"Concerning the Law of Gravitation.—Hitherto we have explained the phaenomena of the heavens and of our sea by the power of gravity, but have not yet assigned the cause of this power. This is certain, that it must proceed from a cause that penetrates to the very centres of the sun and planets, without suffering the least diminution of its force; that operates not according to the quantity of the surfaces of the particles upon which it acts (as mechanical causes use to do), but according to the quantity of the solid matter which they contain, and propagates its virtue on all sides to immense distances, decreasing always in the duplicate proportion of the distances. Gravitation towards the sun is made up out of gravitations towards the several particles of which the body of the sun is composed; and in receding from the sun decreases accurately in the duplicate proportion of the distances as far as the orb of Saturn, as evidently appears from the quiescence of the aphelions of the planets; nay, and even to the remotest aphelions of the comets, if those aphelions are also quiescent. But hitherto I have not been able to discover the cause of these properties of gravity from phaenomena, and I frame no hypotheses; for whatever is not deduced from the phaenomena is to be called an hypothesis; and hypotheses, whether metaphysical or physical, whether of occult qualities or mechanical, have no place in experimental philosophy. In this philosophy particular propositions are inferred from the phaenomena, and afterwards rendered general by induction. Thus it was that the impenetrability, the mobility, and the impulsive force of bodies, and the laws of motion and gravitation were discovered. And to us it is enough that gravity does really exist, and act according to the laws which we have explained, and abundantly serves to account for all the motions of the celestial bodies, and of our sea."

[6] Motte, pp. 77–78.

common time, is some sensible and external (whether accurate or unequable) measure of duration by the means of motion, which is commonly used instead of true time,—such as an hour, a day, a month, a year.

II. Absolute space, in its own nature, without regard to anything external, remains always similar and immoveable. Relative space is some moveable dimension or measure of the absolute spaces; which our senses determine by its position to bodies; and which is vulgarly taken for immoveable space; such is the dimension of a subterraneous, an aereal, or celestial space, determined by its position in respect of the earth. Absolute and relative space are the same in figure and magnitude; but they do not remain always numerically the same. For if the earth, for instance, moves, a space of our air, which relatively and in respect of the earth remains always the same, will at one time be one part of the absolute space into which the air passes; at another time it will be another part of the same, and so, absolutely understood, it will be perpetually mutable.

III. Place is a part of space which a body takes up, and is, according to the space, either absolute or relative. . . . .

IV. Absolute motion is the translation of a body from one absolute place into another; and relative motion, the translation from one relative place into another. . . . .

The six primary planets are revolved about the sun in circles concentric with the sun, and with motions directed towards the same parts, and almost in the same plane. Ten moons are revolved about the earth, Jupiter and Saturn, in circles concentric with them, with the same direction of motion, and nearly in the planes of the orbits of those planets; but it is not to be conceived that mere mechanical causes could give birth to so many regular motions, since the comets range over all parts of the heavens in very eccentric orbits; for by that kind of motion they pass easily through the orbs of the planets, and with great rapidity; and in their aphelions, where they move the slowest, and are detained the long-

[7] Motte, pp. 504 f.

est, they recede to the greatest distances from each other, and thence suffer the least disturbance from their mutual attractions. This most beautiful system of the sun, planets, and comets, could only proceed from the counsel and dominion of an intelligent and powerful Being. And if the fixed stars are the centres of other like systems, these, being formed by the like wise counsel, must be all subject to the dominion of One; especially since the light of the fixed stars is of the same nature with the light of the sun, and from every system light passes into all the other systems: and lest the systems of the fixed stars should, by their gravity, fall on each other mutually, he hath placed those systems at immense distances one from another.

This Being governs all things, not as the soul of the world, but as Lord over all; and on account of his dominion he is wont to be called Lord God παντοκράτωρ, or Universal Ruler; for God is a relative word, and has a respect to servants; and Deity is the dominion of God not over his own body, as those imagine who fancy God to the soul of the world, but over servants. The Supreme God is a Being eternal, infinite, absolutely perfect; but a being, however perfect, without dominion, cannot be said to be Lord God; for we say, my God, your God, the God of Israel, the God of Gods, and Lord of Lords; but we do not say, my Eternal, your Eternal, the Eternal of Israel, the Eternal of Gods; we do not say, my Infinite, or my Perfect; these are titles which have no respect to servants. The word God usually signifies Lord; but every lord is not a God. It is the dominion of a spiritual being which constitutes a God: a true, supreme, or imaginary dominion makes a true, supreme, or imaginary God. And from his true dominion it follows that the true God is a loving, intelligent, and powerful Being; and from his other perfections, that he is supreme, or most perfect. He is eternal and infinite, omnipotent and omniscient; that is, his durations reaches from eternity to eternity; his presence from infinity to infinity; he governs all things, and knows all things that are or can be done. He is not eternity or infinity, but eternal and infinite; he is not duration or space, but he endures and is present. He endures for ever, and is every where present; and by existing always and every where, he constitutes duration and space. Since every particle of space is always, and every indivisible moment of duration is every where, certainly the Maker and Lord of all things cannot be never and no where. Every soul that has perception is, though in different times and in different organs of sense and motion, still the same indivisible person. There are given successive parts in duration, co-existent parts in space, but neither the one nor the other in the person of a man, or his thinking principle; and much less can they be found in the thinking substance of God. Every man, so far as he is a thing that has perception, is one and the same man during his whole life, in all and each of his organs of sense. God is the same God, always and every where. He is omnipresent not virtually only, but also substantially; for virtue cannot subsist without substance. In him are all things contained and moved; yet neither affects the other: God suffers nothing from the motion of bodies; bodies find no resistance from the omnipresence of God. It is allowed by all that the Supreme God exists necessarily; and by the same necessity he exists always and every where. Whence also he is all similar, all eye, all ear, all brain, all arm, all power to perceive, to understand and to act; but in a manner not at all human, in a manner not at all corporeal, in a manner utterly unknown to us. As a blind man has no idea of colours, so we have no idea of the manner by which the all-wise God perceives and understands all things. He is utterly void of all body and bodily figure, and can therefore neither be seen, nor heard, nor touched; nor ought he to be worshipped under the representation of any corporeal thing. We have ideas of his attributes, but what the real substance of any thing is we know not. In bodies, we see only their figures and colours, we hear only the sounds, we touch only their outward surfaces, we smell only the smells, and taste the savours; but their inward substances are not to be known either by our senses, or by any reflex act of our minds: much less, have we any idea of the substance of God. We know him only by his most wise and excellent contrivances of things, and final causes; we admire him for his perfections; but we reverence and adore him on account of his dominion: for we adore him as his servants; and a god without dominion, providence, and final causes, is nothing else but Fate and Nature. Blind metaphysical necessity, which is certainly the same always and every where, could produce no variety of things. All that diversity of natural things which we find suited to different times and places could arise from nothing but the ideas and will of a Being necessarily existing. But, by way of allegory, God is said to see, to speak, to laugh, to love, to hate, to desire, to give, to receive, to rejoice, to be angry, to fight, to frame, to work, to build; for all our notions of God are taken from the ways of mankind by a certain similitude, which, though not perfect, has some likeness, however. And thus much concerning God; to discourse of whom from the appearances of things, does certainly belong to Natural Philosophy.

CHAPTER VI

JOHN LOCKE

John Locke was born at Wrington, near Bristol, in 1632. His father was an adherent of the Parliamentary party of which John was later to write the philosophical defense. Locke was educated at a school of Parliamentary sympathies and then at Christ Church, Oxford. Although he did well in it, he found the accepted classical course of study a tedious affair. "A great part of the learning now in fashion in the schools of Europe and that goes ordinarily into the round of education," he wrote later, "a gentleman may in a good measure be unfurnished with, without any great disparagement to himself or prejudice to his affairs." Locke became a doctor of medicine, though he seldom practiced his profession. But he was actively interested in the development of physical as well as medical science, was well acquainted with Boyle and later with "the incomparable Mr. Newton," and was from 1668 a Fellow of the Royal Society. Locke's political bias is marked by his association with the first Earl of Shaftesbury, dating from 1666—marked so strongly, in fact, that, at Shaftesbury's flight and subsequent death Locke found it expedient, in 1683, to retire quietly to Holland. He returned to England in 1689, on the same ship with the new Queen. From 1691 until his death in 1704 he lived at Oates in the home of his friend Sir Francis Masham. Chief works: *A Letter concerning Toleration* (1689); *An Essay concerning Human Understanding* (1690); *Two Treatises of Government* (1690); *Some Thoughts concerning Education* (1693); *The Reasonableness of Christianity* (1695); *Three Letters to the Lord Bishop of Worcester concerning Some Passages in the Essay concerning Human Understanding* (1697, 1697, 1699); *A Paraphrase and Notes on the Epistles of St. Paul, etc.* (1705, 1706, 1707); *Of the Conduct of the Understanding* (1706 [written about 1697]); *A Discourse of Miracles* (1706 [written 1702–3]); *An Examination of Pere Malebranche's Opinion of Seeing All Things in God* (1706); *Remarks upon Some of Mr. Norris's Books* (1720); *Elements of Natural Philosophy* (1720). Suggested readings: *Philosophical Works* (available in several older editions); *Essay concerning Human Understanding*, ed. Fraser (Oxford, 1894); *Two Treatises of Civil Government* ("Everyman's Ed."; [New York, 1924]). Samuel Alexander, *Locke* (London, 1908); A. C. Fraser, *Locke* (Edinburgh and London, 1890); James Gibson, *Locke's Theory of Knowledge and Its Historical Relations* (Cambridge, 1917); George Santayana, *Some Turns of Thought in Modern Philosophy* (New York, 1933) (includes an essay on "Locke and the Frontiers of Common Sense"); Norman Kemp Smith, *John Locke* (Manchester, 1933).

T HE twenty years during which Locke wrote his *Essay concerning Human Understanding* opened with an incident which he relates in the "Epistle to the Reader":

Were it fit to trouble thee with the history of this Essay, I should tell thee, that five or six friends meeting at my chamber, and discoursing on a subject very remote from this, found themselves quickly at a stand, by the difficulties that rose on every side. After we had a while puzzled ourselves, not coming any nearer solution of those doubts which perplexed us, it came into my thoughts, that we took a wrong course; and that before we set ourselves upon inquiries of that nature, it was necessary to examine our own abilities, and see what objects our understandings were, or were not, fitted to deal with.

The "subject remote from this" was in fact morality and revealed religion. So Locke's initial interest in the examination of the human understanding came from the question whether methods as successful as those of physical science could be applied in the fields of morality and religion. Out of that interest grew his celebrated inquiry into the nature and scope of knowledge.

Locke was a trained (though not a practicing) physician and a member of the Royal Society. He was well acquainted with Boyle, Newton, Sydenham, and others of his distinguished scientific contemporaries; and he was deeply impressed with their attempts to understand nature by "rational experiment and observation" as opposed to bare speculation. To clear the ground for further progress in this direction, Locke was concerned to root out the doctrine of "innate ideas" which seemed to him to give support to some of the vain and pompous doctrines of speculative philosophers (Book I of the *Essay*). And he was likewise concerned to remove "some of the rubbish that lies in the way to knowledge" by eliminating from philosophy "the learned but frivolous use of uncouth, affected, or unintelligible terms." This he endeavored to do by his examination, in the third book of the *Essay*, of the nature and use of names. Both these polemics were incidental to the central task of the *Essay*: the inquiry into the scope and nature of knowledge—executed by what Locke calls the "historical, plain method": that is, by testing the manifold contents of the mind with respect to their origin in "simple ideas." Descartes, it will be remembered, insisted on the necessity of beginning by the elimination of all dubious mental content until we got to a few clear and distinct ideas from which we could then build, always going by steps equally simple and clearly understood. Locke effects a similar reduction to simple elements out of which knowledge is compounded, but with an emphasis that makes the resulting picture look rather different. The change is illustrated by the shift in meaning of the term "idea." In Descartes "idea" vacillates between two meanings. Sometimes it seems to mean content passively present to the mind, sometimes an active comprehension of some concept by the mind. Ultimately, however, Descartes's rationalism leads him to emphasize the active meaning; and Spinoza takes over solely that aspect of the term. For it is in its character of an active conception by the mind that an idea guarantees its own truth. An idea is an activity of mind, truth is a property of ideas; therefore, truth is discovered in some quality (to wit, clarity and distinctness) of those mental activities themselves. If, on the other hand, one takes the term "idea" in its passive sense—if one considers, as Descartes seems to do in the beginning of Meditation III, the objects present "in" one's mind rather than the activity of mind itself—then the obvious question to ask about ideas is not "What distinctive qualities have they in themselves?" but "What right have they to be there?" and "Where do they come from?" Ideas in this sense are tested not by their intrinsic luminosity but by reference to some external source that got them into mind. Thus Locke defines "idea" as any object of thinking, present to a passive understanding; and he proceeds to subject them to his historical plain method, i.e., to test their validity by inquiring into their origin, by asking how they first got into the mind in which they are found to appear.[1]

[1] The Cartesian Malebranche (1638–1715) also changes the meaning of idea in this direction. In fact, ideas are for him so entirely passive pictures presented to mind that they cannot be considered modifications of mind at all. The mind perceives bodies *through* its ideas—fundamentally through the idea of extension. Extension, however, is infinite. But an infinite idea cannot be a modification of a finite mind. It is rather an idea in the infinite divine mind; and it is therefore through such of God's ideas as he chooses to reveal to man that the finite mind perceives things beyond itself. God we know through himself; but we know external things through

Locke starts and finishes with a belief in the Cartesian world of two kinds of finite substances, created by the God of traditional religion. He believes, in other words, in a world of Newtonian physics attached to a world of Christian morality by virtue of their joint creation by a Christian God. He accepts, further, the notion of knowledge as a system of connected ideas having absolute validity in reference to a real world. What he does in the *Essay*, therefore, is to examine ideas with a view to discovering what part of our knowledge of the Cartesian world can really stand as knowledge thus defined, when tested by his historical criterion. After dispelling, in the first book, the notion of "innate ideas," he enumerates (Book II) the kinds of simple ideas we get by sensation and reflection, and the complex ideas we form from them: ideas of modes (or qualities, as distinct from substances), ideas of substance, and ideas of relations. Next (Book III) he considers the use of names, and the general ideas formed in connection with them, insisting that words be used only where there is some well-defined idea to which they are referring. Finally, in the fourth book of the *Essay*, he considers, on the foundation so far established, what knowledge is actually possible to man ("knowledge" understood, again, in terms of connections between ideas, possessing complete validity and significant with reference to a real world). We have, it turns out first of all, knowledge of identity, diversity, and other relations between ideas in themselves; of this character is mathematics, and also the moral knowledge Locke started by inquiring into. Of the real world we have three kinds of knowledge. We know intuitively of our own existence, not as simple and immortal substances, but just as self-conscious beings at moments of such self-consciousness (somewhat in the manner of Descartes's

---

ideas—that is, in God, since all ideas are in him. (We know ourselves, further, through "internal sentiment," and other minds through conjecture.) Thus the skeptical direction given to British philosophy by its interpretation of "ideas" is obviated in Malebranche by his principle that we see all things in God.

"cogito"). We know demonstratively of the existence of God. And we have "sensitive" knowledge, i.e., the consciousness of our sensations as given, in the vividness that distinguishes them from merely remembered sensations. Sensitive knowledge, however, guarantees no permanently existing substances as its causes. True, Locke accepts the current distinction between the primary and secondary qualities of objects; primary qualities being those (like figure, motion, etc.) which we perceive as they actually are in the objects; secondary, those effects of primary qualities which produce in us sensations (of color, sound, etc.) not identical in quality with the actual character of the objects themselves. But even the primary qualities which we actually perceive as they are in things are still qualities *of* substances, not the substances themselves. The latter are, in the case both of mind and of matter, assumed as substrates, not known. The result is that there can be no science, in the strict sense, of nature. Nature is indeed written in mathematical letters, and the incomparable Mr. Newton has gone far to demonstrate those characters in particular fields. But the construction of one all-inclusive natural science is probably beyond our powers. We had better be content with formulating, through careful experiment, such probable judgments as we can concerning the partial appearances to our limited faculties of the great system of nature.

In 1690, the same year which saw the publication of the *Essays*, appeared Locke's *Two Treatises of Civil Government*. They exhibit him, no less in politics than in theory of knowledge, the advocate of moderate and middle-road views. Historically, Locke's *Treatises* appear as an apology for the Glorious Revolution of 1688 and the Whig government that succeeded it. Philosophically, they hold a middle position between the extremes of the absolutist Hobbes and the later democrat Rousseau (1712–78). For Locke the chief end of the state is the preservation of property: i.e., of the life, liberty, and estates of men. The Law of Nature decrees that no man harm another in respect of any of these possessions. In the state of nature, however, men's passions unfortunately prevent the perfect execution of this dictate of reason. Therefore it is to their advantage to enter, by compact with one another, into a political society. For such a society has, by the principle of majority rule, power to act authoritatively for the maintenance of the precious trio of life, liberty, and estates. The magistrates to whom authority is delegated by such a group hold office not absolutely but in trust from the individuals whose property they are delegated to protect; hence they are at least implicitly involved in the contractual relation. As against Hobbes, therefore, Locke's monarch must be constitutional; and the right of revolution against *unjust* force prevails. (This result follows from the changed end of the state: the preservation of liberty and property as well as mere life; for a situation may arise in which the risking of peace, hence of life, is justified for the sake of another of the basic possessions.) At the other extreme, Rousseau, taking over Locke's insistence on the obligations of magistrates under the social contract, will nevertheless declare that there *is* an absolute sovereign created by the contract, to wit, the General Will, that is, the will of the people taken as a whole. Locke declares that a society has, by the principle of majority rule, power to act *as* an individual. Rousseau will hypostatize Locke's "as" and declare that the social body *is* an individual having its own "General Will," the object of which is invariably the general good. (But thereby the role of the majority becomes problematic; for the majority of individuals may resolve on a measure not consonant with the general good, and in that case the majority does not express the General Will. The question then arises: "By what external criterion is an expression of the general will to be recognized?") Between these two conceptions of absolute sovereignty, then—the monarchic and the popular—Locke holds the middle ground. He is the advocate of constitutional government against absolute monarchy,

and in spirit equally against the later, more extreme statement of the doctrine of popular sovereignty which was to
serve as fuel for revolution in eighteenth-century France.

SELECTIONS FROM *AN ESSAY CONCERNING HUMAN UNDERSTANDING*[2]

Book I

CHAPTER I. INTRODUCTION

1. *An inquiry into the understanding, pleasant and useful.*—Since
it is the understanding that sets man above the rest of sensible
beings, and gives him all the advantage and dominion which he
has over them; it is certainly a subject, even for its nobleness,
worth our labour to inquire into. The understanding, like the eye,
whilst it makes us see and perceive all other things, takes no notice
of itself; and it requires art and pains to set it at a distance, and
make it its own object. But whatever be the difficulties that lie
in the way of this inquiry, whatever it be that keeps us so much in
the dark to ourselves, sure I am, that all the light we can let in
upon our own minds, all the acquaintance we can make with our
own understandings, will not only be very pleasant, but bring us
great advantage, in directing our thoughts in the search of other
things.

2. *Design.*—This, therefore, being my purpose, to inquire into
the original, certainty, and extent of human knowledge, together
with the grounds and degrees of belief, opinion, and assent; I
shall not at present meddle with the physical consideration of the
mind. . . . . It shall suffice to my present purpose, to consider the
discerning faculties of a man, as they are employed about the
objects which they have to do with: and I shall imagine I have not
wholly misemployed myself in the thoughts I shall have on this
occasion, if, in this historical, plain method, I can give any account
of the ways whereby our understandings come to attain those

[2] *Locke's Essays: An Essay concerning Human Understanding and A Treatise
on the Conduct of the Understanding*, by John Locke, Gent. (Philadelphia, 1852).
(The text has been checked for errata against the standard edition of Fraser [Oxford,
1894]; but the spelling, punctuation, and chapter headings of the American edition
have been retained.)

notions of things we have, and can set down any measures of the certainty of our knowledge, or the grounds of those persuasions, which are to be found amongst men, so various, different, and wholly contradictory; and yet asserted somewhere or other with such assurance and confidence, that he that shall take a view of the opinions of mankind, observe their opposition, and at the same time consider the fondness and devotion wherewith they are embraced, the resolution and eagerness wherewith they are maintained, may perhaps have reason to suspect, that either there is no such thing as truth at all, or that mankind hath no sufficient means to attain a certain knowledge of it.

3. *Method.*—It is, therefore, worth while to search out the bounds between opinion and knowledge; and examine by what measures, in things, whereof we have no certain knowledge, we ought to regulate our assent, and moderate our persuasions. In order whereunto, I shall pursue this following method.

First, I shall inquire into the original of those ideas, notions, or whatever else you please to call them, which a man observes, and is conscious to himself he has in his mind; and the ways whereby the understanding comes to be furnished with them.

Secondly, I shall endeavour to show what knowledge the understanding hath by those ideas; and the certainty, evidence, and extent of it.

Thirdly, I shall make some inquiry into the nature and grounds of faith or opinion; whereby I mean that assent which we give to any proposition as true, of whose truth yet we have no certain knowledge: and here we shall have occasion to examine the reasons and degrees of assent.

4. *Useful to know the extent of our comprehension.*—If, by this inquiry into the nature of the understanding, I can discover the powers thereof, how far they reach, to what things they are in any degree proportionate, and where they fail us; I suppose it may be of use to prevail with the busy mind of man to be more cautious in meddling with things exceeding its comprehension; to stop when it is at the utmost extent of its tether; and to sit down in a quiet ignorance of those things, which, upon examination, are found to be beyond the reach of our capacities. . . . .

5. *Our capacity suited to our state and concerns.*—For, though the comprehension of our understandings comes exceeding short of the vast extent of things, yet we shall have cause enough to magnify the bountiful Author of our being, for that proportion and degree of knowledge he has bestowed on us, so far above all the rest of the inhabitants of this our mansion. Men have reason to be well satisfied with what God hath thought fit for them, since he has given them (as St. Peter says) πάντα πρὸς ζωὴν και εὐσέβειαν, whatsoever is necessary for the conveniences of life, and information of virtue; and has put within the reach of their discovery the comfortable provision for this life, and the way that leads to a better. . . . . It will be no excuse to an idle and untoward servant, who would not attend his business by candlelight, to plead that he had not broad sunshine. The candle that is set up in us, shines bright enough for all our purposes. The discoveries we can make with this, ought to satisfy us: and we shall then use our understanding right, when we entertain all objects in that way and proportion that they are suited to our faculties, and upon those grounds they are capable of being proposed to us; and not peremptorily or intemperately require demonstration, and demand certainty, where probability only is to be had, and which is sufficient to govern all our concernments. If we will disbelieve every thing, because we cannot certainly know all things, we shall do much-what as wisely as he, who would not use his legs, but sit still and perish, because he had no wings to fly.

6. *Knowledge of our capacity a cure of scepticism and idleness.*— When we know our own strength, we shall the better know what to undertake with hopes of success; and when we have well surveyed the powers of our own minds, and made some estimate what we may expect from them, we shall not be inclined either to sit still, and not set our thoughts on work at all, in despair of knowing any thing; or, on the other side, question every thing, and disclaim all knowledge, because some things are not to be understood. It is of great use to the sailor to know the length of his line, though he cannot with it fathom all the depths of the ocean. It is well he knows that it is long enough to reach the bottom, at such places as are necessary to direct his voyage, and caution him against running upon shoals that may ruin him. Our business here is not to

know all things, but those which concern our conduct. If we can find out those measures whereby a rational creature, put in that state which man is in, in this world, may and ought to govern his opinions, and actions depending thereon, we need not be troubled that some other things escape our knowledge.

7. *Occasion of this Essay.*—This was that which gave the first rise to this essay concerning the understanding. For I thought that the first step towards satisfying several inquiries the mind of man was very apt to run into, was to take a survey of our own understanding, examine our own powers, and see to what things they were adapted. Till that was done, I suspected we began at the wrong end, and in vain sought for satisfaction in a quiet and sure possession of truths that most concerned us, whilst we let loose our thoughts into the vast ocean of being; as if all that boundless extent were the natural and undoubted possession of our understandings, wherein there was nothing exempt from its decisions, or that escaped its comprehension. Thus men, extending their inquiries beyond their capacities, and letting their thoughts wander into those depths where they can find no sure footing, it is no wonder that they raise questions, and multiply disputes, which, never coming to any clear resolution, are proper only to continue and increase their doubts, and to confirm them at last in perfect scepticism. Whereas, were the capacities of our understandings well considered, the extent of our knowledge once discovered, and the horizon found, which sets the bounds between the enlightened and dark parts of things, between what is and what is not comprehensible by us; men would, perhaps, with less scruple acquiesce in the avowed ignorance of the one, and employ their thoughts and discourse with more advantage and satisfaction in the other.

8. *What idea stands for.*—Thus much I thought necessary to say concerning the occasion of this inquiry into human understanding. But, before I proceed on to what I have thought on this subject, I must here in the entrance beg pardon of my reader for the frequent use of the word "idea," which he will find in the following treatise. It being that term which, I think, serves best to stand for whatsoever is the object of the understanding when a man thinks: I have used it to express whatever is meant by phantasm, notion, species, or whatever it is which the mind can be employed about in thinking; and I could not avoid frequently using it.

I presume it will be easily granted me, that there are such ideas in men's minds. Every one is conscious of them in himself, and men's words and actions will satisfy him that they are in others. Our first inquiry then shall be, how they come into the mind.

CHAPTER II. NO INNATE PRINCIPLES IN THE MIND

1. *The way shown how we come by any knowledge, sufficient to prove it not innate.*—It is an established opinion among some men, that there are in the understanding certain innate principles; some primary notions; Κοιναὶ ἔννοιαι, characters as it were, stamped upon the mind of man, which the soul receives in its very first being, and brings into the world with it. It would be sufficient to convince unprejudiced readers of the falseness of this supposition, if I should only show (as I hope I shall in the following parts of this discourse) how men, barely by the use of their natural faculties, may attain to all the knowledge they have, without the help of any innate impressions; and may arrive at certainty, without any such original notions or principles. For I imagine any one will easily grant, that it would be impertinent to suppose the ideas of colour innate in a creature, to whom God hath given sight and a power to receive them by the eyes, from external objects: and no less unreasonable would it be to attribute several truths to the impressions of nature, and innate characters, when we may observe in ourselves faculties fit to attain as easy and certain knowledge of them, as if they were originally imprinted on the mind.

But because a man is not permitted, without censure, to follow his own thoughts in the search of truth, when they lead him ever so little out of the common road, I shall set down the reasons that made me doubt of the truth of that opinion, as an excuse for my mistake, if I be in one; which I leave to be considered by those, who, with me, dispose themselves to embrace truth, wherever they find it.

2. *General assent, the great argument.*—There is nothing more commonly taken for granted, than that there are certain principles, both speculative and practical (for they speak of both) universally agreed upon by all mankind; which, therefore, they argue, must needs be constant impressions which the souls of men receive in their first beings, and which they bring into the world with them, as necessarily and really as they do any of their inherent faculties.

3. *Universal consent proves nothing innate.*—This argument, drawn from universal consent, has this misfortune in it, that if it were true, in matter of fact, that there were certain truths wherein all mankind agreed, it would not prove them innate, if there can be any other way shown how men may come to that universal agreement in the things they do consent in; which I presume may be done.

4. *"What is, is," and "it is impossible for the same thing to be, and not to be," not universally assented to.*—But, which is worse, this argument of universal consent, which is made use of to prove innate principles, seems to me a demonstration that there are none such; because there are none to which all mankind give a universal assent. I shall begin with the speculative, and instance in those magnified principles of demonstration, "whatsoever is, is;" and, "it is impossible for the same thing to be, and not to be;" which, of all others, I think have the most allowed title to innate. These have so settled a reputation of maxims universally received, that it will no doubt be thought strange, if any one should seem to question it. But yet I take liberty to say, that these propositions are so far from having a universal assent, that there are a great part of mankind to whom they are not so much as known.

5. *Not on the mind naturally imprinted, because not known to children, ideots, &c.*—For, first, it is evident, that all children and ideots have not the least apprehension or thought of them; and the want of that is enough to destroy that universal assent, which must needs be the necessary concomitant of all innate truths; it seeming to me near a contradiction to say, that there are truths imprinted on the soul, which it perceives or understands not; imprinting, if it signify any thing, being nothing else but, the making certain truths to be perceived. For, to imprint any thing on the mind, without the mind's perceiving it, seems to me hardly intelligible. If, therefore, children and ideots have souls, have minds, with those impressions upon them, they must unavoidably perceive them, and necessarily know and assent to these truths; which, since they do not, it is evident that there are no such impressions: for if they are not notions naturally imprinted, how can they be innate? and if they are notions imprinted, how can they be unknown? To say a notion is imprinted on the mind, and yet at the

same time to say that the mind is ignorant of it, and never yet took notice of it, is to make this impression nothing. . . . .

22. *Implicitly known before proposing, signifies, that the mind is capable of understanding them, or else signifies nothing.*—If it be said "the understanding hath an implicit knowledge of these principles, but not an explicit, before this first hearing," (as they must, who will say, "that they are in the understanding, before they are known") it will be hard to conceive what is meant by a principle imprinted on the understanding implicitly, unless it be this; that the mind is capable of understanding and assenting firmly to such propositions. And thus all mathematical demonstrations, as well as first principles, must be received as native impressions on the mind; which I fear they will scarce allow them to be, who find it harder to demonstrate a proposition, than assent to it when demonstrated. And few mathematicians will be forward to believe, that all the diagrams they have drawn were but copies of those innate characters which nature had engraven upon their minds.

23. *The argument of assenting on first hearing, is upon a false supposition of no precedent teaching.*—There is, I fear, this further weakness in the foregoing argument, which would persuade us, that therefore those maxims are to be thought innate, which men admit at first hearing because they assent to propositions, which they are not taught, nor do receive from the force of any argument or demonstration, but a bare explication or understanding of the terms. Under which, there seems to me to lie this fallacy; that men are supposed not to be taught, nor to learn any thing *de novo;* when, in truth, they are taught, and do learn something they were ignorant of before. For first, it is evident, that they have learned the terms and their signification, neither of which was born with them. But this is not all the acquired knowledge in the case: the ideas themselves, about which the proposition is, are not born with them, no more than their names, but got afterward. So that in all propositions that are assented to at first hearing, the terms of the proposition, their standing for such ideas, and the ideas themselves that they stand for, being neither of them innate, I would fain know what there is remaining in such propositions that is innate. For I would gladly have any one name that proposition, whose terms or ideas were either of them innate. We by degrees

get ideas and names, and learn their appropriated connexion one with another; and then to propositions made in such terms, whose signification we have learnt, and wherein the agreement or disagreement we can perceive in our ideas, when put together, is expressed, we at first hearing assent; though to other propositions, in themselves as certain and evident, but which are concerning ideas not so soon or so easily got, we are at the same time no way capable of assenting. For though a child quickly assents to this proposition, that "an apple is not fire," when, by familiar acquaintance, he has got the ideas of those two different things distinctly imprinted on his mind, and has learnt that the names apple and fire stand for them; yet, it will be some years after, perhaps, before the same child will assent to this proposition, "that it is impossible for the same thing to be, and not to be;" because, that though, perhaps, the words are as easy to be learnt, yet the signification of them being more large, comprehensive, and abstract, than of the names annexed to those sensible things the child hath to do with, it is longer before he learns their precise meaning, and it requires more time plainly to form in his mind those general ideas they stand for. Till that be done, you will in vain endeavour to make any child assent to a proposition made up of such general terms: but as soon as ever he has got those ideas, and learned their names, he forwardly closes with the one as well as the other of the fore-mentioned propositions, and with both for the same reason, viz. because he finds the ideas he has in his mind to agree or disagree, according as the words standing for them are affirmed or denied one of another in the proposition. But if propositions be brought to him in words, which stand for ideas he has not yet in his mind, to such propositions, however evidently true or false in themselves, he affords neither assent nor dissent, but is ignorant: for words being but empty sounds, any farther than they are signs of our ideas, we cannot but assent to them, as they correspond to those ideas we have, but no farther than that. But the showing by what steps and ways knowledge comes into our minds, and the grounds of several degrees of assent, being the business of the following discourse, it may suffice to have only touched on it here, as one reason that made me doubt of those innate principles.

24. *Not innate, because not universally assented to.*—To conclude this argument of universal consent, I agree, with these defenders of

innate principles, that if they are innate, they must needs have universal assent; for that a truth should be innate, and yet not assented to, is to me as unintelligible, as for a man to know a truth, and be ignorant of it at the same time. But then, by these men's own confession, they cannot be innate; since they are not assented to by those who understand not the terms, nor by a great part of those who do understand them, but have yet never heard nor thought of those propositions; which, I think, is at least one half of mankind. But were the number far less, it would be enough to destroy universal assent, and thereby show these propositions not to be innate, if children alone were ignorant of them.

25. *These maxims not the first known.*—But that I may not be accused to argue from the thoughts of infants, which are unknown to us, and to conclude from what passes in their understandings before they express it; I say next, that these two general propositions are not the truths that first possess the minds of children, nor are antecedent to all acquired and adventitious notions: which, if they were innate, they must needs be. Whether we can determine it or no, it matters not; there is certainly a time when children begin to think, and their words and actions do assure us that they do so. When therefore they are capable of thought, of knowledge, of assent, can it rationally be supposed they can be ignorant of those notions that nature has imprinted, were there any such? Can it be imagined with any appearance of reason, that they perceive the impressions from things without, and be at the same time ignorant of those characters which nature itself has taken care to stamp within? Can they receive and assent to adventitious notions, and be ignorant of those which are supposed woven into the very principles of their being, and imprinted there in indelible characters, to be the foundation and guide of all their acquired knowledge and future reasonings. This would be to make nature take pains to no purpose, or at least, to write very ill; since its characters could not be read by those eyes which saw other things very well; and those are very ill supposed the clearest parts of truth, and the foundations of all our knowledge, which are not first known, and without which the undoubted knowledge of several other things may be had. The child certainly knows that the nurse that feeds it is neither the cat it plays with, nor the blackmoor it is afraid of; that the wormseed or mustard it refuses is not the apple or sugar

it cries for; this it is certainly and undoubtedly assured of: but will any one say, it is by virtue of this principle, "that it is impossible for the same thing to be, and not to be," that it so firmly assents to these and other parts of its knowledge; or that the child has any notion or apprehension of that proposition, at an age, wherein yet, it is plain, it knows a great many other truths? He that will say, children join these general abstract speculations with their sucking bottles, and their rattles, may perhaps with justice, be thought to have more passion and zeal for his opinion, but less sincerity and truth, than one of that age. . . . .

Book II

CHAPTER I.   OF IDEAS IN GENERAL, AND THEIR ORIGINAL

1. *Idea is the object of thinking.*—Every man being conscious to himself that he thinks, and that which his mind is applied about whilst thinking, being the ideas that are there, it is past doubt, that men have in their mind several ideas, such as are those expressed by the words whiteness, hardness, sweetness, thinking, motion, man, elephant, army, drunkenness, and others. It is in the first place then to be inquired, how he comes by them. I know it is a received doctrine, that men have native ideas and original characters stamped upon their minds in their very first being. This opinion I have, at large, examined already; and, I suppose, what I have said, in the foregoing book, will be much more easily admitted, when I have shown whence the understanding may get all, the ideas it has, and by what ways and degrees they may come into the mind; for which I shall appeal to every one's own observation and experience.

2. *All ideas come from sensation or reflection.*—Let us then suppose the mind to be, as we say, white paper, void of all characters, without any ideas; how comes it to be furnished? Whence comes it by that vast store which the busy and boundless fancy of man has painted on it, with an almost endless variety? Whence has it all the materials of reason and knowledge? To this I answer in one word, from experience; in that all our knowledge is founded, and from that it ultimately derives itself. Our observation employed either about external sensible objects, or about the internal operations of our minds, perceived and reflected on by ourselves, is that

which supplies our understandings with all the materials of thinking. These two are the fountains of knowledge, from whence all
the ideas we have, or can naturally have, do spring.

3. *The object of sensation one source of ideas.*—First, Our senses,
conversant about particular sensible objects, do convey into the
mind several distinct perceptions of things, according to those various ways wherein those objects do affect them: and thus we come
by those ideas we have of yellow, white, heat, cold, soft, hard,
bitter, sweet, and all those which we call sensible qualities; which,
when I say the senses convey into the mind, I mean, they, from
external objects, convey into the mind what produces there those
perceptions. This great source of most of the ideas we have, depending wholly upon our senses, and derived by them to the understanding, I call SENSATION.

4. *The operations of our minds the other source of them.*—Secondly, The other fountain from which experience furnisheth the
understanding with ideas, is the perception of the operations of our
own minds within us, as it is employed about the ideas it has got;
which operations when the soul comes to reflect on and consider,
do furnish the understanding with another set of ideas, which
could not be had from things without; and such are perception,
thinking, doubting, believing, reasoning, knowing, willing, and all
the different actings of our own minds; which we being conscious
of, and observing in ourselves, do from these receive into our understandings as distinct ideas, as we do from bodies affecting our
senses. This source of ideas every man has wholly in himself; and
though it be not sense, as having nothing to do with external objects, yet it is very like i , and might properly enough be called
internal sense. But as I call the other sensation, so I call this,
REFLECTION, the ideas it affords being such only as the mind gets
by reflecting on its own operations within itself. By reflection,
then, in the following part of this discourse, I would be understood
to mean that notice which the mind takes of its own operations,
and the manner of them; by reason whereof there come to be ideas
of these operations in the understanding. These two, I say, viz.,
external material things, as the objects of sensation and the operations of our own minds within, as the objects of reflection, are to
me the only originals from whence all our ideas take their beginnings. The term operations here I use in a large sense, as compre-

hending not barely the actions of the mind about its ideas, but some sort of passions arising sometimes from them, such as is the satisfaction or uneasiness arising from any thought.

5. *All our ideas are of the one or the other of these.*—The understanding seems to me not to have the least glimmering of any ideas, which it doth not receive from one of these two. External objects furnish the mind with the ideas of sensible qualities, which are all those different perceptions they produce in us: and the mind furnishes the understanding with ideas of its own operations.

These, when we have taken a full survey of them, and their several modes, combinations, and relations, we shall find to contain all our whole stock of ideas; and that we have nothing in our minds which did not come in one of these two ways. Let any one examine his own thoughts, and thoroughly search into his understanding; and then let him tell me, whether all the original ideas he has there are any other than of the objects of his senses, or of the operations of his mind, considered as objects of his reflection; and how great a mass of knowledge soever he imagines to be lodged there, he will, upon taking a strict view, see that he has not any idea in his mind, but what one of these two have imprinted, though perhaps with infinite variety compounded and enlarged by the understanding, as we shall see hereafter. . . . .

20. *No ideas but from sensation or reflection evident, if we observe children.*—I see no reason, therefore, to believe that the soul thinks before the senses have furnished it with ideas to think on; and as those are increased and retained, so it comes, by exercise, to improve its faculty of thinking, in the several parts of it, as well as afterward, by compounding those ideas, and reflecting on its own operations; it increases its stock as well as facility in remembering, imagining, reasoning, and other modes of thinking.

21. He that will suffer himself to be informed by observation and experience, and not make his own hypothesis the rule of nature, will find few signs of a soul accustomed to much thinking in a new-born child, and much fewer of any reasoning at all. And yet it is hard to imagine, that the rational soul should think so much, and not reason at all. And he that will consider that infants newly come into the world, spend the greatest part of their time in sleep, and are seldom awake, but when either hunger calls for the teat,

or some pain (the most importunate of all sensations), or some other violent impression upon the body, forces the mind to perceive and attend to it: he, I say, who considers this, will, perhaps, find reason to imagine that a foetus in the mother's womb differs not much from the state of a vegetable; but passes the greatest part of its time without perception or thought, doing very little but sleep in a place where it needs not seek for food, and is surrounded with liquor, always equally soft, and near of the same temper; where the eyes have no light, and the ears, so shut up, are not very susceptible of sounds; and where there is little or no variety, or change of objects to move the senses.

22. Follow a child from its birth, and observe the alterations that time makes, and you shall find, as the mind by the senses comes more and more to be furnished with ideas, it comes to be more and more awake; thinks more, the more it has matter to think on. After some time it begins to know the objects, which, being most familiar with it, have made lasting impressions. Thus it comes by degrees to know the persons it daily converses with, and distinguish them from strangers; which are instances and effects of its coming to retain and distinguish the ideas the senses convey to it. And so we may observe how the mind, by degrees, improves in these, and advances to the exercise of those other faculties of enlarging, compounding, and abstracting its ideas, and of reasoning about them, and reflecting upon all these, of which I shall have occasion to speak more hereafter.

23. If it shall be demanded, then, when a man begins to have any ideas? I think the true answer is, when he first has any sensation. For since there appear not to be any ideas in the mind, before the senses have conveyed any in, I conceive that ideas in the understanding are coeval with sensation; which is such an impression or motion, made in some part of the body, as produces some perception in the understanding. It is about these impressions made on our senses by outward objects, that the mind seems first to employ itself in such operations as we call perception, remembering, consideration, reasoning, &c.

24. *The original of all our knowledge.*—In time the mind comes to reflect on its own operations, about the ideas got by sensation, and thereby stores itself with a new set of ideas, which I call ideas of reflection. These are the impressions that are made on our senses

by outward objects, that are extrinsical to the mind, and its own operations, proceeding from powers intrinsical and proper to itself: which, when reflected on by itself, becoming also objects of its contemplation, are, as I have said, the original of all knowledge. Thus, the first capacity of human intellect is that the mind is fitted to receive the impressions made on it, either through the senses, by outward objects, or by its own operations, when it reflects on them. This is the first step a man makes towards the discovery of any thing, and the ground work whereon to build all those notions which ever he shall have naturally in this world. All those sublime thoughts which tower above the clouds, and reach as high as heaven itself, take their rise and footing here: in all that good extent wherein the mind wanders, in those remote speculations it may seem to be elevated with, it stirs not one jot beyond those ideas which sense or reflection have offered for its contemplation.

25. *In the reception of simple ideas, the understanding is for the most part passive.*—In this part the understanding is merely passive; and whether or no it will have these beginnings, and, as it were, materials of knowledge, is not in its own power. For the objects of our senses do, many of them, obtrude their particular ideas upon our minds, whether we will or no: and the operations of our minds will not let us be without, at least some obscure notions of them. No man can be wholly ignorant of what he does when he thinks. These simple ideas, when offered to the mind, the understanding can no more refuse to have, nor alter, when they are imprinted, nor blot them out, and make new ones itself, than a mirror can refuse, alter, or obliterate the images or ideas which the objects set before it do therein produce. As the bodies that surround us do diversely affect our organs, the mind is forced to receive the impressions, and cannot avoid the perception of those ideas that are annexed to them.

CHAPTER II. OF SIMPLE IDEAS

1. *Uncompounded appearances.*—The better to understand the nature, manner, and extent of our knowledge, one thing is carefully to be observed concerning the ideas we have; and that is, that some of them are simple, and some complex.

Though the qualities that affect our senses are, in the things themselves, so united and blended, that there is no separation, no distance between them; yet it is plain the ideas they produce in the mind enter by the senses simple and unmixed: for though the sight and touch often take in from the same object, at the same time, different ideas, as a man sees at once motion and colour, the hand feels softness and warmth in the same piece of wax; yet the simple ideas, thus united in the same subject, are as perfectly distinct as those that come in by different senses; the coldness and hardness which a man feels in a piece of ice being as distinct ideas in the mind as the smell and whiteness of a lily; or as the taste of sugar and smell of a rose. And there is nothing can be plainer to a man than the clear and distinct perceptions he has of those simple ideas; which, being each in itself uncompounded, contains in it nothing but one uniform appearance or conception in the mind, and is not distinguishable into different ideas.

2. *The mind can neither make nor destroy them.*—These simple ideas, the materials of all our knowledge, are suggested and furnished to the mind only by those two ways above mentioned, viz., sensation and reflection. When the understanding is once stored with these simple ideas, it has the power to repeat, compare, and unite them, even to an almost infinite variety; and so can make at pleasure new complex ideas. But it is not in the power of the most exalted wit or enlarged understanding, by any quickness or variety of thought, to invent or frame one new simple idea in the mind, not taken in by the ways before mentioned: nor can any force of the understanding destroy those that are there. . . . . .

CHAPTER III. OF IDEAS OF ONE SENSE

1. *Division of simple ideas.*—The better to conceive the ideas we receive from sensation, it may not be amiss for us to consider them in reference to the different ways whereby they make their approaches to our minds, and make themselves perceivable by us.

First, then, There are some which come into our minds by one sense only.

Secondly, There are others, that convey themselves into the mind by more senses than one.

Thirdly, Others that are had from reflection only.

Fourthly, There are some that make themselves way, and are suggested to the mind by all the ways of sensation and reflection. We shall consider them apart under these several heads.

First, There are some ideas which have admittance only through one sense, which is peculiarly adapted to receive them. Thus light and colours, as white, red, yellow, blue, with their several degrees or shades, and mixtures, as green, scarlet, purple, sea-green, and the rest, come in only by the eyes: all kinds of noises, sounds, and tones, only by the ears: the several tastes and smells, by the nose and palate. And if these organs, or the nerves, which are the conduits to convey them from without to their audience in the brain, the mind's presence-room (as I may so call it), are any of them so disordered, as not to perform their functions, they have no postern to be admitted by; no other way to bring themselves into view, and be received by the understanding.

The most considerable of those belonging to the touch are heat and cold, and solidity; all the rest, consisting almost wholly in the sensible configuration, as smooth and rough, or else more or less firm adhesion of the parts, as hard and soft, tough and brittle, are obvious enough.

2. *Few simple ideas have names.*—I think it will be needless to enumerate all the particular simple ideas belonging to each sense. Nor indeed is it possible, if we would; there being a great many more of them belonging to most of the senses than we have names for. The variety of smells, which are as many almost, if not more, than species of bodies in the world, do most of them want names. Sweet and stinking commonly serve our turn for these ideas, which in effect is little more than to call them pleasing or displeasing; though the smell of a rose and violet, both sweet, are certainly very distinct ideas. Nor are the different tastes, that by our palates we receive ideas of, much better provided with names. Sweet, bitter, sour, harsh, and salt, are almost all the epithets we have to denominate that numberless variety of relishes which are to be found distinct, not only in almost every sort of creatures, but in the different parts of the same plant, fruit, or animal. The same may be said of colours and sounds. I shall therefore, in the account of simple ideas I am here giving, content myself to set down only such as are most material to our present purpose, or are in themselves less apt to be taken notice of, though they are very frequently the

ingredients of our complex ideas, amongst which I think I may well account solidity, which therefore I shall treat of in the next chapter.

1. *We receive this idea from touch.*—The idea of solidity we receive by our touch; and it arises from the resistance which we find in body, to the entrance of any other body into the place it possesses, till it has left it. There is no idea which we receive more constantly from sensation than solidity. Whether we move or rest, in what posture soever we are, we always feel something under us that supports us, and hinders our farther sinking downward: and the bodies which we daily handle make us perceive, that, whilst they remain between them, they do by an insurmountable force hinder the approach of the parts of our hands that press them. That which thus hinders the approach of two bodies, when they are moving one toward another, I call solidity. I will not dispute whether this acceptation of the word solid be nearer to its original signification than that which mathematicians use it in: it suffices, that I think the common notion of solidity, will allow, if not justify, this use of it; but, if any one think it better to call it impenetrability, he has my consent. Only I have thought the term solidity the more proper to express this idea, not only because of its vulgar use in that sense, but also because it carries something more of positive in it than impenetrability, which is negative, and is, perhaps, more a consequence of solidity than solidity itself. This, of all others, seems the idea most intimately connected with, and essential to, body, so as nowhere else to be found or imagined, but only in matter. And though our senses take no notice of it, but in masses of matter, of a bulk sufficient to cause a sensation in us; yet the mind, having once got this idea from such grosser sensible bodies, traces it farther; and considers it, as well as figure, in the minutest particle of matter that can exist; and finds it inseparably inherent in body, wherever or however modified.

2. *Solidity fills space.*—This is the idea which belongs to body, whereby we conceive it to fill space. The idea of which filling of space is, that, where we imagine any space taken up by a solid substance, we conceive it so to possess it, that it excludes all other solid substances; and will for ever hinder any two other bodies, that move toward one another in a straight line, from coming to

touch one another, unless it removes from between them, in a line not parallel to that which they move in. This idea of it the bodies which we ordinary handle sufficiently furnish us with.

3. *Distinct from space.*—This resistance, whereby it keeps other bodies out of the space which it possesses, is so great, that no force, how great soever, can surmount it. All the bodies in the world, pressing a drop of water on all sides, will never be able to overcome the resistance which it will make, soft as it is, to their approaching one another, till it be removed out of their way: whereby our idea of solidity is distinguished both from pure space, which is capable neither of resistance nor motion, and from the ordinary idea of hardness. For a man may conceive two bodies at a distance, so as they may approach one another, without touching or displacing any solid thing, till their superficies come to meet: whereby I think we have the clear idea of space without solidity. For (not to go so far as annihilation of any particular body) I ask, whether a man cannot have the idea of the motion of one single body alone, without any other succeeding immediately into its place? I think it is evident he can: the idea of motion in one body no more including the idea of motion in another, than the idea of a square figure in one body includes the idea of a square figure in another. I do not ask, whether bodies do so exist that the motion of one body cannot really be without the motion of another? To determine this either way, is to beg the question for or against a vacuum. But my question is, whether one cannot have the idea of one body moved, whilst others are at rest? And I think this no one will deny. If so, then the place it deserted gives us the idea of pure space without solidity, whereinto any other body may enter, without either resistance or protrusion of any thing. When the sucker in a pump is drawn, the space it filled in the tube is certainly the same whether any other body follows the motion of the sucker or not: nor does it imply a contradiction that, upon the motion of one body, another that is only contiguous to it should not follow it. The necessity of such a motion is built only on the supposition that the world is full, but not on the distinct ideas of space and solidity; which are as different as resistance and not resistance, protrusion and not protrusion. And that men have ideas of space without a body, their very disputes about a vacuum plainly demonstrate, as is showed in another place. . . . .

6. *What it is.*—If any one ask me what this solidity is? I send him to his senses to inform him; let him put a flint or a football between his hands and then endeavor to join them, and he will know. If he thinks this not a sufficient explication of solidity, what it is, and wherein it consists, I promise to tell him what it is, and wherein it consists, when he tells me what thinking is, or wherein it consists: or explains to me what extension or motion is, which perhaps seems much easier. The simple ideas we have are such as experience teaches them us: but if, beyond that, we endeavour by words to make them clearer in the mind, we shall succeed no better than if we went about to clear up the darkness of a blind man's mind by talking; and to discourse into him the ideas of light and colours. The reason of this I shall show in another place.

CHAPTER V. OF SIMPLE IDEAS OF DIVERS SENSES

The ideas we get by more than one sense are of space or extension, figure, rest and motion; for these make perceivable impressions, both on the eyes and touch: and we can receive and convey into our minds the ideas of the extension, figure, motion, and rest of bodies, both by seeing and feeling. But having occasion to speak more at large of these in another place, I here only enumerate them.

CHAPTER VI. OF SIMPLE IDEAS OF REFLECTION

1. *Simple ideas of reflection are the operations of the mind about its other ideas.*—The mind, receiving the ideas mentioned in the foregoing chapters, from without, when it turns its view inward upon itself, and observes its own actions about those ideas it has, takes from thence other ideas, which are as capable to be the objects of its contemplation as any of those it received from foreign things.

2. *The idea of perception, and idea of willing, we have from reflection.*—The two great and principal actions of the mind, which are most frequently considered, and which are so frequent, that every one that pleases may take notice of them in himself, are these two: perception or thinking, and volition or willing. The power of thinking is called the understanding, and the power of volition is called the will; and these two powers or abilities in the

mind are denominated faculties. Of some of the modes of these simple ideas of reflection, such as are remembrance, discerning, reasoning, judging, knowledge, faith, &c., I shall have occasion to speak hereafter.

CHAPTER VII. OF SIMPLE IDEAS OF BOTH SENSATION
AND REFLECTION

1. *Pleasure and pain.*—There be other simple ideas which convey themselves into the mind by all the ways of sensation and reflection viz. pleasure or delight, and its opposite, pain or uneasiness, power, existence, unity.

2. Delight or uneasiness, one or other of them, join themselves to almost all our ideas both of sensation and reflection; and there is scarce any affection of our senses from without, any retired thought of our mind within, which is not able to produce in us pleasure or pain. By pleasure and pain, I would be understood to signify whatsoever delights or molests us; whether it arises from the thoughts of our minds, or any thing operating on our bodies. For whether we call it satisfaction, delight, pleasure, happiness, &c., on the one side; or uneasiness, trouble, pain, torment, anguish, misery, &c., on the other; they are still but different degrees of the same thing, and belong to the ideas of pleasure and pain, delight or uneasiness; which are the names I shall most commonly use for those two sorts of ideas.

3. The infinite wise Author of our being, having given us the power over several parts of our bodies, to move or keep them at rest as we think fit, and also by the motion of them to move ourselves and other contiguous bodies, in which consist all the actions of our body; having also given a power to our minds, in several instances, to choose amongst its ideas which it will think on, and to pursue the inquiry of this or that subject with consideration and attention, to excite us to these actions of thinking and motion that we are capable of; has been pleased to join to several thoughts and several sensations, a perception of delight. If this were wholly separated from all our outward sensations and inward thoughts, we should have no reason to prefer one thought or action to another; negligence to attention, or motion to rest. And so we should neither stir our bodies, nor employ our minds, but let our thoughts (if I may so call it) run adrift, without any direction or design; and

suffer the ideas of our minds, like unregarded shadows, to make their appearances there as it happened, without attending to them. In which state, man, however furnished with the faculties of understanding and will, would be a very idle unactive creature, and pass his time only in a lazy, lethargic dream. It has therefore pleased our wise Creator to annex to several objects, and to the ideas which we receive from them, as also to several of our thoughts, a concomitant pleasure, and that in several objects, to several degrees: that those faculties which he had endowed us with might not remain wholly idle and unemployed by us. . . . .

7. *Existence and unity.*—Existence and unity are two other ideas that are suggested to the understanding by every object without, and every idea within. When ideas are in our minds, we consider them as being actually there, as well as we consider things to be actually without us: which is, that they exist, or have existence; and whatever we can consider as one thing, whether a real being or idea, suggests to the understanding the idea of unity.

8. *Power.*—Power also is another of those simple ideas which we receive from sensation and reflection. For, observing in ourselves, that we do and can think, and that we can at pleasure move several parts of our bodies which were at rest, the effects also that natural bodies are able to produce in one another occurring every moment to our senses, we both these ways get the idea of power.

9. *Succession.*—Besides these there is another idea, which, though suggested by our senses, yet is more constantly offered us by what passes in our minds; and that is the idea of succession. For if we look immediately into ourselves, and reflect on what is observable there, we shall find our ideas always, whilst we are awake, or have any thought, passing in train, one going and another coming without intermission.

10. *Simple ideas the materials of all our knowledge.*—These, if they are not all, are at least (as I think) the most considerable of those simple ideas which the mind has, and out of which is made all its other knowledge; all which it receives only by the two forementioned ways of sensation and reflection. . . . .

CHAPTER VIII.   SOME FARTHER CONSIDERATIONS
CONCERNING OUR SIMPLE IDEAS . . . .

. . . .

7. *Ideas in the mind, qualities in bodies.*—To discover the nature of our ideas the better, and to discourse of them intelligibly, it will be convenient to distinguish them, as they are ideas or perceptions in our minds, and as they are modifications of matter in the bodies that cause such perceptions in us; that so we may not think (as perhaps usually is done) that they are exactly the images and resemblances of something inherent in the subject; most of those of sensation being in the mind no more the likeness of something existing without us than the names that stand for them are the likeness of our ideas, which yet upon hearing they are apt to excite in us.

8. Whatsoever the mind perceives in itself, or is the immediate object of perception, thought, or understanding, that I call idea; and the power to produce any idea in our mind I call quality of the subject wherein that power is. Thus of snowball having the power to produce in us the ideas of white, cold, and round, the powers to produce those ideas in us as they are in the snowball, I call qualities; and as they are sensations or perceptions in our understandings, I call them ideas; which ideas, if I speak of sometimes as in the things themselves, I would be understood to mean those qualities in the objects which produce them in us.

9. *Primary qualities.*—Qualities thus considered in bodies are, first, such as are utterly inseparable from the body, in what estate soever it be, such as, in all the alterations and changes it suffers, all the force can be used upon it, it constantly keeps; and such as sense constantly finds in every particle of matter which has bulk enough to be perceived, and the mind finds inseparable from every particle of matter, though less than to make itself singly be perceived by our senses: *v. g.* take a grain of wheat, divide it into two parts, each part has still solidity, extension, figure, and mobility; divide it again, and it retains still the same qualities; and so divide it on till the parts become insensible, they must retain still each of them all those qualities: for division (which is all that a mill, or pestle or any other body does upon another, in reducing it to insensible parts) can never take away either solidity, exten-

sion, figure, or mobility from any body, but only makes two or more distinct separate masses of matter of that which was but one before; all which distinct masses, reckoned as so many distinct bodies, after division, make a certain number. These I call original or primary qualities of body, which I think we may observe to produce simple ideas in us, viz. solidity, extension, figure, motion or rest, and number.

10. *Secondary qualities.*—Secondly, such qualities, which in truth are nothing in the objects themselves, but powers to produce various sensations in us by their primary qualities, *i.e.*, by the bulk, figure, texture, and motion of their insensible parts, as colours, sounds, tastes, &c. these I call secondary qualities. To these might be added a third sort, which are allowed to be barely powers, though they are as much real qualities in the subject as those which I, to comply with the common way of speaking, call qualities, but for distinction, secondary qualities. For the power in fire to produce a new colour, or consistency, in wax or clay, by its primary qualities, is as much a quality in fire as the power it has to produce in me a new idea or sensation of warmth or burning, which I felt not before, by the same primary qualities, viz. the bulk, texture, and motion of its insensible parts.

11. *How primary qualities produce their ideas.*—The next thing to be considered is, how bodies produce ideas in us; and that is manifestly by impulse, the only way which we can conceive bodies to operate in.

12. If then external objects be not united to our minds, when they produce ideas therein, and yet we perceive these original qualities in such of them as singly fall under our senses, it is evident that some motion must be thence continued by our nerves or animal spirits, by some parts of our bodies, to the brain, or the seat of sensation, there to produce in our minds the particular ideas we have of them. And since the extension, figure, number, and motion of bodies, of an observable bigness, may be perceived at a distance by the sight, it is evident some singly imperceptible bodies must come from them to the eyes, and thereby convey to the brain some motion, which produces these ideas which we have of them in us.

13. *How secondary.*—After the same manner that the ideas of these original qualities are produced in us, we may conceive that the ideas of secondary qualities are also produced, viz. by the

operation of insensible particles on our senses. For it being manifest that there are bodies, and good store of bodies, each whereof are so small that we cannot, by any of our senses, discover either their bulk, figure, or motion, as is evident in the particles of the air and water, and others extremely smaller than those, perhaps as much smaller than the particles of air and water, as the particles of air and water are smaller than peas or hailstones; let us suppose at present, that the different motions and figures, bulk and number of such particles, affecting the several organs of our senses, produce in us those different sensations, which we have from the colours and smells of bodies; *v.g.* that a violet, by the impulse of such insensible particles of matter of peculiar figures and bulks, and in different degrees and modifications of their motions, causes the ideas of the blue colour and sweet scent of that flower to be produced in our minds, it being no more impossible to conceive that God should annex such ideas to such motions, with which they have no similitude, than that he should annex the idea of pain to the motion of a piece of steel dividing our flesh, with which the idea hath no resemblance.

14. What I have said concerning colours and smells may be understood also of tastes and sounds, and other the like sensible qualities; which, whatever reality we by mistake attribute to them, are in truth nothing in the objects themselves, but powers to produce various sensations in us, and depend on those primary qualities, viz. bulk, figure, texture, and motion of parts, as I have said.

15. *Ideas of primary qualities are resemblances; of secondary, not.* —From whence I think it is easy to draw this observation, that the ideas of primary qualities of bodies are resemblances of them, and their patterns do really exist in the bodies themselves; but the ideas produced in us by these secondary qualities have no resemblance of them at all. . . . .

17. The particular bulk, number, figure, and motion of the parts of fire, or snow, are really in them, whether any one's senses perceive them or no; and therefore they may be called real qualities, because they really exist in those bodies; but light, heat, whiteness, or coldness, are no more really in them than sickness or pain is in manna. Take away the sensation of them; let not the eyes see light or colours, nor the ears hear sounds; let the palate not taste,

nor the nose smell; and all colours, tastes, odours, and sounds, as they are such particular ideas, vanish and cease, and are reduced to their causes, *i. e.* bulk, figure, and motion of parts. . . . .

23. *Three sorts of qualities in bodies.*—The qualities then that are in bodies, rightly considered, are of three sorts:

First. The bulk, figure, number, situation, and motion or rest of their solid parts; those are in them, whether we perceive them or no; and when they are of that size that we can discover them, we have by these ideas of the thing, as it is in itself, as is plain in artificial things. These I call primary qualities.

Secondly. The power that is in any body, by reason of its insensible primary qualities, to operate after a peculiar manner on any of our senses, and thereby produce in us the different ideas of several colours, sounds, smells, tastes, &c. These are usually called sensible qualities.

Thirdly. The power that is in any body, by reason of the particular constitution of its primary qualities, to make such a change in the bulk, figure, texture, and motion of another body, as to make it operate on our senses differently from what it did before. Thus the sun has a power to make wax white, and fire, to make lead fluid. These are usually called powers. . . . .

CHAPTER IX. OF PERCEPTION

1. *Perception the first simple idea of reflection.*—Perception, as it is the first faculty of the mind, exercised about our ideas; so it is the first and simplest idea we have from reflection, and is by some called thinking in general. Though thinking, in the propriety of the English tongue, signifies that sort of operation of the mind about its ideas, wherein the mind is active; where it, with some degree of voluntary attention, considers any thing. For in bare, naked perception, the mind is, for the most part, only passive; and what it perceives, it cannot avoid perceiving.

2. *Perception only when the mind receives the impression.*—What perception is, every one will know better by reflecting on what he does himself, when he sees, hears, feels, &c., or thinks, than by any discourse of mine. Whoever reflects on what passes in his own mind, cannot miss it, and if he does not reflect, all the words in the world cannot make him have any notion of it.

3. This is certain, that whatever alterations are made in the body, if they reach not the mind; whatever impressions are made on the outward parts, if they are not taken notice of within; there is no perception. Fire may burn our bodies, with no other effect than it does a billet, unless the motion be continued to the brain, and there the sense of heat, or idea of pain, be produced in the mind, wherein consists actual perception. . . . .

15. *Perception the inlet of knowledge.*—Perception then being the first step and degree towards knowledge, and the inlet of all the materials of it, the fewer senses any man, as well as any other creature, hath, and the fewer and duller the impressions are that are made by them, and the duller the faculties are that are employed about them, the more remote are they from that knowledge which is to be found in some men. But this being in great variety of degrees (as may be perceived amongst men), cannot certainly be discovered in the several species of animals, much less in their particular individuals. It suffices me only to have remarked here that perception is the first operation of all our intellectual faculties, and the inlet of all knowledge into our minds: and I am apt, too, to imagine that it is perception, in the lowest degree of it, which puts the boundaries between animals and the inferior ranks of creatures. But this I mention only as my conjecture by the by; it being indifferent to the matter in hand which way the learned shall determine of it.

CHAPTER X. OF RETENTION

1. *Contemplation.*—The next faculty of the mind, whereby it makes a farther progress towards knowledge, is that which I call retention, or the keeping of those simple ideas which from sensation or reflection it hath received. This is done two ways; first, by keeping the idea, which is brought into it, for some time actually in view; which is called contemplation.

2. *Memory.*—The other way of retention is the power to revive again in our minds those ideas which, after imprinting, have disappeared, or have been as it were laid aside out of sight: and thus we do, when we conceive heat or light, yellow or sweet, the object being removed. This is memory, which is as it were the store-house of our ideas. . . . .

7. *In remembering, the mind is often active.*—In this secondary perception, as I may so call it, or viewing again the ideas that are lodged in the memory, the mind is oftentimes more than barely passive; the appearances of those dormant pictures depending sometimes on the will. The mind very often sets itself on work in search of some hidden idea, and turns, as it were, the eye of the soul upon it; though sometimes too they start up in our minds of their own accord, and offer themselves to the understanding, and very often are roused and tumbled out of their dark cells into open daylight by turbulent and tempestuous passions, our affections bringing ideas to our memory, which had otherwise lain quiet and unregarded. . . . .

CHAPTER XI.   OF DISCERNING, AND OTHER OPERATIONS OF THE MIND

1. *No knowledge without discernment.*—Another faculty we may take notice of in our minds, is that of discerning and distinguishing between the several ideas it has. It is not enough to have a confused perception of something in general: unless the mind had a distinct perception of different objects and their qualities, it would be capable of very little knowledge, though the bodies that affect us were as busy about us as they are now, and the mind were continually employed in thinking. On this faculty of distinguishing one thing from another depends the evidence and certainty of several, even very general propositions, which have passed for innate truths; because men overlooking the true cause why those propositions find universal assent, impute it wholly to native uniform impressions; whereas in truth it depends upon this clear discerning faculty of the mind, whereby it perceives two ideas to be the same or different. But of this more hereafter. . . . .

4. *Comparing.*—The comparing them one with another, in respect of extent, degrees, time, place, or any other circumstances, is another operation of the mind about its ideas, and is that upon which depends all that large tribe of ideas comprehended under relations; which of how vast an extent it is, I shall have occasion to consider hereafter.

6. *Compounding.*—The next operation we may observe in the mind about its ideas, is composition; whereby it puts together several of those simple ones it has received from sensation and reflection, and combines them into complex ones. Under this of composition may be reckoned also that of enlarging, wherein, though the composition does not so much appear as in more complex ones, yet it is nevertheless a putting several ideas together, though of the same kind. Thus, by adding several units together we make the idea of a dozen, and putting together the repeated ideas of several perches, we frame that of a furlong. . . . .

8. *Naming.*—When children have, by repeated sensations, got ideas fixed in their memories, they begin by degrees to learn the use of signs. And when they have got the skill to apply the organs of speech to the framing of articulate sounds, they begin to make use of words to signify their ideas to others. These verbal signs they sometimes borrow from others, and sometimes make themselves, as one may observe among the new and unusual names children often give to things in their first use of language.

9. *Abstraction.*—The use of words then being to stand as outward marks of our internal ideas, and those ideas being taken from particular things, if every particular idea that we take in should have a distinct name, names must be endless. To prevent this, the mind makes the particular ideas, received from particular objects, to become general; which is done by considering them as they are in the mind such appearances, separate from all other existences, and the circumstances of real existence, as time, place, or any other concomitant ideas. This is called abstraction, whereby ideas, taken from particular beings, become general representatives of all of the same kind, and their names general names, applicable to whatever exists conformable to such abstract ideas. . . . .

15. *These are the beginnings of human knowledge.*—And thus I have given a short, and, I think, true history of the first beginnings of human knowledge, whence the mind has its first objects, and by what steps it makes its progress to the laying in and storing up those ideas, out of which is to be framed all the knowledge it is capable of; wherein I must appeal to experience and observation,

whether I am in the right; the best way to come to truth being to examine things as really they are, and not to conclude they are, as we fancy of ourselves, or have been taught by others to imagine.

16. *Appeal to experience.*—To deal truly, this is the only way that I can discover, whereby the ideas of things are brought into the understanding: if other men have either innate ideas, or infused principles, they have reason to enjoy them; and if they are sure of it, it is impossible for others to deny them the privilege that they have above their neighbours. I can speak but of what I find in myself, and is agreeable to those notions, which, if we will examine the whole course of men in their several ages, countries, and educations, seem to depend on those foundations which I have laid, and to correspond with this method in all the parts and degrees thereof.

17. *Dark room.*—I pretend not to teach, but to inquire, and therefore cannot but confess here again, that external and internal sensation are the only passages that I can find of knowledge to the understanding. These alone, as far as I can discover, are the windows by which light is let into this dark room; for methinks the understanding is not much unlike a closet wholly shut from light, with only some little openings left to let in external visible resemblances, or ideas of things without: would the pictures coming into such a dark room but stay there, and lie so orderly as to be found upon occasion, it would very much resemble the understanding of a man in reference to all objects of sight and the ideas of them.

These are my guesses concerning the means whereby the understanding comes to have and retain simple ideas; and the modes of them, with some other operations about them. I proceed now to examine some of these simple ideas and their modes a little more particularly.

CHAPTER XII. OF COMPLEX IDEAS

1. *Made by the mind out of simple ones.*—We have hitherto considered those ideas, in the reception whereof the mind is only passive which are those simple ones received from sensation and reflection before mentioned, whereof the mind cannot make one to itself, nor have any idea which does not wholly consist of them. But as the mind is wholly passive in the reception of all its simple ideas, so it exerts several acts of its own, whereby, out of its simple ideas,

as the materials and foundations of the rest, the others are framed. The acts of the mind, wherein it exerts its power over its simple ideas, are chiefly these three: 1. Combining several simple ideas into one compound one, and thus all complex ideas are made. 2. The second is bringing two ideas, whether simple or complex, together, and setting them by one another, so as to take a view of them at once, without uniting them into one; by which way it gets all its ideas of relations. 3. The third is separating them from all other ideas that accompany them in their real existence; this is called abstraction: and thus all its general ideas are made. This shows man's power, and its way of operation, to be much-what the same in the material and intellectual world: for the materials in both being such as he has no power over, either to make or destroy, all that man can do is either to unite them together, or to set them by one another, or wholly separate them. I shall here begin with the first of these, in the consideration of complex ideas, and come to the other two in their due places. As simple ideas are observed to exist in several combinations united together, so the mind has a power to consider several of them united together as one idea; and that not only as they are united in external objects, but as itself has joined them. Ideas thus made up of several simple ones put together, I call complex; such as are beauty, gratitude, a man, an army, the universe; which, though complicated of various simple ideas, or complex ideas made up of simple ones, yet are, when the mind pleases, considered each by itself as one entire thing, and signified by one name.

2. *Made voluntarily.*—In this faculty of repeating and joining together its ideas, the mind has great power in varying and multiplying the objects of its thoughts infinitely beyond what sensation or reflection furnished it with; but all this still confined to those simple ideas which it received from those two sources. . . . .

3. *Are either modes, substances, or relations.*—Complex ideas, however compounded and decompounded, though their number be infinite, and the variety endless, wherewith they fill and entertain the thoughts of men; yet, I think, they may be all reduced under these three heads: 1. Modes. 2. Substances. 3. Relations.

4. *Modes.*—First, Modes I call such complex ideas, which, however compounded, contain not in them the supposition of subsisting by themselves, but are considered as dependencies on, or affections of substances: such as are the ideas signified by the words, triangle, gratitude, murder, &c. And if in this I use the word mode in somewhat a different sense from its ordinary signification, I beg pardon: it being unavoidable in discourses, differing from the ordinary received notions, either to make new words, or to use old words in somewhat a new signification: the latter whereof, in our present case, is perhaps the more tolerable of the two.

5. *Simple and mixed modes.*—Of these modes, there are two sorts which deserve distinct consideration. First, there are some which are only variations, or different combinations of the same simple idea, without the mixture of any other, as a dozen or score; which are nothing but the ideas of so many distinct units added together; and these I call simple modes, as being contained within the bounds of one simple idea. Secondly, there are others compounded of simple ideas of several kinds, put together to make one complex one; *v. g.* beauty, consisting of a certain composition of colour and figure, causing delight in the beholder; theft, which being the concealed change of the possession of any thing, without the consent of the proprietor, contains, as is visible, a combination of several ideas of several kinds: and these I call mixed modes.

6. *Substances, single or collective.*—Secondly, the ideas of substances are such combinations of simple ideas as are taken to represent distinct particular things subsisting by themselves; in which the supposed or confused idea of substance, such as it is, is always the first and chief. Thus, if to substance be joined the simple idea of a certain dull whitish colour, with certain degrees of weight, hardness, ductility, and fusibility, we have the idea of lead; and a combination of the ideas of a certain sort of figure, with the powers of motion, thought, and reasoning, joined to substance, make the ordinary idea of a man. Now of substances also there are two sorts of ideas; one of single substances, as they exist separately, as of a man, or a sheep; the other of several of those put together, as an army of men, or flock of sheep; which collective ideas of several substances thus put together, are as much each of them one single idea, as that of a man, or an unit.

7. *Relation.*—Thirdly, the last sort of complex ideas is that we call relation, which consists in the consideration and comparing one idea with another. Of these several kinds we shall treat in their order. . . . .

[*The next chapters deal with such complex ideas of simple modes as space, duration, number, infinity, modes of ideas of thinking, pleasure and pain, etc.*]

CHAPTER XXI. OF POWER

1. *This idea how got.*—The mind being every day informed, by the senses, of the alteration of those simple ideas it observes in things without, and taking notice how one comes to an end, and ceases to be, and another begins to exist which was not before: reflecting also on what passes within itself, and observing a constant change of its ideas, sometimes by the impression of outward objects on the senses, and sometimes by the determination of its own choice; and concluding from what it has so constantly observed to have been, that the like changes will for the future be made in the same things by like agents, and by the like ways; considers in one thing the possibility of having any of its simple ideas changed, and in another the possibility of making that change; and so comes by that idea which we call power. Thus we say, fire has a power to melt gold, *i. e.* to destroy the consistency of its insensible parts, and consequently its hardness, and make it fluid; and gold has a power to be melted; that the sun has a power to blanch wax, and wax a power to be blanched by the sun, whereby the yellowness is destroyed, and whiteness made to exist in its room. In which and the like cases, the power we consider is in reference to the change of perceivable ideas; for we cannot observe any alteration to be made in, or operation upon, any thing, but by the observable change of its sensible ideas; nor conceive any alteration to be made, but by conceiving a change of some of its ideas.

2. *Power active and passive.*—Power, thus considered, is twofold, viz. as able to make, or able to receive, any change; the one may be called active, and the other passive power. Whether matter be not wholly destitute of active power, as its author, God, is truly above all passive power, and whether the intermediate state of created spirits be not that alone which is capable of both active and passive power, may be worth consideration. I shall not now enter into that inquiry; my present business being not to search

into the original of power, but how we come by the idea of it. But since active powers make so great a part of our complex ideas of natural substances (as we shall see hereafter), and I mention them as such, according to common apprehension; yet they being not perhaps so truly active powers, as our hasty thoughts are apt to represent them, I judge it not amiss, by this intimation, to direct our minds to the consideration of God and spirits, for the clearest idea of active power.

3. *Power includes relation.*—I confess power includes in it some kind of relation (a relation to action or change,) as indeed which of our ideas of what kind soever, when attentively considered, does not? For our ideas of extension, duration, and number, do they not all contain in them a secret relation of the parts? Figure and motion have something relative in them much more visibly: and sensible qualities, as colours and smells, &c., what are they but the powers of different bodies, in relation to our perception? &c. And if considered in the things themselves, do they not depend on the bulk, figure, texture, and motion of the parts? all which include some kind of relation in them. Our idea, therefore, of power, I think, may well have a place among other simple ideas, and be considered as one of them, being one of those that make a principal ingredient in our complex ideas of substances, as we shall hereafter have occasion to observe.

4. *The clearest idea of active power had from spirit.*—We are abundantly furnished with the idea of passive power by almost all sorts of sensible things. In most of them we cannot avoid observing their sensible qualities, nay, their very substances, to be in a continual flux: and therefore with reason we look on them as liable still to the same change. Nor have we of active power (which is the more proper signification of the word power) fewer instances: since whatever change is observed, the mind must collect a power somewhere able to make that change, as well as a possibility in the thing itself to receive it. But yet, if we will consider it attentively, bodies, by our senses, do not afford us so clear and distinct an idea of active power as we have from reflection on the operations of our minds. For all power relating to action,—and there being but two sorts of action whereof we have any idea, viz. thinking and motion,—let us consider whence we have the clearest ideas of the powers which produce these actions. 1. Of thinking, body affords

us no idea at all: it is only from reflection that we have that. 2. Neither have we from body any idea of the beginning of motion. A body at rest affords us no idea of any active power to move; and when it is set in motion itself, that motion is rather a passion than an action in it. For when the ball obeys the stroke of a billiard-stick, it is not any action of the ball, but bare passion: also, when by impulse it sets another ball in motion that lay in its way, it only communicates the motion it had received from another, and loses in itself so much as the other received: which gives us but a very obscure idea of an active power of moving in body, whilst we observe it only to transfer, but not produce, any motion. For it is but a very obscure idea of power, which reaches not the production of the action, but the continuation of the passion. For so is motion in a body impelled by another; the continuation of the alteration made in it from rest to motion being little more an action than the continuation of the alteration of its figure by the same blow, is an action. The idea of the beginning of motion we have only from reflection on what passes in ourselves, where we find by experience, that barely by willing it, barely by a thought of the mind, we can move the parts of our bodies which were before at rest. So that it seems to me, we have, from the observation of the operation of bodies by our senses, but a very imperfect obscure idea of active power, since they afford us not any idea in themselves of the power to begin any action, either motion or thought. But if, from the impulse bodies are observed to make one upon another, any one thinks he has a clear idea of power, it serves as well to my purpose, sensation being one of those ways whereby the mind comes by its ideas. Only I thought it worth while to consider here, by the way, whether the mind doth not receive its idea of active power clearer from reflection on its own operations than it doth from any external sensation. . . . .

73. And thus I have, in a short draught, given a view of our original ideas, from whence all the rest are derived, and of which they are made up; which if I would consider as a philosopher, and examine on what causes they depend, and of what they are made, I believe they all might be reduced to these very few primary and original ones, viz. extension, solidity, mobility, or the power of being moved, which by our senses we receive from body; perceptiv-

ity, or the power of perception or thinking: motivity, or the power of moving; which by reflection we receive from our minds. I crave leave to make use of these two new words, to avoid the danger of being mistaken in the use of those which are equivocal. To which if we add existence, duration, number,—which belong both to the one and the other,—we have, perhaps, all the original ideas, on which the rest depend. For, by these, I imagine, might be explained the nature of colours, sounds, tastes, smells, and all other ideas we have, if we had but faculties acute enough to perceive the severally modified extensions and motions of these minute bodies, which produce those several sensations in us. But my present purpose being only to inquire into the knowledge the mind has of things, by those ideas and appearances which God has fitted it to receive from them, and how the mind comes by that knowledge, rather than into their causes or manner of production; I shall not, contrary to the design of this essay, set myself to inquire philosophically into the peculiar constitution of bodies, and the configuration of parts, whereby they have the power to produce in us the ideas of their sensible qualities: I shall not enter any farther into that disquisition, it sufficing to my purpose to observe, that gold or saffron has a power to produce in us the idea of yellow, and snow or milk the idea of white, which we can only have by our sight, without examining the texture of the parts of those bodies, or the particular figures or motion of the particles which rebound from them, to cause in us that particular sensation: though when we go beyond the bare ideas in our minds, and would inquire into their causes, we cannot conceive any thing else to be in any sensible object, whereby it produces different ideas in us, but the different bulk, figure, number, texture, and motion of its insensible parts.

CHAPTER XXII. OF MIXED MODES

I. *Mixed modes, what.*—Having treated of simple modes in the foregoing chapters, and given several instances of some of the most considerable of them, to show what they are, and how we come by them, we are now in the next place to consider those we call mixed modes: such are the complex ideas we mark by the names obligation, drunkenness, a lie, &c. which consisting of several combinations of simple ideas of different kinds, I have called mixed

modes, to distinguish them from the more simple modes, which
consist only of simple ideas of the same kind. These mixed modes
being also such combinations of simple ideas as are not looked
upon to be characteristical marks of any real beings that have a
steady existence, but scattered and independent ideas put together
by the mind, are thereby distinguishable from the complex ideas
of substances. . . . .

9. *How we get the ideas of mixed modes.*—There are . . . .
three ways whereby we get the complex ideas of mixed modes.
1. By experience and observation of things themselves. Thus by
seeing two men wrestle or fence, we get the idea of wrestling or
fencing. 2. By invention, or voluntarily putting together of several
simple ideas in our own minds: so he that first invented printing
or etching, had an idea of it in his mind before it ever existed.
3. Which is the most usual way, by explaining the names of actions
we never saw, or motions we cannot see; and by enumerating, and
thereby, as it were, setting before our imaginations all those ideas
which go to the making them up, and are the constituent parts of
them. For having by sensation and reflection stored our minds
with simple ideas, and by use got the names that stand for them, we
can by those means represent to another any complex idea we
would have him conceive; so that it has in it no simple ideas but
what he knows and has with us the same name for. For all our
complex ideas are ultimately resolvable into simple ideas, of which
they are compounded and originally made up, though perhaps
their immediate ingredients, as I may so say, are also complex
ideas. Thus the mixed mode, which the word lie stands for, is made
up of these simple ideas: 1. Articulate sounds. 2. Certain ideas in
the mind of the speaker. 3. Those words the signs of those ideas.
4. Those signs put together by affirmation or negation, otherwise
than the ideas they stand for, are in the mind of the speaker. . . . .

CHAPTER XXIII. OF OUR COMPLEX IDEAS OF SUBSTANCES

1. *Ideas of substances, how made.*—The mind being, as I have
declared, furnished with a great number of the simple ideas conveyed in by the senses, as they are found in exterior things, or by
reflection on its own operations, takes notice also, that a certain

number of these simple ideas go constantly together; which being presumed to belong to one thing, and words being suited to common apprehensions, and made use of for quick despatch, are called, so united in one subject, by one name; which, by inadvertency, we are apt afterward to talk of, and consider as one simple idea, which indeed is a complication of many ideas together: because, as I have said, not imagining how these simple ideas can subsist by themselves, we accustom ourselves to suppose some *substratum* wherein they do subsist, and from which they do result, which therefore we call *substance*.

2. *Our idea of substance in general.*—So that if any one will examine himself concerning his *notion of pure substance in general*, he will find he has no other idea of it at all, but only a supposition of he knows not what support of such qualities, which are capable of producing simple ideas in us; which qualities are commonly called accidents. If any one should be asked, what is the subject wherein colour or weight inheres? he would have nothing to say, but The solid extended parts: and if he were demanded, what is it that solidity and extension inhere in? he would not be in a much better case than the Indian before mentioned, who, saying that the world was supported by a great elephant, was asked what the elephant rested on? to which his answer was, a great tortoise. But being again pressed to know what gave support to the broad backed tortoise, replied, something, he knew not what. And thus here, as in all other cases where we use words without having clear and distinct ideas, we talk like children; who, being questioned what such a thing is, which they know not, readily give this satisfactory answer, that it is *something*; which, in truth, signifies no more, when so used, either by children or men, but that they know not what; and that the thing they pretend to know and talk of, is what they have no distinct idea of at all, and so are perfectly ignorant of it, and in the dark. The idea, then, we have, to which we give the general name substance, being nothing but the supposed, but unknown, support of those qualities we find existing, which we imagine cannot subsist *sine re substante*, without something to support them, we call that support *substantia*; which, according to the true import of the word, is, in plain English, *standing under, or upholding*.

3. *Of the sorts of substances.*—An obscure and relative idea of substance in general being thus made, we come to have the ideas of particular sorts of substances, by collecting such combinations of simple ideas, as are, by experience and observation of men's senses, taken notice of to exist together, and are therefore supposed to flow from the particular internal constitution, or unknown essence of that substance. Thus we come to have the ideas of a man, horse, gold, water, &c. of which substances, whether any one has any other clear idea, farther than of certain simple ideas co-existing together, I appeal to every one's own experience. It is the ordinary qualities observable in iron, or a diamond, put together, that make the true complex idea of those substances, which a smith or a jeweller commonly knows better than a philosopher; who, whatever substantial forms he may talk of, has no other idea of those substances than what is framed by a collection of those simple ideas which are to be found in them: only we must take notice, that our complex ideas of substances, besides all these simple ideas they are made up of, have always the confused idea of something to which they belong, and in which they subsist. And, therefore, when we speak of any sort of substance, we say it is a thing having such or such qualities; as, body is a thing that is extended, figured, and capable of motion; spirit, a thing capable of thinking; and so hardness, friability, and power to draw iron, we say, are qualities to be found in a loadstone. These, and the like fashions of speaking, intimate that the substance is supposed always something besides the extension, figure, solidity, motion, thinking, or other observable ideas, though we know not what it is.

4. *No clear idea of substance in general.*—Hence, when we talk or think of any particular sort of corporeal substances, as horse, stone, &c., though the idea we have of either of them be but the complication or collection of those several simple ideas of sensible qualities, which we use to find united in the thing called horse or stone; yet because we cannot conceive how they should subsist alone, nor one in another, we suppose them existing in, and supported by, some common subject; *which support we denote by the name substance*, though it be certain we have no clear or distinct idea of that thing we suppose a support.

5. *As clear an idea of spirit as body.*—The same happens concerning the operations of the mind, viz. thinking, reasoning, fearing,

&c. which we, concluding not to subsist of themselves, nor appre-
hending how they can belong to body, or be produced by it, we
are apt to think these the actions of some other substance, which
we call spirit: whereby yet it is evident, that having no other idea
or notion of matter, but *something* wherein those many sensible
qualities which affect our senses, do subsist; by supposing a substance, wherein *thinking, knowing, doubting,* and a power of moving,
&c., do subsist, *we have as clear a notion of the substance of spirit
as we have of body:* the one being supposed to be (without knowing
what it is) the *substratum* to those simple ideas we have from without; and the other supposed (with a like ignorance of what it is)
to be the *substratum* to those operations which we experiment in
ourselves within. It is plain, then, that the idea of corporeal *substance* in matter, is as remote from our conceptions and apprehensions, as that of spiritual *substance*, or *spirit*; and therefore, from
our not having any notion of the *substance* of spirit, we can no more
conclude its nonexistence, then we can, for the same reason, deny
the existence of body: it being as rational to affirm there is no
body, because we have no clear and distinct idea of the *substance*
of matter, as to say there is no spirit, because we have no clear and
distinct idea of the substance of a spirit. . . . .

9. *Three sorts of ideas make our complex ones of substances.*—
The ideas that make our complex ones of corporeal substances are
of these three sorts. First, the ideas of the primary qualities of
things, which are discovered by our senses, and are in them even
when we perceive them not; such are the bulk, figure, number,
situation, and motion of the parts of bodies, which are really in
them, whether we take notice of them or no. Secondly, the sensible
secondary qualities, which depending on these, are nothing but the
powers those substances have to produce several ideas in us by our
senses; which ideas are not in the things themselves, otherwise
than as any thing is in its cause. Thirdly, the aptness we consider
in any substance to give or receive such alterations of primary
qualities, as that the substance so altered should produce in us
different ideas from what it did before; these are called active and
passive powers; all which powers, as far as we have any notice or
notion of them, terminate only in sensible simple ideas. For whatever alteration a loadstone has the power to make in the minute

particles of iron, we should have no notion of any power it had at all to operate on iron, did not its sensible motion discover it: and I doubt not but there are a thousand changes, that bodies we daily handle have a power to cause in one another, which we never suspect, because they never appear in sensible effects.

10. *Powers make a great part of our complex ideas of substances.*— Powers therefore justly make a great part of our complex ideas of substances. He that will examine his complex idea of gold, will find several of its ideas that make it up to be only powers, as the power of being melted, but of not spending itself in the fire; of being dissolved in *aqua regia*; are ideas as necessary to make up our complex idea of gold, as its colour, and weight: which, if duly considered, are also nothing but different powers. For to speak truly, yellowness is not actually in gold; but is a power in gold to produce that idea in us by our eyes, when placed in a due light: and the heat which we cannot leave out of our idea of the sun, is no more really in the sun than the white colour it introduces into wax. These are both equally powers in the sun, operating, by the motion and figure of its insensible parts, so on a man as to make him have the idea of heat; and so on wax, as to make it capable to produce in a man the idea of white.

11. *The now secondary qualities of bodies would disappear, if we could discover the primary ones of their minute parts.*—Had we senses acute enough to discern the minute particles of bodies, and the real constitution on which their sensible qualities depend, I doubt not but they would produce quite different ideas in us; and that which is now the yellow colour of gold would then disappear, and instead of it we should see an admirable texture of parts of a certain size and figure. This microscopes plainly discover to us; for what to our naked eyes produces a certain colour, is, by thus augmenting the acuteness of our senses, discovered to be quite a different thing; and the thus altering, as it were, the proportion of the bulk of the minute parts of a coloured object to our usual sight, produces different ideas from what it did before. Thus sand, or pounded glass, which is opaque, and white to the naked eye, is pellucid in a microscope; and a hair seen this way loses its former colour, and is in a great measure pellucid, with a mixture of some bright sparkling colours, such as appear from the refraction of diamonds, and other pellucid bodies. Blood to the naked eye appears all red; but

by a good microscope, wherein its lesser parts appear, shows only some few globules of red, swimming in a pellucid liquor: and how these red globules would appear, if glasses could be found that yet could magnify them a thousand or ten thousand times more, is uncertain.

12. *Our faculties of discovery suited to our state.*—The infinitely wise contriver of us, and all things about us, hath fitted our senses, faculties and organs to the conveniences of life, and the business we have to do here. We are able, by our senses, to know and distinguish things: and to examine them so far, as to apply them to our uses, and several ways to accommodate the exigencies of this life. We have insight enough into their admirable contrivances and wonderful effects, to admire and magnify the wisdom, power, and goodness of their Author. Such a knowledge as this, which is suited to our present condition, we want not faculties to attain. But it appears not that God intended we should have a perfect, clear, and adequate knowledge of them: that perhaps is not in the comprehension of any finite being. . . . .

CHAPTER XXV. OF RELATION

1. *Relation, what.*—Besides the ideas, whether simple or complex, that the mind has of things, as they are in themselves, there are others it gets from their comparison one with another. The understanding, in the consideration of any thing, is not confined to that precise object: it can carry any idea, as it were, beyond itself, or at least look beyond it, to see how it stands in conformity to any other. When the mind so considers one thing, that it does as it were bring it to and set it by another, and carry its view from one to the other: this is, as the words import, relation and respect; and the denominations given to positive things, intimating that respect, and serving as marks to lead the thoughts beyond the subject itself denominated to something distinct from it, are what we call relatives, and the things, so brought together, related. Thus, when the mind considers Caius as such a positive being, it takes nothing into that idea, but what really exists in Caius; *v.g.* when I consider him as a man, I have nothing in my mind but the complex idea of the species, man. So likewise, when I say Caius is a white man, I have nothing but the bare consideration of a man

who hath that white colour. But when I give Caius the name husband, I intimate some other person; and when I give him the name whiter, I intimate some other thing: in both cases my thought is led to something beyond Caius, and there are two things brought into consideration. And since any idea, whether simple or complex, may be the occasion why the mind thus brings two things together, and as it were takes a view of them at once, though still considered as distinct; therefore any of our ideas may be the foundation of relation. As in the above-mentioned instance, the contract and ceremony of marriage with Sempronia is the occasion of the denomination or relation of husband; and the colour white, the occasion why he is said to be whiter than freestone. . . . .

4. *Relation different from the things related.*—This farther may be observed, that the ideas of relation may be the same in men, who have far different ideas of the things that are related, or that are thus compared; *v. g.* those who have far different ideas of a man, may yet agree in the notion of a father; which is a notion superinduced to the substance, or man, and refers only to an act of that thing called man, whereby he contributed to the generation of one of his own kind, let man be what it will.

5. *Change of relation may be without any change in the subject.*— The nature therefore of relation consists in the referring or comparing two things one to another; from which comparison one or both comes to be denominated. And if either of those things be removed, or cease to be, the relation ceases, and the denomination consequent to it, though the other receive in itself no alteration at all; *v. g.* Caius, whom I consider to-day as a father, ceases to be so to-morrow, only by the death of his son, without any alteration made in himself. Nay, barely by the mind's changing the object to which it compares any thing, the same thing is capable of having contrary denominations at the same time: *v. g.* Caius, compared to several persons, may truly be said to be older and younger, stronger and weaker, &c. . . . . .

CHAPTER XXVI. OF CAUSE AND EFFECT AND OTHER RELATIONS

1. *Whence their ideas got.*—In the notice that our senses take of the constant vicissitude of things, we cannot but observe, that

several particular, both qualities and substances begin to exist; and that they receive this their existence from the due application and operation of some other being. From this observation we get our ideas of cause and effect. That which produces any simple or complex idea we denote by the general name cause; and that which is produced, effect. Thus, finding, that in that substance which we call wax, fluidity, which is a simple idea that was not in it before, is constantly produced by the application of a certain degree of heat; we call the simple idea of heat, in relation to fluidity in wax, the cause of it, and fluidity *the effect*. So also finding that the substance of wood, which is a certain collection of simple ideas so called, by the application of fire is turned into another substance called ashes, *i. e.* another complex idea, consisting of a collection of simple ideas, quite different from that complex idea which we call wood, we consider fire, in relation to ashes, as cause, and the ashes as effect. So that whatever is considered by us to conduce or operate to the producing any particular simple idea, or collection of simple ideas, whether substance or mode, which did not before exist, hath thereby in our minds the relation of a cause, and so is denominated by us. . . . .

3. *Relations of time.*—Time and place are also the foundations of very large relations, and all finite beings at least are concerned in them. But having already shown, in another place, how we get these ideas, it may suffice here to intimate, that most of the denominations of things received from time, are only relations. Thus, when any one says that queen Elizabeth lived sixty-nine, and reigned forty-five years, these words import only the relation of that duration to some other, and mean no more but this, that the duration of her existence was equal to sixty-nine, and the duration of her government to forty-five annual revolutions of the sun; and so are all words, answering, how long. Again, William the Conqueror invaded England about the year 1066, which means this, that taking the duration from our Saviour's time till now, for one entire great length of time, it shows at what distance this invasion was from the two extremes; and so do all words of time, answering to the question when, which show only the distance of any point of time, from the period of a longer duration, from which we measure, and to which we thereby consider it as related. . . . .

5. *Relations of place and extension.*—The relation also that things have to one another in their places and distances, is very obvious to observe; as above, below, a mile distant from Charing-Cross, in England, and in London. But as in duration, so in extension and bulk, there are some ideas that are relative, which we signify by names that are thought positive; as great and little are truly relations. For here also having, by observation, settled in our mind the ideas of the bigness of several species of things from those we have been most accustomed to, we make them, as it were, the standards whereby to denominate the bulk of others. Thus we call a great apple, such a one as is bigger than the ordinary sort of those we have been used to: and a little horse, such a one as comes not up the size of that idea which we have in our minds to belong ordinarily to horses; and that will be a great horse to a Welshman which is but a little one to a Fleming; they two having, from the different breed of their countries, taken several sized ideas to which they compare, and in relation to which they denominate, their great and their little.

6. *Absolute terms often stand for relations.*—So likewise weak and strong are but relative denominations of power, compared to some ideas we have at that time of greater or less power. Thus when we say a weak man, we mean one that has not so much strength or power to move, as usually men have, or usually those of his size have: which is a comparing his strength to the idea we have of the usual strength of men, or men of such a size. The like, when we say the creatures are all weak things; weak, there, is but a relative term, signifying the disproportion there is in the power of God and the creatures. And so abundance of words, in ordinary speech, stand only for relations, (and perhaps the greatest part) which at first seem to have no such signification: *v. g.* the ship has necessary stores. Necessary and stores are both relative words; one having a relation to the accomplishing the voyage intended, and the other to future use. All which relations, how they are confined to and terminate in ideas derived from sensation or reflection, is too obvious to need any explication.

CHAPTER XXVII. OF IDENTITY AND DIVERSITY

1. *Wherein identity consists.*—Another occasion the mind often takes of comparing, is the very being of things: when considering

any thing as existing at any determined time and place, we compare it with itself existing at another time, and thereon form the ideas of identity and diversity. When we see any thing to be in any place in any instant of time, we are sure (be it what it will) that it is that very thing, and not another which at that same time exists in another place, how like and undistinguishable soever it may be in all other respects: and in this consists identity, when the ideas it is attributed to vary not at all from what they were that moment wherein we consider their former existence, and to which we compare the present. For we never finding, nor conceiving it possible that two things of the same kind should exist in the same place at the same time, we rightly conclude, that whatever exists any where at any time, excludes all of the same kind, and is there itself alone. . . . .

9. *Personal identity.*—This being premised, to find wherein personal identity consists, we must consider what person stands for: which, I think, is a thinking intelligent being, that has reason and reflection, and can consider itself as itself, the same thinking thing in different times and places; which it does only by that consciousness which is inseparable from thinking, and as it seems to me essential to it: it being impossible for any one to perceive, without perceiving that he does perceive. When we see, hear, smell, taste, feel, meditate, or will any thing, we know that we do so. Thus it is always as to our present sensations and perceptions: and by this every one is to himself that which he calls self; it not being considered in this case whether the same self be continued in the same or diverse substances. For since consciousness always accompanies thinking, and it is that that makes every one to be what he calls self, and thereby distinguishes himself from all other thinking things; in this alone consists personal identity, *i. e.* the sameness of a rational being: and as far as this consciousness can be extended backwards to any past action or thought, so far reaches the identity of that person; it is the same self now it was then; and it is by the same self with this present one that now reflects on it, that that action was done.

10. *Consciousness makes personal identity.*—But it is farther inquired, whether it be the same identical substance? This few would think they had reason to doubt of, if those perceptions, with their

consciousness, always remained present in the mind, whereby the same thinking thing would be always consciously present, and, as would be thought, evidently the same to itself. But that which seems to make the difficulty is this, that this consciousness being interrupted always by forgetfulness, there being no moment of our lives wherein we have the whole train of all our past actions before our eyes in one view, but even the best memories losing the sight of one part whilst they are viewing another;—and we sometimes, and that the greatest part of our lives, not reflecting on our past selves, being intent on our present thoughts, and in sound sleep having no thoughts at all, or at least none with that consciousness which remarks our waking thoughts;—I say, in all these cases, our consciousness being interrupted, and we losing the sight of our past selves, doubts are raised whether we are the same thinking thing, *i. e.* the same substance, or no. . . . .

25. I agree, the more probable opinion is, that this consciousness is annexed to, and the affection of, one individual immaterial substance.

But let men, according to their diverse hypotheses, resolve of that as they please. This every intelligent being, sensible of happiness or misery, must grant, that there is something that is himself that he is concerned for, and would have happy; that this self has existed in a continued duration more than one instant, and therefore it is possible may exist, as it has done, months and years to come, without any certain bounds to be set to its duration; and may be the same self, by the same consciousness, continued on for the future. And thus, by this consciousness, he finds himself to be the same self which did such or such an action some years since, by which he comes to be happy or miserable now. In all which account of self, the same numerical substance is not considered as making the same self; but the same continued consciousness, in which several substances may have been united, and again separated from it; which, whilst they continued in a vital union with that wherein this consciousness then resided, made a part of that same self. . . . .

CHAPTER XXVIII. OF OTHER RELATIONS

1. *Proportional.*—Besides the before-mentioned occasions of time, place, and casuality of comparing, or referring things one to another, there are, as I have said, infinite others, some whereof I shall mention.

First, The first I shall name, is some one simple idea; which being capable of parts or degrees, affords an occasion of comparing the subjects wherein it is to one another, in respect of that simple idea, *v. g.* whiter, sweeter, bigger, equal, more &c. These relations depending on the equality and excess of the same simple idea, in several subjects, may be called, if one will, proportional: and that these are only conversant about those simple ideas received from sensation or reflection, is so evident, that nothing need be said to evince it.

2. *Natural.*—Secondly, Another occasion of comparing things together, or considering one thing, so as to include in that consideration some other thing, is the circumstances of their origin or beginning; which being not afterwards to be altered, make the relations depending thereon as lasting as the subjects to which they belong; *v. g.* father and son, brothers, cousin-germans, &c. which have their relations by one community of blood, wherein they partake in several degrees; countrymen, *i. e.* those who were born in the same country, or tract of ground; and these I call natural relations. . . . .

3. *Instituted.*—Thirdly, Sometimes the foundation of considering things, with reference to one another, is some act whereby any one comes by a moral right, power, or obligation to do something. Thus a general is one that hath power to command an army: and an army under a general is a collection of armed men obliged to obey one man. A citizen, or a burgher, is one who has a right to certain privileges in this or that place. All this sort, depending upon men's wills, or agreement in society, I call instituted, or voluntary; and may be distinguished from the natural, in that they are most, if not all of them, some way or other alterable, and separable from the persons to whom they have sometimes belonged, though neither of the substances, so related, be destroyed. . . . .

4. *Moral.*—Fourthly, There is another sort of relation, which is the conformity, or disagreement, men's voluntary actions have to a rule to which they are referred, and by which they are judged of; which, I think, may be called moral relation, as being that which denominates our moral actions, and deserves well to be examined; there being no part of knowledge wherein we should be more careful to get determined ideas, and avoid, as much as may be, obscurity and confusion. Human actions, when with their various ends, objects, manners, and circumstances, they are framed into distinct complex ideas, are, as has been shown, so many mixed modes, a great part whereof have names annexed to them. Thus, supposing gratitude to be a readiness to acknowledge and return kindness received; polygamy to be the having more wives than one at once, when we frame these notions thus in our minds, we have there so many determined ideas of mixed modes. But this is not all that concerns our actions; it is not enough to have determined ideas of them, and to know what names belong to such and such combinations of ideas. We have a farther and greater concernment, and that is, to know whether such actions, so made up, are morally good or bad.

5. *Moral good and evil.*—Good and evil, as hath been shown, B. II. Ch. 20, Sect. 2, and Ch. 21, Sect. 42, are nothing but pleasure or pain, or that which occasions or procures pleasure or pain to us. Moral good and evil then is only the conformity or disagreement of our voluntary actions to some law, whereby good or evil is drawn on us by the will and power of the law-maker; which good and evil, pleasure or pain, attending our observance, or breach of the law, by the decree of the lawmaker, is that we call reward and punishment.

6. *Moral rules.*—Of these moral rules, or laws, to which men generally refer, and by which they judge of the rectitude or pravity of their actions, there seem to me to be three sorts, with their three different enforcements, or rewards and punishments. For since it would be utterly in vain to suppose a rule set to the free actions of man, without annexing to it some enforcement of good and evil to determine his will, we must, wherever we suppose a law, suppose also some reward or punishment annexed to that law. It would be in vain for one intelligent being to set a rule to the actions of another, if he had it not in his power to reward

the compliance with, and punish deviation from his rule, by some good and evil, that is not the natural product and consequence of the action itself. For that being a natural convenience, or inconvenience, would operate of itself without a law. This, if I mistake not, is the true nature of all law, properly so called.

7. *Laws.*—The laws that men generally refer their actions to, to judge of their rectitude, or obliquity, seem to me to be these three. 1. The divine law. 2. The civil law. 3. The law of opinion or reputation, if I may so call it. By the relation they bear to the first of these, men judge whether their actions are sins or duties; by the second, whether they be criminal or innocent; and by the third, whether they be virtues or vices.

8. *Divine law, the measure of sin and duty.*—First, The divine law, whereby I mean that law which God has set to the actions of men, whether promulgated to them by the light of nature, or the voice of revelation. That God has given a rule whereby men should govern themselves, I think there is nobody so brutish as to deny. He has a right to do it; we are his creatures: he has goodness and wisdom to direct our actions to that which is best; and he has power to enforce it by rewards and punishments, of infinite weight and duration, in another life; for nobody can take us out of his hands. This is the only true touchstone of moral rectitude, and by comparing them to this law it is that men judge of the most considerable moral good or evil of their actions; that is, whether as duties or sins, they are like to procure them happiness or misery from the hand of the Almighty.

9. *Civil law, the measure of crimes and innocence.*—Secondly, the civil law, the rule set by the commonwealth to the actions of those who belong to it, is another rule, to which men refer their actions, to judge whether they be criminal or no. This law nobody overlooks; the rewards and punishments that enforce it being ready at hand, and suitable to the power that makes it; which is the force of the commonwealth, engaged to protect the lives, liberties, and possessions of those who live according to its laws, and has power to take away life, liberty, or goods, from him who disobeys: which is the punishment of offences committed against this law.

10. *Philosophical law, the measure of virtue and vice.*—Thirdly, the law of opinion or reputation. Virtue and vice are names pretended and supposed every where to stand for actions in their own

nature right and wrong; and as far as they really are so applied, they so far are coincident with the divine law above mentioned. But yet, whatever is pretended, this is visible, that these names, virtue and vice, in the particular instances of their application, through the several nations and societies of men in the world, are constantly attributed only to such actions, as in each country and society are in reputation or discredit. Nor is it to be thought strange, that men every where should give the name of virtue to those actions, which among them are judged praise-worthy; and call that vice, which they account blameable; since otherwise they would condemn themselves if they should think any thing right, to which they allowed not commendation; any thing wrong which they let pass without blame. Thus the measure of what is every where called and esteemed virtue and vice, is the approbation or dislike, praise or blame, which by a secret and tacit consent establishes itself in the several societies, tribes, and clubs of men in the world; whereby several actions come to find credit or disgrace among them according to the judgment, maxims, or fashion of that place. For though men, uniting into politic societies, have resigned up to the public the disposing of all their force, so that they cannot employ it against any fellow-citizens any farther than the law of the country directs; yet they retain still the power of thinking well or ill, approving or disapproving of the actions of those whom they live among, and converse with: and by this approbation and dislike, they establish among themselves what they will call virtue and vice. . . . .

CHAPTER XXIX. OF CLEAR AND OBSCURE, DISTINCT AND CONFUSED IDEAS

1. *Ideas, some clear and distinct, others obscure and confused.*— Having shown the original of our ideas, and taken a view of their several sorts, considered the difference between the simple and the complex, and observed how the complex ones are divided into those of modes, substances, and relations; all which, I think, is necessary to be done by any one who would acquaint himself thoroughly with the progress of the mind in its apprehension and knowledge of things; it will, perhaps, be thought I have dwelt long enough upon the examination of ideas. I must, nevertheless, crave leave to offer some few other considerations concerning them. The first is, that

some are clear, and others obscure; some distinct, and others confused.

2. *Clear and obscure explained by sight.*—The perception of the mind being most aptly explained by words relating to the sight, we shall best understand what is meant by clear and obscure in our ideas by reflecting on what we call clear and obscure in the objects of sight. Light being that which discovers to us visible objects, we give the name of obscure to that which is not placed in a light sufficient to discover minutely to us the figure and colours which are observable in it, and which, in a better light, would be discernible. In like manner our simple ideas are clear when they are such as the objects themselves, from whence they were taken, did or might, in a well-ordered sensation or perception, present them. Whilst the memory retains them thus, and can produce them to the mind, whenever it has occasion to consider them, they are clear ideas. So far as they either want any thing of the original exactness, or have lost any of their first freshness, and are, as it were, faded or tarnished by time, so far are they obscure. Complex ideas, as they are made up of simple ones, so they are clear when the ideas that go to their composition are clear; and the number and order of those simple ideas, that are the ingredients of any complex one, is determinate and certain.

3. *Causes of obscurity.*—The causes of obscurity in simple ideas seem to be either dull organs, or very slight and transient impressions made by the objects, or else a weakness in the memory not able to retain them as received. For to return again to visible objects, to help us to apprehend this matter: if the organs or faculties of perception, like wax, of a temper too soft, will not hold it well when well imprinted; or else supposing the wax of a temper fit, but the seal not applied with a sufficient force to make a clear impression: in any of these cases, the print left by the seal will be obscure. This, I suppose, needs no application to make it plainer.

4. *Distinct and confused, what.*—As a clear idea is that whereof the mind has such a full and evident perception, as it does receive from an outward object operating duly on a well-disposed organ; so a distinct idea is that wherein the mind perceives a difference from all other; and a confused idea is such a one as is not sufficiently distinguishable from another, from which it ought to be different. . . . .

CHAPTER XXX.   OF REAL AND FANTASTICAL IDEAS

1. *Real ideas are conformable to their archetypes.*—Besides what we have already mentioned concerning ideas, other considerations belong to them, in reference to things from whence they are taken, or which they may be supposed to represent: and thus, I think, they may come under a threefold distinction; and are,

First, either real or fantastical.

Secondly, adequate or inadequate.

Thirdly, true or false.

First, by real ideas, I mean such as have a foundation in nature; such as have a conformity with the real being and existence of things, or with their archetypes. Fantastical or chimerical I call such as have no foundation in nature, nor have any conformity to that reality of being to which they are tacitly referred as to their archetypes. If we examine the several sorts of ideas before mentioned, we shall find, that,

2. *Simple ideas all real.*—First, our simple ideas are all real, all agree to the reality of things, not that they are all of them the images or representations of what does exist; the contrary whereof, in all but the primary qualities of bodies, hath been already shown. But though whiteness and coldness are no more in snow than pain is, yet those ideas of whiteness and coldness, pain, &c. being in us the effects of powers in things without us, ordained by our Maker, to produce in us such sensations, they are real ideas in us, whereby we distinguish the qualities that are really in things themselves. For these several appearances being designed to be the marks whereby we are to know and distinguish things which we have to do with, our ideas do as well serve us to that purpose, and are as real distinguishing characters, whether they be only constant effects, or else exact resemblances of something in the things themselves; the reality lying in that steady correspondence they have with the distinct constitutions of real beings. But whether they answer to those constitutions, as to causes or patterns, it matters not; it suffices that they are constantly produced by them. And thus our simple ideas are all real and true, because they answer and agree to those powers of things which produce them in our minds; that being all that is requisite to make them real, and not fictions at pleasure. For in simple ideas (as has been shown) the

mind is wholly confined to the operation of things upon it, and can make to itself no simple idea more than what it has received.

3. *Complex ideas are voluntary combinations.*—Though the mind be wholly passive in respect of its simple ideas, yet I think we may say, it is not so in respect of its complex ideas: for those being combinations of simple ideas put together, and united under one general name, it is plain that the mind of man uses some kind of liberty in forming those complex ideas; how else comes it to pass that one man's idea of gold, or justice, is different from another's? but because he has put in, or left out of his, some simple idea which the other has not. The question then is, which of these are real, and which barely imaginary combinations? What collections agree to the reality of things, and what not? and to this I say, that,

4. *Mixed modes, made of consistent ideas, are real.*—Secondly, mixed modes and relations having no other reality but what they have in the minds of men, there is nothing more required to this kind of ideas to make them real, but that they be so framed, that there be a possibility of existing conformable to them. These ideas themselves being archetypes, cannot differ from their archetypes, and so cannot be chimerical, unless any one will jumble together in them inconsistent ideas. Indeed, as any of them have the names of a known language assigned to them, by which he that has them in his mind would signify them to others, so bare possibility of existing is not enough; they must have a conformity to the ordinary signification of the name that is given them, that they may not be thought fantastical; as if a man would give the name of justice to that idea which common use calls liberality. But this fantasticalness relates more to propriety of speech than reality of ideas: for a man to be undisturbed in danger, sedately to consider what is fittest to be done, and to execute it steadily, is a mixed mode, or a complex idea of an action which may exist. But to be undisturbed in danger, without using one's reason or industry, is what is also possible to be, and so is as real an idea as the other. Though the first of these, having the name courage given to it, may, in respect of that name, be a right or wrong idea: but the other, whilst it has not a common received name of any known language assigned to it, is not capable of any deformity, being made with no reference to any thing but itself.

5. *Ideas of substances are real, when they agree with the existence of things.*—Thirdly, our complex ideas of substances being made all of them in reference to things existing without us, and intended to be representations of substances, as they really are, are no farther real than as they are such combinations of simple ideas as are really united, and co-exist in things without us. On the contrary, those are fantastical, which are made up of such collections of simple ideas as were really never united, never were found together in any substance; *v. g.* a rational creature, consisting of a horse's head, joined to a body of human shape, or such as the centaurs are described: or, a body yellow, very malleable, fusible, and fixed, but lighter than common water: or a uniform, unorganized body, consisting, as to sense, all of similar parts, with perception and voluntary motion joined to it. Whether such substances as these can possibly exist or no, it is probable we do not know: but be that as it will, these ideas of substances being made conformable to no pattern existing that we know, and consisting of such collections of ideas as no substance ever showed us united together, they ought to pass with us for barely imaginary: but much more are those complex ideas so, which contain in them any inconsistency or contradiction of their parts.

CHAPTER XXXI.   OF ADEQUATE AND INADEQUATE IDEAS

1. *Adequate ideas are such as perfectly represent their archetypes.*—Of our real ideas, some are adequate and some are inadequate. Those I call adequate, which perfectly represent those archetypes which the mind supposes them taken from; which it intends them to stand for, and to which it refers them. Inadequate ideas are such which are but a partial or incomplete representation of those archetypes to which they are referred. . . . .

12. *Simple ideas* ἔκτυπα, *and adequate.*—Thus the mind has three sorts of abstract ideas, or nominal essences:

First, simple ideas, which are ἔκτυπα, or copies, but yet certainly adequate. Because being intended to express nothing but the power in things to produce in the mind such a sensation, that sensation, when it is produced, cannot but be the effect of that power. So the paper I write on, having the power, in the light (I speak according to the common notion of light) to produce in me the sensation which I call white, it cannot but be the effect of such a power, in something without the mind; since the mind has not the power to produce any such idea itself, and being meant for nothing else but the effect of such a power, that simple idea is real and adequate: the sensation of white, in my mind, being the effect of that power which is in the paper to produce it, is perfectly adequate to that power, or else that power would produce a different idea.

13. *Ideas of substances are* ἔκτυπα, *inadequate.*—Secondly, the complex ideas of substances are ectypes, copies too; but not perfect ones, not adequate; which is very evident to the mind, in that it plainly perceives that whatever collection of simple ideas it makes of any substance that exists, it cannot be sure that it exactly answers all that are in that substance; since not having tried all the operations of all other substances upon it, and found all the alterations it would receive from, or cause in other substances, it cannot have an exact adequate collection of all its active and passive capacities; and so not have an adequate complex idea of the powers of any substance existing, and its relations, which is that sort of complex idea of substances we have. And, after all, if we could have, and actually had in our complex idea, an exact collection of all the secondary qualities or powers of any substance, we should not yet thereby have an idea of the essence of that thing. For since the powers or qualities that are observable by us, are not the real essence of that substance, but depend on it, and flow from it, any collection whatsoever of these qualities, cannot be the real essence of that thing. Whereby it is plain, that our ideas of substances are not adequate, are not what the mind intends them to be. Besides, a man has no idea of substance in general nor knows what substance is in itself.

14. *Ideas of modes and relations are archetypes, and cannot but be adequate.*—Thirdly, complex ideas of modes and relations are originals and archetypes; are not copies, nor made after the pattern of any real existence, to which the mind intends them to be conformable, and exactly to answer. These being such collections of simple ideas that the mind itself puts together, and such collections, that each of them contains in it precisely all that the mind intends it should, they are archetypes and essences of modes that may exist, and so are designed only for, and belong only to such

modes, as when they do exist, have an exact conformity with those complex ideas. The ideas therefore of modes and relations cannot but be adequate.

CHAPTER XXXII. OF TRUE AND FALSE IDEAS

. . . .

4. *Ideas referred to any thing, may be true or false.*—Whenever the mind refers any of its ideas to any thing extraneous to them, they are then capable to be called true or false. Because the mind in such a reference makes a tacit supposition of their conformity to that thing; which supposition, as it happens to be true or false, so the ideas themselves come to be denominated. . . . .

26. *More properly to be called right or wrong.*—Upon the whole matter, I think that our ideas, as they are considered by the mind, either in reference to the proper signification of their names, or in reference to the reality of things, may very fitly be called right or wrong ideas, according as they agree or disagree to those patterns to which they are referred. But if any one had rather call them true or false, it is fit he use a liberty, which every one has, to call things by those names he thinks best; though, in propriety of speech, truth or falsehood will, I think, scarce agree to them, but as they, some way or other, virtually contain in them some mental proposition. The ideas that are in a man's mind, simply considered, cannot be wrong, unless complex ones, wherein inconsistent parts are jumbled together. All other ideas are in themselves right, and the knowledge about them right and true knowledge: but when we come to refer them to any thing, as to their patterns and archetypes, then they are capable of being wrong, as far as they disagree with such archetypes.

CHAPTER XXXIII. OF THE ASSOCIATION OF IDEAS

. . . .

5. *From a wrong connexion of ideas.*—Some of our ideas have a natural correspondence and connexion one with another: it is the office and excellency of our reason to trace these, and hold them together in that union and correspondence which is founded in their peculiar beings. Besides this, there is another connexion of ideas wholly owing to chance or custom: ideas, that in them-

selves are not all of kin, come to be so united in some men's minds, that it is very hard to separate them; they always keep in company, and the one no sooner at any time comes into the understanding, but its associate appears with it; and if they are more than two, which are thus united, the whole gang, always inseparable, show themselves together.

6. *This connexion how made.*—This strong combination of ideas, not allied by nature, the mind makes in itself either voluntarily or by chance; and hence it comes in different men to be very different, according to their different inclinations, education, interests, &c. Custom settles habits of thinking in the understanding, as well as of determining in the will, and of motions in the body; all which seem to be but trains of motion in the animal spirits, which, once set agoing, continue in the same steps they have been used to, which, by often treading, are worn into a smooth path, and the motion in it becomes easy, and as it were natural. As far as we can comprehend thinking, thus ideas seem to be produced in our minds; or if they are not, this may serve to explain their following one another in an habitual train, when once they are put into their track, as well as it does to explain such motions of the body. A musician used to any tune will find, that let it but once begin in his head, the ideas of the several notes of it will follow one another orderly in his understanding, without any care or attention, as regularly as his fingers move orderly over the keys of the organ to play out the tune he has begun, though his unattentive thoughts be elsewhere a wandering. Whether the natural cause of these ideas, as well as of that regular dancing of his fingers, be the motion of his animal spirits, I will not determine, how probable soever, by this instance, it appears to be so; but this may help us a little to conceive of intellectual habits, and of the tying together of ideas. . . . .

9. *A great cause of errors.*—This wrong connexion in our minds of ideas, in themselves loose and independent one of another, has such an influence, and is of so great force to set us awry in our actions, as well moral as natural passions, reasonings, and notions themselves, that perhaps there is not any one thing that deserves more to be looked after.

10. *Instances.*—The ideas of goblins and sprights have really no more to do with darkness than light: yet let but a foolish maid inculcate these often on the mind of a child, and raise them there together, possibly he shall never be able to separate them again so long as he lives; but darkness shall for ever afterward bring with it those frightful ideas, and they shall be so joined that he can no more bear the one than the other.

11. A man receives a sensible injury from another, thinks on the man and that action over and over; and by ruminating on them strongly, or much in his mind, so cements those two ideas together, that he makes them almost one; never thinks on the man, but the pain and displeasure he suffered come into his mind with it, so that he scarce distinguishes them, but has as much an aversion for the one as the other. Thus hatreds are often begotten from slight and almost innocent occasions, and quarrels propagated and continued in the world.

12. A man has suffered pain or sickness in any place; he saw his friend die in such a room; though these have in nature nothing to do one with another, yet when the idea of the place occurs to his mind, it brings (the impression being once made) that of the pain and displeasure with it; he confounds them in his mind, and can as little bear the one as the other.

13. *Why time cures some disorders in the mind, which reason cannot.*—When this combination is settled, and while it lasts, it is not in the power of reason to help us, and relieve us from the effects of it. Ideas in our minds, when they are there, will operate according to their natures and circumstances; and here we see the cause why time cures certain affections, which reason, though in the right, and allowed to be so, has not power over, nor is able against them to prevail with those who are apt to hearken to it in other cases. The death of a child, that was the daily delight of his mother's eyes, and joy of her soul, rends from her heart the whole comfort of her life, and gives her all the torment imaginable; use the consolations of reason in this case, and you were as good preach ease to one on the rack, and hope to allay, by rational discourses, the pain of his joints tearing asunder. Till time has by disuse separated the sense of that enjoyment, and its loss from the idea of the child returning to her memory, all representations, though ever so reasonable, are in vain; and therefore some, in

whom the union between these ideas is never dissolved, spend their lives in mourning, and carry an incurable sorrow to their graves. . . . .

Book III. Of Words

CHAPTER I. OF WORDS, OR LANGUAGE IN GENERAL

1. *Man fitted to form articulate sounds.*—God having designed man for a sociable creature, made him not only with an inclination, and under a necessity to have fellowship with those of his own kind, but furnished him also with language, which was to be the great instrument and common tie of society. Man, therefore, had by nature his organs so fashioned, as to be fit to frame articulate sounds, which we call words. But this was not enough to produce language; for parrots, and several other birds, will be taught to make articulate sounds distinct enough, which yet, by no means, are capable of language.

2. *To make them signs of ideas.*—Besides articulate sounds, therefore, it was farther necessary that he should be able to use these sounds as signs of internal conceptions; and to make them stand as marks for the ideas within his own mind, whereby they might be made known to others, and the thoughts of men's minds be conveyed from one to another.

3. *To make general signs.*—But neither was this sufficient to make words so useful as they ought to be. It is not enough for the perfection of language, that sounds can be made signs of ideas, unless those signs can be so made use of, as to comprehend several particular things; for the multiplication of words would have perplexed their use, had every particular thing need of a distinct name to be signified by. To remedy this inconvenience, language had yet a farther improvement in the use of general terms, whereby one word was made to mark a multitude of particular existences: which advantageous use of sounds was obtained only by the difference of the ideas they were made signs of; those names becoming general, which are made to stand for general ideas, and those remaining particular, where the ideas they are used for are particular.

4. Besides these names which stand for ideas, there be other words which men make use of, not to signify any idea, but the want or absence of some ideas simple or complex, or all ideas together; such as *nihil* in Latin, and in English *ignorance* and *barrenness*.

All which negative or privitive words cannot be said properly to belong to, or signify no ideas: for then they would be perfectly insignificant sounds; but they relate to positive ideas, and signify their absence.

5. *Words ultimately derived from such as signify sensible ideas.*— It may also lead us a little towards the original of all our notions and knowledge, if we remark how great a dependence our words have on common sensible ideas; and how those, which are made use of to stand for actions and notions quite removed from sense, have their rise from thence, and from obvious sensible ideas are transferred to more abstruse significations, and made to stand for ideas that come not under the cognizance of our senses; *v. g.* to imagine, apprehend, comprehend, adhere, conceive, instil, disgust, disturbance, tranquility, &c. are all words taken from the operations of sensible things, and applied to certain modes of thinking. Spirit, in its primary signification, is breath; angel, a messenger; and I doubt not, but if we could trace them to their sources, we should find, in all languages, the names, which stand for things that fall not under our senses, to have had their first rise from sensible ideas. By which we may give some kind of guess, what kind of notions they were, and whence derived, which filled their minds, who were the first beginners of languages; and how nature, even in the naming of things, unawares suggested to men the originals and principles of all their knowledge; whilst to give names that might make known to others any operations they felt in themselves, or any other ideas that come not under their senses, they were fain to borrow words from ordinary known ideas of sensation, by that means to make others the more easily to conceive those operations they experimented in themselves, which made no outward sensible appearances: and then when they had got known and agreed names, to signify those internal operations of their own minds, they were sufficiently furnished to make known by words all their other ideas; since they could consist of nothing, but either of outward sensible perceptions, or of the inward operations of their minds about them: we having, as has been proved, no ideas at all, but what originally come either from sensible objects without, or what we feel within ourselves, from the inward workings of our own spirits, of which we are conscious to ourselves within.

6. *Distribution.*—But to understand better the use and force of language, as subservient to instruction and knowledge, it will be convenient to consider,

First, To what it is that names, in the use of language, are immediately applied.

Secondly, Since all (except proper) names are general, and so stand not particularly for this or that single thing, but for sorts and ranks of things, it will be necessary to consider, in the next place, what the sorts and kinds, or, if you rather like the Latin names, what the species and genera of things are; wherein they consist, and how they come to be made. These being (as they ought) well looked into, we shall the better come to find the right use of words, the natural advantages and defects of language, and the remedies that ought to be used to avoid the inconveniences of obscurity or uncertainty in the signification of words, without which it is impossible to discourse with any clearness or order concerning knowledge; which being conversant about propositions, and those most commonly universal ones, has greater connexion with words than perhaps is suspected.

These considerations, therefore, shall be the matter of the following chapters.

CHAPTER II. OF THE SIGNIFICATION OF WORDS

1. *Words are sensible signs necessary for communication.*—Man, though he has great variety of thoughts, and such from which others, as well as himself, might receive profit and delight; yet they are all within his own breast, invisible and hidden from others, nor can of themselves be made to appear. The comfort and advantage of society not being to be had without communication of thoughts, it was necessary that man should find out some external sensible signs, whereby those invisible ideas which his thoughts are made up of, might be made known to others. For this purpose nothing was so fit, either for plenty or quickness, as those articulate sounds, which, with so much ease and variety, he found himself able to make. Thus we may conceive how words which were by nature so well adapted to that purpose, come to be made use of by men, as the signs of their ideas; not by any natural connexion that there is between particular articulate sounds, and certain ideas, for then there would be but one language among all men: but by

a voluntary imposition, whereby such a word is made arbitrarily the mark of such an idea. The use then of words is to be sensible marks of ideas; and the ideas they stand for are their proper and immediate signification.

2. *Words are the sensible signs of his ideas who uses them.*—The use men have of these marks being either to record their own thoughts for the assistance of their own memory, or, as it were, to bring out their ideas, and lay them before the view of others; words in their primary or immediate signification stand for nothing but the ideas in the mind of him that uses them, how imperfectly soever or carelessly those ideas are collected from the things which they are supposed to represent. When a man speaks to another, it is that he may be understood; and the end of speech is, that those sounds, as marks, may make known his ideas to the hearer. That then which words are the marks of, are the ideas of the speaker: nor can any one apply them as marks immediately to any thing else but the ideas that he himself hath. For this would be to make them signs of his own conceptions, and yet apply them to other ideas; which would be to make them signs, and not signs of his ideas at the same time; and so, in effect, to have no signification at all. Words being voluntary signs, they cannot be voluntary signs imposed by him on things he knows not. That would be to make them signs of nothing, sounds without signification. A man cannot make his words the signs either of qualities in things, or of conceptions in the mind of another, whereof he has none in his own. Until he has some ideas of his own, he cannot suppose them to correspond with the conceptions of another man; nor can he use any signs for them; for thus they would be the signs of he knows not what, which is, in truth, to be the signs of nothing. But when he represents to himself other men's ideas by some of his own, if he consent to give them the same names that other men do, it is still to his own ideas; to ideas that he has, and not to ideas that he has not.

3. This is so necessary in the use of language, that in this respect the knowing and the ignorant, the learned and unlearned, use the words they speak (with any meaning) all alike. They, in every man's mouth, stand for the ideas he has, and which he would express by them. A child having taken notice of nothing in the metal

he hears called gold, but the bright shining yellow colour, he applies the word gold only to his own idea of that colour, and nothing else; and therefore calls the same colour in a peacock's tail, gold. Another, that hath better observed, adds to shining yellow great weight; and then the sound gold, when he uses it, stands for a complex idea of a shining yellow, and very weighty substance. Another adds to those qualities, fusibility: and then the word gold signifies to him a body, bright, yellow, fusible, and very heavy. Another adds malleability. Each of these uses equally the word gold, when they have occasion to express the idea which they have applied it to; but it is evident, that each can apply it only to his own idea; nor can he make it stand as a sign of such a complex idea as he has not.

4. *Words often secretly referred, first, to the ideas in other men's minds.*—But though words, as they are used by men, can properly and immediately signify nothing but the ideas that are in the mind of the speaker; yet they in their thoughts give them a secret reference to two other things.

First, They suppose their words to be marks of the ideas in the minds also of other men, with whom they communicate: for else they should talk in vain, and could not be understood, if the sounds they applied to one idea were such as by the hearer were applied to another; which is to speak two languages. But in this, men stand not usually to examine whether the idea they and those they discourse with have in their minds be the same: but think it enough that they use the word, as they imagine, in the common acceptation of that language; in which they suppose that the idea they make it a sign of is precisely the same, to which the understanding men of that country apply that name.

5. *Secondly, to the reality of things.*—Secondly, Because men would not be thought to talk barely of their own imaginations, but of things as really they are; therefore they often suppose their words to stand also for the reality of things. But this relating more particularly to substances, and their names, as perhaps the former does to simple ideas and modes, we shall speak of these two different ways of applying words more at large, when we come to treat of the names of mixed modes and substances in particular: though give me leave here to say, that it is a perverting the use of words

and brings unavoidable obscurity and confusion into their signification, whenever we make them stand for any thing but those ideas we have in our own minds. . . . .

CHAPTER III. OF GENERAL TERMS

. . . .

6. *How general words are made.*—The next thing to be considered is, how general words come to be made. For since all things that exist are only particulars, how come we by general terms, or where find we those general natures they are supposed to stand for? Words become general, by being made the signs of general ideas; and ideas become general, by separating from them the circumstances of time, and place, and any other ideas, that may determine them to this or that particular existence. By this way of abstraction, they are made capable of representing more individuals than one; each of which having in it a conformity to that abstract idea, is (as we call it) of that sort.

7. But to deduce this a little more distinctly, it will not perhaps be amiss to trace our notions and names from their beginning, and observe by what degrees we proceed, and by what steps we enlarge our ideas from our first infancy. There is nothing more evident, than that the ideas of the persons children converse with (to instance in them alone) are like the persons themselves, only particular. The ideas of the nurse and the mother are well framed in their minds; and, like pictures of them there, represent only those individuals. The names they first gave to them are confined to these individuals; and the names of nurse and mamma the child uses, determine themselves to those persons. Afterwards, when time and a larger acquaintance have made them observe, that there are a great many other things in the world, that in some common agreements of shape, and several other qualities, resemble their father and mother, and those persons they have been used to, they frame an idea, which they find those many particulars do partake in; and to that they give, with others, the name man for example. And thus they come to have a general name, and a general idea. Wherein they make nothing new, but only leave out the complex idea they had of Peter and James, Mary and Jane, that which is peculiar to each, and retain only what is common to them all.

8. By the same way that they come by the general name and idea of man, they easily advance to more general names and notions. For observing that several things that differ from their idea of man, and cannot therefore be comprehended under that name, have yet certain qualities, wherein they agree with man, by retaining only those qualities, and uniting them into one idea, they have again another and more general idea; to which having given a name, they make a term of a more comprehensive extension: which new idea is made, not by any new addition, but only as before, by leaving out the shape, and some other properties signified by the name man, and retaining only a body, with life, sense, and spontaneous motion, comprehended under the name animal.

9. *General natures are nothing but abstract ideas.*—That this is the way whereby men first formed general ideas, and general names to them, I think, is so evident, that there needs no other proof of it, but the considering of a man's self, or others, and the ordinary proceedings of their minds in knowledge: and he that thinks general natures or notions are any thing else but such abstract and partial ideas of more complex ones, taken at first from particular existences, will, I fear, be at a loss where to find them. For let any one reflect, and then tell me, wherein does his idea of man differ from that of Peter and Paul; or his idea of horse from that of Bucephalus, but in the leaving out something that is peculiar to each individual, and retaining so much of those particular complex ideas of several particular existences as they are found to agree in? Of the complex ideas signified by the names man and horse, leaving out but those particulars wherein they differ, and retaining only those wherein they agree, and of those making a new distinct complex idea, and giving the name animal to it; one has a more general term, that comprehends with man several other creatures. Leave out of the idea of animal, sense and spontaneous motion; and the remaining complex idea, made up of the remaining simple ones of body, life and nourishment, becomes a more general one, under the more comprehensive term *vivens*. And not to dwell longer upon this particular, so evident in itself, by the same way the mind proceeds to body, substance, and at last to being, thing, and such universal terms, which stand for any of our ideas whatsoever. To conclude, this whole mystery of *genera* and *species*, which make such a noise in the schools, and are with justice so little regarded

out of them, is nothing else but abstract ideas, more or less comprehensive, with names annexed to them. In all which this is constant and unvariable, that every more general term stands for such an idea, as is but a part of any of those contained under it. . . . .

11. *General and universal are creatures of the understanding.*—
. . . . It is plain by what has been said, that general and universal belong not to the real existence of things; but are the inventions and creatures of the understanding, made by it, for its own use, and concern only signs, whether words or ideas. Words are general, as has been said, when used for signs of general ideas, and so are applicable indifferently to many particular things: and ideas are general, when they are set up as the representatives of many particular things; but universality belongs not to things themselves, which are all of them particular in their existence; even those words and ideas which in their signification are general. When therefore we quit particulars, the generals that rest are only creatures, of our own making; their general nature being nothing but the capacity they are put into by the understanding, or signifying or representing many particulars. For the signification they have is nothing but a relation, that by the mind of man is added to them. . . . .

CHAPTER VI.   OF THE NAMES OF SUBSTANCES

1. *The common names of substances stand for sorts.*—The common names of substances, as well as other general terms, stand for sorts; which is nothing else but the being made signs of such complex ideas, wherein several particular substances do, or might agree, by virtue of which they are capable of being comprehended in one common conception, and signified by one name. I say, do or might agree: for though there be but one sun existing in the world, yet the idea of it being abstracted, so that more substances (if there were several) might each agree in it; it is as much a sort, as if there were as many suns as there are stars. They want not their reasons who think there are, and that each fixed star would answer the idea the name sun stands for, to one who was placed in a due distance; which, by the way, may show us how much the sorts, or, if you please, genera and species of things (for those Latin terms signify

to me no more than the English word sort) depend on such collections of ideas as men have made, and not on the real nature of
things; since it is not impossible but that, in propriety of speech,
that might be a sun to one, which is a star to another.

2. *The essence of each sort is the abstract idea.*—The measure and
boundary of each sort, or species, whereby it is constituted that
particular sort, and distinguished from others, is that we call its
essence, which is nothing but that abstract idea to which the name
is annexed; so that every thing contained in that idea is essential
to that sort. This, though it be all the essence of natural substances
that we know, or by which we distinguish them into sorts; yet I
call it by a peculiar name, the nominal essence, to distinguish it
from the real constitution of substances, upon which depends this
nominal essence, and all the properties of that sort; which, therefore, as has been said, may be called the real essence: *v. g.* the
nominal essence of gold is that complex idea the word gold stands
for, let it be, for instance, a body yellow, of a certain weight,
malleable, fusible, and fixed. But the real essence is the constitution of the insensible parts of that body, on which those qualities
and all the other properties of gold depend. How far these two
are different, though they are both called essence, is obvious at
first sight to discover.

3. *The nominal and real essence different.*—For though perhaps
voluntary motion, with sense and reason, joined to a body of a
certain shape, be the complex idea to which I, and others, annex
the name man, and so be the nominal essence of the species so
called; yet nobody will say that that complex idea is the real essence and source of all those operations, which are to be found in
any individual of that sort. The foundation of all those qualities,
which are the ingredients of our complex idea, is something quite
different: and had we such a knowledge of that constitution of
man, from which his faculties of moving, sensation, and reasoning,
and other powers flow, and on which his so regular shape depends,
as it is possible angels have, and it is certain his Maker has; we
should have a quite other idea of his essence than what now is contained in our definition of that species, be it what it will: and our
idea of any individual man would be as far different from what it is
now, as is his who knows all the springs and wheels and other contrivances within of the famous clock at Strasburg, from that which

a gazing countryman has of it, who barely sees the motion of the hand, and hears the clock strike, and observes only some of the outward appearances. . . . .

7. *The nominal essence bounds the species.*—The next thing to be considered is, by which of those essences it is that substances are determined into sorts, or species; and that, it is evident, is by the nominal essence. For it is that alone that the name, which is the mark of the sort, signifies. It is impossible, therefore, that any thing should determine the sorts of things which we rank under general names, but that idea which that name is designed as a mark for; which is that, as has been shown, which we call nominal essence. Why do we say, this is a horse, and that a mule; this is an animal, that an herb? How comes any particular thing to be of this or that sort, but because it has that nominal essence, or, which is all one, agrees to that abstract idea that name is annexed to? And I desire any one but to reflect on his own thoughts, when he hears or speaks any of those, or other names of substances, to know what sort of essences they stand for.

8. And that the species of things to us are nothing but the ranking them under distinct names, according to the complex ideas in us, and not according to precise, distinct, real essences in them, is plain from hence, that we find many of the individuals that are ranked into one sort, called by one common name, and so received as being of one species, have yet qualities depending on their real constitutions, as far different one from another, as from others, from which they are accounted to differ specifically. This, as it is easy to be observed by all who have to do with natural bodies; so chemists especially are often, by sad experience, convinced of it, when they, sometimes in vain, seek for the same qualities in one parcel of sulphur, antimony, or vitriol, which they have found in others. For though they are bodies of the same species, having the same nominal essence, under the same name; yet do they often, upon severe ways of examination, betray qualities so different one from another, as to frustrate the expectation and labour of very wary chemists. But if things were distinguished into species, according to their real essences, it would be as impossible to find different properties in any two individual substances of the same species, as it is to find different properties in two circles, or two

equilateral triangles. That is properly the essence to us, which determines every particular to this or that *classis*⁹ or, which is the same thing, to this or that general name; and what can that be else, but that abstract idea, to which that name is annexed? and so has, in truth, a reference, not so much to the being of particular things, as to their general denominations.

9. *Not the real essence, which we know not.*—Nor indeed can we rank and sort things, and consequently (which is the end of sorting) denominate them by their real essences, because we know them not. Our faculties carry us no farther toward the knowledge and distinction of substances, than a collection of those sensible ideas which we observe in them; which, however made with the greatest diligence and exactness we are capable of, yet it is more remote from the true internal constitution from which those qualities flow, than, as I said, a countryman's idea is from the inward contrivance of that famous clock at Strasburgh, whereof he only sees the outward figure and motions. There is not so contemptible a plant or animal, that does not confound the most enlarged understanding. Though the familiar use of things about us take off our wonder, yet it cures not our ignorance. When we come to examine the stones we tread on, or the iron we daily handle, we presently find we know not their make, and can give no reason of the different qualities we find in them. It is evident the internal constitution, whereon their properties depend, is unknown to us. For to go no farther than the grossest and most obvious we can imagine among them, what is that texture of parts, that real essence, that makes lead and antimony fusible; wood and stones not? What makes lead and iron malleable; antimony and stones not? And yet how infinitely these come short of the fine contrivances, and unconceivable real essences of plants or animals, every one knows. The workmanship of the all-wise and powerful God, in the great fabric of the universe, and every part thereof, farther exceeds the capacity and comprehension of the most inquisitive and intelligent man, than the best contrivance of the most ingenious man doth the conceptions of the most ignorant of rational creatures. Therefore we in vain pretend to range things into sorts, and dispose them into certain classes, under names, by their real essences, that are so far from our discovery or comprehension. A blind man may as soon sort things by their colours, and he that has lost his smell as well

distinguish a lily and a rose by their odours, as by those internal constitutions which he knows not. He that thinks he can distinguish sheep and goats by their real essences, that are unknown to him, may be pleased to try his skill in those species, called cassiowary and querechinchio; and by their internal real essences determine the boundaries of those species, without knowing the complex idea of sensible qualities, that each of those names stand for, in the countries where those animals are to be found. . . . .

CHAPTER VIII.   OF ABSTRACT AND CONCRETE TERMS

1. *Abstract terms not predicable one of another, and why.*—The ordinary words of language, and our common use of them, would have given us light into the nature of our ideas, if they had been but considered with attention. The mind, as has been shown, has a power to abstract its ideas, and so they become essences, general essences, whereby the sorts of things are distinguished. Now each abstract idea being distinct, so that of any two the one can never be the other, the mind will, by its intuitive knowledge, perceive their difference; and therefore in propositions no two whole ideas can ever be affirmed one of another. This we see in the common use of language, which permits not any two abstract words, or names of abstract ideas, to be affirmed one of another. For how near of kin soever they may seem to be, and how certain soever it is, that man is an animal, or rational, or white, yet every one at first hearing perceives the falsehood of these propositions; humanity is animality, or rationality, or whiteness: and this is as evident as any of the most allowed maxims. All our affirmations then are only inconcrete, which is the affirming, not one abstract idea to be another, but one abstract idea to be joined to another; which abstract ideas, in substances, may be of any sort; in all the rest, are little else but of relations; and in substances, the most frequent are of powers; *v. g.* "a man is white," signifies, that the thing that has the essence of a man, has also in it the essence of whiteness, which is nothing but a power to produce the idea of whiteness in one, whose eyes can discover ordinary objects; or, "a man is rational," signifies that the same thing that hath the essence of a man, hath also in it the essence of rationality, *i. e.* a power of reasoning.

2. *They show the difference of our ideas.*—This distinction of names shows us also the difference of our ideas: for if we observe

them, we shall find that our simple ideas have all abstract as well as concrete names; the one whereof is (to speak the language of grammarians) a substantive, the other an adjective; as whiteness, white; sweetness, sweet. The like also holds in our ideas of modes and relations, as justice, just; equality, equal; only with this difference, that some of the concrete names of relations, among men, chiefly are substantives; as paternitas, pater; whereof it were easy to render a reason. But as to our ideas of substances, we have very few or no abstract names at all. For though the schools have introduced animalitas, humanitas, corporietas, and some others; yet they hold no proportion with that infinite number of names of substances, to which they never were ridiculous enough to attempt the coining of abstract ones; and those few that the schools forged, and put into the mouths of their scholars, could never yet get admittance into common use, or obtain the license of public approbation. Which seems to me at least to intimate the confession of all mankind, that they have no ideas of the real essences of substances, since they have not names for such ideas; which no doubt they would have had, had not their consciousness to themselves of their ignorance of them kept them from so idle an attempt. And therefore, though they had ideas enough to distinguish gold from a stone, and metal from wood; yet they but timorously ventured on such terms, as aurietas and saxietas, metallietas and lignietas, or the like names, which should pretend to signify the real essences of those substances, whereof they knew they had no ideas. And indeed it was only the doctrine of substantial forms, and the confidence of mistaken pretenders to a knowledge that they had not, which first coined, and then introduced animalitas, and humanitas, and the like; which yet went very little farther than their own schools, and could never get to be current among understanding men. Indeed, humanitas was a word familiar among the Romans, but in a far different sense, and stood not for the abstract essence of any substance; but was the abstracted name of a mode, and its concrete, humanus, not homo.

CHAPTER IX. OF THE IMPERFECTION OF WORDS

1. *Words are used for recording and communicating our thoughts.*— From what has been said in the foregoing chapters, it is easy to

perceive what imperfection there is in language, and how the very nature of words makes it almost unavoidable for many of them to be doubtful and uncertain in their significations. To examine the perfection or imperfection of words it is necessary first to consider their use and end: for as they are more or less fitted to attain that, so are they more or less perfect. We have, in the former part of this discourse, often upon occasion mentioned a double use of words.

First, one for the recording of our own thoughts.

Secondly, the other for the communicating of our thoughts to others.

2. *Any words will serve for recording.*—As to the first of these, for the recording our own thoughts for the help of our own memories, whereby, as it were, we talk to ourselves, any words will serve the turn. For since sounds are voluntary and indifferent signs of any ideas, a man may use what words he pleases, to signify his own ideas to himself; and there will be no imperfection in them, if he constantly use the same sign for the same idea, for then he cannot fail of having his meaning understood, wherein consists the right use and perfection of language.

3. *Communication by words civil or philosophical.*—As to communication of words, that too has a double use.

I. Civil.

II. Philosophical.

First, by their civil use, I mean such a communication of thoughts and ideas by words, as may serve for the upholding common conversation and commerce, about the ordinary affairs and conveniences of civil life, in the societies of men one among another.

Secondly, by the philosophical use of words, I mean such a use of them as may serve to convey the precise notions of things, and to express, in general propositions, certain and undoubted truths, which the mind may rest upon, and be satisfied with, in its search after true knowledge. These two uses are very distinct; and a great deal less exactness will serve in the one than in the other, as we shall see in what follows. . . . .

5. *Causes of their imperfection.*—Words having naturally no signification, the idea which each stands for must be learned and

retained by those who would exchange thoughts, and hold intelligible discourse with others in any language. But this is hardest to be done where,

First, the ideas they stand for are very complex, and made up of a great number of ideas put together.

Secondly, where the ideas they stand for have no certain connexion in nature; and so no settled standard, any where in nature existing, to rectify and adjust them by.

Thirdly, when the signification of the word is referred to a standard, which standard is not easy to be known.

Fourthly, where the signification of the word, and the real essence of the thing, are not exactly the same.

These are difficulties that attend the signification of several words that are intelligible. Those which are not intelligible at all, such as names standing for any simple ideas, which another has not organs or faculties to attain,—as the names of colours to a blind man, or sounds to a deaf man,—need not here be mentioned.

In all these cases we shall find an imperfection in words, which I shall more at large explain, in their particular application to our several sorts of ideas; for if we examine them, we shall find that the names of mixed modes are most liable to doubtfulness and imperfection, for the two first of these reasons; and the names of substances chiefly for the two latter. . . . .

22. *This should teach us moderation, in imposing our own sense of old authors.*—Sure I am, that the signification of words, in all languages, depending very much on the thoughts, notions, and ideas of him that uses them, must unavoidably be of great uncertainty to men of the same language and country. This is so evident in the Greek authors, that he that shall peruse their writings, will find in almost every one of them a distinct language, though the same words. But when to this natural difficulty in every country there shall be added different countries and remote ages, wherein the speakers and writers had very different notions, tempers, customs, ornaments, and figures of speech, &c. every one of which influenced the signification of their words then, though to us now they are lost and unknown; it would become us to be charitable one to another in our interpretations or misunderstanding of those ancient writings; which, though of great concernment

to be understood, are liable to the unavoidable difficulties of speech, which (if we except the names of simple ideas, and some very obvious things) is not capable, without a constant defining the terms, of conveying the sense and intention of the speaker, without any manner of doubt and certainty to the hearer. And in discourses of religion, law, and morality, as they are matters of the highest concernment, so there will be the greatest difficulty. . . . .

Book IV

CHAPTER I. OF KNOWLEDGE IN GENERAL

1. *Our knowledge conversant about our ideas.*—Since the mind, in all its thoughts and reasonings, hath no other immediate object but its own ideas, which it alone does, or can contemplate, it is evident, that our knowledge is only conversant about them.

2. *Knowledge is the perception of the agreement or disagreement of two ideas.*—Knowledge then seems to me to be nothing but the perception of the connexion or agreement, or disagreement and repugnancy of any of our ideas. In this alone it consists. Where this perception is, there is knowledge: and where it is not, there, though we may fancy, guess, or believe, yet we always come short of knowledge. For, when we know that white is not black, what do we else but perceive that these two ideas do not agree? When we possess ourselves with the utmost security of the demonstration, that the three angles of a triangle are equal to two right ones, what do we more but perceive, that equality to two right ones, does necessarily agree to, and is inseparable from, the three angles of a triangle?

3. *This agreement fourfold.*—But, to understand a little more distinctly, wherein this agreement or disagreement consists, I think we may reduce it all to these four sorts: 1. Identity, or diversity. 2. Relation. 3. Coexistence, or necessary connexion. 4. Real existence.

4. 1. *Of identity or diversity.*—First, As to the first sort of agreement or disagreement, viz. identity or diversity. It is the first act of the mind, when it has any sentiments or ideas at all, to perceive its ideas; and, so far as it perceives them, to know each what it is, and thereby also to perceive their difference, and that one is not another. This is so absolutely necessary, that without it there could be no knowledge, no reasoning, no imagination, no

distinct thoughts at all. By this the mind clearly and infallibly perceives each idea to agree with itself, and to be what it is: and all distinct ideas to disagree, *i. e.*, the one not to be the other; and this it does without pains, labour, or deduction; but at first view, by its natural power of perception and distinction. And though men of art have reduced this into those general rules, what is, is; and, it is impossible for the same thing to be and not to be; for ready application in all cases, wherein there may be occasion to reflect on it; yet it is certain, that the first exercise of this faculty is about particular ideas. A man infallibly knows, as soon as ever he has them in his mind, that the ideas he calls white and round, are the very ideas they are, and that they are not other ideas which he calls red or square. Nor can any maxim or proposition in the world make him know it clearer or surer than he did before, and without any such general rule. This then is the first agreement or disagreement, which the mind perceives in its ideas, which it always perceives at first sight: and if there ever happen any doubt about it, it will always be found to be about the names, and not the ideas themselves, whose identity and diversity will always be perceived, as soon and as clearly as the ideas themselves are, nor can it possibly be otherwise.

5. 2. *Relative.*—Secondly, the next sort of agreement or disagreement the mind perceives in any of its ideas, may, I think, be called relative, and is nothing but the perception of the relation between any two ideas, of what kind soever, whether substances, modes, or any other. For since all distinct ideas must eternally be known not to be the same, and so be universally and constantly denied one of another, there could be no room for any positive knowledge at all, if we could not perceive any relation between our ideas, and find out the agreement or disagreement they have one with another, in several ways the mind takes of comparing them.

6. 3. *Of coexistence.*—Thirdly, The third sort of agreement, or disagreement, to be found in our ideas, which the perception of the mind is employed about, is coexistence or non-coexistence in the same subject; and this belongs particularly to substances. Thus, when we pronounce concerning gold that it is fixed, our knowledge of this truth amounts to no more but this, that fixedness, or a power to remain in the fire unconsumed, is an idea that always accompanies and is joined with that particular sort of yellowness,

weight, fusibility, malleableness and solubility in agua regia, which make our complex idea, signified by the word gold.

7. *Fourthly, Of real existence.*—Fourthly, the fourth and last sort is that of actual, real existence agreeing to any idea. Within these four sorts of agreement or disagreement is, I suppose, contained all the knowledge we have, or are capable of: for all the inquiries that we can make concerning any of our ideas, all that we know or can affirm concerning them, is, that it is, or is not, the same with some other; that it does, or does not, always coexist with some other idea in the same subject, that it has this or that relation to some other idea; or that it has a real existence without the mind. Thus, blue is not yellow, is of identity: two triangles upon equal bases between two parallels are equal, is of relation. Iron is susceptible of magnetical impressions, is of coexistence. God is, is of real existence. Though identity and coexistence are truly nothing but relations, yet they are so peculiar ways of agreement or disagreement of our ideas, that they deserve well to be considered as distinct heads, and not under relation in general; since they are so different grounds of affirmation and negation, as will easily appear to any one, who will but reflect on what is said in several places of this essay. I should now proceed to examine the several degrees of our knowledge, but that it is necessary first to consider the different acceptations of the word knowledge.

8. *Knowledge actual or habitual.*—There are several ways wherein the mind is possessed of truth, each of which is called knowledge.

1. There is actual knowledge, which is the present view the mind has of the agreement or disagreement of any of its ideas, or of the relation they have one to another.

2. A man is said to know any proposition, which having been once laid before his thoughts, he evidently perceived the agreement or disagreement of the ideas whereof it consists; and so lodged it in his memory that whenever that proposition comes again to be reflected on, he, without doubt or hesitation, embraces the right side, assents to, and is certain of the truth of it. This, I think, one may call habitual knowledge: and thus a man may be said to know all those truths which are lodged in his memory by a foregoing clear and full perception, whereof the mind is assured past doubt, as often as it has occasion to reflect on them. For our finite understandings being able to think clearly and distinctly but on one

thing at once, if men had no knowledge of any more than what they actually thought on, they would all be very ignorant; and he that knew most would know but one truth, that being all he was able to think on at one time.

9. *Habitual knowledge twofold.*—Of habitual knowledge there are also, vulgarly speaking, two degrees:

First, the one is of such truths laid up in the memory as, whenever they occur to the mind, it actually perceives the relation is between those ideas. And this is in all those truths whereof we have an intuitive knowledge, where the ideas themselves, by an immediate view, discover their agreement or disagreement one with another.

Secondly, the other is of such truths, whereof the mind having been convinced, it retains the memory of the conviction without the proofs. Thus a man that remembers certainly that he once perceived the demonstration that the three angles of a triangle are equal to two right ones, is certain that he knows it, because he cannot doubt the truth of it. In his adherence to a truth, where the demonstration by which it was at first known is forgot, though a man may be thought rather to believe his memory than really to know, and this way of entertaining a truth seemed formerly to me like something between opinion and knowledge; a sort of assurance which exceeds bare belief, for that relies on the testimony of another; yet upon a due examination I find it comes not short of perfect certainty, and is in effect true knowledge. That which is apt to mislead our first thoughts into a mistake in this matter is, that the agreement or disagreement of the ideas in this case is not perceived, as it was at first, by an actual view of all the intermediate ideas, whereby the agreement or disagreement of those in the proposition was at first perceived; but by other intermediate ideas, that show the agreement or disagreement of the ideas contained in the proposition whose certainty we remember. For example, in this proposition, that the three angles of a triangle are equal to two right ones, one who has seen and clearly perceived the demonstration of this truth knows it to be true, when that demonstration has gone out of his mind; so that at present it is not actually in view, and possibly cannot be recollected: but he knows it in a different way from what he did before. The agreement of the two ideas joined in that proposition is perceived, but it is by the intervention of other ideas than those which at first produced that perception. He remembers, *i. e.* he knows (for remembrance is but the reviving of some past knowledge) that he was once certain of the truth of this proposition, that the three angles of a triangle are equal to two right ones. The immutability of the same relations between the same immutable things, is now the idea that shows him, that if the three angles of a triangle were once equal to two right ones, they will always be equal to two right ones. And hence he comes to be certain, that what was once true in the case, is always true; what ideas once agreed, will always agree; and, consequently what he once knew to be true, he will always know to be true, as long as he can remember that he once knew it. Upon this ground it is, that particular demonstrations in mathematics afford general knowledge. If then the perception that the same ideas will eternally have the same habitudes and relations, be not a sufficient ground of knowledge, there could be no knowledge of general propositions in mathematics; for no mathematical demonstration would be any other than particular: and when a man had demonstrated any proposition concerning one triangle or circle, his knowledge would not reach beyond that particular diagram. If he would extend it further, he must renew his demonstration in another instance, before he could know it to be true in another like triangle, and so on: by which means one could never come to the knowledge of any general propositions. Nobody, I think, can deny that Mr. Newton certainly knows any proposition, that he now at any time reads in his book, to be true; though he has not in actual view that admirable chain of intermediate ideas, whereby he at first discovered it to be true. Such a memory as that, able to retain such a train of particulars, may be well thought beyond the reach of human faculties; when the very discovery, perception, and laying together that wonderful connexion of ideas is found to surpass most readers' comprehension. But yet it is evident, the author himself knows the proposition to be true, remembering he one saw the connexion of those ideas, as certainly as he knows such a man wounded another, remembering that he saw him run him through. But because the memory is not always so clear as actual perception, and does in all men more or less decay in length of time, this among other differences is one, which shows that demonstrative knowledge is much more imperfect than intuitive, as we shall see in the following chapter.

CHAPTER II. OF THE DEGREES OF OUR KNOWLEDGE

1. *Intuitive.*—All our knowledge consisting, as I have said, in the view the mind has of its own ideas, which is the utmost light and greatest certainty we, with our faculties and in our way of knowledge, are capable of; it may not be amiss to consider a little the degrees of its evidence. The different clearness of our knowledge seems to me to lie in the different way of perception the mind has of the agreement or disagreement of any of its ideas. For if we will reflect on our own ways of thinking, we shall find that sometimes the mind perceives the agreement or disagreement of two ideas immediately by themselves, without the intervention of any other: and this, I think, we may call intuitive knowledge. For in this the mind is at no pains of proving or examining, but perceives the truth, as the eye doth light, only by being directed towards it. Thus the mind perceives that white is not black, that a circle is not a triangle, that three are more than two, and equal, to one and two. Such kind of truths the mind perceives at the first sight of the ideas together, by bare intuition, without the intervention of any other idea; and this kind of knowledge is the clearest and most certain that human frailty is capable of. This part of knowledge is irresistible, and like bright sunshine, forces itself immediately to be perceived, as soon as ever the mind turns its view that way; and leaves no room for hesitation, doubt or examination, but the mind is presently filled with the clear light of it. It is on this intuition that depends all the certainty and evidence of all our knowledge; which certainty every one finds to be so great, that he cannot imagine, and therefore not require a greater: for a man cannot conceive himself capable of a greater certainty, than to know that any idea in his mind is such as he perceives it to be; and that two ideas, wherein he perceives a difference, are different, and not precisely the same. He that demands a greater certainty than this, demands he knows not what, and shows only that he has a mind to be a sceptic, without being able to be so. Certainty depends so wholly on this intuition, that in the next degree of knowledge, which I call demonstrative, this intuition is necessary in all the connexions of the intermediate ideas, without which we cannot attain knowledge and certainty.

2. *Demonstrative.*—The next degree of knowledge is, where the mind perceives the agreement or disagreement of any ideas, but

not immediately. Though wherever the mind perceives the agreement or disagreement of any of its ideas, there be certain knowledge; yet it does not always happen that the mind sees that agreement or disagreement which there is between them, even where it is discoverable: and in that case remains in ignorance, and at most gets no farther than a probable conjecture. The reason why the mind cannot always perceive presently the agreement or disagreement of two ideas is, because those ideas, concerning whose agreement or disagreement the inquiry is made, cannot by the mind be so put together as to show it. In this case, then, when the mind cannot so bring its ideas together, as by their immediate comparison, and as it were juxtaposition, or application one to another, to perceive their agreement or disagreement, it is fain, by the intervention of other ideas, (one or more, as it happens) to discover the agreement or disagreement which it searches; and this is that which we call reasoning. Thus the mind being willing to know the agreement or disagreement in bigness between the three angles of a triangle and two right ones, cannot, by an immediate view and comparing them do it: because the three angles of a triangle cannot be brought at once, and be compared with any one or two angles: and so of this the mind has no immediate, no intuitive knowledge. In this case the mind is fain to find out some other angles, to which the three angles of a triangle have an equality; and finding those equal to two right ones, comes to know their equality to two right ones. . . . .

7. *Each step must have intuitive evidence.*—Now in every step reason makes in demonstrative knowledge, there is an intuitive knowledge of that agreement or disagreement it seeks with the next intermediate idea, which it uses as a proof: for if it were not so, that yet would need a proof; since without the perception of such agreement or disagreement, there is no knowledge produced. If it be perceived by itself, it is intuitive knowledge: if it cannot be perceived by itself, there is need of some intervening idea, as a common measure to show their agreement or disagreement. By which it is plain, that every step in reasoning that produces knowledge has intuitive certainty; which when the mind perceives, there is no more required, but to remember it, to make the agreement or disagreement of the ideas, concerning which we inquire, visible

and certain. So that to make any thing a demonstration, it is necessary to perceive the immediate agreement of the intervening ideas, whereby the agreement or disagreement of the two ideas under examination (whereof the one is always the first, and the other the last in the account) is found. This intuitive perception of the agreement or disagreement of the intermediate ideas, in each step and progression of the demonstration, must also be carried exactly in the mind, and a man must be sure that no part is left out; which, because in long deductions, and the use of many proofs, the memory does not always so readily and exactly retain; therefore it comes to pass, that this is more imperfect than intuitive knowledge, and men embrace often falsehood for demonstrations.
. . . .

14. *Sensitive knowledge of particular existence.*—These two, viz. intuition and demonstration, are the degrees of our knowledge; whatever comes short of one of these, with what assurance soever embraced, is but faith, or opinion, but not knowledge, at least in all general truths. There is, indeed, another perception of the mind, employed about the particular existence of finite beings without us; which, going beyond bare probability, and yet not reaching perfectly to either of the foregoing degrees of certainty, passes under the name of knowledge. There can be nothing more certain than that the idea we receive from an external object is in our minds; this is intuitive knowledge. But whether there be anything more than barely that idea in our minds, whether we can thence certainly infer the existence of any thing without us, which corresponds to that idea, is that whereof some men think there may be a question made; because men may have such ideas in their minds, when no such thing exists, no such object affects their senses. But yet here, I think, we are provided with an evidence, that puts us past doubting: for I ask any one, whether he be not invincibly conscious to himself of a different perception when he looks on the sun by day, and thinks on it by night; when he actually tastes wormwood, or smells a rose, or only thinks on that savour or odour? We as plainly find the difference there is between any idea revived in our minds by our own memory, and actually coming into our minds by our senses, as we do between any two distinct ideas. If any one say, a dream may do the same thing, and all these ideas

may be produced in us without any external objects; he may please to dream that I make him this answer; 1. That it is no great matter whether I remove his scruple or no: where all is but dream, reasoning and arguments are of no use, truth and knowledge nothing. 2. That I believe he will allow a very manifest difference between dreaming of being in the fire, and being actually in it. But yet if he be resolved to appear so sceptical as to maintain, that what I call being actually in the fire is nothing but a dream, and we cannot thereby certainly know that any such thing as fire actually exists without us, I answer, that we certainly finding that pleasure or pain follows upon the application of certain objects to us, whose existence we perceive, or dream that we perceive, by our senses; this certainty is as great as our happiness or misery, beyond which we have no concernment to know, or to be. So that, I think, we may add to the two former sorts of knowledge, this also, of the existence of particular external objects, by that perception and consciousness we have of the actual entrance of ideas from them, and allow these three degrees of knowledge, viz. intuitive, demonstrative, and sensitive: in each of which there are different degrees and ways of evidence and certainty. . . . . .

CHAPTER III. OF THE EXTENT OF HUMAN KNOWLEDGE

1. Knowledge, as has been said, lying in the perception of the agreement or disagreement of any of our ideas, it follows from hence, that,

1. *No farther than we have ideas.*—First, we can have knowledge no farther than we have ideas.

2. 2. *No farther than we can perceive their agreement or disagreement.*—Secondly, That we can have no knowledge farther than we can have perception of that agreement or disagreement: which perception being, 1. Either by intuition, or the immediate comparing any two ideas; or, 2. By reason, examining the agreement or disagreement of two ideas, by the intervention of some others; or, 3. By sensation, perceiving the existence of particular things: hence it also follows,

3. 3. *Intuitive knowledge extends itself not to all the relations of all our ideas.*—Thirdly, that we cannot have an intuitive knowledge that shall extend itself to all our ideas, and all that we would know

about them; because we cannot examine and perceive all the relations they have one to another, by juxtaposition, or an immediate comparison one with another. Thus having the ideas of an obtuse and an acute angled triangle, both drawn from equal bases, and between parallels, I can, by intuitive knowledge, perceive the one not to be the other, but cannot that way know whether they be equal or no: because their agreement or disagreement in equality can never be perceived by an immediate comparing them: the difference of figure makes their parts incapable of an exact immediate application; and therefore there is need of some intervening qualities to measure them by, which is demonstration or rational knowledge.

4. 4. *Nor demonstrative knowledge.*—Fourthly, it follows also, from what is above observed, that our rational knowledge cannot reach to the whole extent of our ideas; because between two different ideas we would examine, we cannot always find such mediums, as we can connect one to another with an intuitive knowledge, in all the parts of the deduction; and wherever that fails, we come short of knowledge and demonstration.

5. 5. *Sensitive knowledge narrower than either.*—Fifthly, sensitive knowledge reaching no farther than the existence of things actually present to our senses, is yet much narrower than either of the former.

6. 6. *Our knowledge therefore narrower than our ideas.*—From all which it is evident, that the extent of our knowledge comes not only short of the reality of things, but even of the extent of our own ideas. Though our knowledge be limited to our ideas, and cannot exceed them either in extent or perfection; and though these be very narrow bounds, in respect of the extent of all being, and far short of what we may justly imagine to be in some even created understandings, not tied down to the dull and narrow information which is to be received from some few, and not very acute ways of perception, such as are our senses; yet it would be well with us if our knowledge were but as large as our ideas, and there were not many doubts and inquiries concerning the ideas we have, whereof we are not, nor I believe ever shall be, in this world, resolved. . . . .

7. *How far our knowledge reaches.*—The affirmations or negations we make concerning the ideas we have, may, as I have before intimated in general, be reduced to these four sorts, viz. identity, co-

existence, relation, and real existence. I shall examine how far our knowledge extends in each of these.

8. 1. *Our knowledge of identity and diversity, as far as our ideas.* —First, as to identity and diversity, in this way of the agreement or disagreement of ideas, our intuitive knowledge is as far extended as our ideas themselves: and there can be no idea in the mind, which it does not presently, by an intuitive knowledge, perceive to be what it is, and to be different from any other.

9. 2. *Of coexistence, a very little way.*—Secondly, as to the second sort, which is the agreement or disagreement of our ideas in coexistence; in this our knowledge is very short, though in this consists the greatest, and most material part of our knowledge concerning substances. For our ideas of the species of substances being, as I have showed, nothing but certain collections of simple ideas united in one subject, and so coexisting together; *v. g.* our idea of flame is a body hot, luminous, and moving upward; of gold, a body heavy to a certain degree, yellow, malleable, and fusible. These, or some such complex ideas as these in men's minds, do those two names of the different substances, flame and gold, stand for. When we would know any thing farther concerning these, or any other sort of substances, what do we inquire, but what other qualities or powers these substances have or have not? Which is nothing else but to know what other simple ideas do or do not coexist with those that make up that complex idea.

10. *Because the connexion between most simple ideas is unknown.* —This, how weighty and considerable a part soever of human science, is yet very narrow, and scarce any at all. The reason whereof is, that the simple ideas, whereof our complex ideas of substances are made up, are, for the most part, such as carry with them, in their own nature, no visible necessary connexion or inconsistency with any other simple ideas, whose coexistence with them we would inform ourselves about.

11. *Especially of secondary qualities.*—The ideas that our complex ones of substances are made up of, and about which our knowledge concerning substances is most employed, are those of their secondary qualities; which depending all (as has been shown) upon the primary qualities of their minute and insensible parts,—or, if not upon them, upon something yet more remote from our comprehension,—it is impossible we should know which have a necessary

union or inconsistency one with another: for not knowing the root they spring from, not knowing what size, figure, and texture of parts they are, on which depend, and from which result, those qualities which make our complex idea of gold; it is impossible we should know what other qualities result from, or are incompatible with, the same constitution of the insensible parts of gold, and so consequently must always co-exist with that complex idea we have of it, or else are inconsistent with it.

12. *Because all connexion between any secondary and primary qualities is undiscoverable.*—Besides this ignorance of the primary qualities of the insensible parts of bodies, on which depend all their secondary qualities, there is yet another and more incurable part of ignorance, which sets us more remote from a certain knowledge of the coexistence or incoexistence (if I may so say) of different ideas in the same subject: and that is, that there is no discoverable connexion between any secondary quality and those primary qualities which it depends on.

13. That the size, figure, and motion of one body should cause a change in the size, figure, and motion of another body, is not beyond our conception: the separation of the parts of one body upon the intrusion of another, and the change from rest to motion upon impulse,—these and the like seem to have some connexion one with another. And if we knew these primary qualities of bodies, we might have reason to hope we might be able to know a great deal more of these operations of them one upon another: but our minds not being able to discover any connexion betwixt these primary qualities of bodies and the sensations that are produced in us by them, we can never be able to establish certain and undoubted rules of the consequence or coexistence of any secondary qualities, though we could discover the size, figure, or motion of those invisible parts which immediately produce them. We are so far from knowing what figure, size, or motion of parts produce a yellow colour, a sweet taste, or a sharp sound, that we can by no means conceive how any size, figure, or motion of any particles, can possibly produce in us the idea of any colour, taste, or sound whatsoever; there is no conceivable connexion between the one and the other.

14. In vain, therefore, shall we endeavour to discover by our ideas (the only true way of certain and universal knowledge) what other ideas are to be found constantly joined with that of our complex

idea of any substance: since we neither know the real constitution of the minute parts on which their qualities do depend, nor, did we know them, could we discover any necessary connexion between them and any of the secondary qualities; which is necessary to be done before we can certainly know their necessary coexistence. . . . .

15. *Of repugnancy to coexist, larger.*—As to incompatibility or reapugnancy to coexistence; we may know that any subject may have of each sort of primary qualities but one particular at once; *v. g.* each particular extension, figure, number of parts, motion, excludes all other of each kind. The like also is certain of all sensible ideas peculiar to each sense; for whatever of each kind is present in any subject, excludes all other of that sort; *v. g.* no one subject can have two smells or two colours at the same time. To this perhaps will be said, has not an opal, or the infusion of *lignum nephriticum*, two colours at the same time? To which I answer, that these bodies, to eyes differently placed, may, at the same time, afford different colours; but I take liberty also to say, that to eyes differently placed, it is different parts of the object that reflect the particles of light; and therefore it is not the same part of the object, and so not the very same subject, which at the same time appears both yellow and azure. For it is as impossible that the very same particle of any body should at the same time differently modify or reflect the rays of light, as that it should have two different figures and textures at the same time.

16. *Of the coexistence of powers, a very little way.*—But as to the power of substances to change the sensible qualities of other bodies, which makes a great part of our inquiries about them, and is no inconsiderable branch of our knowledge; I doubt, as to these, whether our knowledge reaches much farther than our experience; or whether we can come to the discovery of most of these powers, and be certain that they are in any subject, by the connexion with any of those ideas which to us make its essence. . . . .

17. *Of spirits, yet narrower.*—If we are at a loss in respect of the powers and operations of bodies, I think it is easy to conclude we are much more in the dark in reference to the spirits; whereof we naturally have no ideas but what we draw from that of our own, by reflecting on the operations of our own souls within us, as far as they can come within our observation. . . . .

18. 3. *Of other relations, it is not easy to say how far.*—As to the third sort of our knowledge, viz. the agreement or disagreement of any of our ideas in any other relation: this, as it is the largest field of our knowledge, so it is hard to determine how far it may extend; because the advances that are made in this part of knowledge, depending on our sagacity in finding intermediate ideas, that may show the relations and habitudes of ideas, whose coexistence is not considered, it is a hard matter to tell when we are at an end of such discoveries; and when reason has all the helps it is capable of for the finding of proofs, or examining the agreement or disagreement of remote ideas. They that are ignorant of algebra cannot imagine the wonders in this kind are to be done by it: and what farther improvements and helps, advantageous to other parts of knowledge, the sagacious mind of man may yet find out, it is not easy to determine. This at least I believe, that the ideas of quantity are not those alone that are capable of demonstration and knowledge; and that other, and perhaps more useful, parts of contemplation, would afford us certainty, if vices, passions, and domineering interest did not oppose or menace such endeavours.

The idea of a Supreme Being, infinite in power, goodness, and wisdom, whose workmanship we are, and on whom we depend; and the idea of ourselves, as understanding rational beings, being such as are clear in us, would, I suppose, if duly considered and pursued, afford such foundations of our duty and rules of action, as might place morality among the sciences capable of demonstration: wherein I doubt not but from self-evident propositions, by necessary consequences, as incontestible as those in mathematics, the measures of right and wrong might be made out to any one that will apply himself with the same indifferency and attention to the one, as he does to the other of these sciences. The relation of other modes may certainly be perceived, as well as those of number and extension; and I cannot see why they should not also be capable of demonstration, if due methods were thought on to examine or pursue their agreement or disagreement. Where there is no property, there is no injustice, is a proposition as certain as any demonstration in Euclid: for the idea of property being a right to any thing; and the idea to which the name injustice is given being the invasion or violation of that right; it is evident that these ideas being thus established, and these names annexed to them, I can as certainly know this proposition to be true, as that a triangle has three angles equal to two right ones. Again, "no government allows absolute liberty"; the idea of government being the establishment of society upon certain rules or laws which require conformity to them; and the idea of absolute liberty being for any one to do whatever he pleases; I am as capable of being certain of the truth of this proposition, as of any in the mathematics. . . . .

21. 4. *Of real existence; we have an intuitive knowledge of our own; demonstrative, of God's; sensitive, of some few other things.*—As to the fourth sort of our knowledge, viz. of the real actual existence of things, we have an intuitive knowledge of our own existence; and a demonstrative knowledge of the existence of a God; of the existence of any thing else, we have no other but a sensitive knowledge, which extends not beyond the objects present to our senses.

22. *Our ignorance great.*—Our knowledge being so narrow, as I have showed, it will perhaps give us some light into the present state of our minds, if we look a little into the dark side, and take a view of our ignorance; which, being infinitely larger than our knowledge, may serve much to the quieting of disputes, and improvement of useful knowledge; if discovering how far we have clear and distinct ideas, we confine our thoughts within the contemplation of those things that are within the reach of our understandings, and launch not out into that abyss of darkness (where we have not eyes to see, nor faculties to perceive any thing) out of a presumption that nothing is beyond our comprehension. But to be satisfied of the folly of such a conceit we need not go far. He that knows anything, know this in the first place, that he need not seek long for instances of his ignorance. The meanest and most obvious things that come in our way have dark sides, that the quickest sight cannot penetrate into. The clearest and most enlarged understandings of thinking men find themselves puzzled, and at a loss, in every particle of matter. We shall the less wonder to find it so, when we consider the causes of our ignorance; which, from what has been said, I suppose, will be found to be these three:

First, Want of ideas.

Secondly, Want of a discoverable connexion between the ideas we have.

Thirdly, Want of tracing and examining our ideas.

23. *First, one cause of it, want of ideas, either such as we have no conception of, or such as particularly we have not.*—First, There are some things, and those not a few, that we are ignorant of, for want of ideas. . . . .

26. *Hence no science of bodies.*—And therefore I am apt to doubt, that how far soever human industry may advance useful and experimental philosophy in physical things, scientifical will still be out of our reach; because we want perfect and adequate ideas of those very bodies which are nearest to us, and most under our command. Those which we have ranked into classes under names, and we think ourselves best acquainted with, we have but very imperfect and incomplete ideas of. Distinct ideas of the several sorts of bodies that fall under the examination of our senses perhaps we may have; but adequate ideas, I suspect, we have not of any one among them. And though the former of these will serve us for common use and discourse, yet whilst we want the latter, we are not capable of scientifical knowledge; nor shall ever be able to discover general, instructive, unquestionable truths concerning them. Certainty and demonstration are things we must not, in these matters, pretend to. By the colour, figure, taste, and smell, and other sensible qualities, we have as clear and distinct ideas of sage and hemlock, as we have of a circle and a triangle: but having no ideas of the particular primary qualities of the minute parts of either of these plants, nor of other bodies which we would apply them to, we cannot tell what effects they will produce; nor when we see those effects can we so much as guess, much less know, their manner of production. Thus having no ideas of the particular mechanical affections of the minute parts of bodies that are within our view and reach, we are ignorant of their constitutions, powers, and operations: and of bodies more remote we are yet more ignorant, not knowing so much as their very outward shapes, or the sensible and grosser parts of their constitutions.

27. *Much less of spirits.*—This, at first, will show us how disproportionate our knowledge is to the whole extent even of material beings; to which, if we add the consideration of that infinite number of spirits that may be, and probably are, which are yet more remote from our knowledge, whereof we have no cognizance, nor can frame to ourselves any distinct ideas of their several ranks and

sorts, we shall find this cause of ignorance conceal from us, in an impenetrable obscurity, almost the whole intellectual world; a greater certainty, and more beautiful world than the material. For bating some very few, and those, if I may so call them, superficial ideas of spirit, which by reflection we get of our own, and from thence the best we can collect of the Father of all spirits, the eternal independent Author of them, and us, and all things; we have no certain information, so much as of the existence of other spirits, but by revelation. Angels of all sorts are naturally beyond our discovery: and all those intelligences whereof it is likely there are more orders than corporeal substances, are things whereof our natural faculties give us no certain account at all. That there are minds and thinking beings in other men as well as himself, every man has a reason, from their words and actions, to be satisfied: and the knowledge of his own mind cannot suffer a man, that considers, to be ignorant that there is a God. But that there are degrees of spiritual beings between us and the great God, who is there that by his own search and ability can come to know? Much less have we distinct ideas of their different natures, conditions, states, powers, and several constitutions, wherein they agree or differ from one another, and from us. And therefore in what concerns their different species and properties, we are under an absolute ignorance. . . . .

CHAPTER IV. OF THE REALITY OF HUMAN KNOWLEDGE

1. *Objection. Knowledge placed in ideas, may be all bare vision.*— I doubt not but my reader by this time may be apt to think, that I have been all this while only building a castle in the air; and be ready to say to me, "to what purpose all this stir? Knowledge, say you, is only the perception of the agreement or disagreement of our own ideas: but who knows what those ideas may be? Is there any thing so extravagant as the imaginations of men's brains? Where is the head that has no chimeras in it? Or, if there be a sober and a wise man, what difference will there be, by your rules, between his knowledge and that of the most extravagant fancy in the world? They both have their ideas, and perceive their agreement and disagreement one with another. If there be any difference between them, the advantage will be on the warm-headed man's side, as having the more ideas, and the more lively. . . . .

"But of what use is all this fine knowledge of men's own imaginations to a man that inquires after the reality of things? It matters not what men's fancies are, it is the knowledge of things that is only to be prized: it is this alone gives a value to our reasonings, and preference to one man's knowledge over another's, that it is of things as they really are, and not of dreams and fancies."

2. *Answer, Not so where, ideas agree with things.*—To which I answer, that if our knowledge of our ideas terminate in them, and reach no farther, where there is something farther intended, our most serious thoughts will be of little more use than the reveries of a crazy brain; and the truths built thereon of no more weight than the discourses of a man, who sees things clearly in a dream, and with great assurance utters them. But I hope, before I have done, to make it evident that this way of certainty, by the knowledge of our own ideas, goes a little farther than bare imagination: and I believe it will appear that all the certainty of general truths a man has, lies in nothing else.

3.—It is evident the mind knows not things immediately, but only by the intervention of the ideas it has of them. Our knowledge therefore is real, only so far as there is a conformity between our ideas and the reality of things. But what shall be here the criterion? How shall the mind, when it perceives nothing but its own ideas, know that they agree with things themselves? This, though it seems not to want difficulty, yet I think there be two sorts of ideas that, we may be assured, agree with things.

4. *As* 1. *All simple ideas do.*—First, the first are simple ideas, which, since the mind, as has been shown, can by no means make to itself must necessarily be the product of things operating on the mind in a natural way, and producing therein those perceptions which by the wisdom and will of our Maker they are ordained and adapted to. From whence it follows, that simple ideas are no fictions of our fancies, but the natural and regular productions of things without us, really operating upon us, and so carry with them all the conformity which is intended, or which our state requires; for they represent to us things, under those appearances which they are fitted to produce in us, whereby we are enabled to distinguish the sorts of particular substances, to discern the states they are in, and so to take them for our necessities, and to apply them to our uses. Thus the idea of whiteness, or bitterness, as it

is in the mind, exactly answering that power which is in any body to produce it there, has all the real conformity it can, or ought to have with things without us. And this conformity between our simple ideas, and the existence of things, is sufficient for real knowledge.

5. 2. *All complex ideas, except of substances.*—Secondly, all our complex ideas, except those of substances, being archetypes of the mind's own making, not intended to be the copies of any thing, nor referred to the existence of any thing, as to their originals, cannot want any conformity necessary to real knowledge. For that which is not designed to represent any thing but itself, can never be capable of a wrong representation, nor mislead us from the true apprehension of any thing, by its dislikeness to it; and such, excepting those of substances, are all our complex ideas; which, as I have showed in another place, are combinations of ideas, which the mind, by its free choice, puts together, without considering any connexion they have in nature. And hence it is, that in all these sorts the ideas themselves are considered as the archetypes, and things no otherwise regarded, but as they are conformable to them. So that we cannot but be infallibly certain, that all the knowledge we attain concerning these ideas is real, and reaches things themselves; because in all our thoughts, reasonings, and discourses of this kind, we intend things no farther than as they are conformable to our ideas. So that in these we cannot miss of a certain and undoubted reality.

6. *Hence the reality of mathematical knowledge.*—I doubt not but it will be easily granted, that the knowledge we have of mathematical truths is not only certain, but real knowledge; and not the bare empty vision of vain, insignificant chimeras of the brain; and yet, if we will consider, we shall find that it is only of our own ideas. The mathematician considers the truth and properties belonging to a rectangle, or circle, only as they are in idea in his own mind. For it is possible he never found either of them existing mathematically, *i. e.* precisely true, in his life. But yet the knowledge he has of any truths or properties belonging to a circle, or any other mathematical figure, are never the less true and certain, even of real things existing; because real things are no farther concerned, nor intended to be meant by any such propositions, than as things really agree to those archetypes in his mind. . . . . .

7. *And of moral.*—And hence it follows, that moral knowledge is as capable of real certainty as mathematics. For, certainty being but the perception of the agreement or disagreement of our ideas; and demonstration nothing but the perception of such agreement by the intervention of other ideas, or mediums; our moral ideas, as well as mathematical, being archetypes themselves, and so adequate and complete ideas; all the agreement or disagreement which we shall find in them will produce real knowledge, as well as in mathematical figures. . . . .

9. *Nor will it be less true or certain because moral ideas are of our own making and naming.*—But it will here be said, that if moral knowledge be placed in the contemplation of our own moral ideas, and those, as other modes, be of our own making, what strange notions will there be of justice and temperance! What confusion of virtues and vices, if every one may make what ideas of them he pleases! No confusion nor disorder in the things themselves, nor on the reasonings about them; no more than (in mathematics) there would be a disturbance in the demonstration, or a change in the properties of figures, and their relations one to another, if a man should make a triangle with four corners, or a trapezium with four right angles: that is, in plain English, change the names of the figures, and call that by one name which mathematicians called ordinarily by another. For let a man make to himself the idea of a figure with three angles, whereof one is a right one, and call it, if he pleases, equilaterum or trapezium, or any thing else, the properties of and demonstrations about that idea will be the same, as if he called it a rectangular triangle. I confess the change of the name, by the impropriety of speech, will at first disturb him, who knows not what idea it stands for; but as soon as the figure is drawn, the consequences and demonstrations are plain and clear. Just the same is it in moral knowledge; let a man have the idea of taking from others, without their consent, what their honest industry has possessed them of, and call this justice if he please. He that takes the name here without the idea put to it, will be mistaken, by joining another idea of his own to that name: but strip the idea of that name, or take it, such as it is, in the speaker's mind, and the same things will agree to it, as if you called it injustice. Indeed, wrong names in moral discourses breed usually

more disorder, because they are not so easily rectified as in mathematics, where the figure, once drawn and seen, makes the name useless and of no force. For what need of a sign, when the thing signified is present and in view? But in moral names that cannot be so easily and shortly done, because of the many decompositions that go to the making up the complex ideas of those modes. But yet for all this, miscalling of any of those ideas, contrary to the usual signification of the words of that language, hinders not but that we may have certain and demonstrative knowledge of their several agreements and disagreements, if we will carefully, as in mathematics, keep to the same precise ideas, and trace them in their several relations one to another, without being led away by their names. If we but separate the idea under consideration from the sign that stands for it, our knowledge goes equally on in the discovery of real truth and certainty, whatever sounds we make use of. . . . .

18. *Recapitulation.*—Wherever we perceive the agreement or disagreement of any of our ideas, there is certain knowledge: and wherever we are sure those ideas agree with the reality of things, there is certain real knowledge. Of which agreement of our ideas, with the reality of things, having here given the marks, I think I have shown wherein it is, that certainty, real certainty, consists: which, whatever it was to others, was, I confess, to me, heretofore, one of those desiderata which I found great want of. . . . .

CHAPTER VI. OF UNIVERSAL PROPOSITIONS, THEIR
TRUTH AND CERTAINTY

.   .   .   .

7. The complex ideas, that our names of the species of substances properly stand for, are collections of such qualities as have been observed to coexist in an unknown substratum, which we call substance; but what other qualities necessarily coexist with such combinations we cannot certainly know, unless we can discover their natural dependence; which, in their primary qualities, we can go but a very little way in; and in all their secondary qualities we can discover no connexion at all, for the reasons mentioned, chap. iii.; viz. 1. Because we know not the real constitu-

tions of substances, on which each secondary quality particularly demands. 2. Did we know that, it would serve us only for experimental (not universal) knowledge; and reach with certainty no farther than that bare instance: because our understandings can discover no conceivable connexion between any secondary quality and any modification whatsoever of any of the primary ones. And therefore there are very few general propositions to be made concerning substances, which can carry with them undoubted certainty.

8. *Instance in gold.* All gold is fixed, is a proposition whose truth we cannot be certain of, how universally soever it be believed. For if, according to the useless imagination of the schools, any one supposes the term gold to stand for a species of things, set out by nature, by a real essence belonging to it, it is evident he knows not what particular substances are of that species; and so cannot, with certainty, affirm any thing universally of gold. But if he makes gold stand for a species determined by its nominal essence, let the nominal essence, for example, be the complex idea of a body, of a certain yellow colour, malleable, fusible, and heavier than any other known; in this proper use of the word gold, there is no difficulty to know what is or is not gold. But yet no other quality can with certainty be universally affirmed or denied of gold, but what hath a discoverable connexion or inconsistency with that nominal essence. Fixedness, for example, hàving no necessary connexion, that we can discover, with the colour, weight, or any other simple idea of our complex one, or with the whole combination together; it is impossible that we should certainly know the truth of this proposition, that all gold is fixed. . . . .

CHAPTER IX. OF OUR KNOWLEDGE OF EXISTENCE

1. *General certain propositions concern not existence.*—Hitherto we have only considered the essences of things, which being only abstract ideas, and thereby removed in our thoughts from particular existence (that being the proper operation of the mind in abstraction, to consider an idea under no other existence, but what it has in the understanding) gives us no knowledge of real existence at all. Where by the way we may take notice, that universal propositions, of whose truth or falsehood we can have certain knowledge,

concern not existence; and farther, that all particular affirmations or negations, that would not be certain if they were made general, are only concerning existence; they declaring only the accidental union or separation of ideas in things existing, which, in their abstract natures, have no known necessary union or repugnancy.

2. *A threefold knowledge of existence.*—But, leaving the nature of propositions and different ways of predication to be considered more at large in another place, let us proceed now to inquire concerning our knowledge of the existence of things, and how we come by it. I say then, that we have the knowledge of our own existence by intuition; of the existence of God by demonstration; and of other things by sensation.

3. *Our knowledge of our own existence is intuitive.*—As for our own existence, we perceive it so plainly and so certainly, that it neither needs nor is capable of any proof. For nothing can be more evident to us than our own existence; I think, I reason, I feel pleasure and pain: can any of these be more evident to me than my own existence? If I doubt of all other things, that very doubt makes me perceive my own existence, and will not suffer me to doubt of that. For if I know I feel pain, it is evident I have as certain perception of my own existence, as of the existence of the pain I feel: or if I know I doubt, I have as certain perception of the existence of the thing doubting, as of that thought which I call doubt. Experience then convinces us that we have an intuitive knowledge of our own existence, and an internal infallible perception that we are. In every act of sensation, reasoning, or thinking, we are conscious to ourselves of our own being; and, in this matter, come not short of the highest degree of certainty.

CHAPTER X. OF OUR KNOWLEDGE OF THE EXISTENCE OF A GOD

1. *We are capable of knowing certainly that there is a God.*—Though God has given us no innate ideas of himself; though he has stamped no original characters on our minds, wherein we may read his being; yet having furnished us with those faculties our minds are endowed with, he hath not left himself without witness: since we have sense, perception, and reason, and cannot want a clear proof of him as long as we carry ourselves about us. Nor can we

justly complain of our ignorance in this great point, since he has so plentifully provided us with the means to discover and know him, so far as is necessary to the end of our being, and the great concernment of our happiness. But though this be the most obvious truth that reason discovers; and though its evidence be (if I mistake not) equal to mathematical certainty; yet it requires thought and attention, and the mind must apply itself to a regular eduction of it from some part of our intuitive knowledge, or else we shall be as uncertain and ignorant of this as of other propositions, which are in themselves capable of clear demonstration. To show, therefore, that we are capable of knowing, *i. e.* being certain that there is a God, and how we may come by this certainty, I think we need go no farther than ourselves, and that undoubted knowledge we have of our own existence.

2. *Man knows that he himself is.*—I think it is beyond question, that man has a clear idea of his own being; he knows certainly that he exists, and that he is something. He that can doubt, whether he be any thing or no, I speak not to, no more than I would argue with pure nothing, or endeavour to convince nonentity that it were something. If any one pretends to be so sceptical, as to deny his own existence (for really to doubt of it is manifestly impossible), let him, for me, enjoy his beloved happiness of being nothing, until hunger, or some other pain, convince him of the contrary. This, then, I think, I may take for a truth, which every one's certain knowledge assures him of, beyond the liberty of doubting, viz. that he is something that actually exists.

3. *He knows also that nothing cannot produce a being, therefore something eternal.*—In the next place, man knows by an intuitive certainty, that bare nothing can no more produce any real being than it can be equal to two right angles. If a man knows not that nonentity, or the absence of all being, cannot be equal to two right angles, it is impossible he should know any demonstration in Euclid. If therefore we know there is some real being, and that nonentity cannot produce any real being, it is an evident demonstration, that from eternity there has been something; since what was not from eternity had a beginning; and what had a beginning must be produced by something else.

4. *That eternal being must be most powerful.*—Next, it is evident, that what had its being and beginning from another, must also

have all that which is in, and belongs to its being, from another too. All the powers it has must be owing to, and received from, the same source. This eternal source then of all being must also be the source and original of all power; and so this eternal being must be also the most powerful.

5. *And most knowing.*—Again, a man finds in himself perception and knowledge. We have then got one step farther; and we are certain now that there is not only some being, but some knowing intelligent being in the world.

There was a time, then, when there was no knowing being, and when knowledge began to be; or else there has been also a knowing being from eternity. If it be said, there was a time when no being had any knowledge, when that eternal being was void of all understanding; I reply, that then it was impossible there should ever have been any knowledge: it being as impossible that things wholly void of knowledge, and operating blindly and without any perception, should produce a knowing being, as it is impossible that a triangle should make itself three angles bigger than two right ones. For it is as repugnant to the idea of senseless matter, that it should put into itself sense, perception, and knowledge, as it is repugnant to the idea of a triangle that it should put into itself greater angles than two right ones.

6. *And therefore God.*—Thus from the consideration of ourselves, and what we infallibly find in our own constitutions, our reason leads us to the knowledge of this certain and evident truth, that there is an eternal, most powerful, and most knowing being; which whether any one will please to call God, it matters not. The thing is evident; and from this idea, duly considered, will easily be deduced all those other attributes which we ought to ascribe to this eternal being. If nevertheless any one should be found so senselessly arrogant as to suppose man alone knowing and wise, but yet the product of mere ignorance and chance; and that all the rest of the universe acted only by that blind hap-hazard:— I shall leave with him that very rational and empathical rebuke of Tully, l. ii. De Leg. to be considered at his leisure: "What can be more sillily arrogant and misbecoming than for a man to think that he has a mind and understanding in him, but yet in all the universe beside there is no such thing? Or that those things, which with the

utmost stretch of his reason he can scarce comprehend, should be moved and managed without any reason at all?" . . . .

From what has been said it is plain to me, we have a more certain knowledge of the existence of a God, than of any thing our senses have not immediately discovered to us. Nay, I presume I may say, that we more certainly know that there is a God, than that there is any thing else without us. When I say we know, I mean there is such a knowledge within our reach, which we cannot miss, if we will but apply our minds to that, as we do to several other inquiries. . . . .

CHAPTER XI. OF OUR KNOWLEDGE OF THE EXISTENCE OF OTHER THINGS

1. *It is to be had only by sensation.*—The knowledge of our own being we have by intuition. The existence of a God reason clearly makes known to us, as has been shown.

The knowledge of the existence of any other thing we can have only by sensation: for there being no necessary connexion of real existence with any idea a man hath in his memory, nor of any other existence but that of God, with the existence of any particular man; no particular man can know the existence of any other being, but only when by actual operating upon him it makes itself perceived by him. For the having the idea of any thing in our mind no more proves the existence of that thing, than the picture of a man evidences his being in the world, or the visions of a dream make thereby a true history.

2. *Instance, whiteness of this paper.*—It is therefore the actual receiving of ideas from without, that gives us notice of the existence of other things, and makes us know that something doth exist at that time without us, which causes that idea in us, though perhaps we neither know nor consider how it does it: for it takes not from the certainty of our senses, and the ideas we receive by them, that we know not the manner wherein they are produced, *v. g.* whilst I write this I have, by the paper affecting my eyes, that idea produced in my mind which, whatever object causes, I call white; by which I know that that quality or accident (*i. e.* whose appearance before my eyes always causes that idea) doth really exist, and

hath a being without me. And of this, the greatest assurance I can possibly have, and to which my faculties can attain, is the testimony of my eyes, which are the proper and sole judges of this thing, whose testimony I have reason to rely on as so certain, that I can no more doubt, whilst I write this, that I see white and black, and that something really exists, that causes that sensation in me, than that I write or move my hand: which is a certainty as great as human nature is capable of, concerning the existence of any thing but a man's self alone, and of God.

3. *This, though not so certain as demonstration, yet may be called knowledge, and proves the existence of things without us.*—The notice we have by our senses of the existing of things without us, though it be not altogether so certain as our intuitive knowledge, or the deductions of our reason, employed about the clear abstract ideas of our own minds; yet it is an assurance that deserves the name of knowledge. If we persuade ourselves that our faculties act and inform us right, concerning the existence of those objects that affect them, it cannot pass for an ill-grounded confidence: for I think nobody can, in earnest, be so sceptical as to be uncertain of the existence of those things which he sees and feels. At least, he that can doubt so far (whatever he may have with his own thoughts,) will never have any controversy with me; since he can never be sure I say any thing contrary to his own opinion. As to myself, I think God has given me assurance enough of the existence of things without me; since by their different application I can produce in myself both pleasure and pain, which is one great concernment of my present state. This is certain, the confidence that our faculties do not herein deceive us is the greatest assurance we are capable of, concerning the existence of material beings. For we cannot act any thing but by our faculties; nor talk of knowledge itself, but by the helps of those faculties which are fitted to apprehend even what knowledge is. But besides the assurance we have from our senses themselves, that they do not err in the information they give us, of the existence of things without us, when they are affected by them, we are farther confirmed in this assurance by other concurrent reasons.

4. 1. *Because we cannot have them but by the inlet of the senses.*— First, it is plain those perceptions are produced in us by exterior causes affecting our senses: because those that want the organs

of any sense never can have the ideas belonging to that sense produced in their minds. This is too evident to be doubted: and therefore we cannot but be assured that they come in by the organs of
that sense, and no other way. The organs themselves, it is plain,
do not produce them; for then the eyes of a man in the dark would
produce colours, and his nose smell roses in the winter: but we
see nobody gets the relish of a pineapple till he goes to the Indies,
where it is, and tastes it.

5. 2. *Because an idea from actual sensation, and another from
memory, are very distinct perceptions.*—Secondly, because sometimes
I find that I cannot avoid the having those ideas produced in my
mind. For though when my eyes are shut, or windows fast, I can
at pleasure recall to my mind the ideas of light, or the sun, which
former sensations had lodged in my memory; so I can at pleasure
lay by that idea, and take into my view that of the smell of a rose,
or taste of sugar. But if I turn my eyes at noon towards the sun,
I cannot avoid the ideas which the light, or sun, then produces in
me. So that there is a manifest difference between the ideas laid
up in my memory (over which, if they were there only, I should
have constantly the same power to dispose of them, and lay them
by at pleasure), and those which force themselves upon me, and
I cannot avoid having. And therefore it must needs be some exterior cause, and the brisk acting of some objects without me, whose
efficacy I cannot resist, that produces those ideas in my mind,
whether I will or no. Besides, there is nobody who doth not perceive the difference in himself between contemplating the sun, as
he hath the idea of it in his memory, and actually looking upon it;
of which two his perception is so distinct, that few of his ideas are
more distinguishable one from another. And therefore he hath certain knowledge, that they are not both memory, or the actions of
his mind, and fancies only within him; but that actual seeing hath
a cause without.

6. 3. *Pleasure or pain which accompanies actual sensation, accompanies not the returning of those ideas without the external objects.*—Thirdly, add to this, that many of those ideas are produced
in us with pain, which afterwards we remember without the least
offence. Thus the pain of heat or cold, when the idea of it is revived in our minds, gives us no disturbance; which, when felt, was
very troublesome, and is again, when actually repeated; which is

occasioned by the disorder the external object causes in our bodies when applied to them.

7. 4. *Our senses assist one another's testimony of the existence of outward things.*—Fourthly, our senses in many cases bear witness to the truth of each other's report, concerning the existence of sensible things without us. He that sees a fire may, if he doubt whether it be any thing more than a bare fancy, feel it too; and be convinced by putting his hand in it: which certainly could never be put into such exquisite pain by a bare idea or phantom, unless that the pain be a fancy too, which yet he cannot, when the burn is well, by raising the idea of it, bring upon himself again. . . . .

8. *This certainty is as great as our condition needs.*—But yet, if after all this any one will be so sceptical as to distrust his senses, and to affirm that all we see and hear, feel and taste, think and do, during our whole being, is but the series and deluding appearances of a long dream, whereof there is no reality; and therefore will question the existence of all things, or our knowledge of any thing; I must desire him to consider, that, if all be a dream, then he doth but dream that he makes the question; and so it is not much matter that a waking man should answer him. But yet, if he pleases, he may dream that I make him this answer, that the certainty of things existing in *rerum natura*, when we have the testimony of our senses for it, is not only as great as our frame can attain to, but as our condition needs. For our faculties being suited not to the full extent of being, nor to a perfect, clear, comprehensive knowledge of things, free from all doubt and scruple; but to the preservation of us, in whom they are, and accommodated to the use of life; they serve to our purpose well enough, if they will but give us certain notice of those things which are convenient or inconvenient to us. For he that sees a candle burning, and hath experimented the force of its flame, by putting his finger in it, will little doubt that this is something existing without him, which does him harm, and puts him to great pain: which is assurance enough, when no man requires greater certainty to govern his actions by than what is as certain as his actions themselves. . . . .

9. *But reaches no farther than actual sensation.*—In fine, then, when our senses do actually convey into our understandings any idea, we cannot but be satisfied that there doth something at that

time really exist without us, which doth affect our senses, and by them give notice of itself to our apprehensive faculties, and actually produce that idea which we then perceive: and we cannot so far distrust their testimony as to doubt, that such collections of simple ideas, as we have observed by our senses to be united together, do really exist together. But this knowledge extends as far as the present testimony of our senses, employed about particular objects that do then affect them, and no farther. For I saw such a collection of simple ideas, as is wont to be called man, existing together one minute since, and am now alone, I cannot be certain that the same man exists now, since there is no necessary connexion of his existence a minute since with his existence now: by a thousand ways he may cease to be, since I had the testimony of my senses for his existence. And if I cannot be certain that the man I saw last to-day is now in being, I can less be certain that he is so, who hath been longer removed from my senses, and I have not seen since yesterday, or since the last year: and much less can I be certain of the existence of men that I never saw. And therefore, though it be highly probable that millions of men do now exist, yet, whilst I am alone writing this, I have not that certainty of it which we strictly call knowledge; though the great likelihood of it puts me past doubt, and it be reasonable for me to do several things upon the confidence that there are men (and men also of my acquaintance, with whom I have to do) now in the world: but this is but probability, not knowledge. . . . .

11. *Past existence is known by memory.*—As when our senses are actually employed about any object, we do know that it does exist; so by our memory we may be assured, that heretofore things that affected our senses have existed. And thus we have knowledge of the past existence of several things, whereof our senses having informed us, our memories still retain the ideas; and of this we are past all doubt, so long as we remember well. But this knowledge also reaches no farther, than our senses have formerly assured us. Thus seeing water at this instant, it is an unquestionable truth to me that water doth exist: and remembering that I saw it yesterday, it will also be always true, and, as long as my memory retains it, always an undoubted proposition to me, that water did exist the 10th of July 1688, as it will also be equally true, that a

certain number of very fine colours did exist, which at the same time I saw upon a bubble of that water: but, being now quite out of sight both of the water and bubbles too, it is no more certainly known to me that the water doth now exist, than that the bubbles or colours therein do so; it being no more necessary that water should exist to-day, because it existed yesterday, than that the colours or bubbles exist to-day because they existed yesterday; though it be exceedingly much more probable, because water hath been observed to continue long in existence, but bubbles and the colours on them quickly cease to be.

12. *The existence of spirits not knowable.*—What ideas we have of spirits, and how we come by them, I have already shown. But though we have those ideas in our minds, and know we have them there, the having the ideas of spirits does not make us know that any such things do exist without us, or that there are any finite spirits, or any other spiritual beings but the eternal God. We have ground from revelation, and several other reasons, to believe with assurance that there are such creatures; but, our senses not being able to discover them, we want the means of knowing their particular existences. For we can no more know, that there are finite spirits really existing, by the idea we have of such beings in our minds, than by the ideas any one has of fairies, or centaurs, he can come to know that things answering those ideas do really exist.

And therefore concerning the existence of finite spirits, as well as several other things, we must content ourselves with the evidence of faith; but universal certain propositions concerning this matter are beyond our reach. . . . .

13. *Particular propositions concerning existences are knowable.*— By which it appears that there are two sorts of propositions. (1.) There is one sort of propositions concerning the existence of any thing answerable to such an idea; as having the idea of an elephant, phœnix, motion, or an angel in my mind, the first and natural inquiry is, whether such a thing does any where exist. And this knowledge is only of particulars. No existence of any thing without us, but only of God, can certainly be known farther than our senses inform us. (2). There is another sort of propositions, wherein is expressed the agreement or disagreement of our abstract ideas, and their dependence one on another. Such propositions may be

universal and certain. So having the idea of God and myself, of fear and obedience, I cannot but be sure that God is to be feared and obeyed by me: and this proposition will be certain concerning man in general, if I have made an abstract idea of such a species, whereof I am one particular. But yet this proposition, how certain soever, that men ought to fear and obey God, proves not to me the existence of men in the world, but will be true of all such creatures whenever they do exist: which certainty of such general propositions depends on the agreement or disagreement is to be discovered in those abstract ideas.

14. *And general propositions concerning abstract ideas.*—In the former case, our knowledge is the consequence of the existence of things producing ideas in our minds by our senses: in the latter, knowledge is the consequence of the ideas (be they what they will) that are in our minds, producing their general certain propositions. Many of these are called *æternæ veritates*, and all of them indeed are so; not from being written all or any of them in the minds of all men, or that they were any of them propositions in any one's mind till he, having got the abstract ideas, joined or separated them by affirmation or negation. But wheresoever we can suppose such a creature as man is, endowed with such faculties, and thereby furnished with such ideas as we have, we must conclude, he must needs, when he applies his thoughts to the consideration of his ideas, know the truth of certain propositions, that will arise from the agreement or disagreement which he will perceive in his own ideas. Such propositions are therefore called eternal truths, not because they are eternal propositions actually formed, and antecedent to the understanding, that at any time makes them; nor because they are imprinted on the mind from any patterns, that are anywhere out of the mind, and existed before: but because being once made about abstract ideas, so as to be true, they will whenever they can be supposed to be made again at any time past or to come, by a mind having those ideas, always actually be true. For names being supposed to stand perpetually for the same ideas, and the same ideas having immutably the same habitudes one to another, propositions concerning any abstract ideas that are once true, must needs be eternal verities. . . . .

CHAPTER XIV. OF JUDGMENT

1. *Our knowledge being short, we want something else.*—The under-standing faculties being given to man, not barely for speculation, but also for the conduct of his life, man would be at a great loss if he had nothing to direct him but what has the certainty of true knowledge. For that being very short and scanty, as we have seen, he would be often utterly in the dark, and, in most of the actions of his life, perfectly at a stand, had he nothing to guide him in the absence of clear and certain knowledge. He that will not eat till he has demonstration that it will nourish him; he that will not stir till he infallibly knows the business he goes about will succeed; will have little else to do but to sit still and perish. . . . .

3. *Judgment supplies the want of knowledge.*—The faculty which God has given man to supply the want of clear and certain knowl-edge, in cases where that cannot be had, is judgment; whereby the mind takes its ideas to agree or disagree; or, which is the same, any proposition to be true or false, without perceiving a demonstrative evidence in the proofs. The mind sometimes exercises this judg-ment out of necessity, where demonstrative proofs and certain knowledge are not to be had; and sometimes out of laziness, unskil-fulness, or haste, even where demonstrative and certain proofs are to be had. Men often stay not warily to examine the agreement or disagreement of two ideas, which they are desirous or concerned to know; but, either incapable of such attention as is requisite in a long train of gradations, or impatient of delay, lightly cast their eyes on, or wholly pass by, the proofs; and so without making out the demonstration, determine of the agreement or disagreement of two ideas as it were by a view of them as they are at a distance, and take it to be the one or the other, as seems most likely to them upon such a loose survey. This faculty of the mind, when it is exercised immediately about things, is called judgment; when about truths delivered in words, is most commonly called assent or dis-sent: which being the most usual way wherein the mind has occa-sion to employ this faculty, I shall under these terms treat of it, as least liable in our language to equivocation.

4. *Judgment is the presuming things to be so, without perceiving it.*
—Thus the mind has two faculties, conversant about truth and falsehood.

First, Knowledge, whereby it certainly perceives, and is un-undoubtedly satisfied of, the agreement or disagreement of any ideas.

Secondly, Judgment, which is the putting ideas together, or separating them from one another in the mind, when their certain agreement or disagreement is not perceived, but presumed to be so; which is, as the word imports, taken to be so before it certainly appears. And if it so unites, or separates them, as in reality things are, it is right judgment.

CHAPTER XV. OF PROBABILITY

1. *Probability is the appearance of agreement upon fallible proofs.*
—As demonstration is the showing the agreement or disagreement of two ideas, by the intervention of one or more proofs, which have a constant, immutable, and visible connexion one with another; so probability is nothing but the appearance of such an agreement or disagreement, by the intervention of proofs, whose connexion is not constant and immutable, or at least is not perceived to be so, but is or appears for the most part to be so, and is enough to induce the mind to judge the proposition to be true or false, rather than the contrary. For example: in the demonstration of it a man perceives the certain immutable connexion there is of equality between the three angles of a triangle, and those intermediate ones which are made use of to show their equality to two right ones; and so by an intuitive knowledge of the agreement or disagreement of the intermediate ideas in each step of the progress, the whole series is continued with an evidence which clearly shows the agreement or disagreement of those three angles in equality to two right ones: and thus he has certain knowledge that it is so. But another man, who never took the pains to observe the demonstration, hearing a mathematician, a man of credit, affirm the three angles of a triangle to be equal to two right ones, assents to it, *i. e.* receives it for true. In which case the foundation of his assent is the probability of the thing, the proof being such as for the most part

carries truth with it: the man on whose testimony he receives it not being wont to affirm any thing contrary to, or besides his knowledge, especially in matters of this kind. So that that which causes his assent to this proposition, that the three angles of a triangle are equal to two right ones, that which makes him take these ideas to agree, without knowing them to do so, is the wonted veracity of the speaker in other cases, or his supposed veracity in this.

2. *It is to supply the want of knowledge.*—Our knowledge, as has been shown, being very narrow, and we not happy enough to find certain truth in every thing which we have occasion to consider; most of the propositions we think, reason, discourse, nay act upon, are such, as we cannot have undoubted knowledge of their truth: yet some of them border so near upon certainty, that we make no doubt at all about them; but assent to them as firmly, and act, according to that assent, as resolutely, as if they were infallibly demonstrated, and that our knowledge of them was perfect and certain. But there being degrees herein from the very neighbourhood of certainty and demonstration, quite down to improbability and unlikeness, even to the confines of impossibility; and also degrees of assent from full assurance and confidence, quite down to conjecture, doubt, and distrust: I shall come now (having, as I think, found out the bounds of human knowledge and certainty), in the next place, to consider the several degrees and grounds of probability, and assent or faith.

3. *Being that which makes us presume things to be true before we know them to be so.*—Probability is likeliness to be true, the very notation of the word signifying such a proposition, for which there be arguments or proofs to make it pass or be received for true. The entertainment the mind gives to this sort of propositions is called belief, assent, or opinion, which is the admitting or receiving any proposition for true, upon arguments or proofs that are found to persuade us to receive it as true, without certain knowledge that it is so. And herein lies the difference between probability and certainty, faith and knowledge, that in all the parts of knowledge there is intuition; each immediate idea, each step has its visible and certain connexion; in belief, not so. That which makes me believe something extraneous to the thing I believe; something not evidently joined on both sides to, and so not manifestly showing the

agreement or disagreement of those ideas that are under consideration.

4. *The grounds of probability are two: conformity with our own
experience, or the testimony of others' experience.*—Probability, then,
being to supply the defect of our knowledge, and to guide us where
that fails, is always conversant about propositions, whereof we
have no certainty, but only some inducements to receive them for
true. The grounds of it are, in short, these two following:

First, The conformity of any thing with our own knowledge,
observation, and experience.

Secondly, The testimony of others, vouching their observation
and experience. In the testimony of others is to be considered, 1.
The number. 2. The integrity. 3. The skill of the witnesses. 4.
The design of the author, where it is a testimony out of a book cited.
5. The consistency of the parts and circumstances of the relation.
6. Contrary testimonies.

CHAPTER XXI. OF THE DIVISION OF THE SCIENCES

1. *Three sorts.*—All that can fall within the compass of human
understanding being either, first, the nature of things, as they are
in themselves, their relations, and their manner of operation: or,
secondly, that which man himself ought to do, as a rational and
voluntary agent, for the attainment of any end, especially happiness: or, thirdly, the ways and means whereby the knowledge of
both the one and the other of these is attained and communicated:
I think science may be divided properly into these three sorts.

2. 1. *Physica.*—First, the knowledge of things, as they are in
their own proper beings, their constitution, properties, and operations; whereby I mean not only matter and body, but spirits also,
which have their proper natures, constitutions, and operations, as
well as bodies. This, in a little more enlarged sense of the word, I
call Φυσικη, or natural philosophy. The end of this is bare speculative truth; and whatsoever can afford the mind of man any such,
falls under this branch, whether it be God himself, angels, spirits,
bodies, or any of their affections, as number and figure, etc.

3. 2. *Practica.*—Secondly, Πρακτικη, the skill of right applying
our own powers and actions for the attainment of things good and
useful. The most considerable under this head is ethics, which is the

seeking out those rules and measures of human actions which lead to happiness, and the means to practise them. The end of this is not bare speculation, and the knowledge of truth; but right, and a conduct suitable to it.

4. 3. Σημειωτική.—Thirdly, the third branch may be called Σημειωτική or the doctrine of signs, the most usual whereof being words, it is aptly enough termed also Λογική, logic; the business whereof is to consider the nature of signs the mind makes use of for the understanding of things, or conveying its knowledge to others. For since the things the mind contemplates are none of them, besides itself, present to the understanding, it is necessary that something else, as a sign or representation of the thing it considers, should be present to it: and these are ideas. And because the scene of ideas that makes one man's thoughts, cannot be laid open to the immediate view of another, nor laid up any where but in the memory, a no very sure repository; therefore to communicate our thoughts to one another, as well as record them for our own use, signs of our ideas are also necessary. Those which men have found most convenient, and therefore generally make use of, are articulate sounds. The consideration then of ideas and words, as the great instruments of knowledge, makes no despicable part of their contemplation who would take a view of human knowledge in the whole extent of it. And perhaps if it were distinctly weighed, and duly considered, they would afford us another sort of logic and critic than what we have been hitherto acquainted with.

5. *This is the first division of the objects of knowledge.*—This seems to me the first and most general, as well as natural division of the objects of our understanding. For a man can employ his thoughts about nothing, but either the contemplation of things themselves for the discovery of truth; or about the things in his power, which are his own actions, for the attainment of his own ends; or the signs the mind makes use of both in the one and the other, and the right ordering of them for its clearer information: All which three, viz. things as they are in themselves knowable; actions as they depend on us, in order to happiness; and the right use of signs, in order to knowledge, being *toto coelo* different, they seemed to me to be the three great provinces of the intellectual world, wholly separate and distinct one from another.

JOHN LOCKE

SELECTIONS FROM *TWO TREATISES OF GOVERNMENT*[3]

BOOK II. OF CIVIL GOVERNMENT

CHAPTER I

§ 1. It having been shown in the foregoing discourse,

1. That Adam had not, either by natural right of fatherhood, or by positive donation from God, any such authority over his children, or dominion over the world, as is pretended:

2. That if he had, his heirs yet had no right to it:

3. That if his heirs had, there being no law of nature, nor positive law of God, that determines which is the right heir in all cases that may arise, the right of succession, and consequently of bearing rule, could not have been certainly determined:

4. That if even that had been determined, yet the knowledge of which is the eldest line of Adam's posterity, being so long since utterly lost, that in the races of mankind and families of the world, there remains not to one above another the least pretence to be the eldest house, and to have the right of inheritance:

All these premises having, as I think, been clearly made out, it is impossible that the rulers now on earth should make any benefit, or derive any the least shadow of authority from that, which is held to be the fountain of all power, "Adam's private dominion and paternal jurisdiction;" so that he that will not give just occasion to think that all government in the world is the product only of force and violence, and that men live together by no other rules but that of beasts, where the strongest carries it, and so lay a foundation for perpetual disorder and mischief, tumult, sedition, and rebellion (things that the followers of that hypothesis so loudly cry out against) must of necessity find out another rise of government, another original of political power, and another way of designing and knowing the persons that have it, than what sir Robert Filmer hath taught us.

[3] *Two Treatises of Government, in the Former, the False Principles and Foundation of Sir Robert Filmer, and His Followers, Are Detected and Overthrown; the Latter, Is an Essay concerning the True Original, Extent, and End, of Civil Government. The Works of John Locke* (9 vols.; 12th ed.; London, 1824), IV, 207; Book II: "Of Civil Government," p. 338.

§ 2. To this purpose, I think it may not be amiss to set down what I take to be political power; that the power of a magistrate over a subject may be distinguished from that of a father over his children, a master over his servants, a husband over his wife, and a lord over his slave. All which distinct powers happening sometimes together in the same man, if he be considered under these different relations, it may help us to distinguish these powers one from another, and show the difference betwixt a ruler of a commonwealth, a father of a family, and a captain of a galley.

§ 3. Political power, then, I take to be a right of making laws with penalties of death, and consequently all less penalties for the regulating and preserving of property, and of employing the force of the community, in the execution of such laws, and in the defence of the commonwealth from foreign injury; and all this only for the public good.

CHAPTER II. OF THE STATE OF NATURE

§ 4. To understand political power right, and derive it from its original, we must consider what state all men are naturally in, and that is, a state of perfect freedom to order their actions and dispose of their possessions and persons, as they think fit, within the bounds of the law of nature; without asking leave, or depending upon the will of any other man.

A state also of equality, wherein all the power and jurisdiction is reciprocal, no one having more than another; there being nothing more evident, than that creatures of the same species and rank, promiscuously born to all the same advantages of nature, and the use of the same faculties, should also be equal one amongst another without subordination or subjection: unless the lord and master of them all should, by any manifest declaration of his will, set one above another, and confer on him, by an evident and clear appointment, an undoubted right to dominion and sovereignty.

§ This equality of men by nature, the judicious Hooker looks upon as so evident in itself, and beyond all question, that he makes it the foundation of that obligation to mutual love amongst men, on which he builds the duties we owe one another, and from whence he derives the great maxims of justice and charity. His words are,

"The like natural inducement hath brought men to know, that

it is no less their duty to love others than themselves; for seeing those things which are equal, must needs all have one measure; if I cannot but wish to receive good, even as much at every man's hands, as any man can wish unto his own soul, how should I look to have any part of my desire herein satisfied, unless myself be careful to satisfy the like desire, which is undoubtedly in other men, being of one and the same nature? To have any thing offered them repugnant to this desire, must needs in all respects grieve them as much as me; so that if I do harm, I must look to suffer, there being no reason that others should show greater measure of love to me, than they have by me showed unto them: my desire therefore to be loved of my equals in nature, as much as possibly may be, imposeth upon me a natural duty of bearing to them-ward fully the like affection: from which relation of equality between ourselves and them that are as ourselves, what several rules and canons natural reason hath drawn, for direction of life, no man is ignorant."

§ 6. But though this be a state of liberty, yet it is not a state of licence: though man in that state have an uncontrolable liberty to dispose of his person or possessions, yet he has not liberty to destroy himself, or so much as any creature in his possession, but where some nobler use than its bare preservation calls for it. The state of nature has a law of nature to govern it, which obliges every one: and reason, which is that law, teaches all mankind, who will but consult it, that being all equal and independent, no one ought to harm another in his life, health, liberty, or possessions: for men being all the workmanship of one omnipotent and infinitely wise Maker; all the servants of one sovereign master, sent into the world by his order, and about his business; they are his property, whose workmanship they are, made to last during his, not another's pleasure: and being furnished with like faculties, sharing all in one community of nature, there cannot be supposed any such subordination among us, that may authorize us to destroy another, as if we were made for one another's uses, as the inferior ranks of creatures are for ours. Every one, as he is bound to preserve himself, and not to quit his station wilfully, so by the like reason, when his own preservation comes not in competition, ought he, as much as he can, to preserve the rest of mankind, and may not, unless it be to do justice to an offender, take away or impair the life, or what tends to the preservation of life, the liberty, health, limb, or goods of another.

§ 7. And that all men may be restrained from invading others rights, and from doing hurt to one another, and the law of nature be observed, which willeth the peace and preservation of all mankind, the execution of the law of nature is, in that state, put into every man's hands, whereby every one has a right to punish the transgressors of that law to such a degree as may hinder its violation: for the law of nature would, as all other laws that concern men in this world, be in vain, if there were nobody that in the state of nature had a power to execute that law, and thereby preserve the innocent and restrain offenders. And if any one in the state of nature may punish another for any evil he had done, every one may do so: for in that state of perfect equality, where naturally there is no superiority or jurisdiction of one over another, what any may do in prosecution of that law, every one must needs have a right to do.

§ 8. And thus, in the state of nature, "one man comes by a power over another;" but yet no absolute or arbitrary power, to use a criminal, when he has got him in his hands, according to the passionate heats, or boundless extravagancy of his own will; but only to retribute to him, so far as calm reason and conscience dictate, what is proportionate to his transgression; which is so much as may serve for reparation and restraint: for these two are the only reasons, why one man may lawfully do harm to another, which is that we call punishment. In transgressing the law of nature, the offender declares himself to live by another rule than that of reason and common equity, which is that measure God has set to the actions of men, for their mutual security; and so he becomes dangerous to mankind, the tye, which is to secure them from injury and violence, being slighted and broken by him. Which being a trespass against the whole species, and the peace and safety of it, provided for by the law of nature; every man upon this score, by the right he hath to preserve mankind in general, may restrain, or, where it is necessary, destroy things noxious to them, and so may bring such evil on any one, who hath transgressed that law, as may make him repent the doing of it, and thereby deter him, and by his example others, from doing the like mischief.

And in this case, and upon this ground, "every man hath a right to punish the offender, and be executioner of the law of nature."

§ 9. I doubt not but this will seem a very strange doctrine to some men: but before they condemn it, I desire them to resolve me, by what right any prince or state can put to death, or punish any alien, for any crime he commits in their country. It is certain their laws, by virtue of any sanction they receive from the promulgated will of the legislative, reach not a stranger: they speak not to him, nor, if they did, is he bound to hearken to them. The legislative authority, by which they are in force over the subjects of that commonwealth, hath no power over him. Those who have the supreme power of making laws in England, France, or Holland, are to an Indian but like the rest of the world, men without authority: and therefore, if by the law of nature every man hath not a power to punish offences against it, as he soberly judges the case to require, I see not how the magistrates of any community can punish an alien of another country; since, in reference to him, they can have no more power than what every man naturally may have over another.

§ 10. Besides the crime which consists in violating the law, and varying from the right rule of reason, whereby a man so far becomes degenerate, and declares himself to quit the principles of human nature, and to be a noxious creature, there is commonly injury done to some person or other, and some other man receives damage by his transgression: in which case he who hath received any damage, has, besides the right of punishment common to him with other men, a particular right to seek reparation from him that has done it: and any other person, who finds it just, may also join with him that is injured, and assist him in recovering from the offender so much as may make satisfaction for the harm he has suffered.

§ 11. From these two distinct rights, the one of punishing the crime for restraint, and preventing the like offence, which right of punishing is in every body; the other of taking reparation, which belongs only to the injured party; comes it to pass that the magistrate, who by being magistrate hath the common right of punishing put into his hands, can often, where the public good demands not the execution of the law, remit the punishment of criminal offences by his own authority, but yet cannot remit the satisfaction due to any private man for the damage he has received. That, he who has suffered the damage has a right to demand in his own name, and he alone can remit: the damnified person has this power of appropriating to himself the goods or service of the offender, by right of self-preservation, as every man has a power to punish the crime, to prevent its being committed again, "by the right he had of preserving all mankind"; and doing all reasonable things he can in order to that end: and thus it is, that every man, in the state of nature, has a power to kill a murderer, both to deter others from doing the like injury, which no reparation can compensate, by the example of the punishment that attends it from every body; and also to secure men from the attempts of a criminal, who having renounced reason, the common rule and measure God hath given to mankind, hath, by the unjust violence and slaughter he hath committed upon one, declared war against all mankind; and therefore may be destroyed as a lion or a tiger, one of those wild savage beasts, with whom men can have no society nor security: ,and upon this is grounded that great law of nature, "Whoso sheddeth man's blood, by man shall his blood be shed." And Cain was so fully convinced, that every one had a right to destroy such a criminal, that after the murder of his brother, he cries out, "Every one that findeth me, shall slay me"; so plain was it writ in the hearts of mankind.

§ 12. By the same reason may a man in the state of nature punish the lesser breaches of that law. It will perhaps be demanded, with death? I answer, each transgression may be punished to that degree, and with so much severity, as will suffice to make it an ill bargain to the offender, give him cause to repent, and terrify others from doing the like. Every offence, that can be committed in the state of nature, may in the state of nature be also punished equally, and as far forth, as it may in a commonwealth: for though it would be beside my present purpose, to enter here into the particulars of the law of nature, or its measures of punishment, yet it is certain there is such a law, and that too as intelligible and plain to a rational creature, and a studier of that law, as the positive laws of commonwealths: nay, possibly plainer, as much as reason is easier to be understood, than the fancies and intricate contrivances of men, following contrary and hidden interests put into words; for so truly are a great part of the municipal laws of countries, which are only so far right, as they are founded on the law of nature, by which they are to be regulated and interpreted.

§ 13. To this strange doctrine, viz. That "in the state of nature every one has the executive power" of the law of nature, I doubt not but it will be objected, that it is unreasonable for men to be judges in their own cases, that self love will make men partial to themselves and their friends; and on the other side, that ill-nature, passion, and revenge will carry them too far in punishing others; and hence nothing but confusion and disorder will follow: and that therefore God hath certainly appointed government to restrain the partiality and violence of men. I easily grant, that civil government is the proper remedy for the inconveniences of the state of nature, which must certainly be great, where men may be judges in their own case; since it is easy to be imagined, that he who was so unjust as to do his brother an injury, will scarce be so just as to condemn himself for it: but I shall desire those who make this objection, to remember, that absolute monarchs are but men; and if government is to be the remedy of those evils, which necessarily follow from men's being judges in their own cases, and the state of nature is therefore not to be endured; I desire to know what kind of government that is, and how much better it is than the state of nature, where one man commanding a multitude, has the liberty to be judge in his own case, and may do to all his subjects whatever he pleases, without the least liberty to any one to question or control those who execute his pleasure? and in whatsoever he doth, whether led by reason, mistake or passion, must be submitted to? much better it is in the state of nature, wherein men are not bound to submit to the unjust will of another: and if he that judges, judges amiss in his own, or any other case, he is answerable for it to the rest of mankind.

§ 14. It is often asked as a mighty objection, "where are, or ever were there any men in such a state of nature?" To which it may suffice as an answer at present, that since all princes and rulers of independent governments, all through the world, are in a state of nature, it is plain the world never was, nor ever will be, without numbers of men in that state. I have named all governors of independent communities, whether they are, or are not, in league with others: for it is not every compact that puts an end to the state of nature between men, but only this one of agreeing together mutually to enter into one community, and make one body politic; other promises and compacts men may make one with another, and yet still be in the state of nature. The promises and bargains for truck, &c. between the two men in the desert island, mentioned by Garcilasso de la Vega, in his history of Peru; or between a Swiss and an Indian, in the woods of America; are binding to them, though they are perfectly in a state of nature, in reference to one another: for truth and keeping of faith belongs to men as men, and not as members of society.

§ 15. To those that say, there were never any men in the state of nature, I will not only oppose the authority of the judicious Hooker, Eccl. Pol. lib. 1. sect. 10, where he says, "The laws which have been hitherto mentioned," i.e. the laws of nature, "do bind men absolutely, even as they are men, although they have never any settled fellowship, never any solemn agreement amongst themselves what to do, or not to do; but forasmuch as we are not by ourselves sufficient to furnish ourselves with competent store of things, needful for such a life as our nature doth desire, a life fit for the dignity of man; therefore to supply those defects and imperfections which are in us, as living singly and solely by ourselves, we are naturally induced to seek communion and fellowship with others. This was the cause of men's uniting themselves at first in political societies." But I moreover affirm, that all men are naturally in that state, and remain so, till by their own consents they make themselves members of some politic society; and I doubt not in the sequel of this discourse to make it very clear.

CHAPTER III. OF THE STATE OF WAR

§ 16. The state of war is a state of enmity and destruction: and therefore declaring by word or action, not a passionate and hasty, but a sedate settled design upon another man's life, puts him in a state of war with him against whom he has declared such an intention, and so has exposed his life to the other's power to be taken away by him, or any one that joins with him in his defence, and espouses his quarrel; it being reasonable and just, I should have a right to destroy that which threatens me with destruction; for, by the fundamental law of nature, man being to be preserved as much as possible, when all cannot be preserved, the safety of the innocent is to be preferred: and one may destroy a man who makes war upon him, or has discovered an enmity to his being, for the same reason that he may kill a wolf or a lion; because such men are not under the ties of the common law of reason, have no other rule, but that of force and violence, and so may be treated as beasts of prey, those dangerous and noxious creatures, that will be sure to destroy him whenever he falls into their power.

§ 17. And hence it is, that he who attempts to get another man into his absolute power, does thereby put himself into a state of war with him; it being to be understood as a declaration of a design upon his life: for I have reason to conclude, that he who would get me into his power without my consent, would use me as he pleased when he got me there, and destroy me too when he had a fancy to it; for nobody can desire to have me in his absolute power, unless it be to compel me by force to that which is against the right of my freedom, i.e. make me a slave. To be free from such force is the only security of my preservation; and reason bids me look on him, as an enemy to my preservation, who would take away that freedom which is the fence to it; so that he who makes an attempt to enslave me, thereby puts himself into a state of war with me. He that, in the state of nature, would take away the freedom that belongs to any one in that state, must necessarily be supposed to have a design to take away every thing else, that freedom being the foundation of all the rest; as he that, in the state of society, would take away the freedom belonging to those of that society or commonwealth, must be supposed to design to take away from them every thing else, and so be looked on as in a state of war.

§ 18. This makes it lawful for a man to kill a thief, who has not in the least hurt him, nor declared any design upon his life, any farther than, by the use of force, so to get him in his power, as to take away his money, or what he pleases, from him; because using force, where he has no right, to get me into his power, let his pretence be what it will, I have no reason to suppose, that he, who would take away my liberty, would not, when he had me in his power, take away every thing else. And therefore it is lawful for me to treat him as one who has put himself into a state of war with me, i.e. kill him if I can; for to that hazard does he justly expose himself, whoever introduces a state of war, and is aggressor in it.

§ 19. And here we have the plain "difference between the state of nature and the state of war," which however some men have confounded, are as far distant, as a state of peace, good-will, mutual assistance and preservation, and a state of enmity, malice, violence and mutual destruction, are one from another. Men living together according to reason, without a common superiour on earth, with authority to judge between them, is properly the state of nature. But force, or a declared design of force, upon the person of another, where there is no common superiour on earth to appeal to for relief, is the state of war: and it is the want of such an appeal gives a man the right of war even against an aggressor, though he be in society and a fellow-subject. Thus a thief, whom I cannot harm, but by appeal to the law, for having stolen all that I am worth, I may kill, when he sets on me to rob me but of my horse or coat; because the law, which was made for my preservation, where it cannot interpose to secure my life from present force, which, if lost, is capable of no reparation, permits me my own defence, and the right of war, a liberty to kill the aggressor, because the agressor allows not time to appeal to our common judge, nor the decision of the law, for remedy in a case where the mischief may be irreparable. Want of a common judge with authority, puts all men in a state of nature: force without right, upon a man's person, makes a state of war, both where there is, and is not, a common judge. . . . .

CHAPTER V.   OF PROPERTY

§ 25. Whether we consider natural reason, which tells us, that men, being once born, have a right to their preservation, and consequently to meet and drink, and such other things as nature affords for their subsistence; or revelation, which gives us an account of those grants God made of the world to Adam, and to Noah, and his sons; it is very clear, that God, as king David says, Psal. cxv. 16, "has given the earth to the children of men," given it to mankind in common. But this being supposed, it seems to some a very great difficulty how any one should ever come to have a property in any thing: I will not content myself to answer, that if it be difficult to make out property, upon a supposition, that God gave the world to Adam, and his posterity in common, it is impossible that any man, but one universal monarch, should have any property upon a supposition, that God gave the world to Adam, and his heirs in succession, exclusive of all the rest of his posterity. But I shall endeavour to show, how man might come to have a property in several parts of that which God gave to mankind in common, and that without any express compact of all the commoners.

§ 26. God, who hath given the world to men in common, hath also given them reason to make use of it to the best advantage of life, and convenience. The earth, and all that is therein, is given to men for the support and comfort of their being. And though all the fruits it naturally produces, and beasts it feeds, belong to mankind in common, as they are produced by the spontaneous hand of nature; and nobody has originally a private dominion, exclusive of the rest of mankind, in any of them, as they are thus in their natural state; yet being given for the use of men, there must of necessity be a means to appropriate them some way or other, before they can be of any use, or at all beneficial to any particular man. The fruit, or venison, which nourishes the wild Indian, who knows no enclosure, and is still a tenant in common, must be his, and so his, i.e. a part of him, that another can no longer have any right to it, before it can do him any good for the support of his life.

§ 27. Though the earth, and all inferiour creatures, be common to all men, yet every man has a property in his own person: this nobody has any right to but himself. The labour of his body, and the work of his hands, we may say, are properly his. Whatsoever then he removes out of the state that nature hath provided, and left it in, he hath mixed his labour with, and joined to it something that is his own, and thereby makes it his property. It being by him removed from the common state nature hath placed it in, it hath by this labour something annexed to it, that excludes the common right of other men. For this labour being the unquestionable property of the labourer, no man but he can have a right to what that is once joined to, at least where there is enough, and as good, left in common for others. . . . . .

§ 45. Thus labour, in the beginning, gave a right of property, wherever any one was pleased to employ it upon what was common, which remained a long while the far greater part, and is yet more than mankind makes use of. Men, at first, for the most part, contented themselves with what unassisted nature offered to their necessities: and though afterwards, in some parts of the world, (where the increase of people and stock, with the use of money, had made land scarce, and so of some value) the several communities settled the bounds of their distinct territories, and by laws within themselves regulated the properties of the private men of their society, and so, by compact and agreement, settled the property which labour and industry began: and the leagues that have been made between several states and kingdoms, either expressly or tacitly disowning all claim and right to the land in the others possession, have, by common consent, given up their pretences to their natural common right, which originally they had to those countries, and so have, by positive agreement, settled a property amongst themselves, in distinct parts and parcels of the earth; yet there still are great tracts of ground to be found, which (the inhabitants thereof not having joined with the rest of mankind, in the consent of the use of their common money) lie waste, and are more than the people who dwell on it do, or can make use of, and so still lie in common; though this can scarce happen amongst that part of mankind that have consented to the use of money.

§ 46. The greatest part of things really useful to the life of man, and such as the necessity of subsisting made the first commoners of the world look after, as it doth the Americans now, are generally things of short duration; such as, if they are not consumed by use, will decay and perish of themselves: gold, silver, and diamonds, are things that fancy or agreement hath put the value on, more than real use, and the necessary support of life. Now of those good things which nature hath provided in common, every one had a right, (as hath been said) to as much as he could use, and property in all that he could effect with his labour; all that his industry could extend to, to alter from the state nature had put it in, was his. He that gathered a hundred bushels of acorns or apples, had thereby a property in them, they were his goods as soon as gathered. He was only to look, that he used them before they spoiled, else he took more than his share, and robbed others. And indeed it was a foolish thing, as well as dishonest, to hoard up more than he could make use of. If he gave away a part to any body else, so that it perished not uselessly in his possession, these he also made use of. And if he also bartered away plums, that would have rotted in a week, for nuts that would last good for his eating a whole year, he did no injury; he wasted not the common stock; destroyed no part of the portion of the goods that belonged to others, so long as nothing perished uselessly in his hands. Again, if he would give his nuts for a piece of metal, pleased with its colour; or exchange his sheep for shells, or wool for a sparkling pebble or a diamond, and keep those by him all his life, he invaded not the right of others, he might heap as much of these durable things as he pleased; the exceeding of the bounds of his just property not lying in the largeness of his possession, but the perishing of any thing uselessly in it.

§ 47. And thus came in the use of money, some lasting thing that men might keep without spoiling, and that by mutual consent men would take in exchange for the truly useful, but perishable supports of life. . . . .

CHAPTER VII. OF POLITICAL OR CIVIL SOCIETY

§ 77. God having made man such a creature, that in his own judgment, it was not good for him to be alone, put him under strong obligations of necessity, convenience, and inclination, to drive him into society, as well as fitted him with understanding and language to continue and enjoy it. The first society was between man and wife, which gave beginning to that between parents and children; to which, in time, that between master and servant came to be added: and though all these might, and commonly did meet together, and make up but one family, wherein the master or mistress of it had some sort of rule proper to a family; each of these, or all together, came short of political society, as we shall see, if we consider the different ends, ties, and bounds of each of these. . . . .

§ 87. Man being born, as has been proved, with a title to perfect freedom, and uncontrolled enjoyment of all the rights and privileges of the law of nature, equally with any other man, or number of men in the world, hath by nature a power, not only to preserve his property, that is, his life, liberty, and estate, against the injuries and attempts of other men; but to judge of and punish the breaches of that law in others, as he is persuaded the offence deserves, even with death itself, in crimes where the heinousness of the fact, in his opinion, requires it. But because no political society can be, nor subsist, without having in itself the power to preserve the property, and, in order thereunto, punish the offences of all those of that society; there and there only is political society, where every one of the members hath quitted his natural power, resigned it up into the hands of the community in all cases that excludes him not from appealing for protection to the law established by it. And thus all private judgment of every particular member being excluded, the community comes to be umpire by settled standing rules, indifferent, and the same to all parties; and by men having authority from the community, for the execution of those rules, decides all the differences that may happen between any members of that society concerning any matter of right; and punishes those offences which any member hath committed against the society, with such penalties as the law has established, whereby it is easy to discern, who are, and who are not, in political society together. Those who are united into one body, and have a common established law and judicature to appeal to, with authority to decide controversies between them, and punish offenders, are in civil society one with another: but those who have no such common appeal, I mean on earth, are still in the state of nature, each being, where there is no other, judge for himself, and executioner: which is, as I have before showed, the perfect state of nature.

§ 88. And thus the commonwealth comes by a power to set down what punishment shall belong to the several transgressions which they think worthy of it, committed amongst the members of that society, (which is the power of making laws) as well as it has the power to punish any injury done unto any of its members, by any one that is not of it, (which is the power of war and peace,) and all this for the preservation of the property of all the members of that society, as far as is possible. But though every man who has entered into civil society, and is become a member of any commonwealth, has thereby quitted his power to punish offences against the law of nature, in prosecution of his own private judgment; yet with the judgment of offences, which he has given up to the legislative in all cases, where he can appeal to the magistrate, he has given a right to the commonwealth to employ his force, for the execution of the judgments of the commonwealth, whenever he shall be called to it; which indeed are his own judgments, they being made by himself, or his representative. And herein we have the original of the legislative and executive power of civil society, which is to judge by standing laws, how far offences are to be punished, when committed within the commonwealth; and also to determine, by occasional judgments founded on the present circumstances of the fact, how far injuries from without are to be vindicated; and in both these to employ all the force of all the members, when there shall be need.

§ 89. Whenever therefore any number of men are so united into one society, as to quit every one his executive power of the law of nature, and to resign it to the public, there and there only is a political, or civil society. And this is done, wherever any number of men, in the state of nature, enter into society to make one people, one body politic, under one supreme government; or else when any one joins himself to, and incorporates with any government already made: for hereby he authorizes the society, or, which is all one, the legislative thereof, to make laws for him, as the public good of the society shall require; to the execution whereof, his own assistance (as to his own degrees) is due. And this puts men out of a state of nature into that of a commonwealth, by setting up a judge on earth, with authority to determine all the controversies, and redress the injuries that may happen to any member of the commonwealth: which judge is the legislative, or magistrate appointed by it. And wherever there are any number of men, however associated, that have no such decisive power to appeal to, there they are still in the state of nature.

§ 90. Hence it is evident, that absolute monarchy, which by some men is counted the only government in the world, is indeed inconsistent with civil society, and so can be no form of civil government at all; for the end of civil society being to avoid and remedy these inconveniences of the state of nature, which necessarily follow from every man being judge in his own case, by setting up a known authority, to which every one of that society may appeal upon any injury received, or controversy that may arise, and which every one of the[4] society ought to obey; wherever any

[4] " 'The public power of all society is above every soul contained in the same society; and the principal use of that power is, to give laws unto all that are under

persons are, who have not such an authority to appeal to for the decision of any difference between them, there those persons are still in the state of nature; and so is every absolute prince, in respect of those who are under his dominion. . . . .

CHAPTER VIII.   OF THE BEGINNING OF POLITICAL SOCIETIES

§ 95. Men being, as has been said, by nature, all free, equal, and independent, no one can be put out of this estate, and subjected to the political power of another, without his own consent. The only way, whereby any one divests himself of his natural liberty, and puts on the bonds of civil society, is by agreeing with other men to join and unite into a community, for their comfortable, safe, and peaceable living one amongst another, in a secure enjoyment of their properties, and a greater security against any, that are not of it. This any number of men may do, because it injures not the freedom of the rest; they are left as they were in the liberty of the state of nature. When any number of men have so consented to make one community or government, they are thereby presently incorporated, and make one body politic, wherein the majority have a right to act and conclude the rest.

§ 96. For when any number of men have, by the consent of every individual, made a community, they have thereby made that community one body, with a power to act as one body, which is only by the will and determination of the majority: for that which acts any community, being only the consent of the individuals of it and it being necessary to that which is one body to move one way; it is necessary the body should move that way whither the greater force carries it, which is the consent of the majority: or else it is impossible it should act or continue one body, one community, which the consent of every individual that united into it, agreed that it should; and so every one is bound by that consent to be concluded by the majority. And therefore we see, that in assemblies, impowered to act by positive laws, where no number is set by that positive law which impowers them, the act of the majority passes for the act of the whole, and of course determines; as having, by the law of nature and reason, the power of the whole.

---

it, which laws in such cases we must obey, unless there be reason showed which may necessarily inforce, that the law of reason, or of god, doth enjoin the contrary.' Hook. Eccl. Pol. 1. i. sect. 16.''

§ 97. And thus every man, by consenting with others to make one body politic under one government, puts himself under an obligation, to every one of that society, to submit to the determination of the majority, and to be concluded by it; or else this original compact, whereby he with others incorporate into one society, would signify nothing, and be no compact, if he be left free, and under no other ties than he was in before in the state of nature. For what appearance would there be of any compact? what new engagement if he were no farther tied by any decrees of the society, than he himself thought fit, and did actually consent to? This would be still as great a liberty, as he himself had before his compact, or any one else in the state of nature hath, who may submit himself, and consent to any acts of it if he thinks fit.

§ 98. For if the consent of the majority shall not, in reason, be received as the act of the whole, and conclude every individual; nothing but the consent of every individual can make any thing to be the act of the whole: but such a consent is next to impossible ever to be had, if we consider the infirmities of health, and avocations of business, which in a number, though much less than that of a commonwealth, will necessarily keep many away from the public assembly. To which if we add the variety of opinions, and contrariety of interest, which unavoidably happen in all collections of men, the coming into society upon such terms would be only like Cato's coming into the theatre, only to go out again. Such a constitution as this would make the mighty leviathan of a shorter duration, than the feeblest creatures, and not let it outlast the day it was born in: which cannot be supposed, till we can think, that rational creatures should desire and constitute societies only to be dissolved; for where the majority cannot conclude the rest, there they cannot act as one body, and consequently will be immediately dissolved again.

§ 99. Whosoever therefore out of a state of nature unite into a community, must be understood to give up all the power, necessary to the ends for which they unite into society, to the majority of the community, unless they expressly agreed in any number greater than the majority. And this is done by barely agreeing to unite into one political society, which is all the compact that is, or needs be, between the individuals, that enter into, or make up a commonwealth. And thus that, which begins and actually constitutes any political society, is nothing, but the consent of any number of freemen capable of a majority, to unite and incorporate into such a society. And this is that, and that only, which did, or could give beginning to any lawful government in the world. . . . .

CHAPTER IX. OF THE ENDS OF POLITICAL SOCIETY AND GOVERNMENT

§ 123. If man in the state of nature be so free, as has been said; if he be absolute lord of his own person and possessions, equal to the greatest, and subject to nobody, why will he part with his freedom? why will he give up his empire, and subject himself to the dominion and control of any other power? To which it is obvious to answer, that though in the state of nature he hath such a right, yet the enjoyment of it is very uncertain, and constantly exposed to the invasion of others; for all being kings as much as he, every man his equal, and the greater part no strict observers of equity and justice, the enjoyment of the property he has in this state is very unsafe, very unsecure. This makes him willing to quit a condition, which, however free, is full of fears and continual dangers: and it is not without reason, that he seeks out, and is willing to join in society with others, who are already united, or have a mind to unite, for the mutual preservation of their lives, liberties, and estates, which I call by the general name, property.

§ 124. The great and chief end, therefore, of men's uniting into commonwealths, and putting themselves under government, is the preservation of their property. To which in the state of nature there are many things wanting.

First, There wants an established, settled, known, law, received and allowed by common consent to be the standard of right and wrong, and the common measure to decide all controversies between them: for though the law of nature be plain and intelligible to all rational creatures; yet men being biassed by their interest, as well as ignorant for want of studying it, are not apt to allow of it as a law binding to them in the application of it to their particular cases.

§ 125. Secondly, In the state of nature there wants a known and indifferent judge, with authority to determine all differences according to the established law: for every one in that state being both judge and executioner of the law of nature, men being partial to themselves, passion and revenge is very apt to carry them too far, and with too much heat, in their own cases; as well as negligence, and unconcernedness, to make them too remiss in other men's.

§ 126. Thirdly, In the state of nature, there often wants power to back and support the sentence when right, and to give it due execution. They who by any injustice offend, will seldom fail, where they are able, by force to make good their injustice; such resistance many times makes the punishment dangerous, and frequently destructive, to those who attempt it.

§ 127. Thus mankind, notwithstanding all the privileges of the state of nature, being but in an ill condition, while they remain in it, are quickly driven into society. Hence it comes to pass that we seldom find any number of men live any time together in this state. The inconveniencies that they therein exposed to, by the irregular and uncertain exercise of the power every man has of punishing the transgressions of others, make them take sanctuary under the established laws of government, and therein seek the preservation of their property. It is this makes them so willingly give up every one his single power of punishing, to be exercised by such alone, as shall be appointed to it amongst them; and by such rules as the community, or those authorized by them to that purpose, shall agree on. And in this we have the original right of both the legislative and executive power, as well as of the governments and societies themselves.

§ 128. For in the state of nature, to omit the liberty he has of innocent delights, a man has two powers.

The first is to do whatsoever he thinks fit for the preservation of himself and others within the permission of the law of nature: by which law, common to them all, he and all the rest of mankind are one community, make up one society, distinct from all other creatures. And, were it not for the corruption and viciousness of degenerate men, there would be no need of any other; no necessity that men should separate from this great and natural community, and by positive agreements combine into smaller and divided associations.

The other power a man has in the state of nature, is the power to punish the crimes committed against that law. Both these he gives up, when he joins in a private, if I may so call it, or particular politic society, and incorporates into any commonwealth, separate from the rest of mankind.

§ 129. The first power, viz. "of doing whatsoever he thought fit for the preservation of himself," and the rest of mankind, he gives up to be regulated by laws made by the society, so far forth as the preservation of himself and the rest of that society shall require; which laws of the society in many things confine the liberty he had by the law of nature.

§ 130. Secondly, The power of punishing he wholly gives up, and engages his natural force, (which he might before employ in the execution of the law of nature, by his own single authority, as he thought fit) to assist the executive power of the society, as the law thereof shall require: for being now in a new state, wherein he is to enjoy many conveniences, from the labour, assistance, and society of others in the same community, as well as protection from its whole strength; he is to part also, with as much of his natural liberty, in providing for himself, as the good, prosperity, and safety of the society shall require; which is not only necessary, but just, since the other members of the society do the like.

§ 131. But though men, when they enter into society, give up the equality, liberty, and executive power they had in the state of nature, into the hands of the society, to be so far disposed of by the legislative, as the good of the society shall require; yet it being only with an intention in every one the better to preserve himself, his liberty and property; (for no rational creature can be supposed to change his condition with an intention to be worse) the power of the society, or legislative constituted by them, can never be supposed to extend farther, than the common good; but is obliged to secure every one's property, by providing against those three defects above mentioned, that made the state of nature so unsafe and uneasy. And so whoever has the legislative or supreme power of any commonwealth, is bound to govern by established standing laws, promulgated and known to the people, and not by extemporary decrees; by indifferent and upright judges, who are to decide controversies by those laws; and to employ the force of the community at home, only in the execution of such laws; or abroad to prevent or redress foreign injuries, and secure the community from inroads and invasion. And all this to be directed to no other end, but the peace, safety, and public good of the people.

CHAPTER X. OF THE FORMS OF A COMMONWEALTH

§ 132. The majority having, as has been showed, upon men's first uniting into society, the whole power of the community naturally in them, may employ all that power in making laws for the community from time to time, and executing those laws by officers of their own appointing; and then the form of the government is a perfect democracy: or else may put the power of making laws into the hands of a few select men, and their heirs or successors; and then it is an oligarchy: or else into the hands of one man, and then it is a monarchy: if to him and his heirs, it is an hereditary monarchy: if to him only for life, but upon his death the power only of nominating a successor to return to them; an elective monarchy. And so accordingly of these the community may make compounded and mixed forms of government, as they think good. And if the legislative power be at first given by the majority to one or more persons only for their lives, or any limited time, and then the supreme power to revert to them again; when it is so reverted, the community may dispose of it again anew into what hands they please, and so constitute a new form of government: for the form of government depending upon the placing the supreme power, which is the legislative (it being impossible to conceive that an inferiour power should prescribe to a superiour, or any but the supreme make laws), according as the power of making laws is placed, such is the form of the commonwealth.

§ 133. By commonwealth, I must be understood all along to mean, not a democracy, or any form of government; but any independent community, which the Latines signified by the word civitas; to which the word which best answers in our language, is commonwealth, and most properly expresses such a society of men, which community or city in English does not: for there may be subordinate communities in government; and city amongst us has quite a different notion from commonwealth: and therefore, to avoid ambiguity, I crave leave to use the word commonwealth in that sense, in which I find it used by king James the first: and I take it to be its genuine satisfaction; which if any body dislike, I consent with him to change it for a better.

CHAPTER XI. OF THE EXTENT OF THE LEGISLATIVE POWER

§ 134. The great end of men's entering into society being the enjoyment of their properties in peace and safety, and the great instrument and means of that being the laws established in that society; the first and fundamental positive law of all commonwealths is the establishing of the legislative power; as the first and fundamental natural law, which is to govern even the legislative itself, is the preservation of the society, and (as far as will consist with the public good) of every person in it. This legislative is not only the supreme power of the commonwealth, but sacred and unalterable in the hands where the community have once placed it; nor can any edict of any body else, in what form soever conceived, or by what power soever backed, have the force and obligation of a law, which has not its sanction from that legislative which the public has chosen and appointed; for without this the law could not have that, which is absolutely necessary to its being a law,[5] the consent of the society; over whom nobody can have a power to make laws, but by their own consent, and by authority received from them. And therefore all the obedience, which by the most solemn ties any one can be obliged to pay, ultimately terminates in this supreme power, and is directed by those laws which it enacts; nor can any oaths to any foreign power whatsoever, or any domestic subordinate power, discharge any member of the society from his obedience to the legislative, acting pursuant to their trust; nor oblige him to any obedience contrary to the laws so enacted, or farther than they do allow; it being ridiculous to imagine one can be tied ultimately to obey any power in the society, which is not supreme.

[5] "The lawful power of making laws to command whole politic societies of men, belonging so properly unto the same entire societies, that for any prince or potentate of what kind soever upon earth, to exercise the same of himself, and not by express commission immediately and personally received from God, or else by authority derived at the first from their consent, upon whose persons they impose laws; it is no better than mere tyranny. Laws they are not therefore which public approbation hath not made so." Hooker's Eccl. Pol. 1. i. sect. 10.

"Of this point therefore we are to note, that sith men naturally have no full and perfect power to command whole politic multitudes of men, therefore utterly without our consent, we could in such sort be at no man's commandment living. And to be commanded we do consent, when that society, whereof we be a part, hath at any time before consented, without revoking the same by the like universal argument.

"Laws therefore human, of what kind soever, are available by consent." Ibid

§ 143. The legislative power is that, which has a right to direct how the force of the commonwealth shall be employed for preserving the community and the members of it. But because those laws which are constantly to be executed, and whose force is always to continue, may be made in a little time; therefore there is no need, that the legislative should be always in being, not having always business to do. And because it may be too great a temptation to human frailty, apt to grasp at power, for the same persons, who have the power of making laws, to have also in their hands the power to execute them; whereby they may exempt themselves from obedience to the laws they make, and suit the law, both in its making and execution, to their own private advantage, and thereby come to have a distinct interest from the rest of the community, contrary to the end of society and government: therefore in well ordered commonwealths, where the good of the whole is so considered, as it ought, the legislative power is put into the hands of divers persons, who, duly assembled, have by themselves, or jointly with others, a power to make laws; which when they have done, being separated again, they are themselves subject to the laws they have made; which is a new and near tie upon them, to take care that they make them for the public good.

§ 144. But because the laws, that are at once, and in a short time made, have a constant and lasting force, and need a perpetual execution, or an attendance thereunto: therefore it is necessary there should be a power always in being, which should see to the execution of the laws that are made, and remain in force. And thus the legislative and executive power come often to be separated.

§ 145. There is another power in every commonwealth, which one may call natural, because it is that which answers to the power every man naturally had before he entered into society: for though in a commonwealth, the members of it are distinct persons still in reference to one another, and as such are governed by the laws of the society; yet in reference to the rest of mankind, they make one body, which is, as every member of it before was, still in the state of nature with the rest of mankind. Hence it is, that the controversies that happen between any man of the society with those that are out of it, are managed by the public; and an injury done to a member of their body engages the whole in the reparation of it. So that, under this consideration, the **whole** community is one body in the state of nature, in respect of all other states or persons out of its community.

§ 146. This therefore contains the power of war and peace, leagues and alliances, and all the transactions, with all persons and communities without the commonwealth; and may be called federative, if any one pleases. So the thing be understood, I am indifferent as to the name.

§ 147. These two powers, executive and federative, though they be really distinct in themselves, yet one comprehending the execution of the municipal laws of the society within itself, upon all that are parts of it; the other the management of the security and interest of the public without, with all those that it may receive benefit or damage from; yet they are always almost united. And though this federative power in the well or ill management of it be of great moment to the commonwealth, yet it is much less capable to be directed by antecedent, standing, positive laws, than the executive; and so must necessarily be left to the prudence and wisdom of those whose hands it is in, to be managed for the public good: for the laws that concern subjects one amongst another, being to direct their actions, may well enough precede them. But what is to be done in reference to foreigners, depending much upon their actions, and the variation of designs, and interests, must be left in great part to the prudence of those who have this power committed to them, to be managed by the best of their skill, for the advantage of the commonwealth.

§ 148. Though, as I said, the executive and federative power of every community be really distinct in themselves, yet they are hardly to be separated, and placed at the same time in the hands of distinct persons; for both of them requiring the force of the society for their exercise, it is almost impracticable to place the force of the commonwealth in distinct, and not subordinate hands; or that the executive and federative power should be placed in persons that might act separately, whereby the force of the public would be under different commands: which would be apt some time or other to cause disorder and ruin. . . . .

CHAPTER XVIII. OF TYRANNY

§ 202. Wherever law ends, tyranny begins, if the law be transgressed to another's harm; and whosoever in authority exceeds the power given him by the law, and makes use of the force he has under his command, to compass that upon the subject, which the law allows not, ceases in that to be a magistrate; and, acting without authority, may be opposed as any other man, who by force invades the right of another. This is acknowledged in subordinate magistrates. He that hath authority to seize my person in the street, may be opposed as a thief and a robber if he endeavours to break into my house to execute a writ, notwithstanding that I know he has such a warrant, and such a legal authority, as will impower him to arrest me abroad. And why this should not hold in the highest, as well as in the most inferiour magistrate, I would gladly be informed. Is it reasonable that the eldest brother, because he has the greatest part of his father's estate, should thereby have a right to take away any of his younger brother's portions? or, that a rich man, who possessed a whole country, should from thence have a right to seize, when he pleased, the cottage and garden of his poor neighbour? The being rightfully possessed of great power and riches, exceedingly beyond the greatest part of the sons of Adam, is so far from being an excuse, much less a reason for rapine and oppression, which the endamaging another without authority is, that it is a great aggravation of it: for the exceeding the bounds of authority is no more a right in a great than in a petty officer; no more justifiable in a king than a constable; but is so much the worse in him, in that he has more trust put in him, has already a much greater share than the rest of his brethren, and is supposed, from the advantages of his education, employment, and counsellors, to be more knowing in the measures of right and wrong.

§ 203. "May the commands then of a prince be opposed? may he be resisted as often as any one shall find himself aggrieved, and but imagine he has not right done him? This will unhinge and overturn all polities, and, instead of government and order, leave nothing but anarchy and confusion."

§ 204. To this I answer, that force is to be opposed to nothing but to unjust and unlawful force; whoever makes any opposition in any other case, draws on himself a just condemnation both from God and man; and so no such danger or confusion will follow, as is often suggested. . . . .

CHAPTER XIX.   OF THE DISSOLUTION OF GOVERNMENT

.   .   .   .

§ 223. To this perhaps it will be said, that the people being ignorant, and always discontented, to lay the foundation of government in the unsteady opinion and uncertain humour of the people, is to expose it to certain ruin; and no government will be able long to subsist, if the people may set up a new legislative, whenever they take offence at the old one. To this I answer, quite the contrary. People are not so easily got out of their old forms as some are apt to suggest. They are hardly to be prevailed with to amend the acknowledged faults in the frame they have been accustomed to. And if there be any original defects, or adventitious ones introduced by time, or corruption: it is not an easy thing to get them changed, even when all the world sees there is an opportunity for it. This slowness and aversion in the people to quit their old constitutions, has in the many revolutions which have been seen in this kingdom, in this and former ages, still kept us to, or, after some interval of fruitless attempts, still brought us back again to, our old legislative of king, lords, and commons: and whatever provocations have made the crown be taken from some of our princes heads, they never carried the people so far as to place it in another line.

§ 224. But it will be said, this hypothesis lays a ferment for frequent rebellion. To which I answer,

First, no more than any other hypothesis: for when the people are made miserable, and find themselves exposed to the ill-usage of arbitrary power, cry up their governors as much as you will, for sons of Jupiter; let them be sacred or divine, descended, or authorized from heaven; give them out for whom or what you please, the same will happen. The people generally ill-treated, and contrary to right, will be ready upon any occasion to ease themselves of a burden that sits heavy upon them. They will wish, and seek for the opportunity, which in the change, weakness, and accidents of human affairs, seldom delays long to offer itself. He must have lived but a little while in the world, who has not seen examples of this in his time; and he must have read very little, who cannot produce examples of it in all sorts of governments in the world.

§ 225. Secondly, I answer, such revolutions happen not upon every little mismanagement in public affairs. Great mistakes in the ruling part, many wrong and inconvenient laws, and all the slips of human frailty, will be borne by the people without mutiny or murmur. But if a long train of abuses, prevarications and artifices, all tending the same way, make the design visible to the people, and they cannot but feel what they lie under, and see whither they are going; it is not to be wondered, that they should then rouse themselves, and endeavour to put the rule into such hands which may secure to them the ends for which government was at first erected; and without which, ancient names, and specious forms, are so far from being better, that they are much worse, than the state of nature, or pure anarchy; the inconveniencies being all as great and as near, but the remedy farther off and more difficult.

§ 226. Thirdly, I answer, that this doctrine of a power in the people of providing for their safety anew, by a new legislative, when their legislators have acted contrary to their trust, by invading their property, is the best fence against rebellion, and the probablest means to hinder it: for rebellion being an opposition, not to persons, but authority, which is founded only in the constitutions and laws of the government; those, whoever they be, who by force break through, and by force justify their violation of them, are truly and properly rebels: for when men, by entering into society and civil government, have excluded force, and introduced laws for the preservation of property, peace, and unity amongst themselves; those who set up force again in opposition to the laws do rebellare, that is, bring back again the state of war, and are properly rebels; which they who are in power, (by the pretence they have to authority, the temptation of force they have in their hands, and the flattery of those about them) being likeliest to do; the properest way to prevent the evil, is to show them the danger and injustice of it, who are under the greatest temptation to run into it. . . . .

§ 229. The end of government is the good of mankind: and which is best for mankind, that the people should be always exposed to the boundless will of tyranny; or that the rulers should be sometimes liable to be opposed, when they grow exorbitant in the use of their power, and employ it for the destruction, and not the preservation of the properties of their people?